D0884972

Books By Robert Coles

CHILDREN OF CRISIS I: A STUDY OF COURAGE AND FEAR

STILL HUNGRY IN AMERICA

THE IMAGE IS YOU

UPROOTED CHILDREN

WAGES OF NEGLECT (WITH MARIA PIERS)

DRUGS AND YOUTH (WITH JOSEPH BRENNER AND DERMOT MEAGHER)

ERIK H. ERIKSON: THE GROWTH OF HIS WORK

THE MIDDLE AMERICANS (WITH JON ERIKSON)

THE GEOGRAPHY OF FAITH (WITH DANIEL BERRIGAN)

MIGRANTS, SHARECROPPERS, MOUNTAINEERS (VOLUME II OF CHILDREN OF CR

THE SOUTH GOES NORTH (VOLUME III OF CHILDREN OF CRISIS)

FAREWELL TO THE SOUTH

A SPECTACLE UNTO THE WORLD: THE CATHOLIC WORKER MOVEMENT (WITH
     ERIKSON)

THE OLD ONES OF NEW MEXICO (WITH ALEX HARRIS)

THE BUSES ROLL (WITH CAROL BALDWIN)

THE DARKNESS AND THE LIGHT (WITH DORIS ULMANN)

IRONY IN THE MIND'S LIFE: ESSAYS ON NOVELS BY JAMES AGEE, ELIZABETH BO
     AND GEORGE ELIOT

WILLIAM CARLOS WILLIAMS: THE KNACK OF SURVIVAL IN AMERICA

THE MIND'S FATE: WAYS OF SEEING PSYCHIATRY AND PSYCHOANALYSIS

ESKIMOS, CHICANOS, INDIANS (VOLUME IV OF CHILDREN OF CRISIS)

PRIVILEGED ONES: THE WELL-OFF AND THE RICH IN AMERICA (VOLUME
     CHILDREN OF CRISIS)

A FESTERING SWEETNESS (POEMS)

THE LAST AND FIRST ESKIMOS (WITH ALEX HARRIS)

WOMEN OF CRISIS: LIVES OF STRUGGLE AND HOPE (WITH JANE COLES)

WALKER PERCY: AN AMERICAN SEARCH

For Children

DEAD END SCHOOL

THE GRASS PIPE

SAVING FACE

RIDING FREE

HEADSPARKS

PRIVILEGED ONES

PRIVILEGED ONES

The Well-Off and the Rich in America

Volume V of *Children of Crisis*

ROBERT COLES, M.D.

with illustrations

An Atlantic Monthly Press Book

LITTLE, BROWN AND COMPANY •BOSTON •TORONTO

10   9   8   7   6   5   4   3

Excerpts from this volume have appeared in *The Atlantic* and the
Boston Globe.

An adaptation of some of the material in Part VII appeared in
Learning.

LIBRARY OF CONGRESS CATALOGING IN PUBLICATION DATA

Coles, Robert.
  Privileged ones.

  (His Children of crisis; v. 5)
  "An Atlantic Monthly Press book."
  Bibliography: p.
  Includes index.
  1. Children of the rich—United States. I. Title.
  HC110.P6C56   vol. 5   [HQ792.U5]   309.1'73'092s
  ISBN 0-316-15149-1   [301.43 14'0973]   77-10825

ATLANTIC-LITTLE, BROWN BOOKS
ARE PUBLISHED BY
LITTLE, BROWN AND COMPANY
IN ASSOCIATION WITH
THE ATLANTIC MONTHLY PRESS

MV

Published simultaneously in Canada
by Little, Brown & Company (Canada) Limited

PRINTED IN THE UNITED STATES OF AMERICA

To America's children, rich and well-off as well as poor, in the hope that some day, one day soon, all boys and girls everywhere in the world will have a decent chance to survive, grow, and affirm themselves as human beings.

"And he shewed me a pure river of water of life, clear as crystal, proceeding out of the throne of God and of the Lamb.

"In the midst of the street of it, and on either side of the river was there the tree of life, which bare twelve manner of fruits, and yielded her fruit every month: and the leaves of the tree were for the healing of the nations.

"And there shall be no more curse: but the throne of God and of the Lamb shall be in it; and his servants shall serve him:

"And they shall see his face; and his name shall be in their foreheads.

"And there shall be no night there; and they need no candle, neither light of the sun; for the Lord God giveth them light: and they shall reign for ever and ever."

Revelation 22:1–5

FOREWORD

THIS FOREWORD is a continuation of the forewords for the first four volumes of *Children of Crisis*. The children I first met, twenty years ago, in Arkansas, Louisiana, Georgia, Mississippi, and other Southern states, were struggling with the crisis of school desegregation. They knew far better than I the larger significance of that struggle. They knew how connected their lives were to the lives of others: the men and women who heckled them daily; the teachers who wondered why "the colored" wanted so much to attend school "with our white children"; the lawyers, judges, public officials, and businessmen whose activities and utterances and decisions affected both black and white children in all sorts of ways during that period of time — from 1958, when I was living in Mississippi working with Southern children, to 1965, when segregationist resistance of the fierce, combative, and unyielding kind gave way, only to appear North several years later! As I mentioned in the first volume of this series, I was told rather promptly and forcefully in the late 1950s by a number of black parents that I ought to go talk with those in the mobs who were coming forth with such hate and rage: "They really do need a psychiatrist!" I was also told to go talk with "the rich white folks."

Why the latter, I would ask, with more innocence and ignorance (and maybe self-protective stupidity and perversity)
than I now like to remember. Almost always there would be
no reply. It was 1958, or 1960, and my mere presence, as a
white person, in those homes was itself a remarkable event
— and one that prompted considerable anxiety, fear, and confusion.

Eventually we could become more candid with one another
in those homes, and of course eventually the South would
become a region that allowed far more candid expression
across racial and also class lines. In 1963 one of the black children who pioneered school desegregation in New Orleans,
against terrible obstacles (mobs, threats, violence, a boycott),
asked me yet again how I was "doing with the rich folks." I was
a bit dumbfounded. What did she mean? Only in retrospect
did I realize the limits of my curiosity. I wanted to know about
that girl's family, her private worries and hopes, the specifics
of her educational struggle, the racial difficulties she and others like her had to develop a way of living with, working
against, but surviving under. Yet I abstained consistently from
certain lines of inquiry. When she asked me about the rich
folks she assumed that I was in the midst of "doing" something
"with" them (that is, studying their lives, even as I was studying certain aspects, at least, of hers). She was, I began to realize, making a point to me, making an analysis of my work
— a kind of analysis I hadn't been able to make for myself. I
asked her what she meant, of course. She said: "The rich folks
are the ones who decide how the poor folks live."

I wasn't going to argue with that. I agreed. I remember
thinking to myself: she means the white folks are the ones who
decide how the black folks live. How quickly a child psychiatrist like me can interpret and reinterpret a child's remarks to
suit his own purposes, his own ideological point of view, his

own social and economic comfort, thereby denying the child's
dignity. I had known her for four years, so I felt free enough
to say I thought she meant "white" rather than "rich." No, she
didn't, whereupon she said to me, slowly but pointedly: "You
told me you've been talking to the federal judge and the
school superintendent and some business people. Like my
Daddy says, 'They cough and we feel the house shake.'"

It was only then, in March of 1963, that the work I had
already been doing with relatively well-off and important people became more consciously and explicitly part of my "research." I had started in the late 1950s talking with men and
women whom that black girl would consider "rich"; in fact,
the first people I had seen had been lawyers, a federal judge,
a prominent businessman in New Orleans, a newspaper editor, a college professor. Their words and deeds had decisively
affected the lives of the children, black and white, whom I
visited day after day in New Orleans; and affected their lives,
quite clearly, far more than the frenzied hecklers who shouted
obscenities in front of the schools, which were boycotted for
months. In order for me to reach the black children I had to
speak to prominent blacks, powerful whites.

Why indeed shouldn't a "study" of the lives of poor, vulnerable, harassed children also include a consideration of the purposes, aims, ideas and feelings of those "others," so removed
apparently by "station" in life, yet so involved by virtue of the
money they have, the positions they occupy, the authority
they possess and wield, the influence they exert? I heard it
from a white mother, a fireman's wife, a few months later in
1963, far more bluntly: "You want to know how my children
like going to school with the colored? Why don't you go talk
with the people in the federal government, or the rich people
in the Garden District? Ask them what they think they've
done to us. You can't really know about plain working people

like us, unless you go find out about the big shots. It's their
decisions that end up making us live our lives the way we do."

As for children, she added this: "Have you ever thought to
go talk with the well-off ones — their kids?" I said no, I hadn't.
She said she hoped I would someday. I asked her why —
thinking at the time that she was trying to change the subject.
She told me why; she took a deep breath, and I began to gird
myself for yet another self-justifying tirade, or outburst of
anger, bitterness, resentment. But no, she was brief and a
touch triumphant as she spoke: "You told us you were interested in talking with our children because you wanted to see
how they grow up, and then you'd know more about the
country, something like that. Well, it seems to me if you want
to know a lot about this country, if you want to know about the
people who are running it, and the people who will be running
it in ten or twenty years, then you'd better go visit the big-deal
important people — the well-off and the rich; they're the ones
whose children you should be looking at. Why *aren't* you looking at them?"

Later, with time and knowledge of one another, she and her
husband and my wife and I became more friendly, less prickly
in our talks. Later, she would not say something like that with
quite the sharpness of voice, the edge. But I will never forget
that particular moment. After we left the house, my wife
turned to me and said: "You know, she was right."

I would slowly begin to realize how arbitrary my initial
notion was: a specific stress (school desegregation) produces
specific psychiatric responses, the so-called mechanisms of defense. Eventually, a quite limited "research project" devoted
to the acquisition of more "data" on the nature of "stress"
became something quite else: I joined the civil rights movement; extended my observations to men, women, and children whose various life-situations connect with the ways chil-

dren grow up and see themselves: the jobs their parents hold, the racial and cultural influences that, though acknowledged as "factors" in child development, had not been studied with respect to their pervasive psychological import on a boy's or girl's self-regard, sense of the future, and attitudes toward relatives, friends, neighbors, teachers, or "outsiders."

The first four volumes in this series have attempted to portray the children of the nation's poor — black and white and Chicano and Indian and Eskimo—and also its ordinary working people — teachers, policemen, government officials, foremen who work in factories or farms. In *The Middle Americans,* I enlarged on the presentations of working-class or middle-class people made in the first three volumes of *Children of Crisis.* I have more or less, within the limits of my ability and the way I do my work, paid attention to children from all parts of the country: rural and urban; from each of the major racial and cultural "groups"; and from all the so-called socioeconomic strata or classes — except for the ones I was long ago told to go see and get to know, "the well-off and the rich," to draw again upon the words of the New Orleans woman quoted above. There have been glimpses: the plantation owner in the second volume; the prominent Florida grower in that same volume; the quite well-off suburban woman whose maid speaks in the third volume. But their children are not present, and the adults are there only because they are intimately connected (as happens in the rural South) with the black families or migrant families whose fate and circumstances I was trying to convey.

"Oh, to get by, just to get by, that's what I tell my children I want for them"; so one woman from the mountains of West Virginia used to speak to her sons and daughters. Once she asked me what the owners of the coal mine that employed her husband told their children. I told her that I was trying to find

that out. She said she couldn't even imagine what those children would be told, but it was important for her children that
they know. Why? "Because our children and the mine owner's
children will meet later on; they'll meet in life."

For the past twenty years, I have been involved in the civil
rights movement of the rural South, in the struggle on behalf
of hungry and malnourished children, in various political
efforts on behalf of migrant farm workers or coal miners
ravaged by black lung disease. All the while I have heard some
of this book's "privileged" children keep struggling with their
perceptions of what life is like in America for others, for the
less fortunate. If, at times, the "privileged" seem, in fact,
frightened and guilty and confused and conflicted — in their
own ways victims — then so it goes: the ironies of everyday
life.

As the reader will see, some of the children who appear in
the following pages are impressively thoughtful, decent, sensitive; others are hurt, desperate, worried, callous, confused.
That is how the other "children of crisis" also have turned out
to be. But how justify the inclusion of these utterly privileged
children in a series of this kind, with its title? The "crises" that
come up in the lives of some of the children whose words or
drawings appear in this book are certainly accompanied by
pain, anguish, bewilderment — however privileged the particular boy or girl.

I repeat my indebtedness to the Ford Foundation for its
willingness to let me be, let me wander and wonder and write,
and specifically to Nancy Dennis, Edward Meade, Harold
Howe, and McGeorge Bundy. I want to thank warmly Bonnie
Harris and Kirk Felsman for their constant, tireless help. I
want to thank Peter Davison for the same — years and years
of editorial counsel, tactfully and gracefully rendered. I also

want to thank Dr. Warren Wacker, Director of the Harvard University Health Services, and, before him in the same position, Dr. Dana Farnsworth. For some fifteen years I have had a "berth" at the Health Services, with no obligations other than to do the work this series documents. I could not have done the job without such a place to call home — a place for "rest and rehabilitation" after so much travel. My wife and our three sons each has had a share in the two decades of work that have preceded the completion of this volume. I have done the writing, but my wife's ideas and observations, expressed daily and in dozens of ways, direct and indirect, have been much more than helpful; they inform, maybe the word is suffuse, every page in every one of these five volumes. The various children we have met and worked with have known what it was like when she has not been with me on visits, and so have I. Eventually our own sons grew up enough to enable her to appear and reappear — and sometimes with them. Children being visited had a chance to meet and get to know the visitor's children, who had their own chance to look and listen and think about what they had heard and witnessed.

I can mark the end of this final foreword to the series only with a wish that soon, and in every one of our states, boys and girls like those in the five separate volumes of this series get to meet and know one another. That is not how it is now, obviously; by class and race and nationality and religion and "background" young Americans are all too commonly set apart from one another. I do not argue for a compulsory "melting pot" that denies the many differences among families. But our children learn that someday they will each have a vote, a means of joining the political system and making it work. It might be helpful if they also were enabled, at school, at play, in ways formal and informal, to take the measure of the country socially and culturally as well as politically — to meet others, different from themselves, on some kind of parity. The psychological consequences (not to mention the political and economic ones) might be interesting, indeed, and worth (in some as yet uncertain and seemingly far-off future) a study that might well not require five volumes — or the title *Children of Crisis.*

CONTENTS

(Children's Drawings between pages 289 and 290)

CONTENTS

PART ONE

COMFORTABLE, COMFORTABLE PLACES

DRAMATIC and secluded; old, historic, and architecturally interesting; large and with good grounds; private and palatial; beautifully restored; big, interesting, high up and with an uninterrupted view: so the descriptions go, phrases meant to lift a person's eyebrows, make a person get the point, the facts of money, prestige, position as they come to bear on something called "the real estate market." In the South, the house may be an old plantation manor, made modern, with cool air pouring through tastefully decorated rooms; or an imitation of such a building, designed by an architect and furnished by an interior decorator; or a rambling, nondescript brick or wooden home, contemporary but not conspicuously or outlandishly so; or a self-consciously Tudor home, with wings and maybe a turret; or, far less common and an obvious object of admiration and envy, an antebellum home with an interesting history.

In Appalachia, the home is quite often a heavy brick presence, likely as not with white columns that prompt, or are supposed to, reveries of the Southern landed gentry. The house may be tucked away on the side of a hill, quite visible from the road; or one may have to drive and drive, in seemingly concentric circles, until all of a sudden it is there —

two, maybe three, floors, several large cars, and not much in the way of lawns or gardens, because the woods are immediately nearby and not easily pushed aside. In West Virginia or eastern Kentucky, if the home is located in a town or a city it may be of wood, and less imposing. Out toward the western part of Kentucky, of course, one is no longer in Appalachia, though a number of families that own mines in the eastern counties have taken themselves to "bluegrass" country, to horse farms: gentle hills, rich growing land, an established tradition of leisure — and, through riding or racing, fierce competition. And in the northern part of West Virginia one also leaves Appalachia, approaches Pittsburgh — with it, the Northeast and its cities, near which lie the well-to-do or wealthy suburbs.

In the suburbs and beyond — of Pittsburgh and Philadelphia, of Boston and Hartford, of New York City and Washington, D.C., of Wilmington, Delaware, and Cleveland: towns, townships, villages, stations, even crossings, anything to make it clear that one does not live in the city, that one is outside or away, *well* outside or *well* away, as it is so often put — the houses vary: imitation English castles; French provincial; nineteenth-century American; contemporary one-levels in the tradition of Gropius or Neutra. Sometimes the setting is formal, sometimes one is in view of a farm — animals, rail fences, pasture land, a barn, maybe a shed or two, a flower garden, and, more recently, a few rows of vegetables. Sometimes there is a swimming pool. Sometimes there is a tennis court. Sometimes there is a greenhouse, attached to the house or on its own. Sometimes the house stands on a hill, affords a view for miles around. Sometimes particular trees stand close guard; and beyond them, thick brush and more trees, a jumble of them: no view but complete privacy. Sometimes there is a paved road leading from a street up to the house's entrance.

Sometimes the road is a dusty path, or a trail — the casual countrified scene, prized and jealously guarded. Sometimes the property, as it may be called, is clearly marked. Sometimes no one but the owner seems to know where the "land" ends and someone else's begins, though upon occasion there may be a marker, a fence, a road, a natural boundary like a stream. Sometimes the house is within sight of another house or two or is on a street of large homes surrounded by ample land. Sometimes the house is acres away from the nearest "neighbor." Sometimes life is immediately apparent as one comes near: a barking dog (or two, or three); a watchful cat; children's toys, bicycles, their sandbox — or their pony chewing relentlessly on the grass — a station wagon, another car, still another car. Sometimes there is an eerie silence, and no evidence of anyone — just a long driveway that leads to a home, which seems formidably closed up, even the garage doors tightly closed, and everything neat and tidy, even the flower garden.

The trees matter; so do the grass and the shrubbery. These are not houses in a row, with patches of new grass, fledgling trees, and a bush or two. These are homes that are surrounded by spacious lawns and announced by tall, sturdy trees. Hedges are common, are carefully arranged. The grass is fine yet thick — years of cultivation. And not rarely there is water — a sprinkler system, a nearby pond, a brook running through the land. There are also quite likely wild birds who are fed food, given drink. If the people in the house are their friends and observers, squirrels are their constant competitors. The bird feeders are ingeniously constructed and placed, but squirrels are quick, clever, and, it seems, able to get anywhere. And there are chipmunks, and garden snakes, and colonies of ants, and, in many cases, pheasants — a semirural landscape that particular boys and girls talk about, draw or paint, discuss with a visitor.

Out West, in Texas or in New Mexico, the homes are ranches, big sprawling ones, many rooms in many wings. In the Rio Grande Valley the material may be wood, painted white; in New Mexico it's adobe. The land is wet and fertile throughout the southern part of Texas, so tropical and semi-tropical flowers and trees adorn estates or ranches — acres of land given over to horse trails, gardens, large swimming pools, even landing strips for private airplanes. In New Mexico the large adobe houses abut cacti, corrals, and often stunning views: across a valley, over toward mountains miles and miles away. And the horses: they are not part of a "hunt" club, not exquisitely combed; they are just there, grazing or waiting to be used — and by boys or men as well as girls or women: Western style riding, sometimes bareback. And the cattle. They have to wander far over the stingy land for food — and in the clutch, must be fed grain by quite well-to-do own- ers, who don't worry too much about costs, about profits and losses. And the dogs. Often three or four of them run about — after horses, around the house, up the trails on a scent. Signs announce to anyone who chances to come near that at a cer- tain point a ranch begins — belonging to so-and-so and stretching maybe as far as the eye can see and then some.

Who are the people who live in all those homes, who own all that land — or acreage, as it is sometimes put with just the slightest of commercial implications? How is one to character- ize them, region by region? As rich? As wealthy? As well-to- do? As members of the upper middle class? As affluent or prosperous or well-off, well-off indeed? As advantaged or privi- leged? The words are plentiful, and there are plenty of num- bers to go with them. Clearly the issue is money, and with it social position, and, rather commonly, political leverage. The homes belong to people who have a lot of money, are "success- ful." They are plantation owners, bankers, stockbrokers, business or corporation executives, lawyers, doctors, architects, strip mine operators. They are politicians whose salaries for "public service" only begin to indicate the extent of their resources. They are ranchers and growers. They are entrepeneurs of one sort or another. They are those lucky enough to inherit substantial sums of money. They are sometimes men or women successful in the arts. They are people considered to be "on top," or "the bosses," or very, very "lucky." They are people who, in the middle 1970s, make, say, forty or fifty thousand dollars a year, and up. Some growers in the Rio Grande Valley are many times millionaires, as are mine owners in Appalachia or plantation owners in Louisiana or Mississippi. In cities of the North or Midwest, certain business or professional men bring home seventy-five or a hundred thousand dollars a year — and look up to others who make twice that and therefore are judged and called "better off."

Inside the homes all those dollars have done their work — tastefully or insistently or at times quite gaudily. A formal, nineteenth-century spirit dominates the plantation South — by no means inhabited only by cotton growers, because professional and business men want homes that look like antebellum homes and in some instances have bought "the real thing" and restored it. Mahogany furniture, often heavy, is found in living rooms and dining rooms: solid breakfronts; grand pianos; long and wide eating tables with heavy silver candlesticks; captain's tables; end tables or casual tables on which one finds books that belong to hunters or fishermen — pictures of birds, fish, wildlife; writing tables or desks that boast a gardening lady's books — the flowers of a region beautifully illustrated. Air conditioning is everywhere — entire houses, rather than a room or two. There are exceptions, though — stubborn holdouts: a family in, say, Mountain Brook,

Alabama, that won't, under any conditions, let "good, warm Southern air" be turned into "Yankee weather." Not silly, eccentric people but a distinguished lawyer and his wife who genuinely like summer weather, however hot and humid, and who don't want to surrender themselves to "artificial air."

Cars are everywhere, too; a car for the husband and a car for the wife, a car for each child over sixteen, and often a car that belongs to a maid, to a cook, to a man who "helps" with the garden. The "help" is all black, of course, in the South, and sometimes in the North, too. In the South the swimming pool can be an almost all-year-round center of family life. The pools are lit, are heated. They are guarded by columns of mosquito repellent — steel poles on top of which burn mysterious chemicals that only some people worry about as pollutants. There are many chairs and a table or two — the former bright-colored, the latter usually with a glass top. There is a phone nearby — in a few instances a phone that is mysteriously, miraculously free of wires or cords. There are electrical out-lets, television sets, phonographs, radios, rotisseries, toasters, small refrigerators — a kitchen outside the house's kitchen, all arranged decorously and without clutter.

In Appalachia the pools are more modest; often they are nonexistent. The furniture is likely to be new — North Caroli-na–made imitations of antiques. Not always, however; it de-pends on who has made what money, when, and how. Rather often, simple mountain furniture — part of the region's arts and crafts tradition — gets shunted aside in favor of massive, imposing couches and stereo sets or televisions encased in giant mahogany or cherry cabinets. Cadillacs predominate; Rolls Royces are not unknown. The driveways are occasionally something to see: lights, spaced at intervals, that blaze at night and a certain sweep that goes beyond any requirements of convenience. The garages can be enormous; inside are large

cars, motorized lawn mowers, snowplows, diggers or cultiva-
tors — a warehouse of mechanized equipment. And near the
house, often, a flagpole, used daily. And large television anten-
nae, able to pick up distant signals. And, maybe, a boy's aerial
for a high-powered shortwave radio or a police radio. And
motorbikes; they are fun, and "children" of eleven, say, use
them a lot, indifferent to any law that might urge otherwise.

There is, of course, other wealth in Appalachia — older, self-
consciously understated, Southern in affiliation, or, if near
Pittsburgh, quite Eastern in many respects. In those homes, as
in Southern homes catalogues are often to be found on the
desks of wives and husbands, mothers and fathers: for clothes,
for jams, jellies, fruits, cakes; for hunting or fishing equipment;
for toys; for books or records. And clippings, coupons, advertisements — cut out of magazines like *The New Yorker:* promises of goods and services, bearers of symbolic assurance, rein-
forcements of a family's sense of itself, reminders for anyone
around that there is a national culture (material, at least) for
the upper middle class and wealthy people of this country.
Guns are part of that culture; especially in the rural South and
in Appalachia those guns assert themselves: on walls, in cor-
ners of rooms, in closets, or even outside, in barns or garages
— sometimes almost as numerous as the tennis rackets and
golf clubs.

Golf: a game, but for many a way of life. Some homes are
regarded as especially convenient, because near a golf course.
The weekends become a marathon of golf, interrupted by a
meal or two. The mood of particular parents varies with their
"game," with their scores. And endless discussions are devoted
to experiences in one way or another connected to the sport.
Families travel with a certain golf course in mind. Clothing is
often geared to what is worn on the links. And to move toward
a less sociological and more psychological, even existential,

vein, some well-to-do men and women openly acknowledge that without golf life for them would be unbearable, even hard to imagine.

For others, tennis has the same function — not only a game, a means of exercise, but virtually an organizing principle. Social lives depend on who is playing against whom, when and where. Couples meet other couples. Wives play in the morning, as soon as their husbands and children have left, or right after a housekeeper arrives to care for a preschool child or indeed an infant. On Monday, husbands talk about the sets they played during the weekend; and the memories hold those busy, important men together, so some say, until the next weekend — that is, the ones who are too busy for weekday tennis, increasingly played on indoor courts. The fear of coronary heart disease adds a certain determination to the game, when the opponents are middle-aged professional and business men — who, however, also worry out loud about the competitive intensity they feel as they serve, lob, smash the balls. Will they, on that latter count, be right back where they started, candidates for a sudden and possibly fatal heart attack?

People who make enough money to live a privileged life, socially and economically, spend a considerable amount of time and money making sure that they are near the water. Summer homes are for many of them an utter necessity: Cape Cod, certain stretches of Long Island, Maine, the New Jersey and Delaware coasts, the Carolina beaches, the whole state of Florida, the Gulf Coast, the beaches of the Caribbean islands, Mexico, or the Pacific states. Or lakes: Michigan and Wisconsin, New Hampshire and Vermont, the Northwest and into Canada. Or the Portuguese and Spanish and French resorts, or the islands of the South Seas, not to mention Hawaii. Many families try one place, then another, out of genuine curiosity,

out of a desire to taste different pleasures, or out of a nervous
sense of what is fashionable — or strictly out-of-bounds. Other
families are quite content to stay with a permanent second
home, and pour into it years of lavish devotion: a whole new
set of furniture and electrical gadgets; boats of various kinds;
snorkeling equipment; a tennis court sometimes; often a
movie camera and screen — for rainy days; a special library
(old favorites and recently published books); and almost always
a sampling of records that usually get played more than those
in the "other" house and that have a broad family appeal.
Needless to say, a group of families may stay together, winter
and summer — move from one upper-income community to
another one near an ocean, lake, or mountain. In other cases,
a whole new world of friends and acquaintances awaits a particular family.

There are third homes, too; in order to ski, and avoid the
crowds or disappointments associated with motels, families
purchase condominiums near a particular ski resort, or own
their own lodges. In the upper three New England states, in
Colorado and northern New Mexico and Idaho and Utah and
northern California, and recently in the mountains of western
North Carolina and Tennessee, a winter social and even cultural life centered around the "slopes" has developed and
steadily grown. Shops, moviehouses, even educational programs cluster near ski tows; so do an assortment of restaurants
and bars. Private planes struggle to land amid winter weather
that closes small airports; the alternative, going to a particular
city's jet field, annoys the passengers, who would like ideally
a lot of snow on the ground, but in any case clear weather for
landing, for the departure of Lear jets or more old-fashioned
prop jets. Sometimes a family is torn: to ski at Christmas or to
go to the Caribbean, or Mexico, or Rio de Janeiro, or the warm
and fine beaches of Uruguay? Sometimes both desires are ap-

peased — a week in Switzerland, a week in the Caribbean, where a number of well-to-do Americans keep winter homes. The two seasons most likely spent entirely at home (the main home) are spring and fall, though spring skiing or a last fling or two in the autumn at a summer home are by no means unusual. And there is always a fishing trip, a hunting weekend in the autumn or the spring: a cabin up some chain of mountains or in the middle of woods or near a stream — a place where commonly a man and his friends go, leaving behind wives and children, or a place where an entire family goes a few times a year for yet another change of scene and a sustained effort with guns or rods.

Garages are but one part of a chain of secondary buildings: a shed for bikes and lawn mowers and lawn furniture; a place where barrels are kept; a barn, with horses, hay, grain, saddles; and sometimes yet another building for chickens, maybe a rabbit, maybe some ducks. All that on acres of land *not* considered a farm, but rather a home in a certain village or town, out of which every day men and women travel to cities (by car, by train) in order to work, to shop, to dine, to attend a concert, the theater, a movie. Hunt clubs or, more informally, weekly hunts pursued through woods delightfully untouched except for the paths themselves, or across rolling meadow lands, are an important part of the social life of certain families: the so-called "horse country" of Virginia, New Jersey, or Massachusetts.

In the Southwest and West horses have until recently been part of a culture's mythology as well as the common man's unpretentious but lively and even passionate enjoyment: the rodeo, the fair, the horse show. In Texas, New Mexico, and Arizona boys and girls alike learn to ride, and not only the more well-to-do. The latter, however, are able to indulge their interests in many ways: ranches with many different kinds of horses and ponies; large stables, and individuals to care for them; trails and paths and grazing land; vans to move horses, employees to do the driving, even as they have filled and refilled water pails or containers for grain, and pitched in hay, and shoveled out manure, and spread out shavings on well-put-together wooden floors or on cement ones or, sometimes, the Western earth. For some children and their parents the care of horses as well as the riding of them becomes one of the most important tasks of each day. The "animals" get fed before people do. Even if there are caretakers, and handymen, the children may well go out first thing, talk to their horses, feed them, fill up their water buckets, even groom them a little. Then comes breakfast and "horse talk."

On weekends there are rides, races, or a lot of care: the shoes, the coat, the mane, all in need of work. And a talk with the veterinarian. And a discussion: to go here or there by van on such and such weekend? Some Western ranches are justly famous — beautiful horses, immaculately cared for and trained, ridden on stunning paths that lead up hills, across streams, into valleys or prairies a feast for the eyes. In the East all sorts of social tensions and rivalries get worked at or worked out when horses are mounted in particular places on certain mornings. As with golf, there are clubs and clubs, hunts and hunts, horses and horses, stables and stables. Much has been made of Little League baseball — its searing effect on working- or middle-class children, who fight hard to win; so hard, some claim, that any loss becomes a devastating psychological experience and any victory an exercise in arrogant self-congratulation, accompanied, alas, by a haunting apprehension of future defeat. But among certain quite well-off children the performance at a show or on a hunt can be an occasion for fear, self-doubt, and fierce rivalry. Even a successful morning of dressage can end with tears — the gnawing conviction that one ought *be* better, *do* better, *appear* better.

Sailing, for children of well-off families, also generates

strong competitive demands. The relationship between such families and boats in general is at once apparent: canoes alongside garages of winter homes; sailboats anchored within sight of summer homes; motorboats kept in garages attached to lake-front cottages; and, among the wealthy, yachts of palatial size and equipment. Children take sailing lessons as well as tennis lessons, enter races or regattas, learn every trick they can to pull out front and stay there. Some of those who sail detest motor-driven boats as a noisy, vulgar presence and as the toys of the *nouveaux riches*. In the inland parts of the country Sailfishes or canoes share less socially conscious company with the fast-moving motorboats. Out West, canoes have their own special place — traditionally and symbolically the pioneer's means of navigating swift, treacherous rivers.

A number of children whose parents are quite well-to-do also take an interest in flying and parachuting; a father owns a plane or works in a company that does. Such a family flies privately, perhaps, more than on commercial planes. In the New England states the family finds its way to airports that serve the needs of small planes. There, a spirit of camaraderie exists: families whose planes the same mechanics care for; people who recognize in a way of travel yet another sign of what might be called the apartness that goes with wealth. Among the very rich, there is a pilot, whose work is analogous to a chauffeur's. Among the modestly affluent the husband has learned to pilot the plane and, these days, the wife, too. They may well fly from one of their homes to another — or to visit friends a few hundred miles away for a weekend. And not rarely their children, as they become older, have their eyes on flying lessons and on parachuting.

In the "main home" or "winter home" of such families one sees constant photographic reminders of how diverse life can be, given the money and the will: framed pictures of other houses, or of parents and children riding horses, sailing boats, playing with tennis rackets or golf clubs. Other pictures show tourists in strange lands or about to board planes, disembark from them. There are always new lands, continents to visit. Old, worn Persian carpets are valued, among other reasons, precisely because they give just the slightest impression of shabby gentility to homes owned by people determined to indicate how casual and relaxed they have become with their considerable wealth. In other homes one finds magnificent new Oriental rugs — lush Bokharas, sometimes placed on top of wall-to-wall carpeting, the latter especially prominent in the newer homes of upper-middle-class Southern and Midwestern families. In some homes prayer rugs or Navaho or Pueblo rugs hang on the walls. In some homes the rugs are changed by the season. At times a woman may replace one Oriental rug in midwinter with another: a pleasant change of scene for her and the rest of the family.

The antique market depends heavily on the aspiring tastes of people who regard chairs, tables, clocks, and pictures as important aesthetic objects — and a means of self-definition, self-assertion. Antique shows, auctions, or benefits can be important social occasions. The acquisition of a particular painting, or some piece of Oriental art — jade, a bowl, a tea service — or of a fine old desk becomes, at least for a while, an event in a family's life. The furniture in a young child's room may be old, valuable, rare — or quite new and decidedly ingenious, interesting. Sometimes there are mixtures: a nineteenth-century Windsor chair, resplendent yet fragile, next to a two-level bunk bed, equipped with a ladder, attached lights, pull-out sideboards, and decorated with a patchwork quilt that may have been sewn a hundred years ago and that cost almost as much as the bed itself. Across the spacious room stands a disarmingly "common" roll-top desk, once the unpretentious property of nineteenth-century or early twentieth-century burghers, but now relatively rare to find, as children know and say, echoing their parents' words. The desk is against the wall and not far from a window. The walls of children's rooms in upper-income homes are a vivid contrast indeed to the bare and forsaken surfaces within the homes of not only poor but also working-class people. A child sitting at the roll-top desk can lift his or her head and look at attractively decorated wallpaper, at framed photographs, a painting, curtains that nicely set off the room's windows. The curtains offer their own view — in fact, the room is a room of views, each somehow tastefully connected to the others. And beyond there is the land, there are the trees; everything, it seems, contributes to a child's sense of place, privacy, property, stability. And beyond too there are others, waiting in readiness to serve, to work, to make things as easy as possible.

Many of those "others" work in stores that sell "provisions" as well as regular American food, stores that may take great pains to distinguish themselves from supermarkets. Even supermarkets, for all their uniformity, make exceptions, feature special kinds of meat, canned foods, preserves, bread, fruit, and vegetables. The steaks are the best. Lobsters are available, sometimes flown hundreds of miles. Jams and jellies are English as well as American, or indeed French, Swedish, Spanish. Spices and condiments abound; so does the very best of fruit, plentifully available out of season. In many towns or villages there is a cozy "country store," which despite its name carries all that is convenient and contemporary in packaged food along with various nostalgic offerings — candy in buckets or individually weighed and wrapped; meat specially ordered and cooked; a rotisserie that never seems to stop from morning until evening — indeed, a store that keeps open virtually every day of the year and offers to cater food as well as sell it from the shelf.

Such a store serves a community of people who may not at all take to the notion of large-scale suburban shopping malls. Yes, if need be, one drives a car to those malls, enjoys what they incontestably have to offer, but they are best located elsewhere. The drugstore in a well-to-do village or town may be deliberately old-fashioned in appearance. The hardware store carries feed for animals. The post office is small and informal. The bank is designed not to stand out prominently. There is often a bookstore, a record store. And maybe there is a pleasant restaurant that responds at various times of the day to quite different customers. A point is being made, though no one has ever got up and made it publicly — and, maybe, few have ever done so in private: the people hereabout want to keep the neighborhood where they shop cozy, informal, even intimate. It is as if a minority of Americans had decided that they want to remove themselves, to a degree only, from the twentieth-century commercial actuality of their country and return to the business spirit of another age.

The men, women, and children who come to those stores often do so in what other Americans might call "farm clothes," if not worn-out rags: dungarees, battered khakis, tennis shoes that rarely look white, sweaters with a hole or two in them or at the least well-worn, shirts with sleeves rolled up and not so thoroughly tucked in. Not always, of course; not every successful businessman or lawyer or doctor has the desire to drive a conspicuously old car or wear clothes a garbage collector or factory worker would refuse ever to put on. Nor do the well-to-do always go shopping with little or no money and, at times, no credit cards, either. But in all parts of the country one does see among a significant number of such men and women just those habits and preferences — as if one must act like a nearly indigent farmer, who has barely enough standing in a particular village to secure the necessities of life.

There are men and women worth hundreds of thousands of dollars, maybe millions of them, who make it a habit not to carry money when they go "down" to a nearby group of stores and make various purchases. They look at a man or woman near a cash register, smile, exchange greetings and walk out, their arms full of costly items. In some instances even a milk shake for a child gets charged, but never in such a way that the boy or girl sees or hears anything to prove that such a transaction has in fact taken place. Usually the parent doesn't even have to nod, or look in someone's eyes, let alone suggest the need for payment. Rather, the owner of the store or an employee in it has learned how to be utterly discreet, never do or say anything that so much as implies acknowledgment of a sale, and talk instead about that old reliable, the weather. If something more serious comes up, especially of a political nature, there may well be a smile, and a brilliantly relaxed kind of noncommittal acknowledgment: indeed, indeed, the times are strange and vexing — on that we *all* can agree! Meanwhile, the children are there — walking in and out of such stores, hearing words exchanged, noticing who says what to whom, observing their parents' several cars get filled up, yet never at all observing the gas get paid for, watching their parents take money out of a bank, but not often seeing their parents bring money into the bank.

The very rich have family compounds, but so do merely quite well-off families — many acres, on which may live several families in several homes, none of which is visible to the others. Sometimes among the wealthy there is the large house of a child's grandparents, even great-grandparents; then, farther up the road, a "cottage" or two — substantial, even magnificent, homes in their own right, but offspring of sorts to the "main house." In the "cottages" live a child's parents, uncles and aunts, cousins. If the original tract of land is large enough to accommodate those families in adequate seclusion, they may decide to deed some land to a village for "conservation," in the interests of "ecology," or maybe, recreation. Thus the "character" of many such villages in the East or the South and even in the far West changes more slowly than would otherwise be the case. From the air one sees a cluster of homes, or maybe only one or two, then stretches of woods, streams, meadows, marshes, hills. Or one sees a series of full-fledged farms — belonging to so-called gentlemen farmers, who work in cities and maybe have apartments in them but return nightly or on weekends, at least part of the year, to a cattle farm, or a produce growing one, or both, which an employee (or two, or three, or more) keeps going.

Small private schools are very much part of the landscape. In the beginning it is a nursery, maybe in the basement of an Episcopal church, or maybe in the home of a person who is not rich at all but has earned the confidence and respect of those who are, and wants very much to work with their children. The nursery teacher's home may be nearer the center of the village or town — and smaller, though in keeping with the architectural tradition of the surrounding countryside. The children are transported there as much by housekeepers as by parents, and by the age of four are spending not rarely more than a morning away from home. The school may have a special "orientation" — Montessori, for instance. There are relatively few children, compared to the number of adults who work with them. For older children there are the "country day schools" — dozens of them by that name all over this country, and not dissimilar, be they in New Mexico, Texas, Alabama, West Virginia, or on the Atlantic Seaboard. Those schools, too, enjoy an architectural affinity to the prevailing mode of the neighborhood served. They may be quite well endowed, supported not only by tuition but various fund-raising social events. It is in those schools (their playing fields, their classrooms and eating halls) that a small but important number of American children begin to live, for a few hours at least, with others of their own kind, and begin also to get some sense of what the rest of the nation is like. Often the teachers in those schools are the first adults to give the children sustained, clear expression of their own views — in contrast to the fearful or ingratiating agreement of shopkeepers.

Many upper-income families, however, live in cities and even in the summer prefer travel to Europe, Asia, the Pacific islands, to a country or seaside life. They live in luxury apartments, occasionally in hotels, or in old town houses — on Boston's Beacon Hill, on the East Side of New York, in the Garden District of New Orleans, in the Georgetown district of Washington, D.C., on the Near North Side of Chicago, on Nob Hill in San Francisco, right smack in the middle of downtown Los Angeles, or on Canyon Road, Sante Fe. Those are all well-known neighborhoods, and of course, some of the people who live in them also have country places, Caribbean retreats, ski lodges. But a substantial number of quite privileged parents prefer to live and bring up their children in the city, even shunning at times the actual ownership of a house or an apartment. Young boys and girls who live such a life can be seen walking in city parks, often accompanied by a governess. They can be seen riding bicycles on sidewalks or using swings or playing in sandboxes, again under the watchful eyes of a parent or a housekeeper. They may live in penthouses that have their own gardens and areas for play. They may live in a town house that has a small, open courtyard, also convenient for the activity of children. Some practically never play outside; instead, they spend time in rooms set up for the vigorous, uninhibited energy of the young. Often such children get to know museums, restaurants, department stores. They learn how to dress more formally, restrain themselves in public, be watchful, careful; they do so because for them life is more "public," is more connected to the demands of others — and yes, because of the dangers city life presents. A child learns, at five or six, about taxicabs, waiters who expect to be tipped, policemen, elevator operators — not to mention an elevator that requires those who use it to push the right button, or else. And then there are the doormen, who befriend children, keep an eye on them for brief, and sometimes not so brief, periods — and who, for some boys and girls, become important friends, allies, and teachers.

Those same children may well learn, even at nursery school age, that they possess passports, that they have Social Security cards, that an income accrues to them by the year. The passports enable travel; and some boys and girls know certain foreign places as well as their native city — to the point that in kindergarten or before they talk about various experiences abroad, often more extensive by far than those of their teachers. The schools are often, to outward appearances, homes very much like those many wealthy families own — town houses made into nurseries or elementary schools. The children walk to school or are driven — by cab, by a chauffeur, in a car pool. Some parents want their boys and girls to learn as much as possible about urban living and so encourage them as they get older to take the bus, the streetcar, the subway. Other parents want no part of that life for anyone in their family. Even servants arrive and leave by cab. Occasionally limousines are called into service, driven by chauffeurs hired for the day: a trip to visit someone in the far suburbs or to an airport. Some families keep a car and a chauffeur all year round, however little they are used.

Children learn to amuse and be amused by servants, and also learn to make do in apartment houses or old, restored town houses. They run races up and down stairs, go on expeditions to the boiler room, open and close doors meant to receive trash, learn to make friends with policemen or janitors, develop a keen sense of the dangers as well as the opportunities city life offers. The foyer to a distinguished apartment house can become a virtual playroom, with the doorman (he may be one of several) a casual and inventive overseer. The network of servants in such buildings — maids, cooks, chauffeurs, and those who keep the heat going, the entrances secure — is for children a source of friendship, assistance, and, not rarely, fear or intimidation. A boy may ask who is on duty at some particular station, knowing that if it is one person the morning or afternoon will be fun, if another then best to think of some other way to pass time. And even in the city, time can be spent ice skating, horseback riding, learning to distinguish between various kinds of birds, even fishing. And there is a zoo or an aquarium. There are plays for children and concerts for them, special magic shows, tours, and lectures, in sum: "everything," according to one eight-year-old girl who lives in an apartment house on Lake Shore Drive, Chicago.

Her words provide a useful way of describing and summarizing the way other children of quite well-off parents live, however removed from the cosmopolitan life of America's "second city," or for that matter, its first city, its third city. "Comfortable, comfortable places," she once said, referring to her parents' enormous duplex apartment, a ski lodge they maintain in Aspen, Colorado, and a lovely old New England clapboard home by the ocean toward the end of Cape Cod. She was not bragging; she knew a pleasurable, cozy, even luxurious life when she saw one (*had* one) and was not at all uncomfortable describing its many, consistent comforts. She happened to be sitting on a large sofa as she offered her observation. She touched a nearby pillow, also rather large, then moved it a bit closer to herself. The pillow had many colors, was soft, blended in nicely with the couch's covers yet maintained its own authority. In a rather uncharacteristic burst of proprietary assertiveness, the girl said: "I'd like to keep this pillow for my own house, when I'm grown up."

Children like her have a lot to keep in mind, look after, and, sometimes, feel attached to. At the same time, they may often be overwhelmed with toys, gadgets, presents; and they may wonder why it is that their rooms keep on being redecorated, or whether their family ever stays in one house longer than a year or so. Even within a given home there may be more rooms than a child knows how to make sense of, or come to terms with — at least when he or she is seven or eight. As a result, parts of an apartment or a home become foreign territory, virtually — to be kept at a distance, or entered only with caution and perhaps in the company of a servant or a parent. The same may hold for the surrounding countryside — land that children know to be the property of their parents, but prefer to keep clear of. Better to stay inside; and inside, better to enjoy the "comfortable, comfortable places" — a particular room or two.

There is just so much a child's mind can easily absorb and feel at ease with. Children can be as acquisitive as anyone else, but they prefer to stake out territorial limits, and they also have a stubborn habit of clinging to the familiar, however old and even useless it has become. So it is that children whose parents are wealthy indeed insist upon holding on to a tattered security blanket, a certain pair of worn pants, a dress that no longer really fits. They come home from school, from a walk or a game outside, from lunch with their parents in a restaurant, and they announce that the living room is theirs — but the sitting room or the dining room or the library is utterly out of bounds. After a vacation spent in the South or halfway up a mountain or on another continent they are especially determined to establish their own sovereignty and indicate thereby the limits of their (contemporary) possessiveness.

These are children, after all, who have to contend with, as well as enjoy, enormous couches, pillows virtually as big as chairs, rugs that were once meant to be in palaces of the Middle East, dining room tables bigger than the rooms many American children share with brothers or sisters, and, always, the importance and fragility of objects: a vase, a dish, a tray, a painting or lithograph or pencil sketch, a lamp. A boy or girl who is just beginning to figure out a dependable rhythm of activity and restraint for himself or herself has to stop and wonder how much of a "comfortable, comfortable world" he or she dares include in various journeys or forays through the house. And how much of that world can the young child even comprehend? Sometimes, in a brave, maybe desperate, attempt to bring everything around under control, a child will enumerate (for the benefit of a teacher or a friend) all that is his or hers, all that goes to make up what an observer might call the "setting," the background against which a life is carried on. Large trees get mixed up with globes built into tables; a pond is linked in sequence with a library of thousands of books; a Queen Anne desk shares company with a new motorboat that goes so fast the child's father, no stranger to speed, has begun to have second thoughts about the safety of those who go aboard with him.

Finally, the child may grow weary, abandon the spoken catalogue, and think of one part of his or her life that means *everything:* a snake that can be reliably seen in a certain stretch of mixed grass and shrubbery along the driveway; a pair of pheasants who come every morning to the lawn and appear remarkably relaxed as they find food; a dog or a cat or a pony or a pet bird; a friend who lives near a summer home,

or the son or daughter of a Caribbean cook or maid; a visit to
an amusement park — a visit that, for the child, meant more
than dozens of toys, some virtually untouched since they arrived; or a country remembered above all others — Ireland or
England, France or Switzerland. Posters that commemorate
those voyages are often found in the rooms of such children
— elements of fantasy and pleasure, evocations of what was
seen, heard, and enjoyed, and, not least, reminders of what the
child confidently, realistically expects to see yet again. No
preliminary sketch of the physical "ground-being" (as both
Heidegger and Tillich put it) of upper-middle-class life, or of
the habits of the rich, ought to fail to mention travel as a strong
influence on a select number of children.

Not that the parents of those children necessarily live
uprooted lives; some do, but others have a firm sense of belonging to a particular region and, within it, a given town,
village, or city; and those men and women usually try hard to
give their children a similar sense of themselves. Boys and
girls, when born, get silver cups, engraved with their names
and birthdays. Children are shown family insignia, "trees,"
lines of descent. If a parent's picture appears in the newspaper, a clipping is put on a child's bulletin board, even if he or
she is not yet old enough to read the words. Banners that
fathers had in college rooms appear in the rooms of their
children, as do banners handed down from grandparents or
great-grandparents.

The child can look at himself or herself as a baby, or as a
toddler, or when first going to school, because there are usually many photographs that commemorate moments or events
in his or her life. Indeed, there may be photographs that commemorate similar events in the lives of parents and grandparents. Diaries and family letters of ancestors may well have
been kept, or published for the general public, or privately

printed. An old family home or family compound, long since gone, nevertheless lives in the child's mind through a photograph. In contrast, of course, are those families that have quite a lot of money but few links to the land or to a region's history, or indeed, so far as their loyalties or memories go, to preceding generations. But even children in those families are often taught reasons to feel proud of themselves and, just as well, to feel grateful for what their parents may have done on their own, against great odds and with considerable self-sacrifice.

These children learn to live with *choices:* more clothes, a wider range of food, a greater number of games and toys, than other boys and girls may ever be able to imagine. They learn to grow fond of, or resolutely ignore, dolls and more dolls, large dollhouses and all sorts of utensils and furniture to go in them, enough Lego sets to build yet another house for the adults in the family. They learn to take for granted enormous playrooms, filled to the brim with trains, helicopters, boats, punching bags, Monopoly sets, Ping-Pong tables, miniature tea sets, stoves, sinks, dining sets. They learn to assume instruction — not only at school, but at home — for tennis, for swimming, for dancing, for horse riding. And they learn often enough to feel competent at those sports, in control of themselves while playing them, and, not least, able to move smoothly from one to the other, rather than driven to excel. It is as if, for many such children, the various outdoor sports are like suits of clothing, to be put on, enjoyed, then casually slipped off.

Something else many of these children learn: the newspapers, the radio, the television do not offer news merely about "others," but rather about neighbors, friends, acquaintances of one's parents — or about issues one's parents take seriously, talk about, sometimes get quite involved in. These are children who have discovered that the "news," that events, may well be affected, if not crucially molded, by their parents as individuals or by their parents as members of a particular segment of society. Similarly, parental authority wielded in the world is matched by parental authority exerted at home. Servants are told to do things, are called in, are rung in, are given instructions, or, indeed, replaced summarily. In a way those servants, by whatever name or names they get called, are for these American children a microcosm of the larger world as they will experience it. They are people who provide convenience and comfort. They are people who, by and large, aim to please. Not all of them "live in"; there are cleaning women, delivery people, caretakers, town inspectors, plumbers and carpenters and electricians, carriers of telegrams, of flowers, of special delivery letters. Far more than their parents, the children observe the coming and going, the back-door bustle, the front-door activity of the "staff": teas, cocktail parties, receptions, or just an ordinary meal.

It is a mixed world, a world in which social classes come together, work alongside one another, in ironic ways — a lawyer come to draw up a will or give advice on a business arrangement, being served coffee by a maid, both of them awaiting a child's father, while the child bounces a ball, walks in and out of the room, and decides to ask that he also be given something to drink. It is a world others watch with envy and with curiosity, with awe, with anger, bitterness, resentment. It is a world of decisions — purchases to be made, bids to be offered or taken up, places to go, people to see. It is a world, rather often, of action, of talk believed by the talkers to have meaning and importance, of schedules or timetables. It is a world responsive, of course, in its own way to the cycles of birth and death, to the seasons, to engagements and marraiges, to children and their vicissitudes and triumphs. It is a world in motion — yet, at times, one utterly still: a child in a garden, surrounded by the silence acres of lawn or woods can provide. It is a world of excitement and achievement and eventually inescapably, disaster, tragedy, failure. It is an intensely private world that suddenly can become vulnerable to the notice of others. It is, obviously, a world of money and power — a twentieth-century American version of both. And it is a world in which children grow up, come to terms with their ample surroundings, take to them gladly, deal with them anxiously, and show themselves boys and girls who have their own special circumstances to master — a particular way of life to understand and become part of.

PART TWO

THE METHOD

TWENTY YEARS of work have furnished this book, and still as I write it I wonder whether I can do even a minimum of justice to the special and trying complexities, ambiguities, and inconsistencies that keep arising in connection with the lives of children who come from upper-income families. When I worked with poor children, there were always negatives to evaluate psychologically and try to comprehend: race, extreme poverty, social marginality, cultural isolation or dispersion, the peculiar and sometimes devastating stress of Arctic weather, the consequences of military plunder or political domination, the consequences for a boy or a girl of a hand-to-mouth existence, attendant hunger, malnutrition, lack of proper medical or dental care, inadequate education.

A physician is one who heals, Hippocrates reminded his colleagues and to this day would-be physicians are urged to remind themselves. Despite recent advances in medicine there is still plenty of pathology among children regardless of race or class. The private pavilions of various pediatric hospitals and the centers devoted to the understanding and treatment of children's psychiatric problems are by no means without substantial waiting lists. Some of those lists, as I well remember from my early days as a child psychiatrist, are so long that middle-class children must wait a year or two, or more, for treatment — by which time, alas, a rather new presenting complaint (or complex of symptoms) may have emerged. Even wealthy parents can't always obtain the commitment of time and energy, the promise of experienced intervention, they desire from a particular child psychiatrist or his or her colleagues. There are, after all, only a few hundred such men and women in the entire country.

Against such a background of continuing need for treatment on the part of hundreds of thousands of children, I wonder at times how to justify my two decades of concern with reasonably "normal" children, psychologically speaking, including those whose parents are quite well-to-do. Many of the children whose thoughts and convictions I have tried to present in this volume have known solid homes, psychologically speaking, and in addition belong to families of weight and substance in their particular communities. Why then extend the use of an expression like "children of crisis"?

I actually began the work of this volume without ever contemplating its existence. I happened to come South in 1958 when the doctors' draft landed me in Biloxi, Mississippi, as chief of the neuropsychiatric unit of an air force hospital. I also spent a lot of time in New Orleans, where I went through psychoanalysis and was preparing to go through the necessary seminars and clinical work of the New Orleans Psychoanalytic Training Center, as it was then called. (It is now a full-fledged Institute.) I had originally, before entering psychiatry and child psychiatry, been headed for pediatrics, and had taken hospital work in that field. While working my way through and sometimes reeling from the rigors and perplexities of psychoanalytic experience and study, I felt a need to work with children in Louisiana and Mississippi as I had done in Boston at the Children's Hospital. I volunteered time at several pediatric clinics, and thereby (it was still the 1950s) came to meet and know an exclusively white population, mostly middle-class. I became interested in the differences between those children and the ones I knew in Boston, attributable, I knew, to the mark of regional culture on all of us, even boys and girls not yet in school. I was far less aware, however, of the relationship between a child's social background and his or her psychological development. At the time there wasn't even a field called "social psychiatry." The important book *Social Class and Mental Illness,* by August Hollingshead and Frederick Redlich, appeared in 1958, and marked the beginning of a long struggle to demonstrate the relationship between a person's position in a society and the way he or she is regarded and treated by others, including psychiatrists.

My professional ignorance and narrow-mindedness was soon to be confronted with the increasingly explicit and strongly worded demands of the black people I began to meet and work with and also the repeated admonitions of those working-class white people who so strongly opposed school integration in New Orleans. Again and again, during that city's prolonged agony of the late 1950s and early 1960s, I was asked by the black and white parents whose children I was getting to know — ever so slowly, and at times with great difficulty — why I was "bothering with" them. The same words kept coming up in home after home; and the same resigned, wry conviction: that I was wasting my time, because the people who really mattered, the people who have run and do run and always will run New Orleans live elsewhere, and it is their ideas and thoughts and hopes and worries I'd better go learn about. I was confronted rather firmly with my own previous remarks to those black parents or those working-class white parents — to the effect that it was one thing to work with a child in a clinic, medical or psychiatric, and quite another to get to know about the *lives* of those children.

Too complicated and sophisticated a distinction for "ordinary" people — indeed, not very well educated and quite hard-pressed people? I would have said so unequivocally twenty years ago — *did* say so, in a way, to myself. When a black mother told me that I should go talk with "the big, important, rich white people," I virtually ignored her words. Instead I noted for my records what (I presumed) she was "actually" or "truly" trying to tell me — that she didn't want me around, bothering her and her children with my questions, and my silly requests of her daughter that she draw pictures and more pictures. And then there was the desperately frightened and enraged white father, a factory worker whose salary was low and who was laid off without benefits several times each year; he, also, kept telling me something: "Go see the rich folks and find out what's on their minds, so we'll know what's going to be on *ours* next week!" He was, I said to myself, being evasive and self-protective; he didn't want to talk with me about the hatred he felt for blacks, the personal worries he himself struggled to hold in check. He was suggesting I go see others as a polite way of telling me to leave him alone.

In fact, I didn't have to go see those "others." They came to the neighborhood where I was doing my work in the late 1950s — to the working-class section of New Orleans, near its industrial canal. They came from the fine, upper-income parts of the old port city; they were prominent people, many of them, terribly upset by the violence that first had been threatened and ultimately began to take place. They wanted to be of help, to intervene, to stop what at the time seemed like a headlong rush toward chaos. They came as worried observers who themselves, ironically, felt helpless before the tide of events that was in 1959 and 1960 beginning to overwhelm, it seemed, Louisiana and other Southern states. Doctors, lawyers, businessmen, they wanted their city to be spared humiliation and worse. They weren't in favor of school integration — many of their children were in private schools, anyway — but they were willing to try to "calm the waters," as one of them repeatedly put it. But the prominent citizens, attempting to work quietly and informally, were able to accomplish little. The black and white people who were in awe of them couldn't quite figure out what they would have them do: should the blacks retreat from integration? Should the whites permit integration without raised voices or without shaking outraged fists? The blacks and whites, both poor or at best only not so poor, were incredulous: exactly what did these visitors hope to accomplish, and why didn't they go back and do what they could do any time they wanted — lift their fingers and make things happen?

At first I talked with those influential men and women, because I was naïve enough to wonder whether in fact there was anything to the claim that "the rich," the "big shots," are the ones who "call the punches." Later, I started talking with their children — because I had been so relentlessly teased that I feared if I didn't at least make an effort to comply with an increasingly outspoken demand, I would soon be talking with no parents and no children in the city.

I was alarmed at the shrill protests I heard directed at "the rich people, the important people, the really well-off people," as they were called by a white man who belonged to the Ku Klux Klan, who worked in a brewery, and whose children would *never*, he kept on telling both them and me, go to school with "niggers." I was alarmed, too, at the connections being made for me — to what purpose I could not at the time make out — about the nature of my work as a number of parents I was meeting felt it ought to be. I became alarmed enough, I now realize, to yield — to broaden the work I was doing. And when in those small, old, beaten-down homes, some of them (in a major American city, in the second half of the twentieth century) still without indoor plumbing or proper electricity, I announced that I was, at last, going to the children of well-to-do New Orleans families, I realized, to be honest, that I had indeed bought some time for myself with the poorer people I had originally intended to see exclusively.

Now, many years later, I continue the work begun in New Orleans. Now I realize why it was utterly necessary to go see the privileged ones, who, of course, turn out to be more intimately in touch with the "lower classes" than I had once ever realized. Not that I wasn't told as much right off — in 1959, by a black lawyer in New Orleans who was arguing on behalf of the right of a number of black children to go to neighborhood schools, a scant block or two near their homes but hitherto open only to whites. When I told the lawyer that I was talking with a number of blacks, he asked me about white people. Which of them was I talking with? He knew the answer: with those who heckled the black children, boycotted the desegregated schools. The lawyer had others in mind.

"I think you're missing something important," he began. Then he gave me a speech, an old-fashioned, impassioned oration, after the style, he later acknowledged, of his father's Baptist sermons: "You keep on saying you want to know how the black people live, and how their children grow up. Well, they'll tell you, they'll show you. Even if they don't use the right words, the fancy language, they know what's happening in their lives; and they're good people, and they'll let *you* know what *they* know. But when you tell me that you're trying to talk with the white people, because the way they think affects the way black people live, then I have to ask you: which white people? I think you're going to the wrong people. You can spend ten years with those poor white folks, and what will you discover? You'll discover that they're in a mess, like us, and all they've got to hold onto, all they own, is their hate of us. And that's not much property — not compared to what other people have!

"Do you want to know what I think you should be doing? You say you want to find out as much as you can about black people. If you want to know why black people live the way they do, and how they live, and what's important in their lives, then you'd better go talk with white people all right, but not the ones you've been talking with so far. You'd better go talk with the people who own us, the people we work for, the people who tell us what to do — or else. And those people aren't the ones who are shouting 'nigger' at our children on the way to school. Those people aren't in the Klan, either. Those people own the plantation my granddaddy worked on. They own the factory my brother-in-law works in — nonunion, and he sweeps the floor! They own the stores we go to. (We're lucky if we can get a job sweeping the floors of those stores!) They own everything, and they decide what happens in this city, and in all the other cities. For every black child you talk with, go talk with one of their children. Go see what their sons and daughters think of all this mess we're in. Go see if those kids pay attention to what they hear in church, the way my kids do, and if those kids ask their mothers and fathers the same questions my kids ask my wife and me.

"I wake up in the middle of the night sometimes, and I'm all hot, and I'm in a sweat. You know why? I can't get some question out of my mind that my son Tommy asked me at suppertime. He'll be sitting there, fighting with his sisters, and giving my wife a lot of grief over her cooking, and I'll be ready to hit him one, but I clench my fists and try to keep my cool, and suddenly he'll turn to me and ask me why it is that God lets all this hate in the world keep going on, and why it is that the white people worship Jesus Christ, and say He was a good man, and say He was against hate, and pray to Him, but then they don't pay any attention to Him, not one bit? I don't know how to answer him; he's ten, and I think a lot of the time he doesn't act any more than eight, but when he comes up with those questions he makes *me* feel like ten, or maybe five!

"You ought to go and find out if there aren't some white kids who ask the same questions my son does. After all, there's always some hope in kids; they haven't learned all the rotten lessons their parents want them to learn! You ought to go find out how *they* feel, never mind how *we* feel. We feel rotten and lousy; we feel we've been had — ever since this country got started. The poor whites — they feel rotten and lousy, too. All you have to do is listen to them talking about us, calling us every filthy, crazy name they can come up with, and you know right away how filthy and crazy they feel. They've been driven nuts, trying to figure out this country, and the only thing they can do, is tell the world what's happened to *them* by shouting a lot of garbage talk at *us*. But what about the big-deal, important people, with lots of money and lots of respect, and a 'good name'? They all talk about so-and-so and his 'good name,' or his 'good reputation.' Let's hear what's happening inside those people who are on top. I've heard them talk, but I want to know what they think, and how they justify this life.

"You should go across those railroad tracks that used to divide nigger town and the white trash next door to us from the rich folks in the Mississippi town I was born in. You should go across the city to the Garden District, and knock on some of those doors on Prytania Street and Audubon Place — I've driven by. You should tell them you're mighty interested in them, just like you are in us. You should tell them the same thing you told that Dragon fellow in the Klan, and the same thing you told us black folks. Tell the rich ones that you can't know what's happening in one part of New Orleans, where the poor live, unless you know what's happening in the other part, where the rich live; and that part where the rich live is an important part. It's true, there's only a small number of people with a lot of money there, and here there are thousands and thousands without any money, not a dime to their names, except the checks they cash on payday, if they're lucky and have a job. But you shouldn't ignore the few and concentrate on the many — not when the few whistle, and the many have to come running!"

His promptings were more than echoed on the white side of the street; again and again segregationist parents, or fathers and mothers more frightened of than vehemently opposed to school integration, urged me to go to the city's well-off people — whose children, the working-class whites knew, stood no chance at all of going through the turmoil poorer families lived with almost three years in New Orleans. I asked those white people why I should go elsewhere, when there was a lot to be learned right there from them. Their responses sounded more like the black lawyer's than they would have cared to know. They railed, and sometimes ranted against "the rich" or the "big shots with plenty of money and all the power they want." They insisted that "public policy" is really the decisions that the well-off make, in dozens of ways — in order to accomplish their various purposes, secure their own interests. And if I took issue even tentatively with the sweeping, unqualified nature of such claims, I soon enough noticed how silent my hosts were, how carefully noncommittal about anything and everything they suddenly became — as if to say: all right, we are beginning to get your number, understand where you come from, or the direction of your loyalties and affiliations.

In 1959 — with more than enough already to keep me busy — I began to make some connections between the work I had done with upper-middle-class families who go to private psychiatric hospitals or clinics and the work I had begun with black families (all of them poor) and white working-class families. I did indeed go to the Garden District of the city and to the section near Tulane, where a mixed professional and academic community lives in nice old homes, less imposing and grand than in the Garden District, but quite comfortable to live in. And I started going to Metairie, an upper-income suburb of New Orleans. I had, in connection with my studies at the New Orleans Psychoanalytic Training Center and the pediatric work I had done at Touro Infirmary, met some families who lived there. Through the help of those families and because of events inspired by the city's racial troubles, it was not hard to come in contact with households headed by stockbrokers, cotton or sugar brokers, doctors, lawyers, businessmen, engineers, architects. The city's racial struggle prompted a number of prominent citizens to become actively involved in an effort — ultimately not successful — to spare the city violence. For the most part they did their work quietly, through personal meetings or telephone calls. But in a few instances there were visits to the beleaguered neighborhoods — often at the suggestion of wives. And at one point a group of well-to-do New Orleans women tried to act as intermediaries between the opposing black and white camps.

I recall one unforgettable moment, a turning point in my own work, when a lawyer's wife, never before interested in political matters, came to a meeting of enraged working-class white people, and spoke up, urging what she called "a spirit of Christian reconciliation." She herself became rather quickly a target, and soon had to leave. The abuse directed at her was not random or without a frightening kind of coherence. She was asked where her children were going to school, where her husband worked. She was asked what his income was. She was asked how far she and her friends were willing to go with respect to the integration of their schools, their neighborhoods. She tried to answer politely and thoughtfully, but soon realized that anything she said only seemed to inflame her listeners further. And I realized, only too slowly, how naïve and ignorant I was during that meeting. I had been offended by the rude way a rather fine and thoughtful woman had been treated. Not once had I taken seriously the complaints implied in the questions put to her. Not once had I made an effort to connect her, the others at the meeting, or for that matter myself, to a larger social and economic (never mind racial) situation. In fact, at the very end of the meeting, after the visitor had gone, one white man stood up and jolted at least me (his listeners, far more sophisticated, were not at all surprised) by pointing this out rather tersely: "We don't have anything against *her*. She means well. She's living her life, and we're living ours, and there's a big difference, and that's all. But if we're all going to get mixed up in this city, the colored and the white, then her people, the rich folks, can't just sit back and make the rest of us pay the price, like they do all the time, and then come down here and preach to us to behave ourselves and act the way they want us to act."

A rather wealthy woman had unwittingly become very much a part of the lives of much poorer, more vulnerable people. She never came back to that neighborhood, but she was mentioned all the time — a personal representative, as it were, of many others. Eventually she was replaced, psychologically, by the district federal judge, J. Skelly Wright, who ordered New Orleans to begin school desegregation, and refused to back down, however great the pressure on him to do so. In the first volume of *Children of Crisis* I described those pressures, and tried to suggest that the judge had become a symbol of much more — the judgment thousands of people had made about themselves, their lives, their condition. "We are the ones who take it on the chin for others," the segregationist street demonstrator, who worked in a brewery, kept telling me.

Those were the circumstances under which I began the research for this particular book. To be more specific, in 1960 I started visiting regularly five quite well-to-do New Orleans families — one of them that of the woman who ventured to the meeting mentioned above. These were not the "first" families of New Orleans, but they were far from the last in rank. They were the families of a lawyer, a doctor, a cotton broker, a department store executive, and a college professor who had a substantial inherited fortune. None of the wives, at the time, worked; all of them had their "charities." In four of the five families there were two children; in one, there were four. I began the visits because I wanted to talk with these particular people about what was happening to a lovely city I had grown to know and be quite fond of. I realize now that at the time I felt more assaulted than I could let myself acknowledge by the criticisms I was hearing directed at others — among them, professional men or university-connected people. Though I think I gradually became for many black or working-class white parents and children a certain *person*, I was also and maybe never stopped being a symbol (like the woman who preached "reconciliation") of another class, if not another world.

When I went to the Garden District, Tulane, or Metairie I was in a sense, no matter what my views or my sympathies, going home — visiting with my own kind. But the work with poor blacks and poor whites made me feel increasingly detached from, and sometimes uncomfortable with, upper-middle-class people. If I was ill at ease with the former for one set of reasons, I wasn't exactly having a relaxed time with the latter. For one thing, I increasingly asked myself to be more detached when I visited the upper-income homes. It was all too easy at the time to sit back, drink bourbon, and forget about class and race — discuss ideas, listen to music, talk about a movie or a book. If I was going to learn how the privileged weathered a severe storm, I would have to be more business-like — not bother them with awkward, bothersome, or rude questions but not forget why I was there and what ought be discussed. But in addition, I was bound to be influenced by what I was seeing and hearing every day "across town," in homes where jobless men lived, where women felt desperate about themselves and their children — where "every dollar counts." I can only touch here, on the "problems" encountered by a writer who moves back and forth from one world to another, trying to get close to people different from himself in various respects, trying to learn from them and understand how they feel, but at a certain moment moving away, either literally (the next "research project"!) or figuratively: the writer's need for distance. (There are many kinds of privilege!)

In any event, by 1960 I was engaged in "cross-cultural research" of sorts within my own country — at least, within New Orleans. I spent one day with black children, another with working-class white children, yet another with upper-income children. When I moved to Atlanta in 1961, and studied school desegregation there, I did the same. Actually, in one of the four high schools to which a handful of black youths were admitted, Northside, the predominant student population was upper-middle-class. Consequently, I was working with families different by virtue not only of skin color but of social and economic position. I had originally intended to suggest, in the first volume of *Children of Crisis*, how those differences affected the psychological development of children. But my wife persuaded me to hold off a bit. I did describe what happened in desegregated schools between black children and their new classmates, Southern white children from middle-class families. (In Atlanta and in Charlotte, North Carolina, a substantial number of rather poor black children were assigned to schools attended by children of upper-income families.) I did not, however, in that first volume describe the white children on their own, so to speak. Their racial attitudes, yes; I was ever on the alert for how white children regarded black children, and how, *comparatively,* the two sets of children tended to think about their future, their chances for a fairly decent and worthwhile life.

But I held off until this volume describing the lives, in their own right, of the children who belonged to the well-to-do families I had visited in New Orleans and Atlanta, because I realized that the subject of class as a psychological "variable" required rather more "fieldwork." When I extended my studies, began talking with sharecropper children, or migrant children, or Appalachian children, I made a point of talking with the children of plantation owners (in the Mississippi Delta and in rural Alabama) or of the growers who employ migrant farm workers, or of the people who own the mines of eastern Kentucky and West Virginia. I would see migrant children, for example, through the eyes of other boys and girls who lived a much more comfortable and settled life. I would also learn from those privileged children what kinds of lives they lived, hoped to live — and what thought, if any, they gave to others, far less fortunate.

By 1966, when I moved back to Boston after eight years in the South, I had talked with a significant number of children from the upper middle class; even with some children whose parents were quite wealthy — that is, millionaires several times over. The children lived in urban and suburban New Orleans and Atlanta, in rural areas of the South and Appalachia: the sons and daughters of growers, plantation owners, mine owners, small-town bankers, or insurance executives. Then, when I began increasingly to study the Northern version of America's problems with race and poverty, I knew that I would be talking with well-to-do families as well as those living in the ghettos or working-class neighborhoods of Boston, Hartford, Philadelphia, New York, Chicago, Cleveland. It took, however, a most unnerving evening with a wealthy Florida grower and his wife and their ten-year-old son for me, finally, to realize how critically important it would be for me to visit privileged families, if I was ever going to understand what kind of country migrants (or other vulnerable working people) live in and struggle to make sense of.

The boy had been having some trouble with his father for some time — minor trouble, as children's psychiatric problems go, but serious enough to worry both parents. In school he had been called "rebellious"; he would criticize the teachers for not being attentive to or concerned about the migrant children of the county, many of whom never go to school at all or do so only intermittently — a week or so, followed by an absence of a month, two months. The teachers had sent the boy to a school psychologist, who gave him tests, and declared him "sane" but "obsessive" and struggling with "hostility," which he originally felt toward his parents, especially his father, and now was "displacing" on to various schoolteachers. The parents had been called in, given a summary of the "findings," and told that the boy needed psychotherapy. The diagnosis: "pre-delinquent behavior" in a boy with "rigid personality structure," a "tendency to act out," and "serious problems with authority."

At first the parents were quite horrified by what they heard and naturally agreed to seek psychiatric treatment for their boy. But something in them both rather soon welled up — a tide of their own kind of rebellion. They began to wonder if their son wasn't "sick" but rather, in the father's words, "a believing Christian." They began to regard him as an accuser, a judge of sorts. The father employed, at extremely low wages, hundreds of migrant farm workers, including children. He began to wonder about his life — his values and assumptions. He had started with nothing, become a millionaire. He had always insisted that *his* work made him rich, but suddenly he, like his son, was worrying about Florida's thousands of migrant workers, including the ones who worked for him. And he was acknowledging that it had been *their* work that had made him a wealthy man. Soon he was urging fellow growers to build decent housing for their farm workers — and was doing so himself. Soon he was a thorn in the side of all his friends and increasingly regarded by them as a little "sick" himself, as well as potentially "dangerous." He doubled the wages of his employees. He urged them to form a union. And he began to receive threats on the telephone, by letter. Eventually he sold out — liquidated his considerable assets, moved to Key West, Florida, where he spent his time fishing, reading, and, more than he ever had, talking with his son. In a way, he "cured" his son — changed himself and helped the boy to change. And his wife became a different woman, too. She stopped catering to her husband's needs as a powerful grower (the head of a growers' association). She no longer was afraid to express her own views — about exploited migrant labor, and other matters too.

The three human beings whom I have just mentioned came to exert a strong influence on me. Long ago Freud pointed out that through an understanding of the "psychopathological" we come closer to knowing about the so-called normal; by the same token, this so-called troubled family had come to see things about itself that an outsider like me found more than merely "helpful." I was moved to consider once again why I was talking to such people — especially their children; and what I might want to think about as I went to their homes. Once the father begged and demanded of me: "Go to homes like ours, find out about the suffering children in our homes, find out the costs of success. Find out what happens to *our* children." I was enraged at the time. I had been visiting migrant camps all day, including one on his land. I was there, that particular evening, not to "interview" him or his wife or his son, but to let him know what I had seen among migrant children: the vitamin deficiencies, the malformed bodies, the infectious diseases; in sum, the poor health that went along with wretched living conditions. I had known him long enough to feel able to say my piece strongly, but he was already quite used to such criticisms. Long before I arrived in the county, labor organizers had come to see him — and his own son had for months sounded like a social critic. I had expected a shrug of the shoulders, a resigned acknowledgment that life is hard and unfair, a casual willingness to "look into the matter."

Instead he was almost plaintive, importunate, and I was disarmed. I persisted in my recital of sadness and human misery, only to see him lower his eyes, after which he reiterated his request that I talk more and more with children like his son. Nor was he slyly or unwittingly asking that I only help his son with his "emotional" problems. He was already, in Kierkegaard's phrase, "dangerously meditative." He was, in fact, asking me to respond to his own philosophical self-doubts — and to pay heed to a man's self-probing, a conversion experience prompted by his son's bothersome, unrelenting social conscience. For days afterward I thought about this. I had already spent many hours with his own son and with the children of other growers. But I hadn't until then completely granted that "research effort" a life of its own. From that time on, however, I knew that I would one day try to make sense on its own merits of the work I was doing with privileged children.

My work in certain Northern and Midwestern and far Western cities, covered in *The South Goes North,* brought me constantly in touch with the children of urban and suburban upper-income families. I was studying, among other things, the way black children manage when they are brought to schools attended by well-to-do white children — in wealthy suburbs like Princeton, which years ago initiated school integration. I tried hard to see how children from privileged homes during a few hours a day at school came to regard their new classroom neighbors. But I also tried to gain some appreciation of how those quite advantaged children came to regard themselves, their own prospects, their own situation. I did so initially in towns like Lincoln and Concord, quite well-to-do communities to the west of Boston; in Princeton, New Jersey; in Greenwich and Westport, Connecticut; in Winnetka, Illinois; and in several towns of Westchester County, New York: White Plains, Scarsdale, Hastings-on-Hudson. When we moved to New Mexico in 1971 to work in the Rio Grande Valley of Texas, I interviewed, besides Indian and Chicano children, the sons and daughters of ranch owners or enormously wealthy growers. In Alaska I found not only Eskimo children, but, in the cities, the children of individuals who employed "natives" — and in general had found the state to be an immensely profitable place.

I have worked with the privileged ones just as I did with other children — that is to say, I have visited certain boys and girls at home, talked with them, sat at tables (or often, on the floor) and drawn or painted pictures while they have done the same. I have asked them questions — and very often, especially among some articulate and strong-minded children from the Northeast, been in turn asked countless questions myself. I have spent months, sometimes years, getting to know these children — visiting them twice a week, usually, speaking also with their parents, their schoolteachers, and, not least, their friends. The work, as I have stated in the other volumes of this series, is based upon the observations of a child psychiatrist who has placed himself at a remove from hospitals, clinics, consulting offices. Instead of children visiting him, he visits them, tells them he is interested in their ideas, their observations, and tries later to portray them, to evoke their minds, hearts, spirits as pointedly and suggestively as he can.

I do *not* interview children with tests, tape-recorders, questions. I call upon them as a visitor and eventually, one hopes, a friend. They know that I am a doctor, that I am interested in how various children grow up. Those who are eight and above also find out that I have written some children's books — that I have wanted to write *for* them as well as about them. Especially with privileged children, those five children's books have been of enormous help. These are boys and girls who by and large have been encouraged to do a lot of reading, who possess libraries of their own, some of them quite substantial. They are also children not accustomed, unlike some poor people, to give of themselves to outsiders involuntarily or out of desperate need. There is a psychological analogue, after all, to sociological or economic statistics.

An article in *Business Week* (August 5, 1972) titled "Who Has the Wealth in America" gives a lot of information about the parents of the privileged children. We are told that "personal holdings of wealth are dramatically concentrated at the top of the population heap." We are told that "the richest 20%, which includes many people who do not consider themselves wealthy, has three times the net worth of the bottom 80%." We are told that "the top 5% of U.S. family units holds upward of 40% of all wealth." We are told that "the rich — the top 1% of adult U.S. wealth-holders — own roughly 25% or more of all personal property and financial assets." And, not least, we are told this: "The trouble is that the very rich, as F. Scott Fitzgerald put it, are indeed 'different from you and me.' They are much harder to count or interview than other Americans, and even government economists with access to Internal Revenue Service data have a tough time figuring out the share of the nation's wealth held by the rich."

Not only the "very rich," but the well-to-do, those who belong to the 5 percent mentioned in the article, are not used to being scrutinized the way the poor are — no social workers, welfare workers, police, sheriffs who knock on the door and, if resisted, push it wide open. As the article suggests, money buys privacy, protection, and power: the power to own, to satisfy cravings or desires, and a certain psychological power as well — one is under no obligation whatsoever to let anyone know very much. It is a power backed by lawyers, accountants, advisers, and sometimes by the tax laws with their various "havens." Beyond that, laws provide a form of sanction, even as other laws that enable various outsiders to enter and manipulate the homes of the poor also have a wider psychological effect. And apart from laws, the police, school authorities, city officials obviously respond differently to the well-to-do, as opposed to ordinary working people, let alone the poor.

To be specific about which children I have worked with, and to what degree of familiarity, and over what span of time: I started with the five families in New Orleans, and worked with a total of nine children in them, all between the ages of six and thirteen, for the four years I spent struggling to make sense of that city's racial tensions. In Atlanta, where for three years I worked with black and white children also caught up in the turmoil of desegregation, I selected five children from quite well-off families (in two instances, enormously wealthy — that is, worth many millions of dollars by their own public acknowledgment) and visited them, as I did other children, twice a week.

I worked with children between the ages of five and fourteen from six Appalachian families — rural, eastern Kentucky and Charleston and Huntington, West Virginia; six children ranging in age from five to eleven and belonging to four grower families of Florida; seven children (aged six to ten) from four Mississippi plantation families; from the North and Midwest (Boston, Hartford, New York, Cleveland, Chicago) a total of forty-seven children, some worked with a year, some for three or four years; in Texas, New Mexico, and Alaska, some fifteen children from nine families quite rich from oil or ranching, medicine, law, and insurance. In sum, eighty-five children over a span of about two decades — no number for a mass, even a representative, survey. This work does not depend on questionnaires, but on a long acquaintance, never less than a year in duration, and upon occasion up to four years.

Any reader of my previous volumes may skip the following account of the way I work. It is never really different, never very dramatic or surprising. It is one visit to a home, then another, with no list of questions, with awkward silences followed, thank God, by games played, pictures drawn or painted, and then maybe a little talk — a discussion of the day's news or of a subject the particular child has felt worth bringing up. It is being confused, and at times being self-centered and arrogant and demanding, but quietly so, I suppose — that waiting, waiting, for the child to clear things up. When that happens, when a boy or girl suddenly becomes a quite strong-minded and intelligent teacher, the listener, the observer, the doctor with his ambitions and prejudices and notions, may for a while be healed as well as educated. In the words of one girl, the daughter of a New England industrialist:

"If I'd known you wanted to hear what I thought about the people who work for my Daddy and they got fired, I would have told you a long time ago. We told Daddy, my mother and my older brother and I, what we thought a long time ago, when we were having breakfast." A chapter on method ought to include some mention of the writer's continuing uncertainty, confusion, failure of perception, and yes, inadequacy of faith with respect to the willingness of children to help someone along, make him feel more at ease, teach him, and, not rarely, disabuse him of his misconceptions, his flawed vision.

In the preceding volumes I have described the work that has finally brought me all over the United States of America, to each region, to every state. (The migrant farm workers are especially wide, if wretchedly paid, travelers.) I came to meet the children I write about because I was trying to document for various American children the effects of race and class, the influence of regional culture and environment, the bearing of historical circumstances as well as personal experience upon what is by some abstractly referred to as "child development." In a sense, then, each methodological account I have given of the work I did as a preface to writing a particular volume of *Children of Crisis* is also an account of the work done with some of the children I write about here — and who speak quite on their own here. I apologize for the length — perhaps a million words — in these five volumes; yet, my own self-centeredness aside, the "literature" contains all too few efforts in the direction of *children.*

It has not been as difficult as I expected to get to meet and know the children who appear in this book — perhaps because I never came to their parents as a stranger, suddenly at the door with a brazenly insistent set of inquiries. I met these upper-income families as an outgrowth of work that often they had good reason to know about: as growers and plantation owners; as important citizens in cities faced with traumatic social crises; as lawyers and bankers and industrialists and mine owners and factory owners, whose decisions every day affect black and white poor or working-class people.

If this book has any virtue, the credit rather obviously belongs to a lot of children whose experiences and reflections have finally eroded at least portions of a particular grown-up's ignorance and blindness. One last issue: my political sympathies, my social and economic views, as they come to bear on various children's memories, wishes, dreams, worries. I worked for years in the South with SNCC and CORE, the civil rights movement; in the first volume I described the work with youthful activists (the Mississippi Summer Project) as well as black school children initiating desegregation. With respect to migrants, sharecroppers, and mountaineers, the "subjects" of the second volume, I have been at one time or another a member of the National Advisory Committee on Farm Labor, the National Sharecroppers Fund, the National Committee on Migrant Children, and the Appalachian Volunteers, all quite actively involved in political struggles on behalf of quite impoverished and (for the most part) politically unrepresented people. I dedicated a book I wrote on Erik H. Erikson's psychoanalytic work to Cesar Chavez. I have testified repeatedly on the "condition" of these poorest of our poor before several congressional committees. I have written an assortment of muckraking articles in connection with the social, racial, and economic problems of the South, Appalachia, various ghettos, Texas, New Mexico, the Southwest in general, Alaska. I devoted a whole book to Dorothy Day and the Catholic Worker Movement (*A Spectacle Unto the World*) and spent many days with Daniel Berrigan, when he was underground, trying to spell out the various "positions" one can take (including his and my own) with respect to American society. My heroes

— of this century, at least — are James Agee and George Or-well, Walker Percy and Flannery O'Connor, Simone Weil and Georges Bernanos, William Carlos Williams, and Dorothy Day — none of them great admirers of this nation's upper-income, propertied families.

Nevertheless, I have tried to be as responsive and careful an observer and writer, so far as this part of my work goes, as I hoped to be with other children, other families. I guess the heroes I have just listed have all been a bit troubled, even tortured, by conflicting loyalties, by the fissures and worse within their sensibilities: a concern for the hurt, ailing, and desperate of the world as against a desire to make mention of life's ironies, ambiguities, paradoxes, inconsistencies, and com-plexities, however inconvenient they may turn out to be for anyone's "theory" of man or anyone's ideology, political agenda, or cause. I have wanted in this book to convey as exactly and suggestively as I know how the character of spe-cific lives — those of boys and girls graced indeed by good luck but not untouched by doubt, sadness, apprehension, and even terror, the result of social and political perceptions not always granted to the young by those who have declared themselves authorities or experts on their psychology or psychopathology.

As with earlier volumes of this series, I have edited and drawn together, for the purpose of narration, directness, and emphasis, quotations from various conversations held over months of time. Sometimes I have used a tape-recorder; some-times not. When I left particular homes, I would sit down with a pad of paper and pen and try to reconstruct what was said. I often use the present tense for the sake of immediacy — even though there is a chronological pattern in the individ-ual presentations of various boys and girls. I have tried in all instances to protect the children from the possibility of iden-tification. To do so has required, at times, not only changes of name and place of residence, but substantial alteration of other significant information. The point has been to struggle for representative accounts. I have not hesitated, at times, to condense remarks drastically or to draw upon the experiences of several children in the interest of a composite picture.

PART THREE

IN THE SOUTH

I

WILLFUL DELTA GIRL

S HE IS nine years old, thin, tall for her age, self-possessed, articulate. She moves quickly, runs when others walk, is a busy person — and has dreams of the future that scare the wits out of her parents. They are the lord and lady, virtually, of what looks like an English manor house on the inside, an imitation antebellum home on the outside. The father owns a plantation in the northern part of the Mississippi Delta, not far from Clarksdale, Coahoma County. He is also a banker and has the controlling share in an insurance agency. He has a sister in New Orleans, married to one of that city's most influential lawyers. He has another sister in Memphis, the wife of a doctor. The mother comes from Memphis, too; her father, she will laughingly boast at times, owned half the city, then sold everything, invested in the stock market, and left the country for London, where he owns a home in the Hyde Park section. He returns to Mississippi and Tennessee once a year, bearing gifts. His daughter still thinks of him as the smartest person she knows, her husband included. The mother lost her mother at the age of sixteen and has had three stepmothers since then, the last a woman once married to a duke, and now referred to as "the Duchess" by her husband's Mississippi granddaughter, a girl of nine whose future "plans," as she calls them, include marriage to someone in the royal family of England, a castle in Scotland, a home in the Caribbean, and a career to boot — as a movie actress who works only for English and European directors and never makes any films in this country.

The girl's name is Veronica; she was given the name of her London grandfather's third wife, an Englishwoman who took a fancy to the girl and has continued to correspond with her, even after a divorce and subsequent remarriage to a French businessman. Since then the girl has wanted to learn to speak French, as her former step-grandmother and namesake does so fluently. A schoolteacher in Clarksdale tutors Veronica in French twice a week. She receives weekly piano lessons and weekly lessons to make her already considerable ability at horse riding even more expert. Veronica also has been carefully taught by her mother how to dress, how to take care of the flowers outside the house and the plants inside, located in an enormous sunroom.

What the child craves and has yet to receive is dramatics lessons. There is no one nearby to teach her what she wants to know. She yearns to live, right now, in New Orleans. It is not, she knows, London, or Paris, or, in this country, New York; but she picks up copies of the *Times-Picayune,* and in it she notices mention of theater groups and of dozens of movies, even old ones brought back — all of which she wants to go see. The city's French restaurants also attract her, part of a cosmopolitan atmosphere she very much likes, and misses at home. Her school friends (daughters of lawyers, businessmen) consider her a touch peculiar, but great fun. She shares her hopes and dreams with them and thereby stimulates them. They gather periodically in one of their homes, call themselves a "rat pack," talk of writing letters to Robert Redford, but in the clutch are always stopped cold in their shared, elaborate fantasies by Veronica, who can turn off dreams as well as inspire

them. Who *really* wants to write a letter to Robert Redford,
when there is Marcello Mastroianni to try to track down
— or an English lord or duke or viscount? The friends laugh,
go home and tell their parents, hear Veronica called "too
mature" for her age and also "full of childish daydreams."

At school Veronica does quite well. She doesn't "live in a
world of her own"; she is right there all the time, listening to
her teacher and quite anxious to prove herself a good student.
She goes to a private school, all white and made up of children
whose parents are like hers, quite well-off. Her mother and
father make sure that the girl knows that they are *not* "racists," that they "bear no ill will" against black people. Private
schools are new to the South, most of it — especially to its rural
sections. Segregationist academies were born in the 1960s, as
school desegregation came even to Mississippi, and have by no
means disappeared, even though the state has turned away
from the racial confrontations of the past. A number of poorer
white "academies," catering to working-class families, have
collapsed; but not some of the "better" private schools. A few
of the latter even take a black student or two, but no more.
The white students are told by teachers and parents alike that
they attend because it is important to uphold the highest academic standards possible. The boys and girls nod their heads:
yes, of course. Veronica does, too; but she regards herself as an
astute observer of others — whom she unashamedly calls
"Americans," with tongue only partially in cheek and with
considerable hauteur.

She has this to say about her friends — and others, too: "I
don't think anyone wants to talk about the colored people, not
my friends, and no one else, either. The colored are living in
their world and we're living in ours. It's only in the public
schools that people who come from different homes — the
poor whites and my friends and me, and the colored —

are all supposed to mix. My father says it's a mistake, because
life isn't like that. They started our school, my father and his
friends, because it's no use pretending: if there are a lot of
colored, or poor white kids, then you don't learn much, and
there are fights all the time, and the school is a bad place. My
father said once that if worse came to worse, he'd hire some
tutors, and they could live with us, or they could live in one
of the homes on the plantation — the foreman's place. He
could move out. Then we'd learn at home. My mother didn't
like the idea, but she said there wasn't any choice.

"I had an idea, but I was too young. I wanted to go to
England and study there. My father said all right. But he was
only joking. My mother thought I was serious, and she didn't
like me talking that way. She says that even the school we go
to isn't good enough, and maybe we should *all* go to England!
Then I could get a good education! But she is fooling. She
wants to stay here, and she wants *me* to stay here! Once she
told me that I had a lot of big dreams, and she is glad I do,
but there's a limit! I asked her if we couldn't at least move to
New Orleans, and I could go to a good school there. No; we're
staying in Clarksdale, Mississippi, and that's that! I don't really
care. Our school is a good one. We have drama, and we have
ballet! I'm learning a few French words. A lot of the kids want
to be able to order in French when they go to a restaurant in
New Orleans, and so the principal hired a lady to teach the
younger children French. We have a colored girl in our school
and she's learning French. She's Creole, she says. Her father
has a lot of money. He owns funeral parlors all over the state,
my Daddy says: a rich colored man. His wife is light; my
mother says she's an octoroon — and that means very little
colored blood in her veins. The father is darker — but not as
dark as most of the colored are. He is always dressed up, and
he's very polite. They come to school in a big car, and there's

a colored man driving, and he wears a uniform. My father laughed and told my mother we ought to get Joseph to put on a uniform! Americans aren't like the English. In England our Joseph *would* have a uniform to wear.

"If I was that colored girl, I wouldn't want to come to our school. I don't know why they took her in. We're not supposed to be at school with them. They look different and they live different. Even that colored girl, she's usually by herself. She puts on airs with the other colored kids, my mother says she's heard. But she's not like that at school. She looks as if she wants to talk to everyone, but she never speaks unless spoken to. I'm sure glad I'm not her! I don't want to be anyone else in the world — except maybe a relative of the queen of England! Then I could have a castle, and I would be able to go to Buckingham Palace! I'd rather go there than to the White House! Look at the people who have been living *there* lately! My mother and father don't like to hear me talk against my own people, but I hear them saying they can't stand to visit Washington but they love going to London. Last time they went to Washington, they had their hotel room broken into; they lost money and my mother's watch and my Daddy's camera. The colored are running the city. In London, the police don't carry guns, and still the people behave better. Americans could learn a lot if they went to Europe and tried to be like the English and the French. But my Daddy says I'm wrong and I shouldn't talk like that. He says I'm beginning to be a snob and I'd better watch out! We have a teacher in our school who lived in England for five years. She's from Leeds, Alabama, originally; but lived in England for five years. Everyone looks up to her. My mother does; she says the teacher has the best mixture of accents — Southern and English!"

The girl wants to imitate her teacher, but can't. She worries about her own accent. What would happen if she were living in England, and going to a school in, say, London? Would the other girls laugh at her? Would she fight back, or try hard to sound more like them? And how could she fight back, actually? She has no answers for her questions. They come to mind, then are forgotten. Nor is she always all taken up with English reveries. She has her solidly American moments, long stretches of them. She watches *Emergency* on television; she likes *Adam–12;* she likes to go with the foreman of the plantation and see the cotton being taken in, the cattle being fed, land cleared or dug up or put to rest at the end of the season. She likes to wear dungarees, and ride bareback on her old pony, which she has outgrown, and on her mare, whom she has dubbed Clara, after an old black maid who worked for the family for many years and died just before the horse arrived. She likes also to read books about the West, about cowboys and Indians, as well as about England's royal history. And she likes to look at picture books of old Southern homes, a way of life she has heard praised and hopes one day to be part of. She also likes to go with her father when he shoots ducks or fishes. Her brother, three years older, goes along, too; the father does not try to encourage the girl to stay at home with her mother. Actually, the mother comes upon occasion: hunting or fishing *en famille,* they all say. The girl knows that some of her friends think it "peculiar," the interest a *woman* and a *girl* have in guns and in downing geese, but that is their narrowness or conventionality, and too bad for them. And finally, there is Lego, a game some of Veronica's girl friends say is for boys only. She laughs at her girl friends, scorns their preferences or prohibitions, teases them, argues with them, gives them lectures on "the true aristocrat."

Where did she get that expression? From her father's mother, for whom the black woman Clara worked all her life. Veronica's paternal grandmother was a proud woman —

rich, widely traveled, stubbornly interested in politics at a
time (the earliest part of this century) when for a woman of her
"class" and "background" and especially for a Southern
woman, a Southern *lady,* such a "disposition" was unthink-
able. That is how Veronica's mother describes her own moth-
er-in-law's political concerns — "a disposition toward politics": a strange taste or maybe a constitutional or temper-
amental idiosyncrasy. Even now Veronica has been told by
her father not to "bother" with the ups and downs of the news.
The reason: nothing can be done, anyway, by her or anyone
else to change things. Both her mother and her father constantly emphasize their political helplessness, even their social
vulnerability. Among the richest people in the Delta, maybe
in the state of Mississippi, they tell their children that others
have power, others determine their fate: Yankees up North,
low and dishonest politicians in Jackson, greedy and conniving
manipulators in the grain commodity market, or the gamblers
who move stocks up and down and feel no loyalty to any
particular corporation.

Veronica doesn't know exactly who all those people are,
what they do, but she does realize that her grandmother was
against them, demanded the right to vote so that she could
fight them, and ultimately acknowledged her defeat. In the
grandmother's last years, Veronica's father constantly remembers, there was a marked withdrawal of interest; the old lady
took a personal interest in her garden, cultivated semitropical
flowers, told everyone around her that America was going to
ruin. Her children and even her grandchildren see no reason
to dispute her judgment and certainly don't regard themselves as possible saviors. The only hope is stubborn survival,
as the girl of nine has been told, and in her own way firmly
believes: "You can't stop people from doing what they're
going to do; that's what my Daddy says, and he's right. I told

my cousin not to go into the pool, because he's a poor swimmer; but he did anyway and he near drowned. I had to go get help. He's lucky I'm a fast runner. Afterwards, I asked him why he did it. He started pretending; he said he *fell* in. Well, that's silly. He was walking around and around and showing himself off, telling me he could walk on one leg, and then the other, and sure enough, he stumbled and the next thing I knew he was kicking and splashing and calling for help.

"It's a good thing I was half prepared. I was sitting there on my mother's favorite chair, and with each sip of Coke I said to myself: when will that show-off fool lose his balance and fall in? It didn't take too long. That's what happens. When I told my Daddy, he said a lot of people are like my cousin; they think they know more than they do, and they have to be bailed out by others. The only thing you can do is try to stay clear of trouble. There's plenty of it around, but if you keep your eyes open and watch your step, you can get by. It's like that with my horse; when I ride far out in the fields, I have to keep an eye on the ground ahead, otherwise the horse might step into a hole, and fall and get hurt, and so would I. You get to know the good trails, and what to stay away from. My daddy says his mother was brokenhearted about what started happening to this country a while ago. She said the worst people are taking over, and the only thing to do is hope they'll ignore you, because they're so busy bothering someone else. That's what my father hopes will happen to us — they'll leave us alone, the Yankees and the people moving from the North down here to run the chain stores and the little factories."

She can't quite name a man or woman as an example of the kind of individuals her father fears and detests. She is sure her father could point out a few, were they walking the streets of Clarksdale. But he's too polite, she insists, to point at anyone. He tells the manager of his bank to be "fair to everyone," even to those he wouldn't at all ever want to lay his eyes on, never mind talk with or, God forbid, have in his home. Veronica has often heard that home mentioned as a sanctuary, removed to a degree from the rest of the world. When the girl was five or six she would "pretend" — say she was living in England and that she was going to take a pony ride and meet up with some lords and ladies down the trail. She no longer does so, but she does nod approvingly when she hears her mother and father say in jest that a moat around the house, as in medieval England, might be a great idea — a way of controlling entrances and exits, of establishing some small distance, at least, from an untrustworthy, deteriorating society.

The girl loves to draw or paint pictures of her home as it is, her home as she might want it to be later on — when she is grown up, a wife, a mother. She predicts that fate for herself rather often: early marriage and two children fairly soon thereafter. She would like, years ahead, to have a house very much like that of her parents — located, she estimates, a few miles away, maybe even on their spacious land. But she would also like a "retreat" — in England; a place where she could go to be "really away," with the Atlantic Ocean as a moat. In one drawing she pictures her home in Clarksdale as accurately as she knows how, then considers constructing a moat around it, only to change her mind. She draws several pheasants, places them on the lawn she has put near the house, then remarks that sometimes she feels like the pheasants she watches for minutes at a time from her window: quite easily made afraid by anyone who comes near. She has left food often for them and, to a degree, has tamed them.

She shifts her attention to the sky she has drawn; it was all blue, and she wonders whether she should add a cloud or two. She hesitates. No. Why? She is not sure — can only fall back upon the weather outside that day: clear, sunny, warm. But she is impatient with herself. She decides to talk about her drawing, her view of the surrounding landscape, and, not least, the weather as it was and as she would like it to be: "That's my house. It's a good house. My mother said an architect she knows likes the house and says it's watertight, and even if we had rain for a month, every day, we'd be all right. I don't like a lot of rain, but when it's sunny all the time, that's not good. You need water for the crops. Even if we don't have the sun for a while, Daddy is glad that we're not hurting for water. But when there's too much rain, that's no good. The crops get *too* wet! And even if our house doesn't leak, some other houses do."

The observation is enough to stop her talk, and her work with crayons. She sits and looks at what she has done. She moves her eyes away; they fasten, eventually, on a Chinese plate standing upright in a bookcase. She wonders out loud why such an object is never used. Did the person who made it intend that? She suspects not. She decides to draw the dish, and begins to do so, but interrupts herself. She returns to the drawing she has done of her home. She completes it, decides against clouds, makes the sun's beams more numerous, strengthens the already imposing home by adding a robust chimney; then puts aside the drawing (Figure 1), makes brief mention of "others," as she calls them: "The people who live on our land, the others besides us, come and help us here. They plant the cotton, and run the machines that harvest it. They cut wood and bring it for the fireplace. I'd like to draw a picture of their houses, but I'm not sure I could do a good job. I'd have to go there and look again. I haven't looked too hard."

She changes the subject abruptly. She prefers to talk about England. She asks questions about England's size, population, principal products — the questions a schoolteacher often asks of her — and then goes to the bookcase, brings back a book of pictures: English country homes, English sports, English cars and pubs and roads and hedges and gardens. She wishes that the English countryside were more readily available to her. Why haven't supersonic jets been put into service commercially? Why are distances still so important? Why do passports have to be renewed every few years? Why did this country have to separate itself from England? She isn't interested only in asking questions, however. She has opinions, strong ones. She does not especially like France, though she does want to speak French better. She has been to Paris twice, and each time felt confused. The people speak "too fast" and, of course, with words she can't follow, even though she might recognize particular words or expressions; and anyway, the French are rude, never show Americans any real courtesy. In fact, they are like the Yankees.

She has never forgotten her father's words: "The French and the Yankees are both full of themselves." In contrast, the English have good manners, she points out, and so do Southerners. When she is asked whether her remarks, rather general, are meant to include all the French, Yankees, English (or everyone she knows in Clarksdale, never mind the South as a whole), she smiles and says that she doesn't know many people in Clarksdale, and only one family in Alabama, her mother's cousins. She doesn't want to talk about everyone in the South, or anyplace else — only state her opinion, agree with her father's or mother's opinions. She is sure that there are nice Frenchmen, people who would be as courteous to her as she would be to them, were they to arrive in Clarksdale. As for Yankees, they are not unfamiliar to her. An uncle has ventured north to New York City, and she has gone to visit him, and met her cousins and their friends. Yankee children aren't so bad. They do indeed talk faster than she thinks they ought to, but that is the world — many kinds of people in it. And with that comment she brings herself back home to Mississippi — to her father's plantation.

A number of "the colored" have left for the North, she observes, but some will never go, and those latter are her favorites. She has actually asked her father if she might go visit some of their tenants. The answer was no, and she doesn't want to turn the matter into cause for an argument. She accepts his reasons, chief among them the possibility that her arrival would make "them" rather uncomfortable. She talks at some length about that likelihood: "You have to think of others. They're used to coming here and being with us; but they're not used to us going over there and being with them. My Daddy says he never goes into their houses. They talk outside. Daddy says they like to live the way they do, and you can't change them. It wouldn't be right for us to be giving them long sermons, and telling them to be like us. I asked Sally, our cook, if she preferred the food she makes for us to the food she cooks for her own family, and she said that we eat one kind of food, and her family eats another kind, and they're different. I asked her if she'd mind if I came over to her house and ate with her children, and she laughed, and she said that she didn't think that would be a very good idea. I asked her why not. Well, she said, she thought my mother and my Daddy would be upset, and they'd never let me go. I told her that if I really pushed them, they'd say yes. Then she told me not to; I could see that she really meant it. And she didn't want to talk anymore. She excused herself, and said she had to go outside and get the potatoes we had stored in a shed, and then she had to do a lot of cooking, because company was coming, and so she couldn't talk anymore. I left the kitchen."

She told her parents of the incident, and they had been rather stern with her. Her mother asked her not to "bother"

Sally anymore "that way." Her father had become more specific. He pointed out to her what she remembers him calling
"Sally's point of view." It is not good manners, he told his
daughter, to make someone else feel uncomfortable, to make
them want to leave. Veronica noticed that Sally hadn't gone
to get those potatoes, and later on, that there weren't any
potatoes for supper. The father made explicit what the daughter suspected — that the cook had made up an excuse, then
found it unnecessary once Veronica had left. The father also
told his daughter that people like to be with their own most
of the time, and that for her to visit the cook was to disrupt a
whole pattern of human involvements. The girl paraphrases
her father: "He said there are the colored and the white, and
the tenants and us, and that's how it is in Clarksdale, and all
over the world. He said he'd made a mistake, maybe; he forgot
to tell me to be polite with Sally, and not ask her the kind of
questions I did. But he assumed I knew that it's best to be
polite, but not get too friendly with the people who work for
us. It was all right for me to play with Sally's children when
they came up here with her, and I was younger. But when
you're old enough to go to school, then you're old enough to
know better. I told Daddy I was sorry. And he said he was
sorry, too — but it's best that you get to understand a lot of
things early on, and then later, you'll be spared a lot of trouble."

    She is quite sure that he is right. She has questioned him
since that time; asked him about England and France and
other countries: are there "colored" servants there, and if not,
do the white servants eat different food and dress differently
and talk differently, as is the case with "our colored"? The
father says yes, to a degree, that is how it goes; there are
servants everywhere, and they have similar responsibilities,
and they have their own preferences, styles of living, interests.

It is not a question of skin color, the daughter is told most emphatically. She remembers *that* quite well: "Daddy told me never to forget that it's not bad that a person like Sally works here and that her husband helps on our land; and it's not bad that a person is colored, because God made the colored, and He made us, and He didn't mean for one kind of person to be any better than another kind. We're just different. And if we lived in England, we'd probably have white people working for us, and they wouldn't be any better than the colored. And up North, a lot of the people who help with the house and do the cooking, they're not colored, and they steal, and they walk off the job, and they're bad people, and you can't trust them, the way you can Sally, and all the others over there on our land."

On one occasion she decided that she could, after all, draw a picture of the houses "over there." She started eagerly, reached for the black crayon, began to use it, but didn't get very far — part of one house. Abruptly she stopped, moved toward the top of the paper, switched to a blue crayon, and worked on the sky. She interrupted herself again, however; she abandoned her blue crayon, resumed work with her black crayon — putting it, however, to the sky. She used the crayon, too, when she drew the sun — a circle of black with yellow inside and no rays shining on the countryside. No grass either; she never picked up a green crayon while she constructed that picture, which turned out to offer the viewer three small, rectangular black boxes, each with a window or two, haphazardly placed and all on a straight line of brown, which she did with the aid of a ruler. There were no trees, no flowers, no growing crops, either. Just as she seemed finished, just as she was pushing the drawing away and preparing herself for a resumption of casual conversation, she had an afterthought. She picked up the black crayon again and drew a small animal

— a dog, it turned out to be; then she added a cat, the two near one another and in front of the three houses. She paused, quite evidently thought of going further, then decided no, enough. But she announced her interrupted intention: to picture one or two "colored people," including Sally, the cook. There was no room, however — or so she judged. (Figure 2.)

She decided to draw Sally, after all. She took a fresh piece of paper, looked at it intently. Suddenly she decided to measure the paper with her ruler. When she had done so, and come up with the result (9 1/2" × 11") she remarked that Sally was "big" and was "fat," so maybe there was need for a larger sheet of paper. When that was offered, Veronica laughed and said no, she could manage with the "regular" size — and anyway, she was only trying to be "a little funny." But she couldn't let the matter drop there — let it be that she had made a wry comment and maybe had not been correctly or intelligently heard by her listener. She began to talk about Sally, about her many "sicknesses," about the "sugar in her blood," and the "weakness of her heart," and the severe headaches she gets, "right over her eyes." She recalled the time Sally fainted — a terrible, frightening thud on the floor. Veronica had run to find her mother, who in turn had run to find her husband. By the time he came Sally had awakened and was determined to go back to work. She did so. Veronica saw her parents drive away — at two or three in the afternoon, for a tennis game. She went right away to the kitchen. She asked Sally why she didn't go home. Sally said "because," but no more. The child persisted. The maid (a lady of forty-three) kept being monosyllabically evasive: more "becauses" or a terse "I just don't want to."

Finally, Veronica became demanding, accused the cook of not telling her the truth. Sally was apparently frightened; she apologized, told Veronica that there was a large dinner party coming up in the evening, that it would have to be canceled unless she, Sally, the cook, stayed and did her work, and that "the missus" had in fact asked her to stay if she "possibly could," even though she had just collapsed. The girl remembered that particular account of Sally's: "She told me that my mother leaned over, while she was sitting in the chair and breathing hard and wondering if she was going to pass out again — or maybe, *pass* — and she heard my mother's voice, and she saw my mother's face, and she said yes. It wasn't much longer before she was back in front of the stove and in front of the sink, whipping up her recipes, and she felt real good, I could see that."

A little more talk about those recipes and the girl was ready to begin her portrait. She reached for the black crayon, put it down, reached for the brown one, started using it: the legs, wide and long, the feet on them, the midbody, with a massive, protuberant stomach, and then a long pause. The brown crayon is put down. The black one is summoned, then put down. The blue one is picked up — but not used. Then the brown one, again — and a circle gets drawn, several inches above the torso. For five or ten seconds that is all the child can do. She smiles to herself, decides to make the connection, does so abruptly with one line, then another, and there she is, Sally, the cook: no eyes, ears, nose, mouth; a thick neck that holds a circle of a face and is itself perched precariously on a belly. No effort is made to provide arms. The picture is put aside. (Figure 3.) The child returns to one of the several pictures she has done of her house. She adds a few flowers, puts a knob on the front door, stops. She has no desire to continue. Anyway, it is her mother who is the artist. Maybe she could do an oil painting of Sally.

Veronica remembers the various sketches and oils her mother has done of everyone in the family, of friends and relatives and neighbors. She points out that Sally of course is not among them, has never sat for a portrait. Why not? Obviously, because she is a maid, and has a lot to do. Surely, the child insists, her mother would have nothing against doing a painting of Sally. Often the girl has been told by her mother how fond she is of the cook, how dependent upon her. The child anticipates what her mother would say if a certain question were posed: "If I asked my mother, she'd tell me that it would be wonderful to 'do' Sally, and one day that will happen, but not now. And besides, it might offend Sally if we asked her for permission, because she'd have to say yes even if she didn't feel like it, and that would be wrong — to make her go along with us just because we had our wishes. We wouldn't be taking *her* wishes into consideration. Mother is too considerate sometimes. Sally might want to have her picture painted. Maybe she'd be nervous, though — sitting there and sitting there while Mother paints."

There are other "colored" servants, and the girl keeps an eye on them, too; finds them helpful, reassuring, stimulating. Their stories liven her imagination. She thinks of them at their homes, and makes up conversations between them and their husbands or wives. She seeks them out as friends. Over the years the gardener has helped her dig and construct things in the sandbox, learn to ride a bike. He has also taught her how to plant and care for flowers. The so-called handyman has built a cage, to her specifications, for a rabbit; shown her how to use a hammer, a screwdriver, a saw; and made for her dolls a lovely gazebo of sorts — a large outdoor sitting place for them. The maid, who cleans Veronica's room, is also an adviser: which dress to wear, how to arrange shoes, what to put upon the wall and where.

Not that the child's mother isn't anxious and willing to help her daughter out in countless ways; the two get along rather

well. But the mother, for all her graciousness, is a rather re-
served person and at times solitary by preference. She takes
to her room, reads a lot, and emerges calm, forbearing,
relaxed. Veronica has learned, however — has been asked
— to stay away from the mother during those "private" hours
of hers. Sometimes the girl has a friend over; forgets everyone
else, her mother and the servants alike. Sometimes the girl
calls her father up at his office; chats with him; asks his permission to go here or there, do this or that; tells him how she has
been spending her time. Sometimes she turns to the maid, the
cook, the gardener, the handyman, and of course they gladly
oblige. They often manage adroitly to obtain her cooperation;
she helps them at their work as they talk, and, so doing, she
learns about cooking or the care of the house or its grounds.
Later she tells her mother what she has come to know, and the
mother is quite pleased — even seeks out the particular servant and thanks her. So does the father; he has told his daughter that she has a lot to gain from talking with the servants,
because they are "good people" and "patient," and they
"know the world."

Such remarks are, however, not part of a coherent and explicit "attitude" toward the servants. At times Veronica hears her
parents speak disparagingly of the various people who work
for them: inside the home, outside, in the nearby fields, in the
bank. At other times there are approving smiles, nods, brief
expressions of approval. But when the child tries to find out
more, engage her parents in a general discussion, she comes
against unyielding resistance, and recognizes that fact: "My
mother and father don't like to be overheard talking about the
colored people. Besides, they say it's not right to talk about
people behind their backs. Last week Sally made pancakes
that didn't taste so good, and I said so, and I asked my mother
to ring and send the plate back, but my mother said no, and

she was right. She told me to try to eat what was before me. I did. Then she rang, and when Ruth came to ask what we wanted, mother said she wanted to talk with Sally for a second. I could see on Ruth's face that she was worried. She said yes, ma'am, and went and got Sally, and when Sally came, mother told her she was doing a wonderful job and we always loved her food, but this morning, even though everything was fine, the pancakes were a little flat, and maybe something got left out.

"Sally said she sure was sorry, and she came over and asked me if she could try again. I told her yes, and the pancakes still tasted pretty good, even if they weren't the best. Then she left, and I started crying, but I didn't know why. My mother told me to stop, or I'll embarrass Sally and Ruth. That's when I asked my mother about the colored, and she said there wasn't anything to be said about them: they are they and we are we — she said. I kept hearing her words, and I wrote them down when I got to my room in the afternoon, when school was over. Once I asked my Daddy about 'the colored'; he said the same thing. He didn't use my mother's words, but he said that people are different, and they always have been and they always will be, and it's best not to try to figure out why, because only God knows, and there isn't anything you can do, but try to be good to each other. He's always asking the colored if they're all right, and if their families are all right, and he tells them that he wants to be the first person to know, if there's any trouble. And I believe he *is* the first person to know. When Sally's nephew got into trouble with the police, and ran away and then got caught, Daddy went to see him, and he got a lawyer for him, and he talked to the judge about him, and they let him be free, and now he works for Daddy out in the gin and he does other jobs that come up."

She has not taken much interest in the cotton crop; her

brother goes with the father and says he wants to stay on the plantation, spend his life there, follow in his father's steps. She does take an interest in the spraying of the crops — because she loves to fly in airplanes, her father's small single-engine plane or the jets that have taken her to New Orleans, to New York and Washington, D.C., and to Europe. She has often flown over her father's land with the manager of the plantation, who cares for and operates the plane. She loves looking at the expanse of land that is her family's, loves flying high. The Delta, with its houses, fields, roads, stores, churches, cotton gins, reminds her of a Lego game. Everything is toy size. She also loves flying low, watching places and landmarks emerge, become more distinct, and finally, look lifelike. In the airplane she wonders what visitors to this planet would think — of Clarksdale and other Mississippi towns, of people she knows or is kin to, of herself, and of Sally or Ruth, or their husbands, who are tenant farmers of her father's.

She doesn't remember the incident, but her mother has told her that when she was four or five she once asked both parents whether the black people who in such large numbers are sent here by God from Heaven end up telling the Lord what they have seen while working for the whites. Her parents were surprised, then learned that a television program had inspired the thought: spies from outer space who reported on the Earth's important, powerful people. To whom? To their superiors, who regarded the Earth as a very dangerous place, because its people were setting off terrible explosions and threatening the destruction of the entire universe or, at the least, a significant part of it. Now she has no such question to ask. Now she knows who "the colored" are, what their purpose is. When she draws a picture of what she sees from her father's airplane she includes his land, his home, his bank, and a home or two that belong to her friends. She does not include any of the sharecropper or tenant farmer cabins that also can be sighted from several hundred feet above the ground. She doesn't think to represent, either, the homes of her father's manager and foreman, two white men who she knows keep the plantation going day after day.

But one afternoon, after talking about Sally, and, to a lesser extent, Ruth, she decided to go up in the airplane, figuratively, and include them as well in one of her panoramic views. She closed her eyes for a few seconds — the ascent — and then set to work: the sky and the sun, the ground, the trees, the crops, and then her parents' house, her best friend's house, not far away, and, to the side, a cluster of Clarksdale's buildings. She was through. (Figure 4.) She put her crayons down and began to talk about the joy of flying when suddenly she remembered: "the colored." She said those two words, no more. She picked up her crayon set again, and scrutinized her landscape carefully: where to put "them." After a minute or so she gave up. She said she would have to start in all over again, if she were going to include Sally's house and Ruth's. To do so was more of an effort than she felt able to make. But she did take that opportunity to talk about her house and Sally's house: "We have a nicer home, but Sally told me she was glad she didn't live in it, because there would be so much work to do. Ruth said the same thing — that she doesn't mind cleaning the house, but she's glad to leave it, because if she didn't leave it, she'd always find more and more work to do. I've never been inside their homes, but they are small, and I'll bet they're easy to keep clean. Sometimes my mother gets tired of decorating a room, choosing the curtains or the chair covers, and she tells my father our house is too much for her and she'd like a little cottage someplace on the other side of the plantation. She says I can have the house when I grow up, because when you're young you have a lot of energy and you can keep up with

things, but when you get older you have to slow down. I go
running down the halls and the stairs, but my mother walks.
She gets bursitis sometimes, in her shoulder. It's a good thing
Sally and Ruth don't get bursitis, or our gardener, and the
others. Then we'd really be in trouble."

Has she ever known "trouble"? What would be her idea of
it? She has indeed experienced "trouble"; she can talk about
the time she did, even come up with a rather good definition:
"When you are in pain, and you can't so easily stop it, or when
something bad has happened, and it won't go away after a few
minutes — that's trouble." She remembers one summer when
her father took ill; he had chest pain, and he couldn't breathe.
He was brought to the hospital, told he most likely had suffered a heart attack. But no, the electrocardiogram was negative and the doctors puzzled. Eventually they had him sent to
Jackson, where extensive tests were done — which, however,
were inconclusive. The next stop was New Orleans's Touro
Infirmary. Finally, the doctors figured out what was wrong
— an obscure blood disease that had prompted an anemia,
which in turn had put a serious strain on the heart. The father
was successfully treated and returned home aglow with praise
of doctors, hospitals, nurses, medicines. For Veronica that was
a summer of "trouble" — made all the worse by the concomi-
tant illness of the plantation's manager. He too fell sick, with
high blood pressure. But he refused to follow his doctor's advice, kept working hard and long every day, including great
stretches of the weekends. When her father came home
Veronica was the one who told him that the manager had also
been sick and seen a doctor. Her father asked how he was, and
her mother said he "seemed fine." The father asked how the
plantation was coming along, and the wife again said "fine."
Then the father had remarked that it was all right for him to
get sick, but his manager couldn't, because "without him, everything would fall apart."

The girl could not quite forget those words, that judgment. She was moved, later on, in the presence of her mother, but not her father, to ask what would happen if the manager did, in fact, get even sicker. How would they all deal with that "trouble"? Would the manager go see doctors in Jackson, New Orleans? Would her father take over the manager's responsibilities? The mother told the girl that if "worse came to worse" they would have to get a new manager. The girl became upset, began to repeat her questions about the manager's fate. The mother told her she was "imagining trouble" when it didn't actually exist, and so it was best to change the subject. The girl obliged; but her mind, when left to itself, was less compliant. Once she drew a picture of the manager; in her hands he appeared a small man with eyes and a nose but no mouth and oversize cars. He had only four fingers on his right hand, two on his left. He was pictured talking to a black man even smaller, with eyes and ears, no nose and a rudimentary mouth: Sally's husband. They stood under a large tree, which Veronica identified, upon completion of the picture, as the tree her father has occasionally used for rifle practice: a target tacked to it. She recalls hearing the story of William Tell from her father as she watched him fire and hit the bull's-eye.

Mostly, though, her father goes hunting with his shotgun, driven by the manager and accompanied by a dog. Sometimes Sally's husband comes along; he fetches the fallen prey from the dog. The girl has also gone along, complained about the killing of birds or animals, been reminded that just about every day she eats food derived from slaughtered animals or fish that have been caught. Now in this picture she contemplates adding her father and his gun. No, she won't. Yes, she will, after all. No, there may not be enough room — on a paper only one third used at that point! Yes, she could find the space — and she will. She works on the gun first, has it standing up, as tall as the manager, a little taller, actually. Then she draws her father, his arms thick, his legs stocky, his torso substantial, his face quite large. He gets five fingers on each hand, a mouth with plenty of teeth, a strong nose. In life he tends to be thin, about five feet nine or ten inches tall. In life the manager is the same height, perhaps a half an inch taller. In life Sally's husband is as tall as the manager, stockier than he or Veronica's father — a rather imposing man actually, because of his girth, his exceptionally large eyes, his teeth that feature a good deal of gold, provided for over the years by Veronica's father, who has sent the man to "his" dentist. When the girl has finished with the people, she decides to put ground under them, some grass, a shrub or two. She abandons the blue crayon she'd been working with, uses black, makes the sky dark, forgoes a sun. For a moment she seems through, but soon has an afterthought: a moon gets drawn, a half-moon — with a veil of darkness covering it. Then another afterthought: the dog, a golden retriever.

At last the work is over, completely so (Figure 5); the girl is ready to provide a commentary: "It's around nine at night, and they've been hunting, and they stopped and Daddy is saying good-bye; he's telling the manager and Sally's husband what to do the next morning. He's going to be away; he is taking us to New Orleans and then we'll fly from there to Mexico. He wants to make sure everything is going to be okay on the plantation. I used to think that the colored and the manager and the foreman didn't need to ask Daddy anything, because they knew what to do on their own. But now I realize that they all take their orders from Daddy. He calls in the manager and the foreman and he tells them what to do. Then they tell the colored. Sometimes he goes to the colored himself and talks to them. He knows all about the crops and how the men should work the gin, and he makes them clear the land the way *he* wants and not the way they would if he didn't come and inspect them. We had my uncle and aunt from New Orleans staying with us last week, and Daddy told them one night at supper that the next morning he was going to surprise everyone on the plantation; he'd be up at six and out there when they all came to work. My mother said that he shouldn't go, because it'll make the people uncomfortable, and that wouldn't be nice. Dad said that if Mother found Sally sitting in the kitchen, eating cookies or taking spoons of ice cream when she should be making our supper, then that wouldn't be a good idea, and somebody would have to check up on Sally. My mother said she's sure, by Sally's waist size, that she does that all the time; but we get the supper when we're ready for it, and the food usually tastes pretty good, and so there's no reason to complain or spy on her. My Dad didn't like my mother saying he was a spy; he said he was going to report her to the sheriff, because she was calling him a spy and it was not true, and he was being insulted, and he wanted a million dollars from Mother, and a note of apology, or else she'll have to defend herself in court! My mother said she'd write him out a check later, and wouldn't he accept her apology at the table, and he said yes, and then they talked about our *next* vacation, after this one: to Canada, and then to Ireland."

Veronica has occasionally announced various wishes for her future that prompt skepticism from her parents. But with respect to one of her wishes — that she be a traveling reporter — the parents disagree. Her father says that "no lady ought to do that kind of work." Her mother says that "it wouldn't be a bad life — for a year or two, before marriage." The girl pictures herself a sort of woman's counterpart of Richard Halliburton — romantic adventures in interesting, charming places all over the world, then a writeup of what was seen and heard. She would have to dress "just right" — a trenchcoat, maybe, and a stylish felt hat, rakishly worn. She would have to own and wear a very good, sturdy watch — waterproof, automatic, luminescent. In New Orleans she saw such a watch, was told by her mother that when she is sixteen, she will get it, or one that resembles it. In New York she saw a store full of watches, almost all of which she pictured herself wearing in the future, especially one with a blue background and silver hands. She doesn't want "fancy jewelry," like her mother's — a delicate gold watch, diamond rings. She wants "a big watch, like the ones men wear."

She has been told by her father that "mostly men" become reporters, but she is not at all persuaded by him. A cousin of his, as a matter of fact, writes a society column for one of the Mississippi newspapers, and Veronica has talked with her about colleges and journalism courses. The girl has no interest in writing for the society page. She has no interest in politics, nor does she want to write about the fires or the robberies that take place everywhere. She would like to be at a tennis game, when "someone is really winning by a large score." She would like to "see someone swim a long way up or down the Mississippi," and then interview the person. She would like to fly a plane herself and do stunts with it, maybe parachute from it, then write up her achievements.

Such ambitions, often enough stated, have won over, to a degree, her father. He doesn't expect her really to end up doing what she says she would like to do, but he refers to her as "unconventional," and he has told Veronica that "today" there is "more room" for a lively, imaginative, and willful girl like her than there used to be when he was growing up. He has also told his daughter that "within limits" he is "all in favor" of her wish for what he calls, in front of the girl — usually at the dinner table, during a family conversation — "a temporary career, for a year or two." The girl chafes at the time limit, objects to it, is told in no uncertain terms that two years is a long time, accepts the judgment, drops the subject. The girl's mother is not disposed, either, to wage a fight on speculation. But as the girl weaves her dreams into a family's conversation, the mother and father do a little light sparring, and the child listens attentively, comes to her conclusions, and later on tells what they are: "My father wants me to stay here in Clarksdale and meet a boy who comes from 'a good family'; then, when we get married, my father will send us to England, and I wouldn't be surprised if he said that we should live in London for a year, maybe, before coming home. He says he wishes my mother and he had lived there for a year. He says you have to 'get travel out of your system,' or else you keep trying to go on trips, and you don't appreciate your own home. My mother says that if she had lived in London for ten years, she'd still want to go back a lot of times — every year, if she could — because she likes the stores there, and the hotels, and she likes to go to concerts, and the people aren't dangerous.

"In New York you have to be very careful, but not in London. My mother would like to go to Russia and China, too. My father gets angry when she says so. He says they are terrible countries, and you can't speak your mind in either one. My mother says there are a lot of paintings in a palace in Leningrad, and she'd like to visit the big cities of China, the way our President Nixon did. My father says he wouldn't go if someone paid his way, all expenses; but he'd go if the government told him to go. My brother agrees with my father. My mother says she doesn't disagree with my father; she just wants to say what's on her mind. That's what I like to do — tell what I'll do when I'm grown up, and watch my father look worried, and my brother get annoyed with me, and tell me I'm just 'talking off the top of my head'!"

She has succeeded in gaining a reputation at home and

among her friends and in school as a slightly quixotic girl, at least so far as her *talk* goes. In her behavior, she is willful, but not rebellious or difficult. She wears the same kinds of clothes other girls do — casual around the house, more formal at school and at church. She looks forward, even at her age, to the parties that will celebrate her various adolescent birthdays. She has a "best friend" who is the daughter of a lawyer and former member of the Mississippi legislature. The two girls ride bikes, swim in their families' pools, learn to play tennis — and, as a matter of fact, share dreams of the future: themselves as future tennis champions, for instance: playing at Wimbledon, cheered in Clarksdale, in Jackson, in New Orleans, all over the South, as Dixie winners who have obtained international recognition. They follow tennis in the newspapers, in the national magazines, on television. They like to wear their tennis clothes even when they are not at the courts. Veronica has her own court to use; so does her friend. They like to go to the country club, however, with their mothers; to use the courts there means to meet friends and to learn how much of the game they have mastered and how much they still have to learn.

In the snack bar they order Cokes, drool over rich (hot fudge) sundaes, talk about how lucky they are to be thin, and so able to order and eat anything without embarrassment or self-reproach — a contrast with the dilemma their mothers face. And even though they are indeed thin, they go through "pretend" sequences in which one of them announces she is on a diet, orders food accordingly, and spells out how many pounds are to be lost, within what span of time. The other shows sympathy, gives suggestions or hints, expresses confidence in the eventual outcome of the effort. After a while they both laugh, and abandon the scenario, or choose another one: the celebration, with a soda or a sundae, of two women who have gone away to a weight reduction "spa," and have returned so thin that their husbands have sent them off with instructions to eat two or three desserts at the very least. Alternatively, they have been to New Orleans, have purchased smart dresses, interesting hats, slightly unconventional or suggestive evening clothes, and are now having a time encouraging each other to go ahead, put on the clothes purchased, take the risk of being frowned at, pointed out, envied, asked *where* and *how much*. The girls do a rather nice imitation of what they have seen and heard many times, but sometimes they stop themselves abruptly in disgust or shame: is *that* what it will be like twenty years from now? They make all sorts of vows; Veronica returns to her journalistic dreams and her friend insists that she will go to New York and be a fashion model and come home South only once a year, on Christmas. The two talk about Sophie Newcomb College in New Orleans, the women's part of Tulane: will they go there, as their mothers did, or will they try some other college in another part of the country? They *will* go elsewhere, they insist to one another. A week later they have relented; they see no reason to challenge the traditions of their respective families.

Once Veronica had a dream, and told it to her mother. She has never forgotten the dream. She delights in telling it to her friends, and she wishes she might have similar dreams more often: "I was flying a kite, and it was a good one, so it went way up. The wind was strong, and I knew I'd better pull the kite down or it would pull away from me. But I held on, and the next thing I knew I was up in the air and traveling to the east, toward Alabama. Then I saw the Atlantic Ocean, just like you do in a plane; and soon there was Big Ben and the Thames River. The wind stopped, and I landed in the park — in Hyde Park — and I saw my mother and father. They had flown over to meet me! Then my father said he was convinced I would be a reporter, and I'd go and do stunts and tricks and have good times, and then I'd write stories in the papers and magazines. He said he'd like to fly the kite himself, but my mother said no, it was dangerous, and they told me they wanted to go back to Clarksdale. We took the kite with us, and went to the airport. On the plane I wished I was flying with the kite, and even my mother agreed it's an exciting way to cross the ocean. When we got home, Sally and Ruth and everyone else came and they looked at the kite and said it was great that it could carry me. Then I woke up."

When she talks about the dream she points out that she must have hoped for the trip across the Atlantic, because she chose a highly irregular kite. She is sure that her friends would have shunned that kite. In real life they shun all kites. She became interested in flying kites on her own and has not succeeded in persuading anyone else to join her. She wonders why. Perhaps, she speculates, others are afraid to do the unusual. She has always thought of herself as more adventurous than many of her friends — all of them, she will say in an unguarded moment of pride. One or two of them have, like her, been to Europe, but only she wants to go live there for a while. As she talks about her kite she talks about a certain willfulness, a certain self-confidence in herself, both of which she wants to keep. But she also wonders whether she ought to be so *much* herself, so insistent upon finding a way somewhat different from that others will take.

"I'm a tomboy, that's what one girl called me," she observes. "I'm trying to be an actress, that's what another girl said," she also observes. Her own mother has told her, often, to mind her manners and remember that she soon enough will be "a Southern lady." Her father has reminded her that even a child has to "behave," remember her "responsibilities." But the girl can quite readily, but with a touch of irritation, go through her own list: "I've got to know how to run the house. My mother says her mother prepared her for a long time, so that after marriage it wasn't hard to move in here and get Sally and get Ruth and the others, and keep track of them. If you're not watching them, they begin to sit around, and they look to you and wait for you to speak to them. They're good, and they want to help out, but they need directions. If I ask Sally what she'd do, if she could have any wish she wants, I never hear a real answer from her. She just tells me that she's as happy as can be right now. Even when I promise that I won't let my parents know what she says, there's no difference. She just repeats herself!"

It is impossible to figure out Sally and Ruth, Veronica has reluctantly concluded. Again and again the girl has been told so by her parents — that "the colored" have their own way of thinking. But Veronica is not one to accept such judgments automatically. She has questioned the cook or the maid, presented them with wishes to pick from, fantasies to select. They only humor her, mystify her, even make her rather annoyed. Who do they think they are — smiling but in fact turning sly and evasive? She has asked her mother why it is that "servants sometimes are *too* polite." The mother immediately has told the child to leave "them" alone, go about her own business. But it *is* her business, Veronica reminds her mother, to know how to "deal with" servants.

The girl has learned to distinguish among the various people who work for her parents. The manager drives the children to school on days when the mother decides to sleep late or prepare for an early tennis game. Veronica has learned how to sit quietly in his company, speak when spoken to, or make only the most appropriate and polite of initiatives. She has learned to ask after his wife and his children, to talk about the weather, to compliment him on his promptness, to be respectful when offering her opinions. She has really learned how to distinguish between him and "the colored," and does not hesitate to acknowledge that she does so all the time: "If you're with a white person, that's one thing; if you're with a colored person, it's another. I like Sally, but with her you're in your own home, and you can just relax. With Daddy's manager, you've got to be careful, because he can get his feelings hurt, and then there will be trouble for Daddy. We need the manager. Without him, the colored wouldn't know what to do, and the whole place would begin to fall apart. That's what my father says. The manager is very strict with the tenants, and he's strict with his own children. He has a girl, and she's a year younger than me, and he's always telling me how much he has her do — the dishes and the dusting, and even a lot of cooking. I think his wife works. They need the money, I guess."

She can't understand, though, why they *should* need the money. Her father has made a point of saying how much better off the manager is than the tenants. He earns ten thousand a year — a salary. The tenants get a share of the profits from the crops. The servants who work in or around the house, Veronica knows, get much less than the manager, but she is not sure exactly how much. The reason: her parents don't want her discussing money with those servants, and have told her so. They are afraid she would anyway; so they withhold the information in the hope that their daughter will turn her attention to other matters about which she knows more. To no effect, however; Veronica has openly asked Sally several times what her salary is, only to be told that "salaries are private." The girl persists. The cook resists. The girl doesn't dare complain to her parents. The cook knows the girl doesn't — has been told by those parents to stand up to the girl, so that she will learn to be as "respectful" as she ought be. The girl becomes sullen, sarcastic, teasing. The cook says nothing, even sings softly. The girl gets outraged, turns her back on the cook, plays the radio noisily, to drown out the singing, or stalks from the room. An hour later, the two have met somewhere else in the house and are chatting amiably. In Veronica's words: "If you're going to live in a house like ours, you must learn how to live with Sally. That's what my mother says I have to do, and she says I'm learning."

The cook's daughters are older than Veronica, the youngest of them only by two years. Sally doesn't say much about them, but Veronica asks after them, and expects the noncommittal answers she gets. She has seen the girls, spoken to them briefly. She has gone with her father on Christmas, when he brings presents to the servants — a check, an appliance, or a gift certificate. And a gracious letter of thanks ("for all the help, day after day") from her mother. Once, after she and the father left the cook's house, there was a question from the child: would Sally's girls stay in Clarksdale, or would they move away, later on, when grown up? The father said some would leave and some would stay. Veronica wanted to know why anyone would want to leave Clarksdale. The father told his daughter that "people get wanderlust." He explained to her the meaning of the word. She knew immediately what he was getting at — her own urge to see the world, live in England, travel a lot.

The father did not at all like the comparison; the child was confronted with his annoyance, and a lecture of sorts. She was told emphatically that her reasons were not to be confused with those of Sally's children. If she wanted to go to London or Paris, fine. If Sally's children wanted to leave Clarksdale, that was quite another matter. And he corrected himself: they wouldn't leave because of "wanderlust." They would leave, he let his daughter know, because they "hope to do better in

Chicago, or some other Northern city." The girl remembers the words, the moment, the willingness of her father to be so candid, to go back on his own statement, to share with her his views on a subject of obvious importance to her. It is, the girl knows, the one time he has done so — told her about "the colored," their difficulties and their aspirations. It was not an especially tense or prolonged occasion — rather brief, in fact. She claims to recall his every word: "My Dad said that a white person can't know what a colored person is thinking. He said they have a hard life, and he feels sorry for them. He said that he couldn't really blame them for wanting to leave and go North. He said it wasn't fair to call it wanderlust, like he did. They want to improve themselves. He said he tries to help them; he gives them bonuses and he's always polite to them, and never cusses them out, like a lot of white people do. And my mother doesn't, either. And they both would do anything to help one of Sally's children, or Ruth's, or even a stranger's who was colored. Daddy has taken a lot of colored kids to our doctor — to the doctor I go see when I get sick; he's a pediatrician."

Every once in a while she remembers that occasion, then begins to wonder whether one day she might be able to help "the colored children." Maybe she could be a nurse, or get some money from her parents and relatives and distribute it to "them." Maybe she could even be a doctor herself. Her mother has mentioned a woman doctor she knows in New Orleans. Why not become Clarksdale's first woman physician — and go work among her father's tenants, their children, and other such children who live out of sight, it seems, all over the country? She made that suggestion to her mother one evening, as the mother said good-night. There was no enthusiastic response; quite the contrary. Veronica remembers her mother smiling, and saying that "for a woman to be a doctor is hard" and adding that "there are a lot of exciting things to do" later on, so it's best to "keep an open mind."

The girl got the message: "I don't think my mother would like me to be a doctor, or be worrying too much about Sally and her children. She told me — when I came home from school and said a boy was saying niggers are no good and stupid — that it's best to keep quiet and not get yourself in a lot of trouble. That's the best way. I wouldn't know how to get myself out of the trouble if I got into it, so my mother is right. The same goes for being a doctor; my mother said she wouldn't want to be faced with all the trouble that comes to a doctor, and that's how I feel too. Maybe if you've had a lot of trouble you could be a good doctor, because you've had the experience with trouble. Maybe one of Sally's children could go up North, and become a doctor. I asked her if she'd mind, and she didn't answer me. She asked me if I wanted her to cook me some chocolate chip cookies, and I said yes. She got very busy. Then my mother called me, because I had to go to the dentist."

The dentist is full of magic, she believes. His machines are intriguing rather than frightening to her. He happens to be a kind and friendly man — shrewd too, because the girl is always told what will happen in such a way, apparently, that she looks forward to the event, instead of becoming apprehensive. She has even thought of pursuing his career; but on that score got called down promptly. After leaving the office she told her mother that she wouldn't mind being a dentist, having those machines to use, fixing people's teeth, stopping their aches, joking with patients. No, "it would be a bad idea," her mother told her. That was the end of dentist talk, because the mother had forgotten something, had to call home to be reminded — by Sally. Afterward there was a stop at the hardware store, followed by some ice cream for both of them. Then home, a piano lesson, supper — and so it goes on a weekday afternoon for Veronica, who can with a certain wry detachment describe her life as "too busy," but who admits also to getting easily bored when "there is nothing to do," and who accordingly is glad to keep herself going. "When you've got a lot to do," the child observes (and acknowledges hearing from her mother and father), "there's no time to get upset about a lot of things." Veronica is quite convinced that such a point of view will help her now and in the future; will spare her worry, enable her to get a lot done, even provide her with the kind of moral justification she senses people try to find for themselves — or persuade themselves that they have found.

II

DEFENDER OF
THE GARDEN DISTRICT

NEW ORLEANS has some fine old homes, especially those
that belong to the historic Garden District. Some of the
children who live in them take for granted what others come
from near and far to see: lovely columns, or an especially
attractive portico, or trees and shrubbery and flowers (the
azaleas, the wisteria), which adorn buildings quite appropri-
ately called mansions. But for James, a twelve-year-old resident of the city, those mansions are of endless interest, as are
the city's cemeteries, one of the most beautiful of which is not
far from his home, in the center of the Garden District. The
boy has for a long while hoped to be an architect. His own
home has been turned modern on the inside, with every effort
made to preserve the exterior. He had become (at the age of
six) a good friend of the carpenters, electricians, plumbers, and
painters who worked on the various rooms and from time to
time came back to check on things or do an additional job.

The boy's father is a cotton broker, a man of substantial,
inherited wealth. The boy's mother is an artist whose landscapes have become well known to many residents of the
Garden District; she has had several showings in one of the
city's art galleries. A number of the landscapes — the bayou

country of southern Louisiana — adorn the walls of the artist's home and the nearby homes of her friends. Some paintings, as the boy is proud to announce, have gone to "complete strangers," who have paid "hundreds of dollars." He adds right away that his mother has given the money to charity. Asked what kind of charity, he is quite knowledgeable and forthcoming: "She has a lot of charities, but her favorite is hospitals. She likes to give money to them, and she said that if she didn't have her studio and the pictures she makes, then she'd go and do volunteer work in one of the hospitals. She feels sorry for people who get sick, and she's told us that she wanted to be a nurse when she was a girl, but her mother wouldn't hear of it."

James can walk down one of the Garden District streets and tell which home is the oldest, which home has been recently renovated or restored, which home belongs to what family. He ignores a few homes, sometimes with barely concealed disdain; a "new" family has moved in, he has heard, and he doesn't know (or can't quite remember) their name. But for a year or so he has been more interested in cemeteries than homes; he loves to walk through the former, read what is said about the dead on the aboveground mausoleums. He is not, however, morbid or eccentric. He also likes old watches; he has inherited a family collection, begun by his grandfather, and it is a source of constant fascination to the boy. He is an only son; he points out quite self-consciously and with a touch of boasting that he is also "the last male heir." He is, in fact, referring to his father's family; there are several male heirs on his mother's side, cousins of his whom he sees rather often, because they too live in the Garden District. His father's people have also lived in the Garden District of New Orleans for a long time — though in northern Louisiana there is a family plantation, and in Bay St. Louis, Mississippi, there are several summer "cottages" (rather large oceanfront homes) that belong to his parents and his two uncles.

He is sometimes money-conscious. When he talks about the watches his father and he jointly own and treasure, he makes mention of the hundreds of thousands of dollars the collection is worth. When he points out a home he especially likes, he remembers what he has heard his father say about the value of the place. When he talks about a friend of his, he is apt to call attention to the friend's parents as well — who they *are*, what kind of work the father does, what kind of family the mother comes from. He is not, however, overly preoccupied with "society," not compared to others he plays with or goes to school with. He lives in a city whose upper-income people are quite conscious of where they stand in relationship to each other. The morning newspaper, the *Times-Picayune*, often devotes page after page to social announcements: teas, coffees, lunches, suppers — honoring people, celebrating occasions, and so on. The boy can echo his parents' mixture of delight and chagrin as they go through the pages of the newspaper over breakfast: "My mother usually starts. She tells my father that he should turn from the news to the society page and learn all about what is happening to our friends and our neighbors. Dad doesn't turn; he asks her to tell him. She does, and then they're both unhappy because a lot of the time there's a conflict. They can't be in two places at the same time. They don't like to go out *too* much. They have to pick and choose. My father has a bad back, and my mother tells him never to tell *anyone* that it's better. She writes her 'regrets' notes, and she likes to mention Dad's back pain! Sometimes they both agree that they're going to try to accept every invitation they can, because they like to go out. But Dad gets tired; and my mother says that even now, after all these years, she's still a little shy with people, and so she likes to be at home at least *some* of the time!"

He is not being especially ironic and certainly not sarcastic when he talks that way about his mother. If anything, he is

expressing sympathy for her, and more than a little understanding of how she feels. He is himself rather shy. He has no
close friends, has never had any. He doesn't like to talk very
much with those of his own age, though he is considerably
more open with older people. His maternal grandfather calls
him an "extrovert," but James disowns the description a little
contemptuously. He is not all that close to the old man, who
has (the boy believes) confused his polite conversation made
in the presence of elders with a genuine desire to be with
people. James says he is "most happy" when he is looking at
his watch collection; in second place he puts playing tennis
with his father — provided they go afterward to lunch at a
certain private club whose food the boy especially likes. They
don't often go there; it is a treat and they prepare for the
moment a week or more in advance. There is, first of all, an
announcement of a kind: "My father will tell me that next
week we can go have lunch." When they go alone, it is always
to the club; so the boy has been promised something quite
appealing, by his standards. It is upon those occasions that he
talks about "important subjects"; his father, he says, is his "best
friend," and he likes very much talking with him. He also likes
going with him to buy clothes — another "time" (the boy calls
it) they have together. When Brooks Brothers comes to New
Orleans, James and his father, also James, go to the hotel
where the clothing representatives are staying, and get fitted.

The boy wants to go to Princeton; his father and his grandfather and his great-grandfather went there. He does not want
to go to Tulane. He says unfriendly things about the college,
and thereby irritates classmates of his in the private secondary
school he attends. He criticizes the college's buildings, maintains that the courses there aren't "so good." His source: his
father. When the boy is asked whether there aren't good reasons for some of his family's neighbors to send their children

to Tulane, he says yes, there are. He doesn't know them, but again, he has heard his father speak: "My Dad says it's a city university and it has to serve a lot of people, and the classes are probably bigger than they should be. A lot of people here in New Orleans would die for Tulane. It's a good school. It's got a good reputation. But I'd rather go to Princeton. You should keep up what your ancestors started. My great-grandfather went to Princeton, but he got in some trouble there. He never graduated. I think he fought with a Yankee. That's what my father always tells me. My mother says it may not be the whole truth, but it sounds good — it's a good story! Dad doesn't like her talking that way. Now women can go to Princeton. Dad was against the idea, but he says it had to happen. My grandfather graduated with high honors; he was a lawyer, and he invested in cotton, and he started a brokerage house, too — three professions, my Dad always says. And besides, my grandfather bought a lot of land in northern Louisiana, and he invested in the railroads, and we can go free on them, even now. I think he was a director of the Louisville & Nashville — but who wants to ride on the railroads, the way they are now? I used to have a set, trains going in all directions, a whole room of trains, but I lost interest. Now I like to go out to the airport to meet my Dad when he comes back from a trip: all the jets to see."

James likes to draw planes, mostly large jets, but some smaller ones too, and, rarely, some older planes which he's only seen pictured. When he was younger, eight or nine, he favored struggle — aerial dogfights, formations headed toward formations. But more recently he has abandoned military aircraft for the commercial kind. He sketches 707s, 747s, DC 10s, puts Delta or Eastern or United labels on the fuselages. As he does so he recalls the various flights he has taken — to Atlanta, to Nashville, to New York, to Mexico, to Brazil, to Europe. And he talks about the advantages of comfortable, first-class travel: "My mother said she didn't know how people travel tourist, especially on the long flights across the ocean or up to New York. You can't relax when you are sitting in a narrow seat and there's someone on each side of you. My father's friends, two of them, have their own planes, Lear jets. We've gone with them to Washington, and to Birmingham. I'd like to be a pilot, but I wouldn't want to fly commercial. I'd like to have my own plane, and then if I read the *National Geographic* and there was a city I wanted to see, or a country, I'd just pick up the phone and tell them at the field to get the plane checked out, because I'm coming over soon and I'd like to leave as soon as possible. I'd call up my friends, and the next thing you'd know, we'd be up in the air and headed north over Lake Pontchartrain or south over the Mississippi River. When you're over the clouds, you feel you're on your way. My father has promised that when I'm old enough to take driving lessons, I'll be given flying lessons too, if I still want them. I know I will. I think I'd rather fly than drive. There are too many cars on the road, too many madmen speeding in cars that shouldn't even be allowed to move out of a garage. I once dreamed up an idea: special roads for people who have real good cars and really know how to drive and can afford to pay — first-class roads, they could be called, like the first-class section of an airplane."

He remembers one evening when no amount of money in the world could separate him and his parents from hundreds of other travelers, many of whom he still quite vividly remembers: "I've never seen so many people inside a building. We came into the New York airport from London, and we were the last plane to land — a bad snowstorm. We were supposed to go into the city for a couple of days, but we decided to go right to New Orleans. We couldn't. We just sat there. All these people were sitting there, too. My mother got nervous. She was afraid we'd be robbed. My father says it was one of the worst times he's ever had." He doesn't easily bring up what specifically bothered his parents and himself. He talks about a "bad storm," a "long delay." Finally, he refers to "the crowd," and to "some of the people in the crowd." Then he describes his mother's fears — not only that she'd be held up, but that for some reason violence would break out, a riot would take place, there would be (she was utterly convinced) trouble and more trouble.

The boy volunteered to draw a picture of the waiting room at Kennedy Airport. He thought it would be rather a challenge to recall and evoke that scene through crayons. But he could not really get himself going. He stared at the paper, started to draw, stopped; in the end, he abandoned the project. He decided to draw, instead, particular individuals whom he still could remember — people who belonged to what he calls the "mob" at Kennedy that stormy evening. He contemplates drawing a man in a wheelchair first. That man seemed lost, helpless. The boy had wanted to go help, offer to push the chair — but no, his parents told him to sit with them, not go anywhere or talk with anyone. James decides not to draw the man. The next possible subject is a Texan, the boy was sure — a man headed for Houston and wearing a "cowboy hat." He had come up to them, asked a question or two, been politely denied satisfactory answers. Again, the boy had wanted to be of assistance. Might he go ask a policeman he saw walking in a certain direction? No, he should not, said his father. The boy had seen how much luggage the Texan had, and merely tried to lend a hand, but his parents had by then become quite annoyed. The mother spoke to the father; the father took the boy aside and told him that he must sit down and stop "getting involved with a lot of strangers."

James begins work on the Texan. He draws him quite tall, gives the hat obvious emphasis. The man's hands are made large, his feet also oversize. The mouth is open, toothy. The boy gets curiously agitated as he tries to complete the drawing. He seems satisfied at last, ready to turn to other matters, when suddenly he crosses the effort out with two strokes of a black crayon. (Figure 6.) It is not that he is artistically too critical of himself: "I can't do a good job on any of those people I saw that night. I think I remember them, but I forget them while I'm trying to draw them. I guess I didn't get as good a look at those people as I thought, because if I had, I know I could do good pictures of them. Maybe I obeyed my mother. I remember she told me to close my eyes and think pleasant thoughts. I kept opening my eyes and peeking, but maybe I didn't peek very much."

He has learned over the years to do as his mother suggests — and with less and less desire on his part to peek. Waiting with his father for a cab downtown, he sees someone or something, feels uncomfortable amid the jostle and hustle of the situation, and immediately his eyes close and he thinks, invariably, of his room at home or the inside of his father's club. He is not so much afraid as amused by his ability to spare himself unpleasantness, to create for himself a feeling of well-being: "My mother was right; if you're having trouble or you don't like the people around you, then you can get rid of them. All you have to do is think of some other place! My father says I'm lucky. He can't close his eyes, except when he goes to sleep. He says it can be dangerous, anyway. If you just stand there on the street, with your eyes closed, someone will think you're blind and come up and try to steal from you. The other day I went Christmas shopping with Dad, and I was holding the packages and waiting for him to pay for them. I guess I must have closed my eyes again, because he took hold of my shoulder and said I should pay attention and not 'be in a dream,' or else I'd end up with nothing in my arms, and some colored kid would have a real good Christmas! Or it could be a white kid too!"

His father had in his remarks mentioned only a "colored kid," but the boy wanted to be less specific. He has, in fact, remembered his father's social and racial views quite well and is insistently loyal to them. The father has worried about the impoverished condition of black people, expressed repeated concern for their lot. The father has also denounced the Klan in no uncertain terms — and other "redneck" social groups or activities. Not far from the Garden District live working-class whites (in the city's so-called Irish Channel district); and also not far away are clusters of black people — servants, many of them, to families like his. James has been driven through those neighborhoods, has heard opinions expressed about the people there, and has heard their lives connected to his — as it is and as it will be: "My father says I'll have to learn how to live with the colored, the Negro people, and I'll have to live with the rednecks. We have a lot of rednecks in Louisiana. They can cause trouble. They vote for someone who gets them excited. A lot of people don't know how to keep their tempers, and they go shouting in the streets. The rednecks hate the colored, and the colored hate the rednecks. My mother says she'd rather be with the rednecks, but my father says he trusts the colored more.

"We used to have a governess, she was French — from Paris, not New Orleans. She taught me to speak French. She didn't like a lot of the white people in the city. My father would agree with her, then my mother got angry. She said — she says she'll always say — white is white and black is black. The reason my mother let the governess go was that I was old enough to be in school all day; but my mother says she

would have let her go anyway, because she was more interested in the colored and their troubles than taking care of me.
I think she even joined the colored — the NAACP, my father
said. She used to tell me that it was not the fault of the colored
that they are poor; we made them be, the whites. I told my
father, and he told her to stop talking to me about the races,
and concentrate on the French language. So she did. But
Daddy agrees with her; he says there's good and bad in every
kind, and he says sometimes the worst kind are the rednecks."

But both parents make references to "the colored" as pick-
pockets, thieves; it is the boy who corrects them, reminds
them of their own past observations. Neither parent argues
with the boy. They are both impressed with what they call
their son's "sensitivity." He is not, however, "a bleeding
heart," they reassure themselves. He has heard himself openly
talked about, heard his mother worry, right to his face, that he
would get "too worried" about blacks and their struggles. And
he has heard his father reassure the mother, remind her that
children go through "stages." James doesn't know what a
"stage" really is, but he knows what his father means —
that for a while, but only for a while, it is all right that he worry
a little more than his parents do about blacks or working-class
whites or, indeed, the Indians.

The last have intrigued him for a long time — ever since he
saw some of them being rounded up in a movie and heard his
governess say that "it wasn't only the Negroes." He can still
hear her repeating those words to him, to herself, to the one
friend she had in New Orleans, whom she'd call on the phone,
the boy listening in all the while. The governess read to him
books that gave a chronicle of the fate of various Indian tribes,
and James's parents did not object. But when James, at six,
talked of *becoming* an Indian and fighting on their side against
"the white man," the mother began to ask around: did any of
her friends know of a housekeeper who would be "good" with

a boy like James or, even better, a "girl" from Europe who was here, didn't want to go back, and might enjoy a not too demanding job? The father called in the governess and told her to stop talking to the boy about Indians. By that time the governess was ready to quit, her employers ready to fire her, and James quite ready to abandon all interest in this nation's racial or ethnic minorities. Still, the parents noticed after she was long gone that their son continued to worry over blacks who begged in the street or whites who cussed out blacks. When at eleven James was still applauding the Indians in the Westerns he saw, the parents lost their capacity for detached silence, and spoke out: the Indians were as cruel or brutal in their own way as the white man, and it's not fair to take sides.

The boy has learned that message; says it is a "prejudice" when a person takes sides with one party in a struggle and forgets about the viewpoint or experiences of the other side. But there are times when he abandons the various messages he has heard and plays all-out war. He mobilizes his considerable army of soldiers, tanks, airplanes, and shoots at the enemy. He includes in the enemy blacks, whites, Indians. He declares himself a general defending his territory — one of his father's plantations. His troops have been hired; he isn't calling upon friends or neighbors. They are contemporary Hessians, those men he controls and launches against what he calls "the Americans." Then he explains: "I could be the descendant of a French prince; he came here to Louisiana and then France left, but he held out, and no one noticed, until one day the census people came and spotted the plantation and they started asking a lot of questions. Then the government agents said they wanted us to give up, and let them own the plantation, and we could work for them! That's when I decided to fight! I said *never*, and I hired the troops, and they fought and won."

He goes through the motions — the arrangement and rearrangement of his troops. He pretends that guns are going off, makes noises for the sake of realism, abruptly ends the encounter. He declares himself, thereafter, "a kind prince"; he will not take advantage of those he has vanquished. But he will keep some of "the enemy" on his plantation. They will work the fields, produce good crops, look after the main house, and in return get "all the food they want." Of course they won't be eating his kind of food. They like french fries and sausages and Kool-Aid and candy; he has learned to like grapefruit, cut oranges, fortified cereal, lots of vegetables, and steak from which the fat has been trimmed. He has pecan pie or vanilla ice cream occasionally, but not every day. He takes vitamin pills year round. He uses Vitamin C in winter, as soon as anyone in the house begins to suffer the flu or a cold. He never eats chocolate; takes only a Life Saver occasionally. He used to like popcorn, but now finds it "too salty"; however, he is willing to supply "them," his various employees, with all the popcorn they desire.

It comes to that — the use of a blanket "them" in his story or fable or imaginary game; and also in his "real life," the expression he and many other children use for the day-to-day activity which a boy of his age has learned to take for granted. When he becomes more "realistic," more "grown up," he sees himself as a businessman, an architect who designs and builds shopping centers, a lawyer, a man who buys and sells land in Central America or crops from there. He talks of choosing one of those pursuits, or maybe trying all of them. He talks of becoming an experienced scuba diver. Every year the family goes to Mexico or the Caribbean after Christmas Day — to "unwind." His mother, he knows, has a case of the "nerves." She tires easily, takes to her bed for no discernible reason. She becomes demanding, more critical of the boy than usual. The father intervenes, reassures the child, tells him that time will soon enough bring a change in the mother's "spirits." The father goes further sometimes, insists that the country is going "mad" — so no wonder his wife wants virtually to lock herself up. The boy has heard talk of "therapy," of a possible "rest home," of too many pills. But always, it seems, as things are getting alarming, the mother inexplicably and to everyone's surprise "snaps out of it," an expression the father uses when talking to his son. And when the son wants to know how she has managed to become so much better, so soon, the father gives his reply: willpower.

The boy is told often that he, too, has obligations, must not stumble, has within himself an exacting conscience. There is a time, James knows, for fun and games, for strolls through cemeteries or mock games of a historical and military nature; but there are also times for intensely serious "business." He spells out the demands he has learned to place upon himself: "I'd like to know about the stock market. You can't inherit money and just forget about it. My father goes over the financial pages with me. He points out what's been happening to our money. I have to tell him whether we've lost or gained — the total. He bought me a little calculator, a pocket one, made in Japan. It's great fun, but it's very important business. If you have money, you have to know how to keep it, or you're in big trouble. I have my animals to take care of. I have a dog and I have three white mice. I used to have a snake, but my mother didn't want it around. The maid can't touch my mice, and only I feed the dog and take her for a walk. I have my homework, and that's *very* important. You have to have good marks to get into Princeton. Daddy says he was lucky. When he was young he could just know he'd go there. If I do my work, I will. But I've got to do my work."

He does indeed apply himself. He goes to a first-rate bilingual (English and French) private school, where, as he puts it, "all the kids are from homes like mine." What does he mean by that? He replies tersely at first: "They live in the Garden District." He thinks of an exception or two; then, prompted to explain who the students are and why they have come to his school, he goes into a description of the school's purposes: "There are some other schools that prepare you for college. But we have French as well as English. Some parents drive their children a long way to get them here. I'm lucky, I can walk. We have a colored girl in the school. She doesn't pay tuition, I hear. If you have a few kids different from yourself, then you learn from them. The colored girl — her father is a professor at a college, I think. There's a boy who is Chinese. I don't know how the Chinese got here in Louisiana. My Daddy says they're all over, and they came a long time ago. I think this boy is the son of a businessman who owns a motel. But mostly the kids are regular, and I know a lot of them well, because they live nearby or their parents know my parents."

When he does his homework he likes to stop after a bout of concentration and look out the window. He will see someone standing or walking and quickly do a sketch of the person. He will doodle, then put a big circle around the doodles, then throw them out. He will pick up a board with nails driven into it and arrange elastics around the nails, to make up various patterns. He will look at a map of the world, and wonder where he will go in the course of his life. He expects firmly and without qualification to visit every single continent before he is twenty-one. His father has told him so, because the father also wants to get to see every continent — before *he* reaches the age of forty-five. Left to be seen are Australia, Africa, and Asia; but the boy knows that "it only would take two trips at the most" for the goal he and his father have set. Once in a while he doodles like a geographer; he sketches North and South America, or Africa. He puts in a river or two, makes note, through dots, of certain cities he happens to think of, then abandons the diversion for a mathematics assignment or a composition he is struggling to write. He has trouble writing; he is quite fussy about language — is constantly asking his mother or his father about the meanings of various words or looking them up in the dictionary. Though he talks well, he finds it hard to write about his personal thoughts or ideas.

Nor is the boy unaware of the possible reasons he has for holding back, for struggling hard to achieve a more impersonal essay than an English teacher may have in mind as desirable: "My father says that once you've put something down on paper, you're committed to it. When you're committed, you're really on the line — you can't just forget about the whole business. My father once wrote a letter to the newspaper; he said that he was against the colored people going to our schools, but the law is the law, and if the judge said they had to go, then we should all obey the judge. Well, we had to disconnect the phone, and we got letters from people saying they were going to kill us. We were scared. The police came, and they looked at the letters. They had a police car near the house for a few days. My father hired a detective to watch the house. My mother drove me the two blocks to school. When it was all over, my father said there was one lesson to learn: if you have an opinion, keep it to yourself. My mother said she didn't agree, because if no one expressed any opinions, it would be like living in a dictatorship. But Daddy said that he wasn't against *speaking* your opinion; he just thinks that there are a lot of no-good people around, and they are ignorant, and they are violent, and if they don't like what they hear from a person, they're as likely to try to hurt him, or even kill him, as not. So, the best thing to do is stay out of their way — the mob."

That word "mob" has interested him for some time. In one

of his doodles he drew a mob, a lot of people pressed against one another, their bodies not distinguishable, their faces small and sometimes twisted. He used shading to connect faces, or stray hands and legs and torsos — a rather powerful sketch, actually. (Figure 7.) And he didn't throw it out as he often has done. He gave it a title, "The Mob," and put it on his bulletin board. He has read about mobs in history books — the mobs that turned the French Revolution into an orgy of killing, with the innocent suffering as much as the guilty. He has heard his father talk about "mob rule," the danger in a democracy. He has seen a mob, too; the frenzied white men and women who heckled black children of his own age when they tried to enter previously all-white schools. For days, weeks, months, that mob persisted, aided and abetted by a city's indifference, a state's defiance of federal laws, and, for a long time, a national government's (in 1960, under President Eisenhower) reluctance to move quickly or effectively. James was taken by his parents to the scene of the riots and mob formation, will never forget what he saw and heard — from the mob, and from his parents, as they drove away and reflected upon what they had seen: "The women were calling the little colored girls bad names. The men were threatening the girls. A lot of people had posters, telling the girls to stay away and never come near the school. The police were just standing there, and my father said he thought the police were joking with the mob, and encouraging them, instead of telling them to cut it out. When the girls were gone — inside the school building — the mob stayed and they cheered and shouted and said they'd be back in the morning. On the way home my father said that there's a great danger in a country like ours that mobs will take over, because there are a lot of ignorant people, and they listen to ignorant politicians, and the next thing you know, there's a lot of trouble. My mother said she never wanted to see that neighborhood again. My father said he agreed, but mobs can move into any neighborhood, even ours."

He was younger then; the words above, spoken five years later, have to do with memories that still linger. A city's turmoil became for a rich and prominent family the basis of an emotional series of discussions which the child did not so easily shake off. The father took the boy back, just the two of them. They never left the car, but they saw once again the hate and threatening violence. Afterwards, the father repeated to his son certain philosophical premises, which the boy in subsequent years has fashioned into a way of looking at the city of New Orleans, the state of Louisiana, the United States of America.

When he had completed his drawing of a mob scene, and drawn a circle around it, he pinned the paper to the cork of his "message to myself center," as he calls the bulletin board, and began to talk about his views: "If that mob broke through the circle, we'd all be in trouble. My father says there's always that danger. When we go downtown to his club, the people you meet on the streets and coming out of the stores — a lot of them look as if they might join a mob if something got them upset. They push and shove; Dad says they're already half a mob — the way they act when they go into the department stores. Even in the good restaurants you'll meet people who push when they're standing in line, and they make a lot of noise, and they could cause trouble, if they weren't in a good mood. That's why the city has to have policemen who know how to keep control, and that's why the state has its own police, and the government has the troops, and there's the National Guard.

"My father was a colonel in the army. He says a strong army is important. If we didn't have the army, the Russians would invade us. And there'd be mobs all over, and the country wouldn't be the same. A lot of people don't believe in obeying the law. They want to steal and rob; or they want to hit someone; or they want to march up and down on the streets and scare people. If the police don't stop mobs from forming, then the city begins to fall apart. We almost had the whole city of New Orleans become a huge mob a few years ago, and it could happen again."

He draws a picture of a policeman, makes him tall, burly, wide-eyed. He provides the man with a billy club in one hand, a gun in the other. The reason: he has just seen a thief and is going to take after him, catch him, apprehend him. The officer has another gun in a holster. He has a large badge on his chest. James shows no interest in turning the portrait of the man into a street scene. He does not provide, either, a sky or any ground for the officer to stand on. (Figure 8.) He explains the reason he doesn't want to show an actual chase: "I've seen the police, and I talk a lot with one policeman who stands near our school, but I've never seen any thieves, so I don't know what they look like. I've asked my father if he has ever seen a thief, and he said no — but then he changed his mind and said he's probably seen thousands of them, but not when they're actually stealing something, or being chased by the police." And anyway, he wouldn't want to draw a thief even if he had caught a glimpse of one. He prefers to draw pictures of friends or allies rather than enemies.

There was a time when he himself thought about becoming a policeman. He mentioned his idea to his parents, and was not actively discouraged. His father knows the chief of the New Orleans police, and so the boy was brought to headquarters and shown around; he met a number of officers, got a ride in a cruiser, and even saw a few rookies being given training. When a year or so passed, and James was still talking about the glories of a policeman's life and his own intention of sharing in those glories later on, the mother began to have second thoughts and to speak them. She was sure there were other boys who would grow up to be quite satisfactory policemen; James had "better things to do." The boy couldn't imagine what they were. The mother came up with a few suggestions: law, business, or the boy's long-standing interest in architecture. But James would not budge; he was going to be a policeman. He remembers telling his mother that "there is no work more important than a police officer's"; and he remembers telling her who told him so: his father.

And it was the father who carefully remained loyal to his earlier pronouncements. He told the boy that he agreed — the police do indeed "hold everything together." He bought him two children's books that try to tell boys and girls about the working lives of the police. He allowed the boy to watch television programs that featured the activities of the police. And gradually he began to tell the boy how the police in turn need others to help *them* — prosecuting attorneys, judges who are not "soft" but utterly determined to "protect the public," and, not least, "ordinary citizens," who will back the police, if need be, against their enemies. The boy learned, with respect to "enemies," that the police not only have to hunt down criminals but to deal with the attacks of all sorts of "dangerous people." Who? The father has been both vague and precise. He has referred to "lawless people," and to mobs, of course; also to the Ku Klux Klan, but no less to "civil rights agitators."

Eventually James began to lose interest in the police — so far as a career for himself was concerned. At eleven he had even decided that the police had failed to curb various "mobs"; they therefore may be part of the nation's problem. He has wondered out loud repeatedly why Princeton University doesn't train police officers — who would, he is sure, be much more competent and effective than many now on the force. His father has agreed but tried to explain to the boy what is meant by the expression "division of labor." The boy tries hard and with considerable success to explain the concept: "Some people are good at being carpenters and some people are good at being architects. The carpenter doesn't know what to do in a house that is being built unless the architect makes his plans, a blueprint, and shows the carpenter what has to be done. That's division of labor. Princeton University is where you learn to be an architect, or a lawyer. If you want to be a carpenter, then you don't go to Princeton. You can learn that in a high school or from a carpenter who will teach you. The policeman is like a carpenter; he doesn't need to go to college. If you went up to a policeman — to most New Orleans cops — and asked them if they would have liked to go to Princeton, they'd think you were some nut, trying to be funny. They wouldn't even know, a lot of them, about Princeton; it's too far away. And my father says they don't like Tulane, and that's right here in our city."

The mob he saw as a child is the mob he thinks about when he stresses the importance of the police to New Orleans. When a Tulane professor criticized the city's police for being heavy-handed in the way they dealt with blacks or poor people, regardless of race, the boy rallied to the defense of the police — after hearing his father do likewise. At such moments James stakes out an interesting position. He condemns Tulane, condemns the people of both races who complain against the police, declares himself only too anxious to leave the city and attend Princeton when the time comes. But he will come back, and then, he hopes, the police will be at his side — protecting the Garden District, he says bluntly and unashamedly, from the people who "want to take away what we own here." His father has said as much: "Dad says that when people want to cut down on the number of police we have, and cripple them with rules and regulations, it's because those people don't want the city protected. Once the police are gone, the mobs will start marching, and they'll come here and break into the homes. We'll lose all we've got."

James has heard his mother argue time and again that the family ought to sell their city home, go live upstate on their plantation year around — or, alternatively, take an apartment, in which they would be "less exposed." The father has said no, he will not budge; he insists that once fear obtains that degree of leverage over the lives of people, they won't know when to stop running. He wants to stand and fight. He has several guns in the home, two rifles and a handgun. He does target practice on weekends, when he and his family do indeed go to their plantation or their oceanside home in Mississippi. His son has also learned how to shoot, possesses a lightweight rifle, enjoys using it in the woods of northern Louisiana.

Upon occasion James has thought up a rather spirited if harrowing scenario of what might prompt him to aim a weapon and pull its trigger inside the New Orleans house. In a picture drawn at the age of ten he showed himself at the window of his Garden District home, with his newly acquired gun. The street outside was filled with another of his "mobs," and the assault was obviously directed toward his family's property. The house seems vulnerable indeed, not the sturdy, even imposing, building he sometimes draws — as if the mob had already won part of its objective simply by putting in an appearance. The boy is prepared to fight to ward off the enemy. The mother, the boy explained later, is in the kitchen preparing for the necessity of flight — cooking food, filling up a thermos or two, packing a suitcase. There is a lot of smoke coming out of the chimney, more than one expects, since the home is in New Orleans, not known for its cold weather. The sky is cloudy; no sun is shown. (Figure 9.) The boy explains the smoke — and much more: "I think my mother would probably be burning some family papers. My father says we shouldn't keep anything important at home. But my mother doesn't like to go back and forth to the bank. She keeps her papers in her desk. She's told us that if a robber wants to find out how much stocks she inherited from her father, that's all right. But if a mob tried to break in, I'll bet my mother wouldn't want them poking into her papers!"

A year later, as he talked yet another time about the police and a recent news story of a robbery in a Garden District home, James began to speak of envy — his envy. If only he were "one of those poor colored kids" he had seen five years earlier, walking past a mob into school; then he wouldn't be worried about thieves and robbers and mobs and the destruction of his home. It is an anxious and fearful life, the one he has inherited from his parents — or so he was beginning to believe. Better to be poor; one has little or nothing to lose! Nevertheless, he had no choice but to do the best he could under the circumstances — try to gird himself for future hazards, stresses, times of outright danger, if not disaster.

"I know that I've got a lot of advantages," he announced a week before turning twelve. "But it's not all easy for us, here in the Garden District," he went on. And he knew exactly why: "The more you have, the more people want what you have. My Dad says he wakes up, and he's dreamed that he's been robbed and lost his watch, his wallet, his key chain, and even the coins in his pocket. I've had the same dream: a kid came — he was white, I believe, but he could be colored — and he took away my model planes and my Tonka toys. My father said it was just me saying I was too old for those toys. I told him I disagreed. I said a lot of kids want my toys, just like a lot of grown-ups want his wallet! He said I was right. Then my mother asked him again if we couldn't please move away to the country. And he said no. And she wouldn't talk to us anymore. She asked to be excused, and she rang and had her breakfast brought upstairs to her bedroom. And she wasn't too nice later on, either. She was working on her plants until a minute before supper, and then she said she didn't feel too good, so she was going to skip eating. But Dad went upstairs and persuaded her to come down, and the cook had made a good supper — her favorite red snapper — and we forgot about the trouble. It's always around the corner, though — the trouble that comes when one of our neighbors tells us that someone tried to break in; and then mother gets upset. She's had three locks put on all our doors. And we have an alarm that's supposed to be the best. Dad says he'd hire a private detective to watch the house at night, if it would make mother feel better; but he says it's crazy to do that now, and if he ever really has to do it, then he *will* sell the house and we'll leave the whole United States, not just New Orleans, because by that time there will be mobs in the small towns, too!"

The boy is sure that there are some poor children, black and white, who will never grow up to be greedy, lawbreaking, violent people. He recalls quite vividly the dignity of "the colored kids" who started school desegregation. He recalls the "nice" children of his parents' servants — boys and girls whom he has, however, seen only occasionally, because their mothers or fathers are not prone to bring them to work. He wishes there were more like "them" — those children of his family's maid and laundress and gardener and handyman, who also serves as a butler at formal parties: "They are polite. They look at you with real respect in their eyes. I told my cousin that the colored kids are the equal of their parents. My cousin is going to Princeton next year. He said the colored up North aren't as

nice as they are down here. My Dad says the children of our
servants would naturally be good, but some other colored kids
in New Orleans aren't so good. My mother says she's never
met a bad colored kid from the country; the city makes the
colored greedy and they lose their manners and they get in
trouble with the law. I asked her about the children we've
met, the children of our servants, and she said they're special.

"We go to their houses every Christmas; my father was
brought up to do that. On Christmas Day we bring gifts to the
servants before we open up our own presents. We've been
going for years. I was once given a long lecture, because my
father said I was rude when we went to the servants' homes.
I didn't ask after them, and I didn't try to make conversation
with them. I guess I just stood there. I must have been about
six. I remember it was when those colored kids were having
all the trouble with the mobs. The next year I was much
better. I got so friendly with one colored boy, our maid's son,
that I asked him to come over and play with my Lego. He said
he'd like to, but his mother said no. My father said he'd try to
get us together one day, the colored boy and me; but afterwards, in the car, I got another lecture. I realize now that I was
too young to realize how to behave. It was a bad thing to do,
because it really embarrassed the maid's whole family, and the
boy must have felt bad. My father was sure that the maid gave
her son a whipping. She talks a lot about whipping her children when they don't behave. I asked my father if he wouldn't
turn around, please, and let me go back in the house and
apologize, and ask the maid to leave her son alone. But my
Dad said no, if we tried that there'd be even more trouble, and
they'd all be in a real scared state over there, and they
wouldn't know what to say or do. So, we drove on, and I
realized then and there how careful you've got to be when
you're talking with colored people, and it's our responsibility."

The word "responsibility" is one he has learned to use with increasing frequency. When he was six years old, and his parents were upset by the racial struggle and near chaos facing New Orleans, there was a lot of talk in front of him about "responsibility." When the boy was taken to see the mob in action, his father told him afterward, day after day, that it was the "responsibility" of families like theirs to fight for "law and order," to resist "mob rule," to prevent "violence" from spreading — to the point that the city becomes "a jungle." The boy still links together in his mind those various words or phrases. He talks about a safari his cousin went on; then goes on to remark upon how "violent" the jungle is and how hard it must have been for the white men who explored Africa to come to terms with the various tribes, as well as the animals. So with our own settlers, who came West against the opposition of Indians, some of them violent. His uncle worked for a while in Latin America as an executive of a major American corporation and has told James and his father a number of times how "primitive" the people are in countries like Brazil, Colombia, Venezuela, and how much "responsibility" an American company incurs as it tries to "raise the standard of living," "stay in business," and "make a reasonable profit."

James has heard, and will not forget, that there are a lot of people in this country who have never been within a thousand miles of "a jungle" or "an underdeveloped nation" and have no idea what the people of such places are like — but who are against all American companies on principle, and "make a lot of noise" to that effect here and abroad. The same holds nearer at home, the boy knows, at the age of eleven. He is worried about his nation's future: "My uncle told us that he tried to get the people near the jungle of Colombia to be clean and to take medicines, so they wouldn't be tired and they wouldn't feel so bad, and they could work better and live better. But they suspected him, and they were very superstitious. They need a lot of education, and that takes years. That's why the colored in our country should go into the same schools as whites do; then the colored will begin to learn a lot more than they once did, and they will be better off. The trouble is, a lot of white people aren't too good either. You'd think white people would know better, but they don't. It depends on who the white person is. The same with the colored: my father says there are some very smart colored people, and they're more civilized than the white. Dad told Mother he wouldn't mind going to lunch at his club with a colored man, if he was the president of a colored university, or a doctor, a surgeon. There's supposed to be a very good colored surgeon in Nashville, my mother heard someone say. She says she's never been convinced the colored should go to school with whites; she says they should civilize themselves, like the surgeon did, and stay away from the rednecks. Dad says *they're* the *most* uncivilized — worse than any colored are.

"My father went to a meeting; he talked with judges and he met the chief of police, and he said they all agreed that America is in trouble. By the time I grow up New Orleans might need an army to keep the peace. The colored have become more violent. They're not as polite as they used to be, except for our servants and some people like them. The rednecks are looking for fights with the colored. My father says we've got to do all we can to be umpires; it's our responsibility. My uncle says that he used to think he was crazy for going to South America and trying to live there, but now he's sorry he's become vice-president and lives here, because it's safer in the jungle than in downtown New Orleans; and it's getting worse here, and you can't be sure that even in your own neighborhood you're safe. People want the government to take everything away from the people who have earned it, and they want a lot of things for nothing, so it's like the jungle, with everyone trying to beat out everyone else — only in the jungle, when you come there from this country, and you have your bulldozers and rifles, and you bring food and medicine for the natives, then you can make them work, and they live better than ever before, and it's pretty safe down there. Up here it's getting more and more dangerous. My uncle says he's glad he's lived most of his life; the way it's going in America, everyone will soon be nervous about being robbed. But my father says I shouldn't pay any attention to talk like that, because there's always going to be *some* trouble, and if you read the diaries of my grandfather and my great-grandfather, they were in a lot of trouble too, but they didn't retreat, and they knew how to live up to their responsibilities, and they did right well, so it's not all so bad."

No, indeed; he has wonderful times throughout the year. He goes north to the family's plantation on weekends; there he fishes, learns to shoot and hunt, swims in a pool that is heated (hence usable all year), goes horse riding, learns to play tennis. In addition to family travel abroad, there are other trips, too; James occasionally goes skiing in Colorado with his parents on long winter weekends, missing a day or so of school, or goes to the family's home on the Gulf Coast, where he has learned to sail. In fact, as he has noted often, the family's "main home" (his expression) seems like a stopping place: a place among places — all very reassuring, actually, for people who have increasing doubts about city life, however privileged it be.

But the city at least offers the excellent private school he attends, and the teachers there are quite accommodating as well as serious-minded and demanding. "They expect us to miss school," he observes. As a result, they keep high standards, get a lot of work done with each child when he or she is in attendance, and assign a lot of homework to someone going away with his or her parents. The headmaster has even told the children that absences are not all that detrimental, so long as the student really takes advantage of the time spent in school: "He said he knows our families are living busy lives, and have a lot to do, and places they have to go, so he doesn't get upset when our mothers or fathers write letters saying we're going to be out for a couple of days, or even a week. He says that we're all from good homes, and our parents have gone to college, and they're successful, and they want us to be successful, so they'll keep us working and make sure we don't lose out if we miss school. My father does keep me working, too; no matter where we go on a weekend, he makes sure I have my books with me, and either he or my mother go over the work. My spelling has never been very good, and my father is always asking me to spell words. We'll be driving, and he'll say: 'James, how do you spell "restaurant"?' Then I do, and then my mother says to him: "You must be hungry!' I think I've learned how to spell from my father more than from my teachers. They say you have to keep practicing, and my father makes sure I do. Even at breakfast, he'll look up from his paper and ask me a word. When we're skiing or way over in Europe, he remembers to 'give me a word.' He'll stop what he's been doing and say: 'James, let me give you another word.' I tell him okay, I'm ready."

James looks forward to the future — when he will be the father and a child of his will be asked how to spell. He assumes he will have a son; he bears the number III after his name, and he wishes that one day the number IV will appear after the name of a newborn baby in the family. The family will persist, he is sure; it has for centuries — through wars, revolutions, natural and man-made disasters. Maybe there will be a strategic retreat: the abandonment of New Orleans, even of Louisiana. But the father has said that this will not be necessary. In the event of a disaster, however, there are always the mountains of east Tennessee or of Colorado.

The son is reassured as he contemplates the safety of the mountains, but he hopes never to leave New Orleans. He remarks upon the affection he feels for his Garden District home, predicts that his own children will love going there and visiting his old room. He might, one day, have a house nearby, well placed in the District, and so his parents and his future wife and their children would be quite *intime,* as his mother puts it. And maybe "the colored" and "the rednecks" by then would be the ones to have left New Orleans. After all, as his parents keep mentioning, cities are expensive places to live in. James has wondered why the poorer people don't move out, find cheaper places to live. His father has explained that people stay in the city because they can get work more easily there than in the small towns or the country. But the father has also mentioned repeatedly that the unemployment rate is high in New Orleans, so the boy has felt puzzled.

He has asked what the poor who can't find work do. He was told that "a lot of them don't do anything, they just loaf around." James suggested that they might eventually get tired of "loafing around" in the city. They might pick themselves up and go back to places like northern Louisiana or the Mississippi Delta. At least they will be able to hunt and fish — and so eat rather well. In the small towns or the countryside they'd feel better, live better, and if they got into trouble, they'd know the sheriff, and he'd give them a second chance and keep a friendly eye on them. The father heard the boy out, said nothing for a while, then decided that his son was a social prophet, a young person of hope and wisdom. When he acknowledged as much out loud, the boy smiled, asked his father if he was "just fooling" or "trying to be nice." No, the man was quite serious. Well, if that is the case, won't the Garden District soon be as safe at night as the homes his parents owned elsewhere? The father shook his head, told his son that it may take decades for his prediction to come true — for the poor and potentially troublesome ones to be gone from New Orleans. Meanwhile, they had to gird themselves for more trouble, rather than less. The son asked when he might own a pistol as well as a beginner's rifle. Soon, he was told. The boy left for his room, where he looked at a gun catalogue and made a selection, which he showed to his father, who said yes, one day the two of them would go make the purchase.

When James has recalled the mob scene he saw at the age of six, he has wondered repeatedly whether the parents of the black children had guns at home, or on them as they walked with their children — "just in case." The father used to say each time that he doubted very much "any colored person would pull a gun on a white mob." But more recently he has changed his mind. The city has seen crowds of blacks stand up and assert themselves rather forcefully, so the father is quite sure that never again will he or his son see what they once saw — terrorized children and parents heckled mercilessly, with no apparent inclination to fight back. The boy goes a step further, speculates that blacks have been secretly "practicing," hiding guns and using them to aim at targets, on the assumption that one day there might be an awful confrontation. He would fight to death to defend his home, his neighborhood, and has imagined himself doing so. Blacks would, too. That is the bottom line, he is sure — defense of one's place of residence against mob assault.

III

TAMED REBEL

L ARRY has been, according to his father and mother, a
constant, unflagging critic. When he was six, he asked his
father why some children of his age were working in the fields,
helping their parents pick the crops, while he was doing nothing of the kind. The father explained that he owned the land,
was a grower, and paid money to others in exchange for their
labor. Later on, maybe at seven or eight, the boy asked about
the houses the father owned, in which the migrants lived: why
were those houses in such bad repair, so "broken-down," he
called them, whereas his family lived in such fine style? The
father is one of Florida's leading growers, the owner, actually,
of an "agribusiness" — growing fields, packinghouses, wholesale distribution outlets, even supermarkets. The boy is named
after his grandfather, who at eighty-one still described himself
as a "dirt-poor farmer who made good." The grandfather
wants even his son and grandson to call him Larry. The old
man lost his oldest son, also named Larry, in the Second World
War. His second son, Edward, called Ted, agreed to give his
first son the name Larry. But for a long while the agreement
seemed of remote significance: one girl after another was
born. Ted and his wife Brenda, herself the daughter of a
grower, tried one more time, in their hearts resigned to a sixth

and last girl. But no; Larry was born on November 11, 1962. The father said on the boy's tenth birthday: "You'd think he'd remember that he was born on Armistice Day! Instead, he's always looking for a fight. Even when he was a baby, he was a scrapper. He cried a lot, and he always wanted his own way. My wife told the pediatrician when Larry was three that he was as stubborn as a mule. The doctor said it sometimes happens like that: a kid develops a mind of his own when he's very young, and there's nothing you can do about it. The doctor was one hundred percent correct!"

The boy Larry may have been willful as a young child, but he was also active, energetic, and obviously quite intelligent. In the first weeks of kindergarten he showed himself able to read, much to the surprise of his teacher. He also had, even then, what his parents and his grandfather called "ideas." The boy would watch migrants pick oranges, carry baskets of them under the hot sun, then wonder out loud to his mother or father why those men, women, and children didn't stop every once in a while to take and eat an orange. After all, oranges were always being urged upon *him!* Nor were his parents' answers satisfactory. They said that the farmhands weren't there to eat the "produce" but to harvest it. They also said that the migrant laborers were "too ignorant" to know about the value of orange juice. For the boy, during part of his childhood, at least, such ignorance seemed enviable indeed. He began telling his parents at breakfast time that he wished he were a migrant child, then he wouldn't have to drink fresh orange juice, or eat the carefully cut sections placed before him by Anita.

Anita is the sister of a migrant worker, the wife of a former migrant worker, who is now crippled for life as the result of an injury sustained "on the road." She is also the mother of five children — three grown and become migrants, two who live with her. One of those two, Fred, is a year older than young Larry, and at the ages of three, four, five, they played together. In fact, Larry's parents look back at that circumstance as one of the more harmful psychological experiences of their son's childhood. The father gives a retrospective account of his son's early years, along with a fairly accurate description of what in the son's "behavior" upsets his parents: "My boy was all right to begin with. The doctor told us he was a big, husky, normal child. When Larry was one year old, I remember my father saying we had a future fullback of the Notre Dame football team. He used to eat anything we put before him. I guess I wanted a son so badly I got too wrapped up with the kid. I even fed him a lot, once he was able to eat solid food. My daughters didn't like me doing it. They said I was partial to Larry; and they were right. But then I cut down; I had to pay so much attention to my business, because we were growing so fast, that I had less and less time even for Larry. My wife says I never paid enough attention to our girls. Well, I evened it out: I didn't give Larry any more attention than I gave to the girls. And the wife began to get involved in all her "charities," and the boy was left to be looked after by Anita.

"The next thing we knew our Larry and her boy Fred were bosom buddies. I asked my wife once if she thought we ought to step in and do something. No, she said, 'Let things be.' She kept insisting Larry would outgrow the friendship. Even though Larry doesn't see that Fred anymore, the friendship in my opinion, has *marked* my son. He talks, a lot of the time, as if *he's* Fred — a kid who's going to work in the fields all his life. First it was the orange and grapefruit trouble: he didn't want to eat them, because Fred didn't. I remember asking Larry why he has to copy Fred. I never got a satisfactory answer, just that Fred was his friend. Finally I told Anita to keep her son away from this house, or I'd fire her. She got all upset, and got my wife to come and tell me to be more 'kind' and 'under-standing.' My wife is always doing that; if it's not one excuse, it's another, for her to come at me with the 'understanding' routine.

"My wife is a good woman; she just lives a sheltered life. That Anita is a good cook, and she's a good maid, and so I've let the whole thing drop. She can stay here until she's too old to stand up to the stove or push the vacuum cleaner, and then I'll give her a huge pension. But I know she exerts an influence on my wife, just like her son did on my son. That Fred boy, I'm sure, got my son Larry going on all this 'unfair' business. 'It's not fair'; that's what I've been hearing all these years — since the boy was five or six. That's why I finally decided to go see our doctor. Larry was eight, and he was driving me out of my mind with his questions, and even his mother was getting upset. So we sat down with Larry one day and asked him what was wrong and what we could do to make life easier for him — and for us. Well, he had a lot to tell us; and then I decided that either I lost my temper and started a bad, bad fight with my only son, or I tried to find a neutral party to help us settle the matter — like in business, an arbitrator. So we went to the doctor, and that was only the beginning!"

The child had quite another sense of what was happening to him when he first was taken to a doctor he had known for years — through the thick and thin of colds, yearly checkups, a bout of surgery for a mild hernia: a boy's normal moments of difficulty. A lively, sharp-eyed but often smiling boy, Larry remembers his first visit to the pediatrician quite well: "He examined me; then he told me there was nothing wrong with me. He asked me to sit down, because he wanted to talk with me. I did. He did the talking; he told me my parents were worried about me, and they didn't know what to think about my 'views.' I asked him what 'views.' He said he wasn't sure,

but I must know which ones! I said I didn't! Then we didn't
have too much to say. He asked me if I ever saw much of
Anita's boy, Fred, now that I was in the second grade, going
on the third, and I said no, I didn't. That was about all. He said
he wanted me to come back next week, and I asked what for,
and he said to talk. I didn't say I would and I didn't say I
wouldn't. I waited until I got home, and when my father asked
if I'd had a good talk with the doctor, I said yes. Then my
mother said she was glad, and that she'd be driving me there
next week, because Daddy would be out of town. Then I told
them I wouldn't be going."

He smiles. He isn't interested in reciting the subsequent
uproar: the efforts at persuasion, and bribery; the pleas followed by threats; and eventually the command. He bowed. He
went. He became, for the most part, silent or monosyllabically
polite when in the doctor's office. He went once a week for ten
weeks. The doctor finally called it quits; they were "getting
nowhere." The boy insisted, at the end, that he still liked the
doctor, but he couldn't see why his parents wanted him to go
see the man, or why the doctor kept asking all those questions.
Shortly after the visits had been ended, Larry drew a picture
of the doctor: a tall man, given a smiling face, a well-propor-
tioned body, a nicely clothed and pleasant appearance. Impul-
sively, as the picture was being set aside, the boy put a large
black question mark near the doctor's head — as if to question
his intentions or purposes. (Figure 10.) The boy then drew his
own father: shorter, less smiling, but no object of scorn or
terror. He has his father standing near a field, which he leaves
dug up, but without standing crops — as at the end of a harvest. The sky is blue, the sun in mid-sky, no clouds. There are
no trees, either, or houses. The man has his back to the viewer;
he is looking at his land, taking satisfaction (one is later told)
in the achievements of his business. His hands are in his pock-

ets. His ears are rather small. His feet are planted firmly in the earth, a little wide apart, and even a bit below ground level, as if they had been dug in somewhat more successfully than intended. (Figure 11.)

The father loves that earth. He is an eager, rather sophisticated photographer, and has taken dozens of pictures of his land, the crops, the various buildings. Some of the photographs have been in color; they have been enlarged and mounted. In one room a dramatic aerial view of the land covers an entire wall. Larry has done his best to draw his version of that land. But he is more interested in the people who work on the hundreds of acres of land his father owns than in the majesty of the view: row upon row of citrus trees, or neatly arranged lettuce or celery, all converging upon gray hulks of buildings — the packinghouses. The father's photographs show the crops, the expanse of territory, the complicated machinery that helps sort the produce, pack it, send it on the way to the market. The boy, on the other hand, wants to show whose labor enables the entire "operation." In one drawing, done when Larry was nine, the rows of crops are shown, but looming over them are human beings; the picture is really concerned with them. They too are lined up in rows! There may be plenty of sun in Florida, but the boy chooses to leave the sun out of this picture, emphasize the dark clouds above. (Figure 12.) He did another picture about a week later in which he put the sun. His father had seen the first picture and asked the boy why he had denied the crops sun. Larry smiled and said it wasn't sunny *every* day in Florida. The father replied: "Most days it is — in the spring." The boy drew a group of migrants bent over, cutting celery; he placed directly over them an enormous sun, its rays beating down relentlessly on the rows of huddled farmhands — almost touching them. (Figure 13.) The father did not like that picture, either: "The sun is exaggerated."

Larry's concern for the lives of migrant farm workers became increasingly obvious to others, outside the family, when he was about nine years old. He began to tell his friends that when he grew up he'd build new houses for the migrants. He would get rid of all outhouses. He would provide running water. He would give each family a television set. Why? "If they can work so hard for us," he explained about a month before his ninth birthday, "we can give them television sets that work." He had the interest in, had taken the time to find out, how migrants live and what they do with their evenings. His parents had arranged to keep Anita's son away from the house, but not Anita herself or a gardener who took care of flowers and semitropical plants. Young Larry had a way of making casual conversation with them but in the course of it asking at least one pointed question. Gradually he had learned about a whole way of life, a social and economic phenomenon. At nine he took to speaking up, when the opportunity arose, in school. The teacher was surprised, became increasingly apprehensive as Larry said more and more. She eventually called in the parents for a conference. They were not at all surprised. They had known all along of their son's continuing interest in "labor problems," as the father put it. When the pediatrician gave up, they did, too. They decided to let him watch the crops and the workers, let him even carry on his various conversations with migrant men and women. They did, however, refuse to allow him to play with migrant children. They tried to keep him busy — music lessons, Cub Scouts, bowling, sports, the movies — and increasingly to get him away: trips on weekends to Florida's cities, to Atlanta, to New Orleans, to the Caribbean. The parents, no great lovers of travel or cities, began to feel that *they* were becoming migrants.

Larry was sardonically aware: "I think my mother and father would stay home if only I'd stop bothering them about the people out there in the field. My mother started crying and she said I should stop being so much trouble. I told her I wasn't trying to cause trouble. I don't even bring up the subject; it's my father who keeps on asking me if I'm 'still worrying about those folks out there.' I told him I wasn't worrying. I told him I felt sorry for them, but it wasn't my business to worry over them, it was his business, and if he didn't want to, then there wasn't anything I could do. We were riding in his jeep. He stopped right in the middle of the road, and he asked me if I wanted a jeep like that one some day. I said I sure did. Then he said I could have more than the jeep; I could have the whole place, and he'd be only too glad to retire, like his Daddy did, and see me running everything. I said I'd be glad to help out. But then he brought up the 'labor problems' he was having, and he started telling me about how much it costs to run the place, and get the work done, and how he only makes a little bit on the crops, and it's not like a factory, where you can count on a certain profit. There's always the chance of a freeze, and he could be ruined for the season."

The boy did not contemplate such a disaster with sadistic glee. He appeared worried and sad at the prospect. He had memories of previous struggles waged by his father and grandfather against the elements — hurricanes and torrential rains as well as sudden, dramatic drops in the temperature. And over the years he had heard, especially from his grandfather, the family saga: a poor man with five acres of land, who decided to farm for a living; his hard labor, his sacrifices; his gradual acquisition of land; his risks and losses; and eventually, during the Second World War, when the price of food began to rise, his stunning success. The old man can still scarcely believe that it was he who initiated what now has come to be a vast and influential commercial enterprise. He gives credit to his son, who knew to expand further, purchase packinghouses, buy into a supermarket chain, and not least, cultivate a large "pool" of migrant labor, managed by tough crew leaders utterly loyal to their boss and "dependable as the Florida sun," to quote that boss. The son, in turn, once had hopes for his son — young Larry. The boy could move into the firm right after college — the first in the family to go "right through." The boy Larry would take "a business course," then run one of the "spinoffs": the supermarket chain, most likely; or if he wished, a nonagricultural enterprise, the combined car-washing and laundromat "operation" the father had made such a go of — "the perfect thing," he has observed, for Florida, with its elderly people "who like clean cars and clean clothes."

And Larry, for all his so-called rebelliousness, has never turned his back on the future offered him by doting, but increasingly apprehensive, parents. He has told his father on more than one occasion that it would be "fun" to learn to drive the various harvesting machines; and fun to work on the assembly line of the packing plant, sorting the good from the bad produce; or, for that matter, fun to have a job in one of the places where cars are washed by those machines. But the father says: "I think the boy has to realize the difference between himself and a lot of other people. He thinks he's just anyone — the same as a colored kid whose father picks oranges, or a white kid whose father works in one of our stores. You can't have a boy thinking like that. What will happen later? Someone has got to take over this business eventually. I'm afraid my son would want to take it over, then give it away for free. I'm not joking, either!"

Larry knows quite well that his father is not joking. The boy wrote a composition when he was eleven that made clear his understanding of his father's views, even as an effort was made to differ with them. "I am lucky," the composition began. But immediately there was a counterassertion: "I am unlucky, too." Then came the explanation: "My father has made a lot of money, and like he says, a lot of people have jobs because he's made jobs for them. But a lot of the people who work for him are very poor, and they couldn't be much worse off. My father says they should work harder and make more money. I've seen them work, and they can't work much harder than they do. My father says I can be the boss when I'm grown up, but I don't think I can be a good boss. I hope I can think of another job to do. If I don't, I'll be in the same bad shape our colored people out in the fields are. When I ride my bike and try to talk with them, they look at me funny. So does my father!"

The teacher had corrected some spelling mistakes, broken up a long statement into two paragraphs, and reprimanded Larry in a note for writing on "the wrong subject" — because the composition was supposed to be about an "experience," and the child had written about "the future." The boy took issue with the teacher, insisted that he had written about "experiences" he had been having with his father — conversations, disagreements. The teacher was not at all convinced. She told the parents later, at a conference, that the boy seemed determined to have his own way — with her as well as in life. She wondered whether the pediatrician should be consulted again. Perhaps the boy would now be (at eleven and a half) "more reasonable." The school authorities knew that Larry was "difficult" at home, though not, in the teacher's words, a "real behavior problem." It was his "ideas" that bothered his parents; and in time his teachers too.

At twelve, in the seventh grade, Larry wrote a major essay on the state of Florida, with particular reference to its agricultural development. He went to the public library, to the school library, and ultimately, at his request, was driven by his mother to a more useful library in a larger town. After giving a historical account of the early years of Florida's land boom, the boy addressed himself to the relationship between his own family and the migrant families that labor in the fields bought years ago by his grandfather: "My grandfather and I have the same name. He built up the business my father runs. My grandfather is now an old man. He tells me that he wants to live to see me start working with my father, and then he will die in peace. I don't know what I will be when I grow up. I think I would like to be a doctor, or a teacher. I would like to help the poor people of Florida. They don't have the luck I have. I could afford to help them without asking them for money, because my grandfather told me that I have money, and when I am twenty-one I will be able to use it. I told my grandfather not to worry, I won't spend the money on foolish things. He's afraid that I'll throw the money away. I tell him I won't. But I'd like to give some money to the poor. I'd like the people who work for us to be friendly with us. Right now, they are afraid of my father. They are afraid of the crew leaders, who work for my father. They are even afraid of my old grandfather, when he comes to watch them work. I have to be honest; I think they are afraid of me, too. When I come near them on my bike, they stop talking, and they work very hard, and they keep on looking up at me, to see if I'm still there. When I go, I can hear them start talking to each other again, and I don't even want to turn around and look, because if they see me looking, they'll stop talking again. I'd rather be me than them. I guess they would rather be me, too!"

The teacher put a large question mark beside that long, personal statement. She called Larry to her during a study period and asked him why he had decided to put his family's "private business" into an essay that concerned itself mainly with Florida's history. The boy told her that he believed his family's experiences are part of Florida's history. The teacher told him that a composition had to be "consistent," and not be a hodgepodge of social history, economics, and autobiographical comment. The boy said "Yes, ma'am"; he was always polite. Once Larry drew pictures of his teacher. He was almost twelve when he did so. He had not attempted to hide his dislike of his teacher — whose large question marks at the sides of his various compositions had become standard fare. She had no understanding of what he was trying to say, or so he felt. He watched her when his parents came to find out how he was doing, and concluded that she was entirely too nice toward them. In his brief account: "They talk and she nods her head."

He showed her doing so in his drawing; her head was bent, the neck long and quite agile — a Modigliani neck that connected, however, a far from sensitive and appealing face to a rather bulky torso. At first sight her arms seemed absent, or deliberately portrayed as stumps; but the boy explained that he intended to place her hands behind her back. Her legs are short, much shorter than they are in real life, and her shoes are almost sabots. Her face comes across as grotesque: large eyes that seize the viewer's attention immediately and in fact, dominate the portrait; the thinnest of mouths; ears big and pricked up; nondescript, slightly frizzly hair. Larry provides no background at first, then decides to draw with a black crayon a few wandering, wavy lines. He stops and seems done. But no; he works a little longer and the result is a small window — detached, seemingly floating in space. Again he has a second thought. He puts a slanted roof over the woman's head, makes a haphazard effort to connect the roof to walls, which he begins to construct from the ground up. The walls don't intersect, however, with the roof. The building seems both solid (the walls) and disconnected and insubstantial (the spaces between the roof and the walls, the absence of any floor).

Who is the person portrayed? (Figure 14.) She is, in reality, a woman of forty-two, considered by most parents one of the very best teachers in the school — intelligent, attentive, responsive to the children, rather gentle with them. The boy does not contradict that judgment; he considers it only part of the story: "I can see why a lot of people, a lot of kids, like her. She's popular with the parents, and she's popular with many in my class. She tries to be friendly. At first I thought I'd get along real fine with her. But I decided to speak up, after I'd heard her repeat herself about five times one week — about the migrants; and ever since then we've had trouble."

What did she say? Larry is that anxious to repeat the words. He says that he tries to forget painful moments in his life. But he hasn't been able to forget one sentence of his teacher's original criticism: "Where would the migrants be if your father didn't have jobs for them?" He had no answer; she had asked a theoretical question. She was reprimanding him because he — of all people! — had chosen to speak skeptically about the condition of farm laborers in the nearby area. He, in turn, did not knuckle under. He had spoken words which marked him. As a matter of fact, his words created a rush of whispering gossip. He had raised his hand, and simply asked: "Why are you worrying about the growers? Why don't you worry about the migrant people? Just because people have a lot of money, does that mean everyone should be on their side?"

The teacher, some of Larry's classmates say, had turned red, said nothing for an embarrassingly long time. Finally, she turned to another subject. Later in the day, however, during a mathematics period, she had recognized Larry, because his hand was the only one up — in response to a question of hers

put to the class. When he answered incorrectly, she went after
him with scorn, much to his dismay and even apprehension:
"I didn't know what she was talking about, at first. She said
that if you're rich, you can afford to forget about money. If you
overdraw a check, the bank doesn't bounce the check. I don't
remember all she said. All I know is that she was angry at me.
It was hard for us to know what was bothering her. She mentioned the migrants; she said they're lazy, and they drink a lot,
and they don't know how to live clean, and no matter what
kind of houses the growers would build, the migrants would
ruin them in a month or so. When she said that, I knew she
hadn't forgotten what I'd asked in the morning. Now she was
practically shouting at me. The whole class was upset. They
couldn't understand why she talked on and on.

"Finally she stopped. I was so surprised, I guess, by what she
said, that I forgot I was still standing. She glared at me, after
she sat down; and then she told me to sit down, and not to
move until she gave me permission! I felt like getting up and
running away. I thought to myself: she's going nuts. I decided
to stay there and say nothing and not move either — except
to breathe! In a few minutes she was back to our arithmetic,
and I decided that she'd forgotten about me. But then I had
to go to the bathroom. I raised my hand. She started shouting
again: hadn't she told me *not to move?* I said, 'Yes, but.' She
interrupted me, and said that I'd better learn to obey *her*,
even if I don't obey my mother and father! That's when *I* got
excited. I shouted at her: 'You leave my mother and father out
of this!' She banged her ruler down on the desk, and she began
to talk, but I just got up and walked right out of the school
building. I even forgot that I'd wanted to go to the john. I
walked all the way home. It took me almost an hour."

He came home to an empty house — or rather a house with
only the servants there. He tried to avoid them, unusual for
him. Later he would say quite openly that he was afraid he

might start crying and tell Anita what had happened, and thereby cause her pain and sadness. She is, he knows, a proud, sensitive woman. Once upstairs he turned on the television in his room and watched a baseball game — with the sound off. In the middle of the fifth inning he became bored, put off the set, began to play with his Corgi automobiles, became bored again, went to lie down on his bed — and fell asleep. The next thing he knew, his father was standing over him, nudging him, calling his name. The phone had rung: Larry's teacher, an account of "trouble," of the boy's "insubordination," his departure from the school. The father went to check the boy's room — and there he was, asleep.

Larry remembers clearly a second of hesitation: what to say, how to explain himself, the earlier events, the teacher's words, his own? He said nothing. His father, in the face of continuing silence, became angry. The boy now remained silent out of his own anger. The more the father hurled questions, the more the boy stared at the ceiling. Finally the father exploded, shouted obscenities, left the room. The boy wanted to go get him, ask him to come back. But he could not seem to move; and any hope that his father would calm down and return and try at least to talk, proved futile. Larry began to think again about running away from home. He pictured an even more enraged father; and he pictured his mother, cross and sullen — familiarly silent but disapproving. He pictured himself at his father's side walking back to school, the principal's office, the teacher's room — apologies and more apologies. No, he would not, never; he would indeed run away. And he did.

He remembers, months later, his every step, it seems. As he moved away from the house, he asked himself *where:* back to school, or toward his father's field, or in the direction of the town, or, for that matter, away from the town and toward an interstate highway? He decided in favor of the last, did so because a thought, for a few moments an obsession, seized

him: he would become a migrant farm worker himself. And
why not? A perfect way, he reasoned, to prove himself consistent. He could end the criticism he felt coming at him from
all directions, even from Anita, who, he sensed, was beginning
to feel the burden of his own partisanship on behalf of her
people. Perhaps he would finally convince his parents and his
grandfather and his teachers and his friends that he wasn't "a
spoiled rich kid," as his father had once called him, who was
"patting the poor on the head," as the father had also insisted
the boy was doing, "because he had nothing better to do with
his time." Larry envisioned himself spending several months
"on the road" — the expression he'd heard his father's labor-
ing men and women use to describe the migrant life. He
would go perhaps up to New England, work on various farms.
He would by then have enough money to fly home. He would
from time to time call his parents and let them know that he
was all right. But he would not tell them where he was, and
they wouldn't in their wildest dreams think of him as phoning
from a pay station near someone's large field of vegetables.

After a half an hour of walking Larry began to have second
thoughts. Where would he go first — to which grower's migrant crew? Why hadn't he thought to take some money with
him? His father gave him two dollars a week spending money,
and he'd left a pile of bills, maybe forty or fifty dollars, on his
desk. Ought he go back and get the money? No, if he did he'd
be spotted immediately. The police might be already looking
for him. Should he wait until school was out, go visit a friend
of his, ask him for a loan — maybe even ask him if he wanted
to come along on an adventure that in the long run their
parents might actually approve of? In a moment he recognized the absurdity of his various fantasies, and soon enough
he was walking very slowly indeed and preparing himself to
return. The only question still open to him was where: home,

school, maybe the police?

He decided upon school, for reasons he remembered quite well, many weeks later: "I decided that the best thing to do was go back there, where it all started that day, and let them do what they wanted to do to me. If I went home there'd be a fight with my father. I can't answer him back the way I'd like to. He talks better than I do. He's probably right in what he says. He's lived longer; and my mother says I'm always forgetting how hard he works and how much he knows about his business, and how much the migrant people look up to Dad. But I couldn't face a lecture from him, not then. I turned around and began to go home, but I changed my mind. I saw a friend of my mother's driving, and luckily she saw me. I waved her down. I asked her if she'd mind driving me to school. She wanted to know what I was doing out of school in the first place. I didn't know what to say then. Finally I told her that I'd thought I was sick, and had gone home, and then I'd felt better, and had decided to take a walk, but I'd realized I ought to go back to school, if I was feeling better. She believed me, I think. She took me right to school. On the way she asked after my mother and father, and told me she and my mother are very good friends, and they work together on the flower show, and the United Fund. She asked me if I was in the Cub Scouts, and I said no. She said I should join. Her son was now a Boy Scout, and she was proud of him.

"When we got to the school, I almost told her please turn around and take me home, fast. But I didn't dare. I figured I'd just take the punishment. I thanked her, and got out, and went inside, and headed straight for the principal's office. When I got there, I had one last thought of turning around and running away. But it was too late. I was right there, and there was no use wasting time; I opened the door, and that was it. From then on, I try to forget. The principal's secretary looked at me

as if I'd been in prison, and had escaped, and was going to hold
her up, something like that! She looked me over as if she was
looking for my gun! Then she buzzed him, and he came out,
and he began his speech. I half listened, and half thought of
what it would be like if I was 'on the road.' At least I wouldn't
be listening to that principal! I might be hungry, and have no
place to sleep, but I wouldn't be standing there hearing myself
called all those bad things: 'spoiled' and 'ungrateful' — when
my father is 'one of the best people in the whole state of
Florida.' I didn't say anything. He kept asking me what I had
to say. Finally, I said I didn't have anything to say. He said I
usually do, and that was the trouble! I said I didn't want to
cause any trouble. He said he was glad I had changed my
mind, because a while ago I had been looking for trouble, he
knew, because my teacher had told him all the things I'd said.
I didn't say anything more. He stopped his talking, and he told
me he was going to call my parents in for a big conference, and
meanwhile he wanted me to go right back to my class and
apologize to the teacher. I didn't say I would, and I didn't say
I wouldn't. I looked at the door, and I guess he decided he'd
had enough of me, so he told me to go, and I sure did, zoom.

"I was going to walk right out of the school again, but I
didn't. I figured the worst was over — the principal's lecture.
I went to my classroom and went in, and there she was, waiting. I think they'd buzzed her and told her I was coming,
because she wasn't surprised; she seemed to be waiting for me,
and the whole class had been told I was coming, I found out
later. She didn't say anything, just told me to sit down. She
stared at me, though; and so did the kids. They smiled, and a
couple of them laughed, and that got her going — but at least
she was angry with them, and not me. She told them it was bad
enough 'one person had misbehaved'; now 'others' thought it
was 'funny'! And then she said the trouble with a lot of us was

that our fathers had too much money, and we didn't know about life, and we lived in 'castles,' and had no idea how other people lived, and one day we'd find out, and then we'd realize how silly we'd been, and we'd grow up — and the sooner that happened the better it would be. We didn't know what to say. We couldn't say anything. She didn't want to hear anything from us, anyway. She slammed that ruler of hers down, like she does when she's angry, and she told us to 'take a study period' until the bell rang and school was over. So, that was the end of it, for me — at least until I got home."

Larry conveyed the above intermittently, working all the while on a rather large painting of his school building. The building is, in fact, of tan stucco, but he chose to substitute red bricks. He built an enormous wall, leaving spaces as he worked for a window or two. The wall grew higher and higher, but did stop short of the top of the paper. There was room enough for a relatively thin blue line, the sky. The bottom of the wall rested on the bottom of the paper — no ground at all. The door was placed in the center of the wall — very small, though. The windows also were small. No shrubbery or lawn — both quite extensive in real life — were painted; there was no room for them on the paper. Out of one of the windows a small face peered — featureless. There was no other sign of life. (Figure 15.)

The boy decided to draw a picture of the principal — a small figure, put in the corner of a rather large piece of paper. His eyes were emphasized — big black circles — and then glasses, two more black circles. His mouth was surprisingly small for one who had lectured Larry so long and hard; it was, however, wide open. No teeth were bared; in fact, it can be said that nothing is shown *but* an open mouth. The face lacked ears, also went without a nose. An already balding man was denied any hair. He also had no neck, short arms, two right fingers and one left finger, an undersized torso, big feet presumably planted in large shoes, which in turn had no ground under them. A boy who could draw his mother, his father, himself in settings of land, grass, the sky, the sun, clouds, a building nearby, some flowers, had no interest in suggesting where the principal was, where he might usually be seen, where he belonged. (Figure 16.)

Not that Larry has been all that certain where he himself belongs. He has not been too kind to himself, either, when he has drawn his own picture. He always gives himself ears, but he has been likely to forget an arm, overlook all features — the face an empty oval. He represents himself small enough to be mistaken, in the context of the particular drawing or painting, for an animal or a piece of shrubbery. In one painting he identified himself after he was finished as *that* — part of a small fence, it seemed, which stood to the side of a meadow. (Figure 17.) The fence he had in mind was a particular one, and he described it as follows: "My mother remembers her grandmother's house; it was in north Georgia, and there was a lot of grass and it had a fence around it, part way. When mother was a kid, she was told not to go any further than the fence, because if she did, there might be trouble. I think there might have been a stream beyond the fence, or maybe a sewer pipe. Mother doesn't remember, because her family moved when she was little; but she remembers the fence, and she used to think, I guess, that the world began at the other side of the fence. We don't have any fences near our house, though the trees and the shrubs have been planted so as to give us privacy. There is a big fence, though, at the beginning of the road that leads to Daddy's land. That's the fence in the picture. He has his men patrol there. He doesn't want trouble from people, trespassers he calls them. His men will fire, if they need to; they tell people that it's private property and to stay away."

He doesn't know exactly which people; but he has heard his father talk about "social worker types," people who try to "stir up trouble" among the migrants, try to organize them into unions or investigate their living and working conditions. Larry's father has resisted all such efforts with everything at his disposal — armed guards, the sheriff's assistance, the legal efforts of the best lawyers, and the intervention of friendly state legislators. But the struggle has not ended, and the boy has heard his father say that "eventually" he expects to lose, to be dealing with "the unions." The grandfather hates the unions — they represent to him the greed of lazy people who want, as the old man puts it, "something for nothing." The father is more philosophical — and canny; he is not ready to fight the unions in such a way that "things get worse rather than better." Best to give in at times, increase wages a bit, tell the crew leaders to be careful about the quality of the food sold to the workers for lunches, make sure the water is clean and pure, try to improve the "living conditions" in the houses, and in general work toward "smoother labor relations." The grandfather regards such efforts as disastrous compromises, a surrender of principle. The father thinks otherwise; and Larry is not without his own ability to make a kind of social and political analysis: "My father wants to see the migrants work. My grandfather gets so upset with them, he'd fire them all, and the next thing we'd be without anyone working here, and there'd be crops out there, and they'd rot away. That's what my father doesn't want to see happen. He tells my mother that he tries to keep my grandfather from knowing too much about the 'labor problems' we have. The only trouble is my grandfather goes and talks with the head crew leader and the other crew leaders, and they tell him things. Then he comes back and starts arguing with my father. But my father convinces him, every time, that it's best to give in a little — at least he convinces him while they're talking. My father says the migrants aren't the real problem; the real problem is the outside people who come down here and want to make trouble, and use the migrants to cause trouble.

"I think no one could cause any trouble if we didn't have trouble already. I've heard the migrants talk behind my father's back — behind the crew leaders' backs. I've been standing in the woods, behind the migrants, and they're having some soda pop on one of their work breaks, and they don't know anyone is nearby listening, and they say some pretty bad things about the crew leaders and about my father and my grandfather. They're afraid of them. They don't like them. They say they're being cheated and robbed and deductions of money are made, but the migrants don't know why. They don't get the money they should, and if they could only get better jobs, they'd leave here, but they can't find work. They're scared of the growers. They're scared of my father. I've heard them say so. I'm sure my father could get them locked up. He knows the sheriff, and I've heard him pick up the phone, and the sheriff comes over right away and they talk, and the sheriff goes and does what he's 'supposed to do.' That means: arrest someone, and hold him until he stops complaining. My father tells my mother a lot of times that we've got a 'good' sheriff, and that he does 'what he's supposed to do.' I don't think the sheriff cares very much about the migrants. He doesn't like them. I've heard him saying so to my father. He told my father that the only time we'd have real peace here in the county is when my father will be able to replace every single migrant with those big machines being built to harvest the different crops, and then the sheriff said he could 'clear the county of them.' I guess he'd tell the migrants to get out or he'll arrest them. He'd have to build a lot of jails to hold them!"

The boy once drew a picture of the sheriff. The man's brawn is made obvious; in real life hefty, he is made fat. In real life slightly above average in height, he is made enormous. In real life a hunter, a fisherman, he is provided with a gun that is almost as big as he, and might prove more than adequate as a bazooka. In the picture the eyes are narrow, a bit slanted, and possess pinpoint pupils. The nose is big, broad, the nostrils prominent. The ears are also large. Brawny arms do not taper at the wrist; the fingers are long and wide. The belly protrudes, has a wide leather belt wrapped around it. Some bullets are on the belt, as well as two holsters, with guns jutting out — apart from the rifle in the right hand. The legs are brawny; again, they don't taper at the ankle. One sees no feet or toes, only enormous boots, their size and strength emphasized by the heavy black coloration given them. The man is standing on a thick layer of earth — bare of any softening touches like grass, flowers, leaves, shrubs. A man of the earth; a man of guns; an enormous, stocky man; a man to be reckoned with. The badge on his chest is put there almost as an afterthought — as if the artist felt the sheriff needed no identification. (Figure 18.) Larry is not reluctant to talk about the man he has drawn: "I don't want to be the sheriff of this county, or any other county. My friends say they would like to be cops, they would like to be the sheriff. Not for me; I told my father a long time ago that I didn't like the sheriff. I saw him beat up some people. He hit them with a stick. Then he laughed. He told us that he could have hit them more."

The "us" was Larry and Tom, a boy of Larry's age. Tom is Larry's best friend — his only real friend. Tom's father is also a grower, and they are in the same class at school. They talk rather candidly with each other, and have visited back and forth for years. (They live two miles apart.) They happened one day to see an encounter between the sheriff and some labor union organizers. The latter were eventually arrested, but not until they had stood their ground, been threatened for doing so, and then beaten up because they dared speak back to the sheriff, who later charged them with "threatening an officer of the law." The two boys were frightened by what they saw — and have never forgotten the scene.

As the sheriff drove off, followed by his deputies and the seven men and women who had been arrested, Larry turned to his friend Tom and suggested that they each go home and ask for help. Larry remembers the discussion quite well: "I thought that if I asked my father to call up the sheriff, and Tom asked his, and if both fathers did, then those people would be let out of that jail right away. Tom said he was afraid to ask his father, because his father sometimes says he'd like to shoot the 'labor people.' I said my father talks like that, too; but he won't shoot *me,* for asking. And I told Tom his father wouldn't shoot him. Tom said yes, he knew that; but his father *would* get upset. I said my father would be upset too — but he wouldn't send me to jail, and Tom's father wouldn't send him to jail, so at least we're better off than the labor people! Tom said we couldn't do anything for them, even if we tried. I said we could. We argued for five or ten minutes, then we quit arguing. Tom said he knew why his mother told him I was a troublemaker. I told Tom he should learn to be a troublemaker himself! He laughed, and asked me if I'd teach him how! I said yes; and that's what I was trying to do.

"We were getting ready to go home. Suddenly we saw the sheriff; he was back for some reason. I guess he was checking up — looking for any labor people who had escaped him the first time. We were the only ones there, though. He came up and asked us if we'd seen people carrying posters and looking for trouble. Tom said no. I said we'd seen him arrest some people a while ago and we wondered why. He gave me a bad look. Tom started walking away, but I wasn't going to move. I figured: let him arrest me. I wished he would arrest me. I was trying to think of a way to get arrested. Then, if I was in jail, my father would come to see me, and I could introduce him to the labor people, and maybe he'd feel sorry for them, and he'd be on their side, and not the sheriff's side. But I couldn't say a word. I just stared at his guns, and his badge. He asked me what I was staring at. I said nothing. He turned to Tom and asked him if he'd seen anyone 'suspicious' around. Tom said no. I was going to say yes, we had. Then if he'd asked who, I would have said him — the sheriff! But I didn't say a word. He left us a minute or so later. He got into that car of his and he went speeding off; his red light on top of his car was going around and around.

"Tom said he wouldn't mind being a sheriff. I asked him why. He said because he'd like to ride in that car. I said I'd like to be a sheriff; then I could ride in the car — but I could do other things, too. I could make sure the labor people are left alone. That's when Tom and I had a fight. He said I was nuts, the way I worry about the labor people and the migrants. He said that if I didn't watch out, there'd be real trouble for me when I got older, because the sheriff is tough, and even my father hasn't got him in his pocket. I laughed. I started bragging about my father. I said my father had pretty big pockets, and that Tom might be surprised at who he'd find in those pockets. Then he laughed; he said I was against my father one minute, and ready to take his help the next, and that wasn't right. I didn't see why it was wrong to ask for my father's help. He always says he doesn't want me to say yes, yes, yes; he says he likes it when I disagree. But when I *do* disagree, he gets angry. Tom said my father would begin to crack down on me, when I get older. I told him I didn't want to argue anymore. I just wanted to go home. We didn't say another word to each other. We just walked to my house, and my mother drove him home. I came along. When he got out of the car, I said, 'Good-bye, sheriff'; he said, 'Good-bye, sheriff,' to me, and that's how we made up."

Later that day Larry did indeed tell his father what the sheriff had done. The father was interested, at first; he asked the boy a number of questions. But when he saw what the boy was beginning to put into words, the father said he had to leave. The boy was quite willing to go along, keep his father company. But no, the latter would not have the boy along. The father had been told a month or so earlier by a lawyer friend to ignore his son's efforts to get into discussions or arguments over migrants or labor organizers. The father left so abruptly the boy became frightened: an emergency of some kind. He began to wonder whether in fact the emergency wasn't the arrest of the labor organizers. Was his father rushing to the jail, and if so, for what reason? Would he arrive there as friend or foe of the farm workers? The boy was sure of the answer to the second question. He called up his friend Tom, said that his father was "completely against" the labor organizers, and had left the house immediately for the sheriff's office. Tom was sure his own father would have reacted similarly. They talked of other matters, said good-bye. Just as he hung up, Larry heard his father's voice downstairs. He was talking to Anita, expressing a hope that she would cook a certain special dish of hers soon. Larry went down, and when he saw his father, said, "Hello." Then he asked his father where he'd gone. The father insisted he'd gone to do an errand. The boy was sure his father had gone to the sheriff's. The father exploded with anger, denounced his son, frightened Anita to the point that she left the room and hid for a while.

Larry still remembers that afternoon, that outburst of his father's. A year later, when nearly thirteen, the boy claimed to remember almost every word his father said. It was the most decisive occasion of his young life. He is convinced that when he is fifty or seventy-five, if he lives to one or the other of those ages, he will recall his father's words, his own response.

The father started out with questions. Had the boy seen the sheriff? If so, what had been happening? When the father learned what indeed had been happening, he began his tirade, the boy remembers, with an accusation: "He asked me why I was there in the first place, and why I was always looking for trouble, and when would I grow up, and what was the matter with me, and why wasn't I like Tom, and how much longer would I keep on bothering him and embarrassing him — my own father. I didn't know what to say. I had my mouth half open, but he began again. He didn't ask me any questions. He said I was going to get into trouble soon, he knew it, and there wasn't a thing he could do about it. He said he'd already warned my mother to expect the worst. Then he started raising his voice and shouting. He said I was more trouble than the colored, and more trouble than the Mexicans, and more trouble than the Yankee communists who came down here trying to fool the migrants into joining a union. He said there are times when he's convinced someone is slipping me ten dollars or more, just to upset him — maybe a union troublemaker. He said he'd been waiting for me to grow up, and he'd been waiting, and he'd been waiting, but I still was talking nonsense, and he was losing all his patience, and there wasn't anything he could do now, but tell me never, never again to talk to him about the migrants, or the union people, or anyone like them. He said they didn't know what to make of me in school, and he and my mother and my grandfather don't know what to make of me, and the doctor doesn't know, so it's hopeless. He called me a nuisance, and two or three times, hitting his hand on the counter, he said I was a nuisance, a nuisance, a *big* nuisance.

"I guess I started crying. Anita was listening outside. She came in and took me out. She took me up to my room. She told me to stay there, and wait until my mother came home. She told me she was leaving, because she was afraid she might be tempted to pick up a dish and throw it at my father, and she didn't want to do that. I didn't want her to go. I asked her to stay. She said no, and she just closed the door and left. I sat on my bed and I cried. Then I stopped. I got up and went to the door. I couldn't hear anything. I decided to open the door. I did. I went down the hall, and from the top of the stairs I could hear my father on the phone. Everything that he said to me he was saying to someone else. At first I thought it was my mother. Who else would it be? Not my grandfather, because he'd get too upset; and not a stranger. But then I heard him say the word *sheriff.* He said, 'Yes, sheriff.' I thought I was hearing things, but I wasn't. I heard him say it again: 'Yes, sheriff.' I didn't want to hear any more. I was more scared than I'd ever been. I was afraid my father might get the sheriff to come after me! I guess I was thinking wrong. I was starting to cry again. I went back to my room and closed the door. I sat on the bed, and I thought of running away again. But I didn't. I just sat there and thought of poor Anita. She can't run away! She'd be in the kitchen soon, saying yes, sir and yes, ma'am, and she'd be smiling all the time. I said to myself that if Anita can stay, I can stay. And if she can be polite, I can try to copy her. I promised myself that when I grow up I'll try to be a friend to Anita's kids, and to the migrants, and to the labor people. I hope I can be their friend one day."

He apologized to his father later that afternoon. He has never since mentioned migrants or labor people. He has stopped writing or saying what his sixth-grade teacher called "provocative comments." He has become, in his father's words, "a normal boy." He still spends a lot of time talking with Anita, and he is more deferential to her, complimentary of her cooking, than anyone else in the house. He still rides his bike all over this father's land — on the same dusty, unpaved roads hundreds of migrant men, women, and children use as they go from their cabins to the fields and back again. As he rides along he notices out of the corner of his eye the people bending and stooping, or climbing on ladders or crawling on their knees — picking, cutting, pulling: harvesters. And he notices the shacks, the broken windows, the outhouses, the pools of stagnant water mixed with garbage.

When he turned thirteen his father took one of those bike rides with him. They talked about growing up, about being at last a teenager, about the terminal illness of Larry's grandfather: cancer of the pancreas. The father asked the boy whether one day he might want to help in running "the business"; the boy knew to say yes. But he did add that he might want to go to law school first. The father was enthusiastic, pleased: everything is so complicated and difficult these days; one can scarcely move without the need for a lawyer; it would be wonderful to have a lawyer in the family. The boy agreed. But a day afterward he added a subdued but candid afterthought.

He told his mother, not his father, that he might want to be a lawyer "all the time," rather than a lawyer-grower; and he might not be a lawyer on the side of the growers of the county or the sheriff — "it would all depend." The mother told the boy to hush, to keep his "ideas" to himself. And the boy agreed that he would, that he should — that there would be plenty of time, a decade or more in the future, to come to terms with the specifics of his career, not to mention with his father. The boy thanked his mother for her good advice and recalled, a month later, and a year later, and two years later, an unforgettable gesture of hers: a wink, as she thanked him for being "understanding" and "wise" enough to "wait awhile" until he reveals his plans. The boy winked back, knew he was signing a pact. He became thereafter the increasingly agreeable companion to his grower father as, together, they often drove across the acres of Florida land, thousands of them, and looked after their business realm.

PART FOUR

IN APPALACHIA,
THE SOUTHWEST,
AND ALASKA

I

GRANDCHILD OF A MINE OWNER

FOUR DAUGHTERS, and each so different; everyone comes up with words to that effect. The mother is delighted with her girls, the father has long since given up being annoyed that he has no "heir," a word he once summoned with a certain bitterness and now uses casually — such as when he reminds his wife that the girls will marry someday and maybe provide a grandson or two. But that is all in the future. Right now the oldest girl, Marjorie, is a mere twelve. She has an eleven-year-old sister, a seven-year-old sister, and a five-year-old sister, who cheerfully announces, often, that after her "they gave up." Their father is quite willing to tell them all his theory of why they have no brother. Their generation, he has informed them several times, is the first one in the family that lacks male offspring. There has to be a reason, and the father wonders whether it is the move to Charleston (West Virginia) that accounts for, in his phrase, the "chain of girls."

The father first heard the theory proposed by his father, a mine owner who likes to visit Charleston, but prefers to live in Mingo County, where he owns several mines. The grandfather is not a "first-generation owner," as he refers to some newly rich mountain men who have recently (in the 1970s) made a lot of money stripping the land mercilessly, or going after second- or third-rate coal in hazardous seams — anything to find the stuff and send it on to a newly profitable market. No, the grandfather of "those four Charleston girls," as he playfully calls them upon occasion, was himself born "pretty well-off." *His* father owned a store, a small mine, and, late in life, an automobile agency. The grandfather went to West Virginia University in Morgantown and thought of going to law school, living in Charleston, as his son eventually did.

But there were family investments and interests to be looked after, and as the grandfather has pointed out, it was a good thing he did go back home after college: "We're not one of America's richest families, by any means, but we're quite well-off, and by the standards of West Virginia, of Appalachia, we're wealthy. I guess we're wealthy by national standards; we have several million salted away — it's no secret. But we've worked for the money. I'm no fly-by-night strip miner. I've never wanted to squeeze profits, just make them! I try to be a responsible man, and I try to think of my son and my grandchildren. My people have been in this state for many generations, and I hope the family never leaves. I didn't mind my son becoming a lawyer and leaving Mingo County. If I'd done that, we wouldn't have the money we all have now. My father was born dirt-poor, a subsistence farmer the census people would call him, from up a hollow. But he came down from that hollow and he borrowed money and he bought land and there was coal under it and he just kept on making money and investing it. I had about a hundred thousand dollars to play with when he died, a lot of money in the nineteen-thirties. I didn't gamble and I didn't drink, and I knew how to take risks — *good* risks; so I made a lot more than a hundred thousand dollars. The times got good, especially during the Second World War and afterwards. We needed coal, and I had it to sell. Also, I spotted IBM and Xerox and Polaroid, companies like those, right at the beginning; I put my money in them. I bet on free enterprise!

"Things haven't been so good in the nineteen-seventies. I'll tell you, I've pulled a little out of the stock market, and put my money back in land, where it all started — our family's rise from poverty, you could call it. My son says I should forget about making money. He says we've got enough — plenty, as a matter of fact — and the best thing to do is keep it in good securities and enjoy ourselves. But that's him; I'm me. You don't change an old dog; he's younger, and he's different. Up there in Charleston they live a fancier life, and they don't want to be caught *crawling* for money, the way we do out here. But I've never had to compromise my principles; maybe my father did — if he did, he never told me. I'll bet my son doesn't even mention the word 'money' to his girls."

He is correct. The son is a prominent West Virginia lawyer, a member of several corporate boards, an influential stockholder in a number of local companies — and of course not without substantial shares in national companies. But he doesn't like to talk about such matters, nor does his wife, the daughter of a West Virginia bank president. Their daughter Marjorie wrote a composition for her sixth-grade teacher about the future, and never indicated how she'd be able to do all the things mentioned. The girl wrote about ballet lessons, a trip around the world, a spell in Holland, where she would learn about various cheeses and wear wooden shoes, a year or two on a ranch out West, with several horses to ride. Marjorie's teacher surprised the girl with this comment: "A very nice paper, full of interesting plans. But do you have the money for all this?" The teacher was being a bit facetious, but Marjorie did not respond with a smile. She was confused, upset. She came home and showed the paper to her mother and father, then with a touch of anxiety, asked them whether in fact the teacher was suggesting that there wasn't enough money in the family to support the aspirations of the children? The girl's mother contributed to at least an hour or two of apprehension and uncertainty by saying she didn't "know anything about money," and so "Daddy will explain everything later." That evening Marjorie's Dad told her not to worry, there was "enough money" so that she could go ahead and "have her dreams."

But the father had no desire to sit down and talk at any length with his daughter about money. She remembers a somewhat awkward, even tense time of it: "Daddy said I shouldn't be thinking about money, because there are more important things in the world. He said the teacher was just pulling my leg. If she wasn't, he'd get her fired. He asked me about the horse riding, and I told him I was doing real good; the jumping was getting better and better. Then he asked me if I wanted more allowance. I said no, a dollar and a half a week was still enough. I don't even spend that, a lot of weeks. He told me it's a good idea to learn how to save, and if I wanted, he'd open up an account for me in the bank and I could put away some of my allowance. He said if I put a lot of the allowance away, he might add some of his own money to my account, 'a matching amount.' Then we started talking about my room, and how it should be neater, and it wasn't fair to expect the maid to clean up after us all the time. I told him that when I grow up and I have my own house, I would like to have a maid, but it *was* 'good discipline' for us girls to know how to clean our own rooms. I asked him if I'd be able to afford a maid. That's when he got annoyed with me. He slapped his knee and said it was getting time for me to go up to bed, because I had school the next day and a ballet lesson after-wards. I told him I was just trying to ask a question, but he wouldn't answer. He said he didn't like all this talk of money, and I should keep my room neat — and he might go talk with my teacher so she wouldn't make another comment like the one she did about money on the composition I wrote. Then I said good-night."

Marjorie didn't let the matter drop, though. She tried to have a talk with her mother. She told her mother that she thought that Daddy had been upset by the questions she put to him. The mother said yes, that was true. Her father had said later that night (to his wife) that he hoped none of his daughters became "money conscious," because it's "not at all nice for a girl to be like that." When the mother had finished telling her daughter what the father had said, the girl immediately asked this: "If I was a boy, then would Daddy want me not to be asking him a lot of questions about money?" The mother didn't answer right off, but she did say, finally, that "it makes no difference, boy or girl; it's wrong to have your mind dwelling on money." Marjorie gave in, said she didn't really care about money; she had just become curious as a result of her teacher's remark.

But the girl was not convinced by her own words; she had, anyway, asked her mother several times how much money her father made each year. The mother had said she didn't know, and the girl was persuaded that was so: "My mother told me that if our lives depended on it, she couldn't tell someone how much money Daddy makes, because she doesn't know — and she doesn't really want to know. I told her I didn't want to know; it's just that you hear kids talking, and they'll say my father owns this, and my father makes that, and then you begin wondering — what does *my* father do? My father is a lawyer, I know. In our social studies class the teacher asked us to put down in the papers we wrote what our fathers did and what we would like to do when we grow up. We were writing about the state of West Virginia, and the teacher told us a lot about the state, and she told us that it was coal that is our biggest asset. She said that if any of us come from families that make money from coal, we should write that down too. I didn't think I should write down that we made money from coal, because Daddy is a lawyer. I started worrying later, though — because my grandfather owns some mines. But that's his money, and not Daddy's, I think. Anyway, I said Daddy is a lawyer, and I'd like to be part of a ballet company.

"I don't think I could be a leading ballerina, like I once wanted to be. The ballet teacher says I don't concentrate enough and work hard enough. She said you have to be *possessed*. I asked her what she meant, and she laughed and said if I knew then I'd be a future ballerina! I didn't know what she was talking about, so she explained to me that there are very few good ballerinas in the whole world, and to be one you have to give your whole life to dancing, and that's too much for most people to give — even for her, and she's a good ballet dancer. That's right; I'd like to do other things as well. But I would like to dance in a ballet company, for a year or two, maybe. My mother says I might change my mind later, but if I didn't, she'd back me up. She says my father might not like the idea of ballet as an *occupation* — that he'd rather I take ballet lessons, but do something else: go to college, I guess. Maybe that's what I'll do, go to college. But the ballet teacher says that you can't work part-time for a ballet company. So, if I want to be part of a company, I'll have to postpone college."

Marjorie does rather well at ballet; she is the most committed of her friends. Her mother has taken her to New York City three times to attend the ballet there and also go shopping. They stay at the Plaza, dine at various French restaurants, go shopping in Bergdorf Goodman's and Saks Fifth Avenue. Marjorie was ten when she first went; at eleven she went twice; and she has her mother's promise of an annual visit. The mother went to Vassar and knows New York City well. She also believes in taking each child off alone, as the particular girl gets old enough, and since Marjorie loves ballet and New York City is where ballet is most commonly available, it is there her mother takes her.

Marjorie is quick to point out how flexible and versatile her mother is. For example, Susan, the daughter a year younger than Marjorie, loves the outdoors, is an excellent horse rider, has already won several prizes in shows, and loves as well to go on long hikes with a friend or two, even camp out. The girls take a bare minimum of food, have learned to cook outdoors, make do without matches, find safe and relatively comfortable places to sleep. Susan and her mother go on "overnights" alone, setting out from a "camp" the family has about an hour out of Charleston and wandering through paths, up hills, along a stream or two, and then back. Marjorie has no such interests or inclinations; she likes to ride, but "for pleasure," not "to compete"; and she prefers the city to the country. The family lives outside Charleston, actually; the girls don't get into the city all that much. Even their mother stays away except for certain evenings — a play, a concert. When Marjorie talks of the city, she has in mind not Charleston, West Virginia, but New York City, or Pittsburgh, or Washington, D.C. Her father has taken the family repeatedly to the last two cities; he has board meetings, and while he attends them, his wife and daughters (and a maid, who comes along to help out) "have a good time," as Marjorie sees it. They go shopping. They go to the movies. They visit museums. They eat in elegant restaurants. They romp through fine hotels, and especially enjoy room service.

How can Susan have any doubt that such a life is the very best one imaginable? Marjorie asks that question often — but answers, she knows, only for herself. She and Susan have

always disagreed, have fought constantly, have entirely different hopes and plans, or so one tells the other on many occasions. When Marjorie was nine she drew a picture of herself,
another of her sister. Marjorie's self-portrait shows a limber-
legged ballerina in a conventional pose — one leg up, the
other only barely touching the floor. She is smiling, has light
blue eyes that are open, stretches her arms upward to the
ceiling of what turns out to be a stage when the drawing is
done. (Figure 19.) As for Susan, she is shown under a cluster of
trees, and near some bushes, holding a horse by the reins. She
is looking down at the ground, and the viewer doesn't actually
get a direct look at the girl's face. Rain is falling, the rider and
her horse have stopped for a moment to take cover. (Figure
20.)

Marjorie was willing to make more distinctions than those
she acknowledged and portrayed in her drawings: "My sister
says she hates fancy clothes, and she doesn't like to get dressed
up at all, even for church. My mother has to insist. Sometimes
she talks back to Mom, and then Daddy steps in. I like to get
new dresses. I like my ballet clothes, and I go with Mom when
she buys her clothes, and she buys some for me. Susie won't
go. Mother has to order clothes for Susie, and get our sewing
lady to fix them up. The lady comes once a week. She does the
laundry, and she sews. My mother was taught to sew, but she
doesn't like to do it. She says she won't even teach me, because
she can tell that I'm going to be like her; but Susie is a great
friend of the sewing lady, and Susie says *she* wouldn't mind
being a sewing lady herself! She would work one day a week,
then ride her horse or go camping on the other days! We had
a talk at the supper table once. Susie told Daddy of her plan,
and he laughed and said she'd change her mind when she got
older — because she'd never make enough, with one day of
sewing, to live the rest of the week and be able to pay her bills.

She told Daddy that she wouldn't be spending much, just enough for snacks, and she'd camp out a lot. Daddy asked her where she'd *live*, and she said here at home, of course. Then he laughed again and told her that he *hoped* she did, because if she didn't, she'd be in real trouble, trying to get by.

"Susie didn't like what Daddy said. She told him she could camp out all week, even in the winter. Then Daddy started listing all the expenses she'd run up, and he asked her about the worst winter days, or the summer days, with the mosquitoes. She didn't give in. She argued with Daddy until he got angry, and he told her to stop talking because she didn't know what she was talking about. That's when Susie had her temper; she told Daddy she didn't want to live the way we do. He asked her what she meant, and she said 'like rich people.' He turned to Mother and asked her where Susie got the idea we're rich. Mother said she never talks with us about money. I spoke up; I told Daddy that Mom was telling the truth. Susie said we were all playing pretend, the way she would when she was five or six. She turned to me and told me I was rich, and she said she was, and she said everyone in the family was. My father said he was glad our younger sisters had eaten and were being put in bed. He told Mother that Susie and I should eat with them for a while, until we knew what to say at the table and what not to say.

"I started to cry. I hadn't said anything, really. Mother defended me. She told Dad that it wasn't fair to blame *both* Susie and me, when it was Susie who was doing the talking. Then Susie said she couldn't see what she'd done that was so wrong. Daddy decided to give us a lecture. He said we might as well understand who we are and why we live the way we do. He told us about his grandfather and his father, and how they worked hard, and how they didn't work so we would just sit around and do nothing. He said he sets his alarm for six in the morning and he likes to read over his work for a half an hour before he comes down for breakfast. He eats little in the morning, just fruit, toast, and coffee — because he wants to be in 'top shape' for the office. He said he didn't *have* to work. He said he could just sit at home and watch television and read the newspaper. Then he wouldn't be doing anything for anyone else, only living like a lazy person does. He said he could play golf all day. But if he did, it wouldn't be any better than watching the television set. He said we had to learn the difference between a hobby and work. It's a hobby to go for a walk, or ride on one of our horses, but it's work when you have a job, and you go every day to the office."

There was much more to the lecture, but the girl didn't hear any more; she complained of a headache, a stomachache, a sore throat — all three! — and left, followed by her mother. Her father stayed with her sister, and they apparently kept on talking for a half hour or so, Marjorie learned the next morning. Not that she had any clearer idea, then, what her father meant when he talked about their collective "responsibility" as a family to provide "leadership." She knew when she was in the first grade that her father was an important person in Charleston, West Virginia. He was on the school's board of trustees, and her teachers obviously deferred to him when he came to visit the classroom. During one recess period she was overheard by the teacher telling another child that her Daddy was a lawyer; the teacher added, "a prominent lawyer." Marjorie didn't know exactly what "prominent" meant; at the supper table that evening she asked — and heard about the "responsibilities" that go with prominence.

When she was seven she drew prominence, so to speak; she made a painting of an office building, made it quite tall, and placed her father on top of the building. He was almost as tall as the building, and his head quite literally touched the sky.

The sun seemed like a neighbor of his. The earth appeared as a distant object, perhaps of little concern, because the father's head was turned upward. (Figure 21.) The girl's explanation for that posture was quite direct: "Daddy likes to listen to the wind. There's a lot of wind on top of tall buildings. He's probably thinking while the wind blows. Daddy likes to climb up hills and mountains. He says he thinks better, when he's climbed to the top of a hill, and he can see for miles, and the wind is strong, and he's away from all the things he has to do down below."

Five years later, at twelve, she still had only a vague sense of what those "things" were; but she could take comfort in the fact that her mother was not all that sure, either, of the man's various obligations: "My mother tells me that a woman shouldn't be poking into a man's business, and the same goes vice versa. She said that when they got married, she and Daddy made a pact, and she recommends that I make one, too, with my husband, when I get married: stay out of each other's hair, but try to be of help, when there's need for help."

But Marjorie knows that her father belongs to various committees, is a trustee of various institutions. She has heard him talking on the phone, recognizes the influence he wields, the authority in his voice. She has heard him talking to her mother, heard the latter express her unqualified confidence in his ability to "get things done." She has seen his picture in the newspaper repeatedly, and watched her mother clip the articles, paste them in a scrapbook, which the family upon occasion looks at together. And she has thought of her own future: what kind of man will she marry?

She said at nine that she couldn't possibly imagine the man. She said at eleven that she couldn't be "too exact," but she did have some ideas. She is partial to blond men, for instance; and would like to marry a tall man. Unashamedly she indicates the connection between her father's appearance (tall, sandy hair) and her own preferences. But she has some reservations, too; she doesn't want her future husband to be as "busy" as her father is. He has too many duties — burdens, really. He gets too many requests, has to take far too many phone calls, must deal with a heavy correspondence. He himself has sometimes wondered out loud how he manages to do all he does. His oldest daughter wonders whether she might one day meet a "farmer," fall in love with him, whatever her prejudices in favor of the city. At least, if that should happen, she would know what her mother refers to, wistfully, as "peace and quiet." But she doubts such an outcome is in store for her. She will "probably" marry a lawyer, she suspects, or "maybe" a businessman. Her best friend is the daughter of a surgeon, and he is also an enormously overworked man. Marjorie has emphatically crossed surgeons off her list of prospective successful suitors. She would be "too lonely," like her friend's mother.

Since she was in the third grade Marjorie has been described as an imaginative and expressive child, who has a knack of describing what she thinks and feels in vivid and strong language. When some forty miners were killed in a serious disaster north of Charleston, the girl was saddened and prompted to become reflective in her sixth-grade English composition class. The title of her brief essay was "Dying Underground," and it went as follows: "I read in the paper that forty miners died the other day. They were digging coal, and suddenly there was an explosion. On television the man said the miners must have been killed right away. I wondered what the men thought when they heard the explosion, and they knew they were going to die. They must have thought of their wives and their children. They must have prayed to God. They must have said good-bye to each other. They must have thought that it's not fair, for people to die like that. I hope the coal company gives the families of the men a lot of money. They deserve it. I hope we don't have more explosions like that one. We should have more mine safety, like the newspaper said. A lot of people are poor. They have hard jobs. They suffer. Sometimes they even die. Then the rest of us feel sorry for them. We should worry about them when they're alive."

For that effort she got an "excellent," though her teacher wrote this comment on the paper: "You must understand, Marjorie, that explosions are accidents, and sometimes there's nothing anyone can do to prevent an accident." The girl brought the composition home, and of course, her mother and father read her words, and her teacher's words, with great interest. The mother hugged her daughter, told her she was a "good Christian," and said she hoped the compassion expressed so eloquently would last the child's lifetime. The father said he loved his daughter's "sincerity," and agreed with her about the miners — the sadness of their death; but he also agreed with the teacher. "The fact is," the father reminded his daughter, "miners often cause a mine disaster, because they are careless; they don't pay attention to the safety rules."

The girl remembered her father's analysis and felt even more troubled. A day or two afterward she brought up the subject again; she asked her father whether it wasn't true that "it's very dangerous down the mines, and no matter how careful you are, there can be an explosion." He replied by asking his daughter why she was "still talking" about the accident. The girl was silent for a while, but did come up with an answer: "The newspapers and television are still talking about the disaster, too, so it's hard to forget." Her father agreed, but became rather stern, as the girl remembered: "He told me that the newspapers can make a lot of mistakes, and I shouldn't believe everything I read in them. Mother said she was sure I didn't. Then Daddy explained what really happened in the coal mine; and he knows, because he's on the board of directors, and the president of the company got his job because Daddy recommended him. The president says he's been told that one of the miners must have done something wrong. Daddy says everyone feels sorry for the miners who died, but if one of them caused the accident, then he's the one to blame, and not the company.

"On television they're always criticizing the company and in the newspapers, too; that's what Daddy decided — and that's why he called up the owner of the paper, and he told him that it wasn't fair, the way the reporters were writing their stories. The publisher told Daddy that he'd call him back, but first he wanted to investigate. And Daddy had an answer for him; he told the publisher that he'd send over a file, with all the facts, right away. The publisher said thank you, but he didn't need the file. My father thinks the publisher is afraid of the editor, and doesn't run his own business the way he should. It would be like someone working in my father's office, one of his law clerks, telling my father what to say, and my father going along, and not ever disagreeing.

"We have a man who comes and works in the garden. He planted some roses and my mother didn't like them, but she wasn't going to say anything, because she knew how hard the man had worked, and he told her the roses would last for a long time, and they are a good color to have. When my father heard my mother tell my sister and me about the roses, he got very upset. He was in the hall, but he came into my mother's sewing room, and he said that we had to have one thing settled in our house — that the servants were taking orders from us, and not telling us what to do. He said that Mother should fire the gardener right on the spot, when he starts telling her what to do, and the same goes for the maid — or anyone else. I was upset, and so was my sister. He left right away, and we thought he was mad at us, but mother said no, he wasn't. She said he had to go to an important meeting — and it was about the mine disaster, she was sure. That's when I asked her if Daddy was right in what he said — that the miners could be the ones who caused the disaster. She said she didn't know. She told me and my sister that our father is a lawyer, and he is honest, and he'd never tell a lie, and if he believed something, it was because he had the proof. So I said he was probably right. When I said that, she said I shouldn't say *probably*, I should say *definitely*. I did. My sister asked her about the gardener, and she said she'd try to be tougher, but it wasn't in her nature to be like Daddy. I told her *she* could be right, and Daddy wrong — because, like the teacher says, *everyone* makes a mistake sometime. Mother said she can't remember when Daddy had ever made one!"

The roses attracted Marjorie's interest after that episode. She looked them over carefully, came to be fond of them. She had been interested in flowers and plants for several years; she kept several cacti in her room, and a month or so before the gardener had made so bold as to take the initiative with certain rose bushes, he had obtained for Marjorie three quite lovely plants, or so she had judged them. Did her father have quite another opinion? She was afraid to ask. She was afraid even to ask her mother. But the maid also loved plants. Why not ask her? She could innocently enough ask her father what he thought of his daughter Marjorie's plants. The maid did ask the girl's father, and reported back that he had indeed noticed them and pronounced them quite lovely. Shortly thereafter the father brought the subject up at the dinner table, told Marjorie how very much he liked her room, how pleased he was to see the care she gave to it, and how particularly fond he was of her three plants. Then he turned to the mother — saying nothing, but smiling and nodding, as if to send her a compliment, also: the one who, no doubt, selected the three plants and gave them to the girl. The mother said that she did agree with her husband's judgment, but in all fairness had to admit that it was the gardener who had selected the plants and given them to Marjorie. A moment of nervous silence, then a smile from the father, a relaxation of everyone's apprehension, and a statement from the man at the head of the table: "I think we are all becoming the gardener's protégés. I must sign up myself!"

A month later Marjorie used paints to indicate her approval of the lush late summer garden outside the house. She was especially drawn to the roses, but also to some enormous and beautifully arranged sunflowers — a stunning column of them, astride rows of vegetables. They were so "lucky," she reminded herself, to have a gardener of such skill and devotion. He grew beautiful flowers all year around (the mother had a hothouse, attached to the stable) and he also had an exceptional way with lettuce, tomatoes, carrots, and squash, which wandered and flowered and intrigued Marjorie by their independent ways. The gardener also helped out with the horses — kept an eye on "everything outdoors."

Marjorie tried hard to do justice to the beauty the gardener had made possible near her home, but worried that she was not a good enough artist. She was especially anxious to make the sunflowers the commanding presence they were for her. Each one received her closest attention. And she topped them off, so to speak, with the sky's sun — in her words, "the sunflower that makes all other sunflowers grow." She decided at the last minute to put the gardener in the painting, but abruptly changed her mind: best to leave people out of it. As she put the painting aside (Figure 22), she gave herself some credit, but was still humbled by her self-acknowledged inadequacies. If only she could become even a half-competent

amateur artist one day! But she has no gift in that direction
— unlike two of her sisters. Yet, she loved to look at the flowers
outside the house, and she could at least learn to grow them,
care for them, keep them reasonably healthy and attractive.
Now she had a thought: the ground, the earth that nourished
the gardener's flowers, her family's flowers, the earth she had
rather quickly suggested with a few strokes of brown paint,
was the very same earth, not too far away, that men dug and
cut into — miners in search of coal.

She began to wonder out loud about coal: "There might be
coal right under our house; if we dug up the garden and kept
digging, we might find coal. I've never seen a coal mine. I
asked my father, after the forty men died in the disaster, if he
would take me to a coal mine — a safe one! — so that I could
see the coal being dug and carried up. My father said no, there
are more important things for me to see. I asked him if he'd
ever gone down a mine, and he said no. He said there are a
lot of things he hasn't done. He didn't want us in a mine, he
told me, and I shouldn't ask anymore! I did ask my mother, the
next day; I was sure she could just take us to some mine, and
they'd show us how it works. But she said no, you can't just
drive up to a mine and expect the miners to stop work and
become your guides! My mother gave me a talk — on how I
was growing up and ought to be more considerate and think
of others. She was right! They work hard down in mines, and
they don't want people staring at them and asking them a lot
of questions. I'll bet my grandfather could show me a lot of
mines, down where he lives. But maybe he wouldn't. Mother
says it's the same there; he has to hire very strong men to do
the work, and they wouldn't like to be bothered by me and my
sisters! And we'd be staring at them, and it wouldn't be polite,
and you can't just go and see anything you want to see.

"The mines are off limits to everyone except the people who

work in them. What if someone older went down there, and he lit a cigarette? There'd be an explosion! You have to be trained not to do a lot of things you might be tempted to do — if you're going to work in the mines. It's like being in an airplane; you don't smoke, if you're older, when they tell you not to smoke. I told my mother that I wouldn't smoke, anyway, but she said there might be other mistakes I could make, and so I still couldn't go visit a mine. She didn't know what the mistakes might be; maybe I would kick over a lamp, and then a fire would get going."

Marjorie has, however, seen pictures of a mine — of miners, at least, at work in West Virginia. The occasion: a social studies course — a book in it meant to "bring life in the United States closer to the young reader." Marjorie asked the teacher where in the state the mine shown is. The teacher said she didn't know. Marjorie thought of asking the teacher how the class might find out, might go visit the mine, but she did not. Another child did, a boy she didn't know well — "only his name." What had the teacher said? She said no, it would not be possible. The boy had asked why, only to be ignored. The class had to "move on." Marjorie started paying attention to the boy; his name, Miles, began to interest her. She knew no one but him with that name. She had never said anything to him, not even hello. He sat on the other side of the room — "and besides, he's a boy." But a day or so after the incident mentioned, Marjorie approached Miles and asked him if he'd ever visited any mine, anywhere. He said no. Had she? She said no. Would *she* like to do so, also? Yes — and she liked hearing him say that he would. The boy confided in her: his uncle was the vice-president of a coal company. It was located in Alabama, however, and the boy had never gone to the state, let alone a mine within the state. The girl told *him* something, in exchange: her grandfather owned several mines, and they were located right in West Virginia. But she had never been to a mine, either. She had been to her grandfather's home; she had gone fishing with him, and had taken walks with him, but she had not even seen his office. As for the mines, her own father had not seen "one of Granddaddy's mines." She wasn't even sure that Granddaddy himself had actually gone down any of his mines. She had asked her father that question; he had said "probably." Miles and she decided that "it must be very dangerous to go where the miners go" and for that reason "no one really wants to go there."

But the two of them could not quite forget that for some people there is no choice: "Miles said he saw the people on television, the families of the men who got killed, and he asked his father if there wasn't some way to prevent mines from having explosions inside them. His father said no, there are always accidents. I told Miles that my father said the same thing. My father said the miners can cause the trouble, and it's not fair that everyone gets mad at the owners of the company. Miles said that was the way his father looked at the trouble, too. We both said it was no good — that all those miners should die.

"I once thought I would like to try being a miner for a few weeks. I didn't tell anyone except my sister, and we both told our mother, and she just laughed. My sister Susie really wouldn't mind marrying a miner one day; that's what she told me the other day! She said she'd like to live way out on a farm, and if there was a mine nearby, and her husband worked in it, she would like the idea of him working hard and coming home covered with coal dust. She would have a hot shower ready to go, and she'd cook him food they'd grown themselves. I don't think I'll ever meet a miner or a miner's son. I told Susie I don't think she will either. I asked Miles if he thought he would, and he said no, that he wouldn't. If my father had to go down the mines every day, I'd be plenty worried. If my husband was the one, I'd be worried. If I knew a miner, I'd worry about him.

"My mother said the other day that anyone can get into an accident. Look at the number of automobile accidents every year. But it's worse being a miner — more dangerous. Mother said I'm making a mountain out of a molehill, but I told her I'm glad Daddy doesn't work in a mine. She said Daddy carries a lot of burdens on his shoulders; he has worries, and he's always in a rush, because of the cases he has in court and the meetings he has to go to. Even so, he doesn't have to worry that there will be a spark, and it will make some gases explode, and that will be the end. Miles said he told his father that he didn't want to have a job even near a mine; he'd rather be in a submarine than down a mine. Miles says we're both lucky. He wants to learn how to ski and go live in Switzerland; his uncle goes there every year to ski. Miles says if you go all the way over every year, you might as well live there."

Marjorie's family has a summer home in the Adirondacks and regularly rents a home on the West Coast of Florida, near Venice, for two weeks every February. Marjorie likes those two homes a lot, but wishes there were yet another one, a permanent apartment in New York City. A classmate of hers speaks of such a place — the property of a law firm that does a lot of litigation in New York, and in West Virginia for companies located in New York. The companies are coal companies, and the lawyers in Charleston go back and forth, mostly getting instructions in New York and carrying out agreed-upon efforts "back home." Marjorie has asked her father why his firm doesn't rent such an apartment. She has been told that his particular firm handles other "accounts" — railroads, utilities, various wholesale distribution outlets. Those companies don't all have offices in New York City.

The firm does not, surprisingly, handle her grandfather's legal problems. The girl is not sure why, but knows what she has heard and been told: "My father wasn't supposed to live here. He was supposed to stay home in Mingo County and help my grandfather — be his lawyer. He would become the boss himself when my grandfather got too old or else died. But my father didn't want to go back. He kept stalling after he got out of law school. He met my mother, and she didn't want to go back with him. I think she once wanted to be an actress. She wanted to live in New York City. She made a compromise with my father: if he agreed not to go back to Mingo County, she would agree to give up the idea of going to New York. She asked him for a long time to take a job in a law firm up there, and he almost did. But he was afraid of the big city, my mother thinks. She says she's glad, now. She says she wouldn't have wanted to bring us up in a big city. But she likes to go up there on visits. My father says he wouldn't rent an apartment in New York, even if he had to spend half of every week in the city — not when he can go to the Plaza, and they know him there, and he and my mother have a much better time in the hotel than they would in an apartment, and it all gets written off as expenses."

The question of income taxes prompts from Marjorie a thought about money: "Some have a lot, and some have none, and it's not right that people should have none." Her father strongly believes in private charities, as opposed to government-sponsored welfare programs of various kinds. He proudly tells his wife and children that he tithes himself, as his father and grandfather did before him: 10 percent of his gross income goes to assorted causes — the Presbyterian Church, the United Fund, a program directed at "problem children." After the mine disaster Marjorie wondered out loud at the supper table whether her parents would be sending any money to the survivors of the men killed. She was told the answer immediately and abruptly: no. She did not ask her father why. The next day, characteristically, she turned to her mother for information. The mother was rather tense herself. She told the girl that it is her father's "decision" where the charity money goes. The girl was insistent: why not try to help such obvious victims? The mother again called upon her husband's authority and his rights: it is his money, and he has every justification to spend it as he pleases. What might she want to do with the money, if he gave her the chance to spend it as she pleased? The mother could not come up with an answer. She would have to "do some thinking." The child asked if, in the course of her reflections, she might, just might, consider the survivors of the dead miners possible candidates for charity. The mother said yes, they were possible beneficiaries.

But the mother never gave any money to the survivors of that particular mine accident, or to any miners, or to their families. And Marjorie learned her mother's reasons — learned over a period of a year or so to stop being interested in such people and their difficulties. When Marjorie turned thirteen her grandfather became gravely ill, was flown to Charleston in a private plane, became a patient in a hospital there, was operated upon, and almost died. When he had recovered enough to begin contemplating his future, Marjorie asked him whether he would go back to Mingo County and resume his work, which was to keep an eye on several quite profitable businesses there. No, he would not. He was tired of "the smell of coal," he told his granddaughter. He was tired of workers making demands and "outsiders" coming into the county, seeking him out, and also making demands — of him. He wanted rest and "peace" during his final months.

But he did not want to live with his son: "My grandfather told me there would be fights between him and Daddy if they both lived under the same roof. Daddy was supposed to stay in Mingo County, but he didn't. My grandfather is going to sell the mines he owns down there. He can't leave them to my father, and there's no one else in the family either who wants to run them. I have an aunt in Pittsburgh, and she is married to a stockbroker, and they don't want to leave Pittsburgh. I have another aunt in Beckley, West Virginia, and her husband owns a shopping center, I think, and they like living where they are. Like my grandfather says: there's no one to take over. Anyway, there's a lot of trouble now in the coal fields. It's no joke owning a mine. Some of the owners have to hire bodyguards. There's a lot of violence. My grandfather says on some days he feels like he's just sitting and waiting for the union men to come and get him. He practices shooting his guns, and he keeps them near him. He has an alarm that can detect anyone even coming *near* the house, and he has a rifle right beside his bed. He's a light sleeper. The doctor told him that's another reason for him to stay in Charleston; he won't sleep well at home, and he'll get weak. But my grandfather says he'd really like to face down some of the union organizers and show them how he can shoot to kill."

Marjorie would hate to see that kind of confrontation. She has told that to her grandfather, and he has not argued with her. He has, rather, told her that she is a "girl," and that he can understand how she would abhor "gun-shooting." Still, she must know "the facts of life"; and he has supplied them to her — long statements about the "rights of mine operators" and the "violence" that the miners have been visiting upon West Virginia in the name of "progress." For him it has been a painful decade; yet he is no quitter and only regrets that someone in his family isn't prepared to take a continuing stand against "them," the United Mine Workers and their various "sympathizers," not to mention the "agitators."

His granddaughter had begun to lose interest in drawings by

the time she was thirteen, but she did initiate one out of a certain frustration she felt when asking questions of him: "I love him," she would say, "but he is a hard man to pin down." She had in mind the various questions she'd asked of him: for instance, what do the miners look like when they come out of his mines? What do they say to him when he talks with them — or indeed, has he ever talked with *them,* as opposed to the union officials who are their representatives? Marjorie drew a picture of him standing upright and ready for action, his gun at his side. His eyes were wide and attentive, his ears large and meant to be alert. He was, she pointed out, "just waiting," but he was also fully prepared to "raise the gun and shoot." The gun is rather large, almost his size — in real life, a half inch or so under six feet. And beyond him stretch, somewhat shapeless, the surging masses, it would appear, bent on having their say, getting a number of concessions he was unwilling to make. In the background are smoke, shadowy buildings, a chimney or two, a gray, bleak sky with no sun. When the young lady had finished her drawing (Figure 23) she gave it a final look, pushed it aside, spoke one sentence: "Too bad for Granddaddy and too bad for those miners."

Then she turned her attention elsewhere, began to wonder whether her grandfather would accompany her parents, herself, her sisters, to Colonial Williamsburg in Virginia. Her father had to attend a meeting being held there, and he thought it would be a fine occasion for the entire family to go away and glimpse an earlier America, "when life was simpler." She rather suspected her grandfather would jump at the chance to take this particular trip, would enjoy it enormously, would get on very well in Williamsburg with his family and with everyone else, and might even, she added at the very end, insist upon "paying for everyone, even Daddy." There would be a fight over that matter, but the girl had no fear that a gun would be used. Her father would yield, she was sure. Her father liked to stand up to his father, but she was sure that "on money" there wouldn't be "trouble" — because several times she had overheard her parents talking about the money to be left them by the grandfather, and both her mother and her father seemed quite anxious to get the money, rather than keeping it at a remove for the sake of their independence. And as she said: "You can't blame them." She even went further. She insisted that there wasn't anyone she knew who would blame them.

II

NEW MEXICO TWINS

TWINS, a boy and a girl. Though each makes clear his or her willingness to disagree with the other, yet they are very close, and they do make an effort to have conversations about any number of issues. Their names begin with the same letter — Alice and Alexander. They have not let their parents forget *that* decision; each has threatened a change of name — though neither was given a middle name as an alternative. It is not that they actually dislike their names; it is a certain cuteness that the two children find unattractive. Alice would have liked her brother to be named William, after their father; Alexander would have liked his sister to be named Joan, after an aunt he likes very much. But at eight years of age they had learned to live with their names, had found other sources of discontent. Their parents own a large and beautifully maintained ranch in the so-called North Valley of Albuquerque. The house is adobe, with strong wooden beams at crucial junctures. Several trees, tall and ample, provide shade from the strong southwestern sun, never absent for long. The house wanders — a new wing to the left and a new one to the right of the main, older building, and a new wing to the rear as well. There are sixteen rooms, all air-conditioned by three separate systems. Inside one finds Navaho rugs, paintings that have been purchased in Mexico and depict rural life there, and antiques purchased in New Orleans and San Francisco — like those found in the Parke-Bernet galleries of New York or in Sotheby's of London, the mother will point out.

She collects antiques, subscribes to periodicals that advertise and display them, goes on trips to buy them, but has never herself made a purchase in either New York City or London. She has a dealer in Santa Fe who helps her. He has traveled at her expense to those cities, in search of a particular "object" or "piece." The mother does not, however, want her children — the twins or their younger brother, Edmund — to feel "imprisoned" by the rather significant "collection" she has amassed over the years. Her daughter, then in the third grade, made quite clear what she had heard and overheard: "My mother doesn't want us to act as if we're living in a museum. We should forget about the furniture, just be as careful as we can remember to be. I scratched one of the chairs in the dining room; I was pushing my Tonka truck too fast. My mother said she was sad but she wasn't going to punish me. She told me to be more careful, and she said I must never play with the truck or the bulldozer in the dining room or the living room, only my bedroom or the playroom. In the playroom we can crash into anything. They bought special furniture and they made the walls special too — so that if we crash into them, we don't get hurt. My father said we are lucky. He told my mother we get too many toys. But then he'll go and buy us some toys himself, when he feels good."

The father is a prominent New Mexican; he was born in Portales, a city in the eastern section of the state known as "Little Texas." And his father had indeed migrated from Galveston "clear across Texas and into New Mexico" at the end of the First World War. He is still alive, "a tough man of Texas," he calls himself sometimes when playing with his grandchildren. He loves to tell them stories. Their ancestors were Southern, he keeps reminding the twins — from Alabama. Several ancestors fought and got killed in the Civil War. A few who survived left the South for Texas, in search of "a future." They "worked their way up," became "prosperous" several times, only to lose their money again and again because of the repeated "depressions" the country had in the nineteenth and early twentieth centuries. The grandfather's father owned a hardware store and a grocery store in Galveston and was sheriff there too — but he "gave away" his money to people, all sorts of people, who knew him as a "soft touch." His mother was "driven to an early grave" by her husband's spendthrift generosity. He helped take care of his younger brother and his two younger sisters. His father remarried a rather tough and calculating woman who "reined him in" and indeed "cured him," even made him a "tightwad." And finally, because it was hard to get along with "the new woman," the grandfather, then a young man, left "to seek a fortune farther West."

As Alice and Alexander listen to their grandfather, they know full well that he succeeded. He became, by his own description, "the richest man in Portales." He opened a general store, began buying real estate, invested in the stock market, became a "silent rancher" — through money lent to those who did the work — and eventually started a career as a builder: homes, office buildings, shopping centers, in eastern New Mexico. He underestimates himself, for all his moments of self-assurance, even braggadoccio; he is one of the richest men in New Mexico, though he has taken pains, as he puts it, "not to advertise the fact." He still lives in Portales, but he comes to Albuquerque often on business, stays with his son, spends a good deal of time with his grandchildren. He especially enjoys going on horse rides with them or, in the winter, watching them ski on the slopes of the Sandia Mountains, which stand constant watch over Albuquerque. The children love having him around, as does his son, who is also in the real estate business. The son buys and sells land, "develops" it, is active in the planning and building of commercial and residential "property," and besides all that manages both his and his father's stock market assets.

Alice comments, at the age of nine, on the strong bond between her father and her grandfather: "They're always talking on the phone, when Granddaddy isn't here. They're as close as Alex and I are. My mother says they are twins, just like we are. They think alike. I don't think my brother and I do think alike, actually. He wants to be a skier and I want to be a movie actress, or maybe a model. My mother lets me have her old magazines. *Vogue* is my favorite. Once my father told me he didn't like me always looking at 'that magazine.' He said I should forget about 'fancy Eastern clothes,' and enjoy my 'New Mexico dungarees.' I told him he was wrong, because a lot of people in the East wear dungarees now. He wanted to know how *I* knew. I reminded him that I'd been there — with him! We've gone to New York City three times, and I remember each time seeing a lot of people there in dungarees. I liked New York. My father hates the East. He says New York is a bad, bad city. He says Washington is full of crooks. My grandfather says people aren't as honest in the East as they are out here. My father always says 'the crooked East will kill us.' Daddy and Granddaddy tell us they see eye to eye. Last year they both had to go to a meeting in Chicago, and when they came back they said they'd never leave New Mexico again, except to go to Texas or Colorado or Arizona."

But they did not live up to their vow; a month later they took the family to Canada — Vancouver and adjoining territory. They wanted to see Alaska, but decided not to go so far away. The mountains of western Canada reminded them of the mountains of Colorado and northern New Mexico. Neither the grandfather nor the father has ever left North America. The mother has gone to Europe with her sister and the children; "the men," as she sometimes refers to the father and grandfather, stayed resolutely at home. Alice is sure she knows why. Although her father has said repeatedly that he does indeed want to see Europe before he dies, the girl believes he is afraid to leave the United States for long. Canada and Mexico are close enough to assuage his fears, but they are the limit for him: "I've told Alex that Daddy loves it here in New Mexico, and he thinks that when he's in Chicago or New York, he's 'out of the country.' That's what he says. He gets upset and wants to come back here. He got homesick in Canada when he saw those mountains. He got homesick in Mexico, when he saw the desert, and some mountains way off. He says that mother is foolish to want to travel, when we've got everything we want or need right here in New Mexico. I don't believe Daddy and Mother agree on the antiques she buys. My Granddaddy said that Daddy wants Mother to be happy, and if she wants the furniture, she can have it. My grandfather says all he wants is a good bed and a stove he can use to cook on. But Mother laughs when we tell her what Granddaddy says; she reminded us that he has a real big house and it's full of expensive Indian rugs he's collected for a long time."

The girl knows that both her father and her grandfather have long been involved in various ways with Indians. The Pueblo people have land, and her family has had an interest in land, a willingness to buy it, sell it, build on it, divide it up, display it, advertise it, promote its virtues, and, she knows, overlook (at the very least) its deficiencies. She has walked with her father, seen him looking at land, heard him talking about it. She and her brother have asked him many questions about his work, and he has usually been rather reticent. He once made a terse summary: "It's mostly the land — I try to help people get what they need out of it." The children listen and ask more questions, but he has few answers. When they ask him how much land he owns, he tells them that he doesn't know, that only his accountant probably knows. When they ask him whether he owns land outside New Mexico, he says yes, but he's not sure he can tell them exactly how much or precisely where. When they ask for one or two examples, he mentions Colorado and Arizona, but cautions them not to get too particular, because he would then have to mention the names of counties they would not have heard of anyway. Alice says her father is "too busy to remember little details." Her brother Alex has another interpretation: "I heard Daddy telling Mother that he didn't want to tell her about some of the business he's been doing with one of the Indian tribes; he's afraid people will find out, and then there will be trouble, and he might lose out. Mother promised him she'd tell no one. I told him I wouldn't tell anyone, and besides I didn't know what he'd actually told Mother. But I know it's important."

The twins have gone to see the Indian pueblos north of Albuquerque. They were taken by their schoolteachers once, by their grandfather once, by their mother and father once. They recall each time vividly. They remember the different tone or spirit of each visit. Alex talks of his crusty grandfather's response to Pueblo life: "He said they are nice people, but they don't ever amount to much, because they've got no real *fight* in them. That was the trouble with the Pueblos; they gave up rather than fight. Other Indians won over the Pueblos, and so did the Spanish. He said he knows the Pueblos better than any Anglo he's ever met. He used to sell to them. He owned a grocery store. He didn't run the store; he had a manager. But he kept his eyes on the Indians. He'd go riding on their land.

That was when he'd moved to Albuquerque, and he'd just got married. But then he went back to Portales. He once owned land next to Indians, and he wanted to sell them the land, but they didn't have the money. He says he wishes he'd held on to that land; he could sell it for a half a million dollars or more today."

Alice recalls the visit sponsored by the school she and her brother attend: "It was the best time we've had on a trip. We've gone to museums and to the state parks, but to go visit the Indians was a real treat. They look like nice people. I don't think they're as lazy as Granddaddy says they are. They are very polite. They smile at you. I saw some kids of my age. I wanted to go talk with them, but I didn't have the nerve. They're happy on their reservation. It belongs to them. That's what the teacher says. They're scared of the Anglos, some Indians are. But it's wrong for them to be like that. In this country, everyone is equal. The Indians have their own place to live, so they're separate from us, but they're still part of this country. Our teacher said we've got to try to understand them; they're different from us. You shouldn't think you're better than the Indians. They have their own religion, and they try to make a living the best they can. A lot of them don't have jobs, though; that's what the teacher said."

Her brother Alex remembers the time they all went to Cochiti Pueblo. Their father had business there. He was helping to arrange for the construction of an apartment complex for well-to-do Anglos, located on land owned by the Indians. He had to talk with the governor of the pueblo, and decided to take his wife and children. Alex remembers the governor and some other Pueblos, including children of his age — he was then ten. The governor liked Alex, squeezed his shoulder and said a warm welcome to the boy, who felt himself, in response, rather tongue-tied: "I didn't know whether to thank him for being nice to me, or whether to say nothing, because my father had already thanked him for all of us. I couldn't find anything to say, but the governor was still friendly with me. He showed me things — the house where his old mother lived, and his own house, and the kiva, which is where they pray, I think, and we're not allowed in it. Later I asked my father if being governor of a pueblo is like being governor of New Mexico, and he said no, because the governor of New Mexico has a more important job. I guess so. There are more Anglos than Indians, and the Indians are pretty poor."

He drew a picture of the Pueblo governor he had met a couple of days earlier. He made the man's face quite round and gave him black hair, black eyes, a closed mouth, a small nose. He made him a short man, smaller by far than the man beside him, his father. He decided to show the two of them talking, but it is his father whose mouth is open. The father is comparatively tall, with yellow hair, a longish face, and a toothy and wide-eyed look. The father has no ears at first, an absence the boy eventually corrects, but with no intention of stressing their presence. Certainly the Indian's ears are larger. His hands are also larger, as are his feet. It is his legs and arms and torso that come across as noticeably short. The arms hang close to the body; the legs are also near each other. His father, in contrast, is obviously pointing to someone or something, and his legs are rather wide apart.

In the distance stand the mountains, green to indicate the summer. The sun shines brilliantly on the two men. Some of the reservation's houses are suggested rather than defined with precision. (Figure 24.) The boy tells what is going on: "My father is telling the governor that if he'll let the apartment houses be built, a lot of money will come into the reservation, and the Indians will be better off. I didn't hear my father say that, but I know he did. My mother told me so. When they went off and talked, I asked her what they were talking about, and she said they were talking 'business.' Then Alice asked, 'What kind of business?' Mother said we shouldn't be too curious! But she told us. She said Daddy was trying to arrange a real big deal, and if he did, the Indians would be better off, and a lot of people would have beautiful homes to live in. That's how Daddy works; he tries to help as many people as he can. If he didn't get the governor to agree, the Indians would be even poorer than they are, and there'd be no apartment houses there, and no lake. They made a lake. They built a dam and made a lake."

Alex stops. He decides to draw a picture of the Rio Grande, of the dam and the lake behind it. He has fond memories of the river — walks beside it, a governess watching over him. His home is near the river, and he has always been drawn to it. He likes to throw rocks in it, ride alongside it on his horse. His father owns a small propeller plane, and they often fly over the river, follow it far north toward Colorado. The river becomes fuller, wider, upstream, and the boy dreams of navigating it on a raft or a kayak. He is a good swimmer, has thought of going to a college located near the Pacific Ocean when of age, so that he might be able to contend with waves and surf. In New Mexico there are a few lakes, but mostly it has been his family's swimming pool where he perfects various strokes. He uses a large piece of paper, and decides to depict a rather long stretch of the river. He will make a map, and let it be dominated by the Rio Grande. He works carefully, indicates what section of the river he is doing with the name of a town or two, attends to some topographical features — a lake, some mountains, a stretch of rather barren semidesert — and then works hard on the Rio Grande itself, moving it through the countryside, giving it twists and turns, showing how its width varies.

Soon he has brought the river to Albuquerque. He abruptly terminates the project at that point, puts the drawing aside (Figure 25), begins to talk about skiing. The dam has been left out. Cochiti Pueblo is left unmarked. No pueblos, for that matter, are mentioned. As he talks about skiing one could imagine him in Switzerland, New England, Scandinavia; the emphasis is on technique rather than the particular country-side he knows so well. Suddenly he stops himself and makes a more sociological comment: "I've never seen any Indians skiing. I guess they don't know how; or maybe they have their own places to ski, though I doubt it. I would like to have an Indian friend, a boy my age. I would take him skiing with me. I saw some Indian kids on the reservation when I last went there, and they seemed to be nice. They were watching us, but they didn't say hello when we did; they just stared. I told my mother on the way home that I would like to talk with some Indian kids, and she said it would be all right, but they keep to themselves, and they don't like white people very much. My father said they'll do business with you sometimes, but they never get friendly. He's been in their homes, but they won't even offer him a glass of water or a cup of coffee. He had to ask for water once, because he was thirsty, and they looked at him as if he'd done something wrong, but they gave him the water. My mother said they were probably scared to be friendly, but Daddy says they're *not* friendly. He says he doesn't think they're even friendly with each other. But the kids seemed friendly with each other — when they weren't staring at us."

He looks out of the window. He notices a breeze moving its way through the trees outside his window. He comments on the Sandia Mountains: plenty of snow there. He thinks of the river he has just drawn. He wonders if the Indians of the various pueblos to the north of Albuquerque are as fond of the river as he is. He is sure, upon reflection, that they are. They *must* be. Weren't they great lovers of the natural world years ago? They surely continue to feel close to the world around them. The history teacher has declared them to be good people, who have suffered a lot. It is a sad commentary on our nation that they continue to suffer. He has asked his father whether he thinks the Indians actually do suffer, and has been told no, they don't — or don't any more than others do. His father's strongly worded views have (but only tentatively) become his. Every once in a while Alexander has a moment or two of disagreement. Every once in a while he takes issue with his father. Not to his face, however; he tells Alice about *his* opinion, as against his father's. And she says yes, he ought stick to his guns, even go speak up to their parents, let them know what one of their children thinks. He has not followed her suggestion, though.

He explains why: "My father knows more about the Indians than the teacher. He says he talks with them face-to-face about business, and the teacher only gets her information from books. Daddy says he doesn't like some of the ideas the teachers tell us. He thinks they are biased in favor of the Indians and the poor people. He told Mother he was thinking of taking us out of the school and letting us go to a public school. But it would be a long bus ride. And we might have a lot of trouble in a public school. The teachers there aren't very good, and you can get into a lot of fights. Alice will probably ask to go to a public school one of these days, just because she likes to argue with Daddy. She tells him she thinks he's wrong sometimes! He smiles and says she's young and she will change her mind later on. She asked him last week what would happen if she *didn't* change her mind. He said nothing for a while, then he said she would, even if she thinks she won't.

"She'd heard someone on television talk about white people

marrying black people, so she asked Daddy what he thought. He said he was against it. She asked Daddy about Indians: would he mind if she married one? He said she wouldn't. She said yes, but what if she decided she wanted to. He told her to stop asking him a lot of silly questions. She got upset, because he was really angry with her, and she could tell. That's why I don't want to argue about the Indians with my parents or my grandfather. They think the Indians aren't the same as the white people, and we should stay away from them, just like they stay away from us. The teachers have a different opinion; they like the Indians. So does my best friend's father. He's a doctor, and he says the Indians have a lot of diseases, and they should go to the hospital, but they have no money, and the government is supposed to have doctors taking care of Indians, but there aren't enough doctors, and it's bad to be born an Indian, because you might die very young. I told my mother what he said, and she said it's sad, but it can be the fault of an Indian mother: she doesn't keep a clean house, and she doesn't know the right food to feed her kids, so then they get sick. She said my grandfather is right when he says that the Lord helps the people who try to help themselves."

The boy wonders whether Indians pray to the same God his parents ask him to beseech before going to sleep. His parents are Presbyterians, attend church with their children every Sunday, and encourage in them prayer at the table and upon retiring. The father or mother says grace before each meal. In that regard, the children are encouraged to take the initiative upon occasion. Alice will ask the Lord's "kindness" to descend to animals she loves — horses, dogs, cats, a bird — and to "the poor people." So will Alex. He even specifies who they are — "the Indians and the Spanish." The latter are, of course (in New Mexico), men and women and children who have, most likely, been Americans for many generations; in some in-

194 IN APPALACHIA, THE SOUTHWEST, AND ALASKA

stances going back to the seventeenth or eighteenth century. The parents say nothing, but the twins know that their concern for the impoverished or the socially and racially "different" is theirs alone at the table. The father has often commented upon how "different" Indians or Spanish-speaking people are. The differences, to him, go quite deep, have to do with what he calls "mentality" as well as social or historical experience, and are ultimately (he has argued) spiritual, hence derived from that hard to comprehend source (for children, certainly, and maybe for grown-ups as well): God's Will.

At the age of twelve Alex remembers that phrase as he talks about an Indian boy he saw win a rodeo contest: "I got to meet him afterwards. I knew his father; he has come to talk with my father about land. His father will be the governor of one of the pueblos, my father says; it's a matter of time. The boy's name is Jack, and he's friendly. I wanted to ask him over to our ranch, but I knew I couldn't. He'd be even better if he could ride horses like ours. He needs some lessons. I just wish I was as tough as he is, though. He holds on. I don't dare ride a horse I can't control. He said he'd get on any horse, and then he'd worry about staying on when he was already on. I told him it's the other way around with me; I was taught to find out about the horse first. I asked Daddy later if he thought it would be all right if I ever had an Indian kid play here at home. I didn't tell him who I was thinking about. He said he doubted I'd ever meet an Indian boy I'd want to have here, because they're 'different,' and that's how it is, God's Will. I think he's right, because when I tried to talk with the Indian kid, he didn't really talk very much on his own; he just answered my questions.

"The Indians have their reservations, and they've never wanted to leave them — most Indians. Some have left. There is a man who comes and helps with our horses. He's always got a fence to repair, or the stalls to fix up, because a horse has kicked at a wall, or he works out in the pasture land, or the yard, doing jobs Mother or Daddy have told him to do. He's half Indian. He looks more white than Indian, though. Our maid is Spanish-American, she says. She told my father that she wished they closed the border with Mexico: too many Mexicans are coming into Texas and New Mexico. She doesn't like the people she sees in Albuquerque — Mexican-Americans. Some of them aren't here legally. They could be sent back if the police discovered them. The maid brings her son and her daughter with her sometimes, when her mother isn't feeling good and can't cook for them. We play with her kids. We try to be friendly. They're a year or two younger than us. They seem even younger than they are. My mother says it's because they don't go to good schools. They don't talk the way we do. They are shy, maybe that's the trouble. They don't let you know what's on their minds. I think the Spanish people and the Indians don't trust us. The Anglos make them scared. But they scare us, too. I don't know why, but they do. I wouldn't want to be alone on a reservation, even if I was visiting a friend there.

"We have the migrants come through here and help us harvest our fruit. They are very good at climbing the trees and getting the apples and pears and cherries. They are Mexicans, or they're Americans who originally came from Mexico. We only need them for a week. Our orchard isn't as big as some. I don't feel safe near them, either. My father hires a private detective to watch the house the week they're around. They might come into the house and steal. They seem very poor and they don't take good care of themselves. We always find some beer cans or wine bottles around, after they've gone. Daddy says, each year, he'd like to deduct money from their checks to pay for cleaning up after them. But the maid's kids are clean; we take them to our playroom, and they like to build with Lego. We just leave them there alone, and they don't cause any trouble. I think they feel better when we're gone than when we're there with them. They keep on glancing at us."

Alex and Alice are fond of the mother of those children. Her name is Maria, and she is especially fond of Alice, who returns the affection. Alice has often expressed the wish that Maria stay with the family, rather than go home every night. When Maria has a day off — she never takes two days in a row off — Alice wonders what supper will be like or how her mother will manage the house. Maria helps with the cooking, makes sure each room looks clean and neat. When she is off, or on vacation, the children know that the chances they will go out for supper are improved considerably. Moreover, their mother is apt to be less interested in how tidy they keep their bedrooms. She tends to "let things go" until Maria comes back. There is another woman who comes in occasionally — when guests have arrived, or a party is to be held, or when Maria is away sick or on vacation. But she is not Maria, as the children keep saying. She does not smile. Maria always seems to do so. She speaks hard-to-understand English. Maria has a Spanish accent, but she is quite intelligible. And she doesn't work as efficiently, as tactfully as Maria does. The children acknowledge fear of her. The taciturn face makes them wonder about her thoughts. She seems sad, they say. She seems worried, they observe. She seems unhappy, or even angry, they venture. What is the matter with her? they ask. Why does she even come to work, they wonder, when she obviously takes no pleasure in the work, in meeting with and talking to the people who live there — the children and their parents? What does she say to her husband when she gets home? they ask themselves.

Alice even imagines herself an invisible presence in the woman's home: "She probably steps inside, sits down, asks her children to bring her some cold water, and starts telling them all the bad things she can remember about us. Yesterday was my tenth birthday and Alex's, and she came to help Maria, because we had the birthday party, and all my friends came over, and Granddaddy, and some businessmen friends of Daddy's who just came into Albuquerque and stayed for supper. Maria made me a pot holder; she knows I'd like to learn how to cook, so she gave me something to use when picking up hot dishes or pans. She gave me a hug, and told me that she hopes she's around to see me twice ten; by then I may have a boyfriend, and I may want to marry him, she said! The other maid didn't say very much. She wished me a happy birthday, but she kept looking out the window. Her name is Mary, not Maria; but we don't really call her anything. We just speak to her without using her name. I think she tells her children that we are spoiled. I heard her say so to Maria, and Maria said she should keep quiet. I went to my room and wondered what I'd done to make someone say I'm spoiled. My mother has been telling us ever since I remember that she won't let us get spoiled. She makes us take care of our room, and she makes us eat what's before us on the table. My father is even tougher; he gets mad when we ask him for a lot of toys, or an extra dollar allowance. He says we're lucky, and we should know it, not take advantage of it. He will lend us some money once in a while, but we have to pay it back. And he doesn't forget. I'll bet he's harder on us than the maid who helps Maria is on her kids. I've seen them, and they go running to her, and they cry a lot, and she's always trying to get them to stop by giving them candy. She brings the candy with her. Our mother won't let us eat candy, except at special times."

She has spent enough time thinking about the differences

between the two maids to want to draw pictures of them. But she finds herself not able to begin the job without a reservation: she would fail to make Maria as "nice" as she is. The reason: Maria is "not very pretty." Mary, on the other hand, "looks very nice," but "it's the expression on her face" that makes her, for the child, at least, rather unappealing. The young artist decides to concentrate on the face. She draws a round circle for Maria, puts in it large black eyes, a smiling mouth, black hair, and modest ears. She remembers the nose at the end — small and almost unnoticeable. The other maid's face is rendered carefully: more oval, narrow eyes, a closed mouth, a more prominent nose, larger ears, abundant black hair. The girl decides each of them deserves a body. She sets to work with her black crayon. She draws a few lines, makes a semblance only of a body for each maid. They get sticks for arms and legs, and boxes for the torso. They are left suspended in air — no ground, no sky. (Figure 26.) She has drawn others she knows far more accurately, and she has always put them somewhere, given them land to walk on, a river or a sky to look at, a tree or two for shade, a horse or dog for company: her brother, for instance, or a girl friend, Lila.

The girl friend she has pictured lives in a nearby ranch and is Alice's best friend. Alice often talks about Lila — and about the English governess who attends to Lila and her two younger sisters. Lila's mother is herself English. Lila's father is from New Mexico. He met the mother while visiting England, and stayed there to pursue and win her hand. Alice loves to talk to her own parents about the romantic stories of that courtship; Lila has recited them often. Alice makes clear the envy she feels, and the hope that her own life will somehow be "different." She will go to Europe. She will meet a man from England perhaps. Maybe a Frenchman; but no, her parents don't like Frenchmen. Who do they like? She is not sure, because they don't really speak well of the English, either. They are critical, actually, of the English governess who helped bring up Lila: "My mother says she puts on a lot of airs, and she makes Lila do the same. Lila doesn't put on any airs with me, but she does with some other kids, I agree. The governess has an English accent, and she *tells* you what to do, instead of asking, the way Maria will. My mother says a maid should be a maid and not try to run the house. But the woman is *not* a maid, she's a governess; that means she's supposed to take care of the kids. They have a maid who does what our maid does. She's not as nice as Maria. She's more like our Mary. She gives you a bad look, and she watches you a lot. Lila doesn't like her. Lila told her mother that she'd be glad to do what the maid does, and then they could fire the maid. But her mother wouldn't agree. She said Lila has to go to school, and doesn't have the time to be a maid, and besides, it's not right. I agree with Lila's mother.

"It's no fun being a maid, anyway. I wouldn't want to have Maria's job. Sometimes I watch her; I even follow her around. I'll talk with her. Or I'll find things to do while she's working. I feel sorry for her. She told me she used to have dreams, when she was my age, of finishing school and going to college and 'becoming somebody,' that's what she keeps on saying — that she wished she could have 'become somebody.' I told her she is wrong to talk that way; she *is* 'somebody' to us. My mother has told her many times that she keeps us all organized, and that without her the house would fall apart. But she doesn't believe what she hears, I guess. My brother says it's unfair, that she should live the way we do. But he can't figure out how she ever will, and I can't, either. We asked Daddy whether he thought that the day will come that Maria and her family are better off than they are. Daddy said we pay her more than anyone else like her in Albuquerque gets —

maybe in all New Mexico. He asked us how much we thought she should get. We didn't know. He said he used to worry about the poor Indians and the poor Spanish people, but when you grow up you begin to realize that even if you gave away every penny you have, there would be no change in the world: the rich and the poor would still be there.

"Daddy keeps telling Alex and me one very important thing; he says it would be very bad if we ever stopped thanking Maria or stopped showing her our appreciation. We buy her Christmas presents from our own allowance — besides the ones Mother and Daddy give her. A lot of the time we go up to her and tell her how much we like her. I would tell her more often, but I don't think she really likes to hear me compliment her. She asks me please to stop. Mother says she's shy. I'm not sure she is. I heard her tell Mary that she likes us, but she'd rather not work at all. Her youngest boy — he's six, I think — is sick, and she'd rather take care of him than us. My mother paid for an operation the boy had, and he's better now, the doctor said. But Maria worries. My mother told her she really shouldn't be worrying, and it's a good thing she's not at home with him all day, because she'd spoil him and pamper him and he'd be much worse off than he is now. Anyway, he goes to school all day, and so she doesn't have to be there with him. Before this year her sister took care of him. She's a widow. Her children are older. They live next door.

"Maria's mother died three years ago. I remember when it happened. Mother and Daddy went to the funeral. Alex and I wanted to go, but they said no. We'd met the mother a few times. She even would come over here and help Maria — when there was a party, and we needed three or four people. I think Maria's father died a long time ago. He was dead before we ever got to meet Maria. They were very poor a long time ago, but now they're not so poor. Daddy says they do better than a lot of their neighbors, he's sure. I asked him why they don't move out of their neighborhood. He said they're comfortable there; they like it, and they wouldn't be comfortable here. He knew I was going to ask him why they don't live near here! Alex once asked why we don't build a home on our land for Maria and her husband and their kids. But the husband would have a lot of trouble going to work, because he works in a store, a supermarket, on the other side of the city. He helps keep the store clean. I think he puts things on the shelves, after the customers have left or before they come in the morning. That's one of Maria's problems: she comes home and he has to leave; then she has to leave and he's just coming home. It's no good, she told me. I'd asked what her husband did. I said: has he still got the same job? She didn't like my question; I knew that right after I'd asked. But she told me; she said yes, he had the same old job. She said that he'd *always* have that job. Then she left the room. She told me she had to go clean the kitchen. But she hadn't finished doing my room. I was going to run after her and tell her there was more to do in my room, but I decided not to."

Over the years Alice has given Maria pictures drawn in school or things made there. Once, at the age of nine, she gave Maria an ashtray, done in a pottery class. Once, at the age of ten, she painted a picture at home for Maria. She earnestly wanted the picture to be "pretty," so that it would offer a touch of beauty to the maid's house. Even as she worked with her paints, she envisioned the painting hung up on a wall of that house. She worked long and hard at the job — and did so in secret, lest the maid see what she was doing. She would go to her mother's studio, which the maid never was allowed to clean up — the one place in the house permitted to stay messy. The mother is an amateur artist, and Alice had hoped that she too might be called one after finishing the painting for Maria.

Alice had a landscape in mind as she set to work; for inspiration, she looked out the window at an expanse of semiarid meadow land that stretches toward a mesa and is cut into by the Rio Grande. The point was to provide Maria with a pleasant scene that would help sustain her, would please and gratify her. The girl had seen the maid looking out that window, staring for many seconds at the rather striking view the living room window afforded. Why not evoke the view with paints? But when Alice had finished, she was not altogether happy with her work. (Figure 27.) Perhaps she ought get her father to take one of his fine photographs — in color. How could she ever hope to rival the work of a camera? On the other hand, she reasoned, with some self-confidence, Maria might enjoy having a painting — done by someone she knows and appears to be fond of. And in fact, the maid had confided to the girl a preference for her: "You are the one I like to talk with when I come here." The girl, in return, had many times told the maid how much her work is appreciated by the family. The maid had even volunteered to help the girl take care of her horse — brush the coat or work in the stall. No, that was not necessary. But the girl certainly appreciated the offer.

When Alice had finished the painting, she waited several days for the right moment to offer it to Maria. But the girl kept having misgivings, second thoughts. Ought she not put some person in the scene, or, at the least, animals — signs of life? Is there some other scene that might appeal to Maria far more? And wouldn't it have been wiser to have asked her in advance what she would like? Alice never came up with satisfactory answers for those questions. She decided abruptly one day to add her horse to the painting, and did so with enthusiasm. The mare was given a prominent place. When that was done the girl had a new issue to confront: whether to put herself on the horse's back — and make thereby a more personal gift than she had previously thought of offering. She called upon her mother for advice. The mother said yes, of course — why not? Wouldn't Maria be glad to see Alice? Don't they get along rather well? So Alice added herself. And a day later the gift was presented.

Moments later the girl had seen on the maid's face the response: "She was surprised. She stared at what I'd done. I couldn't tell what she was thinking. I waited for her to smile, but she didn't. She just thanked me. I guess I wanted her to tell me that I'd done a good job. But she didn't say so. She looked out the window, and then she looked at the picture again, and she thanked me again. She said that now she could show her children what she sees every day at our house. I was disappointed. I told my brother that she seemed a little sad when she was looking at the painting. Alex said maybe she didn't want to be reminded of our house when she goes back to her own house. I had never thought of that. It was then I knew I'd made a mistake. I was going to go ask Maria for the painting; I had an excuse in my mind: it needed some 'finishing touches' — my mother's words. But I didn't have the nerve. I tried to stay away from Maria. I went out for a long ride on my horse. I wished that we weren't on vacation; then I wouldn't be expected home for lunch. I knew she would give us lunch, because Mother was packing to go with Daddy to Denver for two days. Finally I came home. I wondered whether she'd take the painting home with her. But I'd forgotten that she was going to stay with us until our parents came back.

"I decided to forget about the painting. I tried to talk with Maria at the supper table, when she was serving us; and she was friendly. She seemed to have forgotten about the painting too. She didn't mention it while she stayed with us. When she was ready to leave — after my parents came back — I wondered if she'd remember to take the picture. It was in my room; she likes to go there to sit and catch her breath. She's told my mother it's her favorite room in the house. She even leaves her coat or her pocketbook in my closet. She went to the room to get the coat and the pocketbook and her little suitcase that Daddy bought for her. But she didn't take the painting. I wasn't surprised. By then I was glad. Alex had taught me a lesson. He's smarter than I am a lot of the times. He doesn't have much to do with Maria; he says he feels sorry for her and he wishes we didn't take her away from her own children. I guess he knows her better than I do. After she left I took my painting and put it in the closet of my mother's studio. Then Maria wouldn't see it, and we both could forget about it."

Her brother had, a week or so afterwards, given her a rather stern lecture. It was a painting, Alex pointed out, that Maria's children would have had to look at every day: a painting done by another child, a painting *of* another child, and, at that, a child who saw more of their mother than they did. Not that Alice was inclined to accept her brother's critical observations without protest. She emphasized her goodwill, protested the injustice of such an interpretation — her brother's or Maria's. Yet she agreed quite willingly with Alex's insistence that *something* had bothered Maria, had turned her quiet, evasive, even grim. Alice wanted to bring the matter to the attention of her parents, but her brother cautioned her not to do so and she tended to agree with him. They had both heard their parents talk about Maria, had argued with them on various occasions about her, had argued even more heatedly with their outspoken and upon occasion splenetic grandfather, who felt that everyone in the house was too deferential to the maid, to the hired hands who worked on the ranch, to people who work in stores, to "all the people who are paid, dammit, to give the best service possible, and don't anymore."

Best to let the whole episode be forgotten. Best to talk with her brother and learn to think about Maria in a different way. Best to hope and pray that when she, Alice, is older, when she is a wife and mother, things will be different: "Alex and I have both decided that we won't let other people do our work. We'll do our own work. I don't want anyone to help me with my horse. I try to clean up my room; Mother makes us do that. When I'm a grown-up, I'll try to take care of my house. The only trouble is — I keep telling my brother — Maria might not be very happy if she could stay at home, but she didn't have any money to go buy food with. She'd say we weren't being of much help to her that way! My brother says she could go and get a job if she needed money. But that's what she's done. That's why she's here. That's how she came to us, because she needed money. Maybe if the rich people gave some money to the poor people, Maria would be better off. But Alex says he doesn't think they will give enough."

III

YOUNG LAST-DITCH AMERICAN

I N THE Rio Grande Valley of Texas Anglo families are, almost without exception, better off than almost all the thousands of Chicanos who have crossed the river for the privilege of working at low salaries on large farms and ranches, or in stores and gas stations and an occasional nonunion small factory. ("Migrant labor" and "menial labor" are the phrases used with no embarrassment at all.) In some towns, in some counties even, Chicanos make up as much as 80 or 90 percent of the population. They are under the authority of Anglo foremen or "managers," who are, in turn, employed by "the big boss," a phrase sometimes used by Anglos themselves as well as Chicano "field hands" or "help" — two other phrases that get used a lot.

Near Crystal City in the Valley one "big boss" manages to straddle several worlds: he owns a large expanse of fertile land, on which is grown vegetables and, quite profitably, flowers; he also owns a small factory, where raincoats and rainhats are made; and he is, as he puts it, "a leader in the community," by which phrase he refers to activities like membership on the board of directors of the county's bank, trusteeship at the county's hospital, and involvement in the activities of the American Legion, the Red Cross, the Boy Scouts, and the Girl

Scouts. He has a son, Peter, Junior, usually called Young Peter when the father is present, and a daughter named Paula. The mother's name is Pauline. When Peter was seven and Paula was five their parents began to make frequent reference to the larger (commercial and charitable) world they take such a significant part in. The mother, for instance, works as a most conscientious volunteer, four to five days a week, in the hospital. She helps at the blood bank, pushes a "book wagon" around, works in the laboratory, sterilizing and sorting out instruments and glassware. The mother had wanted to be a nurse but was instead sent to college at the University of Texas. She left Austin within a few months, again tried to win permission to be a nurse, but to no avail. Her father was a doctor. He told her that if she wouldn't go to college, she'd have to go abroad. She did, with a maiden aunt — for six months. When she came back she was willing to try college. She did — for two years. And there she met her future husband, who also was no great enthusiast for higher education. They both refused to go up to Austin for their senior year, and each went to work in Crystal City — she in her father's office, he in his father's office, a real estate agency. They got married within months, soon thereafter decided to start a family.

The rest is a history their son, at the age of ten, was able to give a rather detailed account of: "They weren't poor when they were married, but they didn't have a lot of money. My mother's family was large; she had seven brothers and sisters. My grandfather was good to his patients. He'd sometimes lend them money, instead of sending them bills. And he didn't get repaid most of the time. My grandmother used to tell my mother that it was no good, the way everyone got money except her. My mother says she's glad Daddy isn't like her father. He keeps his money. It's all locked up in the bank, and in other places. He started with his father in the real estate office. Then he decided he wasn't going to help *other people* buy and sell land; he was going to get some land for himself. So he did. Then he sold it, and made a lot of money. Then he bought more land. This time he didn't sell; he got a man to come and start growing crops, and that's how the money got made. Then he bought more land, and he hired more people to work on the crops. He's had a lot of people working for him ever since. Later on he *expanded;* he tells us at supper a lot of times that in business you either keep *expanding,* keep moving and growing, or you're in real trouble, because in America nothing stays still. He learned how to fly, and he's going to teach me how in a few years. We have a plane for dusting the crops, and we have another plane for taking trips. It's an old prop jet. My father won't buy a company jet yet. He says he can't afford it. He says maybe someday he will have enough money to get a jet; but he won't buy one except for cash. It's dangerous to owe a lot of money.

"Daddy makes money in his new business, the factory. He met a man at a Chamber of Commerce meeting, and the man said someone from Chicago wrote to him and was thinking of coming down to Texas and building a place here where he could get people to work and still make a living himself. He was going broke in Chicago, my father said, because he was paying all his money to his workers, and they were always asking for more, and then more, and they were lazy, on top of it. They weren't grateful for having a job, the way our people are down here. I guess my father decided to do something about helping the man from Chicago. Pretty soon the man came down here; my father wrote to him and called him up. They became partners. They built a factory, and my father got some of his people, the Mexicans, to go work in it. They were glad to have new jobs, and they got better pay. They could stay here all year around, instead of going way up North in the summer to harvest crops when it's too hot here to grow much. A lot of Mexicans would rather work in a factory than pick the crops. My father says he can't figure out what goes on in their heads, because you'd think they would like working outdoors. It's what they're used to doing back in Mexico. They get a little more money, that's probably why. My mother says she thinks they hope they'll get more money, and they'll learn a skill, and improve themselves. Daddy gives them raises every year. He doesn't want the union coming around, causing trouble."

The boy knows that, in fact, "the union" has been coming around. Organizers have talked with his father's workers. His father's partner, from Chicago, became very nervous when those organizers appeared; eventually, he sold his share of the business to the boy's father. Peter has contempt for "labor people," and also for the former co-owner of the plant. Why did he run so quickly? What kind of "guts" does he have — or rather, not have? And how foolish he was — to give up a half share in a quite profitable enterprise. The boy talks with disdain of outsiders who are ignorant or cowardly, like the former partner; or malevolent, like the "labor people." The boy also looks forward to taking on such individuals. His father is a tough, even combative, man, and the boy wants very much to emulate him. Moreover, the boy is convinced that the ones who "lose" in this world are those who lack patience, stubbornness, and "savvy," a quality he has often heard his father claim for himself and deny to others.

It was "savvy" that brought the raincoat (and, later, umbrella) factory to "the Valley"; it was "savvy" that converted a risky venture into a flourishing enterprise; and it was "savvy" that "saved everything" (the boy is sure). At just the right moment his father took complete control, sent his frightened partner away, and made a stand that the boy likens to the

Alamo: "Daddy was outnumbered. There was just him. They came about ten strong, and they were going to picket, and they had these threats that they told to Daddy: give in, or we'll cause a lot of trouble for you, and there won't be any business before too long. Daddy told them to get away, fast. They didn't go away. They stood around, and they tried talking with the Mexicans working for Daddy. That's when his partner pulled out. He was afraid there'd be a fight. He ran from Chicago to here, and he left here and went back to Chicago. My father says that if people like him had come to Texas a hundred years ago, or more, then we'd still have Indians riding around in north Texas and Spain would own south Texas. Daddy told his partner good-bye, and he called the sheriff in, and the sheriff promised to help out, and he did.

"The 'labor people' started pushing hard, and they violated the law; they trespassed. They got themselves arrested. Daddy hired some real big tough Mexicans to fight the labor people. They saw they weren't going to get far. The whole county was upset. They had reporters here from as far away as San Antonio. Everyone agreed that Daddy was right. The whole Chamber of Commerce met, every single member; and they voted to support Daddy. The newspaper said they should run the labor people out of Texas, and send them back to New York, where they all came from. The sheriff came over to see Daddy one night and he told us — we were all there in the living room — that he'd use his deputies, and if need be, get more deputies, and it would be a no-fooling gun battle, if those union people didn't clear out right away. They did, too. They did make some more threats. And they had someone get the governor to call up the sheriff and ask him what he was going to do. My father says the sheriff told the governor he wouldn't kill a single one of them, but he'd lock them up and hold them in his jail until they got good and tired. That's what he did.

They got their lawyers down here from Austin, I believe, but it took them time to get the labor people out. The judge is a good friend of Daddy's, and he called him up and said: 'Don't you worry, I'm feeling tired these days, and it's going to take me a real long time before I lift a finger to get those fellows out on bail, and by the time they do get out, they'll be having some second thoughts.' "

He expresses anger that the judge let the "labor people" out at all, then says he was "only kidding"; he knows full well that even judges have limited power. In any event, it was his father who "won"; his father and the loyal Mexicans; and his mother too — because she kept giving advice to her husband. The advice was direct and simple: tell the workers that he would pay any of them "a fair wage," but he would never under any circumstances yield to the pressure of the unions. The Mexicans who work for him were willing to fight for him, his son makes clear. A war was in the making. But it was averted; the enemy retreated, have not yet returned. They will, young Peter knows. At ten he was quite ready to go fight, should the occasion arise. He was also prepared for the longer future: the day when he would himself be grown, a partner of his father's — and, again, one prepared at any moment to take up arms. "I'd take them on, if I had to," he said after coming home from a friend's birthday party. The friend had just turned ten, four months after Peter had done so. But Peter was looking forward to being eleven, twelve, thirteen — sixteen. Then he would be able to drive, and he would be in a position to get help — the sheriff and his deputies. In the event of an all-out confrontation, a son who drives would be a great asset: his father could send him on errands, and he'd get to his destination fast.

Peter took time that day to draw up a battle plan, in the event of "trouble." He worked hard on the scene, using only pencil — no crayons, no paints, both of which were available. He built the factory with care and affection, spoke warmly of his father's initiatives as a businessman and of "the Mexicans" who remained loyal to his father "during the trouble." He provided the building with many windows — a modern and airy structure. His father had said that one day he would build such a structure. His father would never be pushed or intimidated in any way by those who call his present "operation" a "sweatshop," but his father would indeed (on his own and at a time of his choosing) make a more comfortable working life for "his people," for "the Mexicans." The boy praises his father's essential honor and decency as he works with his pencil. And as he finishes (Figure 28), portrays a "fight" outside the factory — men facing down other men with drawn guns — he praises his father even more strongly. He calls him "brave," because he demonstrated the courage to face threats and possibly worse. He calls him "honest," because he demonstrated the willingness to sit down with his family, with his workers, with his enemies, and make quite clear what he would do, "if crossed." He calls him "kind," because he buys many presents for his children and his wife, provides all sorts of benefits for "his Mexicans," contributes rather substantial sums of money to various "charities."

Not that his father shows off. It is the boy's mother who has told him a lot about her husband's generosity and thoughtfulness, his "character," in her words. The boy says: "I know my mother is prejudiced in favor of my father. A friend of mine told me that, and I laughed at him. I said: 'Do you think you're so smart that you're telling me something I don't already know?' But my mother knows the facts; she knows how much money Daddy gives to the hospital, and to the church, and to the Red Cross, and to the Visiting Nurse people. He gives them a lot, because my mother wanted to be a nurse, and he thinks the nurses do a lot for the Mexicans. He gives his people food and bonuses — the people who work in the fields, and the people in the plant. My mother even tells my father sometimes that she'd like him to stop giving so much money away. But he tells her he has to, or else he won't have much money left. He says you have to give a lot, if you want to make a lot. If he kept all his money, and didn't give the pickers and the people who work in the factory some extra money every once in a while, they'd get upset and they'd listen to the union people. Like it is now, they listen to Daddy instead. If they don't, he fires them."

The boy loves to play games with his father. They play "pitch and catch," their version of baseball practice. It is a game of some originality and imagination, because each of them pretends to have a team at his side, to be called in at various times for an assist. In so doing the person calls out what he will do in fantasy (throw a ball from the outfield to a particular base, for instance) and then the father and the son decide whether, in fact, the ball thrown only in their minds does or does not arrive at the base in time. Actually, the imagined plays are usually called upon when one or the other of the two wants to add a touch of excitement. But there is another purpose, too; the father or the son may want to indicate that nothing can be taken for granted, that there are always surprises, that one has to be on guard constantly. That is how life is, the father believes. That is how life is, the son has come to believe.

At the age of eleven, however, the boy had a teacher (in the sixth grade) who had slightly different ideas about what one ought to expect from others (and oneself) in this world. She was a teacher of high reputation, much liked by some children and by their parents as well. In the middle of the school year, however, Peter went through what his mother called "a difficulty," which, without question, she attributed to the teacher. The teacher had given her class a lesson on "minorities." She had told the children that they ought to think of others who look or talk or dress or live differently from themselves — think of them with kindness and affection. No one took exception to that exhortation; it is made routinely in the church Peter's family attends — and with the sanction of Jesus Christ. But the teacher would not let the matter drop there. She insisted upon getting specific, local. She insisted upon looking right outside the windows of her classroom. She talked about Chicanos, not Mexicans or Mexican-Americans, and she indicated her disapproval of the way they live, the wages they get, their social and educational isolation.

The boy remembered "almost every word she spoke," or so he claimed a few days afterward. "I used to think she was a real good teacher. I told everyone that she was fair, just as fair as could be. She tried to be nice to everyone in the class. She had no favorites. She seemed a lot better than last year's teacher. That's why I was so surprised when we started getting a 'sermon,' Daddy called it, on the Mexicans. The teacher said we ought to think about other people, even the ones we don't know. She said it's a *shame*, what's going on here in the Valley. She didn't wait for anyone to raise a hand and ask why. She just went on and on, telling us we were doing bad by the Mexicans, and asking us if we'd ever thought of *their side* — how they feel toward us. I wanted to raise my hand, but I was afraid to do it. I thought of what my Daddy would say. I could hear him talking while she was talking. He would have told her a few things! He would have told her off! She said the Anglos don't do right by the Mexicans. She said it's unfair, and we're not doing what Jesus Christ says we ought to be doing. She said maybe one day the Mexicans will get into a fit, and they'll blow up at us, the Anglos, and they'll try to take away

what we have for themselves. That's when I *did* speak up. I
raised my hand. She said later I didn't, but I did. I raised my
hand, and I started talking, because she wasn't paying any
attention to me, and I wanted to get my word in. I wanted to
go home and tell my Daddy and my mother that I didn't just
sit by and listen to all of us being bad-mouthed. That's what
Daddy says she was doing — bad-mouthing us, her own people. It's not right."

He is less certain of his own words than hers. He dismisses
his protest as insignificant, though he recognizes that everyone in the class was upset. He spoke out — that is all. Someone
had to speak out. He remembers clearly what crossed his mind
just before he opened his mouth: "I could see my father
pounding his fist on the table, the way he does when he reads
something in a magazine he doesn't agree with, or the way he
did when he got a letter from the union people, and they told
him to expect trouble, because he is a 'bad employer.' I think
it was right that I said something. All I did was say there is
another side to the story, and she wasn't telling it to us, and
my father would, if she didn't. She told me I was out of order;
she said I should ask for permission to speak. Then she said I
could speak anyway. But I didn't. I'd already said all I had to
say. I couldn't think of anything more to say. I tried to talk, but
nothing would come out. I think that's when I must have
started crying. She came and tried to be nice to me, but I got
angry and I lost my temper. I didn't want her standing there,
telling me she liked me, and all that. I just swore, I guess, and
I pushed my books off the desk, and I ran out of the room. I
changed my mind and came back in right away, but the bell
rang, and we all went home."

When he got home he told his mother immediately what
had happened. He told their Chicano maid, too. Both were
upset. It was the maid, actually, who suggested that the father

be phoned at his factory. The boy remembers her saying: "Some Anglos are very bad; that teacher must be very bad." He remembers being made nervous by the observation, but grateful for the maid's support. He has often called her "a good Mexican — the best." So does his mother; so does his father. Still, when his father came home, and he did so immediately, the boy asked if they could talk "in private," meaning away from the maid. The father was puzzled at first. Why? The boy had no answer, only a second request that his parents go with him to his room. They did, of course, and soon enough the father was excited, angry, full of plans, if not plots: "Somehow that teacher's got to go." The boy remembers his father saying that over and over again.

A couple of years later, when the boy was almost thirteen and preparing to leave for San Antonio, to participate in an "all-Texas debating competition," the boy would remember those words of his father's: "My Dad was determined to get that teacher I had in the sixth grade fired. He kept telling us that somehow she had to go, and the next thing we all knew, she did go. I tried to find out why she left, but no one would tell me. Dad said he didn't know. Mom said she didn't know. My friends said their parents didn't know, either. Our maid said she didn't know — but she did say something that made me suspicious; she told me not to keep asking questions, because it might get me into trouble. I couldn't figure out what she meant for a while. I knew she was always afraid; no matter what happens in the house, she gets worried. My mother is always telling her to calm down, because everything is going to be all right. I guess I decided she was just being nervous, as usual. But I knew my father had done something. I knew he'd spoken to the principal, probably — maybe the school board. He was once the chairman of the school board. I knew it was no accident the teacher left. I was glad she was gone. But now

I'm worried, because the principal in our school called me over to his office and told me that I'd better be careful, because there are a lot of 'flaming liberals and radicals' up there in San Antonio, and one of them is going to be a judge in the debating contest — my sixth-grade teacher. He wasn't sure whether she'd judge me; there will be a lot of judges, I guess. If my old teacher turns out to be my judge, I'll just go ahead and debate, and hope the other judges will stand up to her. I know she'd remember me, and she'd probably vote against me. I'm pretty sure that my father was the one who got her fired. Or maybe she just quit when she saw that she couldn't win, not with Dad against her. I'd hate to have my father as an enemy! I'd even hate to debate with my father. He could win up there in San Antonio; he could become the champion Texas debater. I think he already is. My mother says he can outtalk everyone, and when she doesn't agree with him, she says he can make black seem white and white seem black."

The teacher was indeed there. Peter saw her name on the program. He saw her. He debated while she was on the stage, looking, listening, judging. He won. On behalf of the judges she told him he had won. He said thank you. She smiled and told him he had done a good job arguing. (Resolved: That Texas ought not separate from the United States and become an independent nation.) He went on to the next "level" of competition, lost, went to a cousin's house for a day and night, returned to the Valley, and told his parents how it had gone in San Antonio. When the subject of the former teacher came up, the boy was hesitant but forthcoming. His father questioned him carefully, was satisfied that there was "no prejudice." If anything, the boy felt, there was an inclination on the teacher's part to favor him. The father explained to the boy why that might indeed have been the case. The boy was grateful for the analysis: "Dad told me that you have to understand the liberals. They're always preaching to people. They're always worried about other people. They can't mind their own business. He says my sixth-grade teacher will probably talk about me and what she did in the debating competition for five years. She'll tell everyone how fair she is. I think Dad is right; she was so *nice* to me.

"I don't understand why she didn't try to get tough with me. If I was in her shoes, I think I would have been tough. I wouldn't have smiled, and I would have listened to every word and been waiting for a slip-up. My mother says people are different, and that's the only explanation there is. My father says if you're going to get ahead in the world, or stay ahead in the world, you can't be like that schoolteacher. It's all right for her, he says, but if he was like her, we wouldn't have the kind of life we do. I'm sure I'll work with Dad in his business when I'm grown up. If that schoolteacher ever lost her job again, and wanted to come back here in the Valley to live, we could give her a job, maybe. But I don't think he'd hire the teacher; and I don't think she'll ever come back to the county."

She did, however — a short six months later. She came back as a political organizer, as another one of those "labor people." She surprised and enraged the boy's father by calling on him. One day his secretary told him that a lady was outside who said she knew him and had taught his son. The secretary was told to show her in. She entered, said hello, introduced herself, and told him that she and others would begin picketing his factory the next morning quite early, unless he saw fit to come to an accommodation, whereby his workers would be allowed to join a union and obtain certain benefits hitherto denied them. He was silent, unbelieving, stunned — not by her demands or threats, but by the fact of her presence.

Peter says he will never forget what happened when his father came home: "He wasn't angry. He wasn't upset. He had a smile on his face. He called Mother and me into his study and he said he'd just had a real crazy experience. He told us that my old teacher had shown up in town again, and he told us what had happened. I guess he never said more than a few words to her. He said he was so amazed that she'd dare show up in his factory and talk to him like she did that he couldn't think of anything to say, except no, he'd never agree to a union being formed, and she'd might as well leave town, because she was wasting her time. He said he thought of reaching for the phone and getting the sheriff and having him come over and arrest her. But he just couldn't get over the shock — a woman, an Anglo, a sixth-grade schoolteacher, who'd been fired and left the county years ago, now coming back and behaving like some wise-guy Mexican. So, he *asked* her if she wouldn't *please* leave, because he had other business to do, and she did, and she was polite, and she even asked after me!"

When the father told his wife and son what had happened, he was not his usual decisive self. He couldn't understand the former teacher's motives, and the more he tried, the more confused he became. His cardinal measuring rod had always been the question: What's in it for so-and-so? The boy had repeated those words of his father's many times — especially in San Antonio during the debating competition, when he asked himself repeatedly why the teacher should be so kind and considerate toward him. There was nothing, after all, "in it" for her. Now the father was confused. Hadn't the teacher left quietly and quickly several years ago? Hadn't she only recently been rather nice to his son? Wasn't she from "a good Anglo Valley family"? Didn't her brother manage a nearby grower's rather profitable enterprise?

"She knows the score," he kept on saying, perhaps to convince himself. When Peter wanted his father to enumerate and explain the particular elements that go to make up the "score," the father refused, and even became angry at his son: "My Dad told me to stop asking stupid questions. He was right. I shouldn't have bothered him when he was under pressure. (That's what my mother told me later.) He stopped talking to us and went to call his lawyer. He called the sheriff too. He called the owner of the newspaper. He called our congressman. He called a friend of his in Austin; he told the friend to go talk with the governor. He told everyone he talked with that he couldn't figure out what that teacher was up to, but he was worried, because the Mexicans aren't too smart, but she's 'brassy,' and she has 'good connections' through her family, and he wants to be ready for the worst."

The worst turned out to be nothing too difficult for Peter's father. Within forty-eight hours after the picketing of the factory had begun, the teacher and three "Mexican labor people" were under arrest — and faced with the alternative of jail for "disorderly conduct" or an enforced departure from the county. The teacher was at first prepared to fight Peter's father with every ounce of resistance. But she soon realized how futile her opposition would be. Her father refused her help. She had saved over four thousand dollars but could not find a local lawyer to take her case. There would be legal help from San Antonio, eventually — but the judge was threatening her with prolonged imprisonment; he had indicated he might set high bail.

She made the mistake of going back to see Peter's father, this time in a more plaintive frame of mind. Wouldn't he sit down and talk with her? Wasn't he really a generous and thoughtful man, anxious in his own way to befriend Chicanos? Couldn't their differences be resolved — perhaps with the help of a mediator or arbitrator? The father no longer had any hesitations about what was "in it" for her. Nor did his son: "Daddy told us what she'd said to him. He finally realized that she wasn't so smart, after all. She's just a troublemaker. She wanted to come back here and show everyone how big and important she is; instead, she saw she'd end up in a jail. She's a coward. She tried to bargain with my father, and he told her she'd best leave the county while she could. He gave her twenty-four hours. He says she was out of here in an hour! The Mexicans had already left. The sheriff scared them. He threatened to ship them back to Mexico. They didn't cause any trouble. The Mexicans are usually pretty good. The trouble starts when an Anglo decides to use them. The teacher was a big shot — for a couple of days. But she crumbled. Daddy says they all do, the labor people."

By the age of fourteen Peter foresaw what was in store for himself. He would finish high school, and heed his father's advice: college and, after that, law school. The father had once thought that his son need not take the considerable risks of college, let alone graduate school: the frivolity or the leftist political atmosphere of Austin, Texas. But the boy had been, all along, a loyal son; and the father could not forget that his taxes helped support the University of Texas. The place ought to "belong" to him rather than to the "kooky professors"; a fight must be waged against "radical types" in Austin as well as outside the factory in the Rio Grande Valley. Moreover, the father had girded himself for a rather long haul of what he called "guerrilla war." So it would be good to have a lawyer in the family.

No need for Peter to go to business school, as his mother had suggested. The father thought "business school types" too "cautious"; they are the kind who would sit down and talk and start bargaining with "labor people." They are the kind who "give in all the time." They are "overeducated." They have lost all their "self-respect." They have read too many books, forgotten how to fight. Lawyers know how to fight. Peter as a lawyer would be a good ally to his father, the grower and the factory owner.

A high school freshman, Peter already knew how to argue well. He was also a good football player — a sturdy lineman. And he had sharp eyes, attentive ears. One afternoon he heard several workers saying "bad things" about the factory, without realizing that he was around the corner of the building, trying to put the slipped chain of his bike back on. He didn't know their names, but he had gone out of his way to catch a glimpse of them. Later, the father thanked the son for his "good work" and told him to keep their faces in his mind, just in case of any future trouble. The boy said he would, and he did. He wished he had been able to photograph the three men. He wished that he was a good enough artist to sketch their faces, as is done, he'd read, by the police. Instead he walked casually, every now and then, through the plant, and looked at the men. He kept his memory "refreshed."

Neither he nor his father wanted to ask the foreman the names of the men. The point was to be ready — but not give one's readiness away, even to a presumed ally. The chances were strong that those discontented workers would never cause any trouble. And Peter was glad to hear his father say that so emphatically. No one wants to tattle on people, the youth would insist. He would even go further and proclaim his sympathy for the men. They work hard; they are entitled to their petulant moments. "So long as they don't move from words to actions," he emphasizes, "everything will be all right." And just in case anyone should be tempted to credit him with that social, political, economic, and legal appraisal, he acknowledges cheerfully the father who keeps uttering those words — the man who regards himself and his son as two "last-ditch Americans."

IV

YOUNG WHITE NATIVE OF ALASKA

PEOPLE in the rest of the United States ("the lower forty-eight" which, with Hawaii's admission to the Union, have actually become the lower forty-nine — though the former expression persists) tend to ignore or not even know about her and others like her. She made that complaint at the age of nine. (She is now thirteen.) She was telling her teacher in an Anchorage, Alaska, classroom what, in fact, the teacher had told her and her classmates — that for many, maybe most, American children of her age, Alaska meant Eskimos and Indians, hunters and trappers and fishermen, polar bears and igloos, and perhaps, these days, oil pipes or ice breakers. But Pam is an Alaskan, was born there and will most likely die there. And her parents are native Alaskans, with the same expectations — a full, long life as residents of Anchorage. It would be nice, Pam told the teacher and wrote in her brief composition, if her life and the lives of others like her were celebrated in books for young readers like herself, not to mention in newspaper stories or magazine articles. Here is what Pam wrote: "I come from Alaska. I am not an Eskimo. My father was born here. My mother was born here. We are natives, just like they call the Eskimos and the Indians. Daddy is a lawyer. Mummy taught school before my brother was born.

I'm two years younger than he is. I would like to visit the lower 48 one day."

Her grandparents, she knows, were born in Terre Haute, Indiana. The grandfather came to Alaska alone as a young man. He was poor and could not find a job in Terre Haute or, later, in Indianapolis. He went to Chicago and drifted. He began to hate the city. He obtained a job as a dishwasher and saved until he had enough money to purchase a railroad ticket to Seattle. He hoped to obtain a job through a cousin who lived there, and began a new life in the state of Washington. In Seattle he was still unhappy. The cousin was himself unemployed; the Great Depression of the 1930s was in full swing. Pam's grandfather tried hard to find work, refused to consider going "on relief," soon exhausted all his funds. At a soup kitchen he met a man who was going to "hitch" a ride on the railroad up to Alaska. Yes, he would go along with that man; and he did. In Alaska he became a rather self-reliant hunter and trapper; he also took odd jobs, began to save money, and, for virtually nothing, bought land just outside Anchorage. He began writing to a girl he had gone to elementary school with. Would she come visit him? Would she consider marrying him? The answer came: she would do both. She rather quickly and gladly left Indiana, using everything he and she had to purchase a railroad ticket. Neither of them would ever return to the lower forty-eight.

Pam's father was born in 1937. Her mother was born to a couple not unlike her father's parents, though originally from Arkansas. Pam calls them "hillbillies," without pejorative intent. They were proud yeomen from the Ozarks — caught up in the agricultural calamity of the late 1920s and early 1930s. They too had gone West, had been migrants for a year or so, had tried to settle down in California, had become disgusted with the prospects life offered, and had managed an escape to

Alaska — the man first, and later (when sent for) his wife. They too would never return to what the maternal grandmother often tells Pam is "the old part of America." And they too, as of the late 1930s and certainly the early 1940s, were beginning to prosper. They had worked in a small grocery store, grown some of their food, become good at hunting and fishing. The owner of the store, a bachelor, died; he left the store to them. The year: 1939, the same year Pam's mother was born.

Pam thinks of her father's origins and her mother's every once in a while; she is quite interested in distinguishing between her own roots and those of other Alaskans, as well as of people in the lower forty-eight: "I don't like a lot of the people who have been coming up here to Alaska lately. They don't want to stay. They come, and then they're ready to leave before you know it. It isn't just the oil pipe people. Even before, there'd be visitors, and they'd say they really want to live up here, but after a year or two they'd go back to California, someplace like that. My grandparents say that Alaska became their home as soon as they got here. They never wanted to go back to Indiana or Arkansas. They had a bad time in those places. My mother and Dad were all set to go to the lower forty-eight once, but they changed their mind. They aren't interested in Arkansas or Indiana. They only have distant kin in those places, I think.

"Franklin Delano Roosevelt was one of the best Presidents we've ever had; both my parents say so. He helped the poor people in Arkansas and Indiana. I told the teacher that, and she said a lot of people would agree, but a lot wouldn't. I asked her who wouldn't. She said she knew a few people. But she wouldn't give me their names! I'll bet they're not real Alaskans! Real Alaskans are the Eskimos and the Indians and the white people who came up here and stayed and didn't leave after a few months, or maybe a year or two. President Roosevelt sent money up here, and he helped the people of Alaska, and during the Second World War they built bases here, for the army and navy, and my parents were here, and they started to make a lot of money then, I think. They say they were here at just the right time, when the state burst open and you could make a good living. But my parents didn't come up here because there was a boom; they were here before then. They are natives. I suppose they are white natives!"

She uses that last word often and insistently. She has been taught to do so. She will argue (has argued repeatedly) with anyone — a teacher usually — who calls only Eskimos and Indians "native Alaskans." She regards Alaska as a nation within a nation — a place which some people "really live in," and others "just come to visit." Among the latter are tourists, of course; but they are joined by "hoodlums" or "bums," who think they can "find gold" or simply "loaf and get paid for loafing." And there are "troublemakers," too — men and women, usually young, who come up to Alaska and go as fast as possible to Eskimo or Indian villages, where they "say bad things about the white people," and thereby start trouble. Pam has heard her parents denounce such young people, call them "radicals." She has also been told that some of them have "infiltrated" the Anchorage school system — the whole state of Alaska, actually. And it is a pity, because once there was "harmony," her father puts it, among all the state's people. Now there is "more and more trouble." That last word comes up often as she has talked of her life, her ideas, her hopes for herself and the huge state she loves so much and is so proud to call her home.

When she was nine, she once gazed at a map of the state she had tacked on her bedroom wall and spoke at some length about what she saw happening to Anchorage, to Alaska, and more immediately, to her own family: "My father says the time may come when we'll leave; the only problem is, where will we go? Daddy says Anchorage is becoming too crowded. The more people who come, the worse it gets. We have to lock our doors now. People steal. There are a lot of loafers; they're on welfare. Daddy says they should all be shipped back to the lower forty-eight. Daddy has made a lot of money, since people started coming up here. Some land he bought became more and more valuable, and he sold part, and he has more money than he ever dreamed he'd have.

"He doesn't know what to do about his travel agency. He started it a long time ago, before so many people started coming here. He was a guide himself, in the beginning; that's how he made a living. Then he'd meet people, and they wanted to sell their land, because they were living alone, a lot of them, and they were going to die soon, they'd tell Daddy; so if he'd pay them something and let them stay where they were, he could have their land. Daddy figured he couldn't lose; he loved every inch of Alaska, and he didn't want to do any harm to the land, the way some people say. He just liked owning it. When Daddy bought his land, he just left it as it was; he never ruined any land. The people who bought his land are ruining it now. Daddy wishes Alaska was still the place it used to be. He says he'd give away every cent he owns, if only all the tourists and the oil people and the loafers would go away and leave us alone. It used to be that my parents said they wished we could go live near the Eskimos; then we'd be away from all the new people coming up here. But the Eskimos aren't the same anymore. They've become different people. They've become lazy. My mother says she feels sorry for them. She says they're becoming like children. My grandfather says that's what is happening: the Eskimos are getting to be like the colored; it's like it used to be in Arkansas, when he was a boy."

Her maternal grandfather owns a large store in Anchorage.

Her paternal grandfather owns an airline company — small single- and double-engine planes that serve Alaskans like taxis, and are an important part of the state's commercial life. Her father is one of the state's leading businessmen — an "old" Alaskan, politically conservative, a man who has indeed, as his children have sensed, entertained serious notions of "pulling out." It is an expression Pam uses often; she too criticizes recent trends in the state, and wonders what will happen in the future. The father's doubts and misgivings have become influential enough to cause the girl more apprehension than he or his wife had anticipated. They reprimanded Pam, told her to let them do the worrying about Alaska, while she attends to growing up to be "a good girl." But Alaska is becoming "bad," Pam muses rather too often; and she worries that everyone, herself included, will get caught up in the "badness," just as the Eskimos have.

She has become quite interested in the Eskimos, has worried about their fate as if it were her own. Her parents have tried to dampen that concern, too, but without success. Pam keeps referring to Eskimos when she talks, ostensibly, about her own life: "My Daddy says the Eskimos lived by themselves and they were different. They were very nice and polite. They liked to have visitors. My mother and Dad used to go to Eskimo villages, and they would come back and say that the Eskimos are the best people in the world, much better than white people. But it's all gone now — the way Eskimos used to live. According to our teacher in school, the Eskimos want more money. According to my father, they want to be like all the white people who are coming up here. They eat canned food and frozen food, instead of hunting and fishing, like they once did. They sit around all day, waiting for their welfare checks, or for the money they're getting from the oil companies. They're always trying to get more out of the state of Alaska. When the Eskimo goes sour, my Daddy says, it's the worst thing you can ever want to see. Some of them talk as though all they want is to become as rich as the white man. When they do, they won't be Eskimos any more. They'll be welfare bums and loafers; that's what my father says they're turning into.

"I don't agree with my father — that there's no hope. The Eskimos we know are very nice. An Eskimo lady named Mary helps in the house. We've gone to her village and met her people. They are very good people. They would give you the shirt off their backs, my father says. They can't be *all* bad! They still go fishing; I saw the salmon drying in the sun. They go hunting too. But they are on welfare, like Daddy says. And Mary says she's as worried about her own people as Daddy is; she says the village is beginning to fall apart — because people are fighting a lot with each other. She says that the more the Eskimo gets from the white man, the less the Eskimo thinks of himself — and it's no good when you don't think good of yourself."

When Pam was younger she was friendly with Mary's daughter, a year her junior. She even spent several weeks with the daughter's family "back in the village." A grandmother was taking care of the daughter while Mary took care of Pam and her family. When the mother went home on vacation, Pam asked to go with her — she was seven — and the maid said yes. At the age of ten Pam still remembered with pleasure the experience, but wondered whether Mary had, in fact, assented as willingly and enthusiastically as had seemed to be the case. Maybe she was "pretending." Maybe she was "afraid to say no to Mum." Maybe Eskimos are "like that" — traditionally hospitable to a degree and in ways surprising to white people. Pam realizes she will never really be able to find out how the maid felt then, or feels now, three years later: "She has to be nice, I guess."

Rather than talk about Mary, about Eskimos, about Alaska,

Pam has often tried to draw or paint people, places, scenes. She is an eager, industrious artist; she has for a long time enjoyed looking at the world, or inward, for that matter, and then using crayons or paints to indicate what she sees or considers important. Her first drawing of Mary was done at the age of seven, just before the trip to the village. The woman's face is enigmatic, virtually featureless: two circles for eyes and that is all. The emphasis is on the chunky body (true to life) and the sturdy hands. The woman has a broom in her right hand, but is given no world to be part of. (Figure 29.) A year later she was shown taller, thinner, with a nose and mouth as well as eyes, and leaning against a wall. To her left and right are small wall pictures. She stands in a room. Outside there is a sky, a sun, some dirty snow. (Figure 30.) How better to show snow, the artist asks as she works, than to let some mud get worked into it? Pam wants to make sure that the viewer understands where her subject is — in an Eskimo home, and not a quite well-off Anchorage estate, owned by one of Alaska's most influential businessmen. Outside the room one sees salmon drying, and some husky dogs. Neither is to be found near Pam's home.

At the age of ten she draws Mary with great care and delicacy. She seems to be a thoughtful, introspective person. Her eyes are large, the pupils with a slightly downward and sideward direction. She is still a bit heavy, but carries her weight with a good deal of grace. She has nothing in her hands; they are clasped in front of her. Beside her is a chair. She is in the artist's home, because the chair is one of her favorites, a sturdy straight-back wooden one in her bedroom, on which she often places her pants or a blouse. Through a large window one views the sea. There are fine curtains to set the window off. (Figure 31.) The girl has this in mind: "She is in my room, thinking. I can see her standing there. She is all alone. She has fixed the bed and cleaned up after me. She has done what I should have done myself. She is not annoyed. She is thinking of her village — her husband and her four sons and her daughter. She loves the boys. She not only loves her daughter but thinks of her often. I will see her looking out the window, and I know what is in her mind — *who* is in her mind. I like her daughter too. I've wondered a lot of times what it would be like to be her daughter. The maid has told me that her daughter thinks of me. The maid believes our thoughts meet in the sky, halfway between here and where her daughter is.

"One day we were talking, and Mary seemed not to be listening to me. I was telling her that I'd like to go home with her again, the way I did a few years ago; and I said it would be nice if I could convince my mother that when I came back I would come back with my Eskimo friend. Suddenly the maid went to the window and looked out, and she saw a cloud in the sky. She called me over. She pointed to the cloud. She said the sky has been clear all morning, but now there was this one big cloud, and she was sure it was my mother's voice speaking to both of us, saying no. I didn't catch what she meant. I laughed, because I thought she was trying to be funny. But she was serious, and she didn't like my attitude. She lowered her head; I knew that means she doesn't want to talk anymore. I told her I was sorry. Then she explained to me that my mother wouldn't want me to come home with 'just anybody.' I didn't say anything. I felt a little sick to my stomach. I told the maid that I had to go get some ginger ale, because I wasn't feeling well, and I left."

She drew a picture of Mary's daughter a month or so afterward, along with a self-portrait. The Eskimo girl is shown standing near a husky dog, and is scarcely taller than the dog, a serious underestimate of her height. She is in life smaller than Pam, but only an inch or two; and the artist was about four feet ten at the time she made the drawing. The figure drawn is curiously fragile, not at all like the solid, slightly obese girl of real life. Her right arm and hand hang close indeed to her body, but her left hand reaches toward the dog, as if to pat it, maybe to be linked with it. The sky is cloudy, the sun immersed in clouds. A sled is placed near the dog but is over-shadowed by a snowmobile, which actually dominates the en-tire picture. The girl's features are small, unremarkable. The artist comments, as she finishes her work, that "it may start snowing soon, and the girl will have to go inside, and stay there for a long time." There is no house in the picture, however. The artist wonders: ought she construct one? She readies her-self to do so, has reservations, surveys the scene. Where? How big? She decides to draw the house on another piece of paper, then link the two with Scotch tape. (Figure 32.) She does so. The house is quite small, almost a doll's house — or a dog's house — when viewed beside the earlier drawing. That is to say, the house is no bigger than the child or the animal nearby. And the house is given no distinctive features; it comes across as ramshackle and unadorned. The pine trees that are near the house in real life are missing. So is a wooden boardwalk con-structed to give some relief from the mud of the spring thaw. No neighboring buildings are shown, even though the artist surely knows they exist. The impression is one of desolation, abandonment — a miniature building surrounded by mud under no sky, all alone, almost unapproachable, certainly un-desirable.

When the maid saw the picture, she said nothing, smiled tactfully, asked quietly what the season was, and upon being told (the spring) wondered what had happened to the potted plants placed in the ledge of the front window once the sun came in strength. The girl, of course, had forgotten. She made a motion to add the plants, but was told not to do so by the maid. No point paying attention to someone else's ideas for a picture; best to leave it as it is. Pam felt the observation as a reprimand, apologized, and rather quickly turned to a self-portrait. She gave no evidence of being shy about herself or modest when connecting what she was drawing to what the future would offer her. Her picture of herself was done with obvious care, relish, and precision. She filled an entire piece of paper with herself. She went to the mirror once to look at herself before beginning in earnest. She worked slowly — at times, it seemed, hesitantly. She was anxious to give her face just the right expression, her hair just the right color; and, too, she wanted a certain dress on herself — her favorite, purchased from San Francisco by mail.

As she was finishing (Figure 33) she started talking about that dress and, soon enough, a number of other matters: "I like that dress, because it has a lot of color in it, and orange is my favorite color. The dress makes me think of the sun. We miss the sun here in the winter; but we get a lot of it in the summer. My father says he wonders whether we all shouldn't leave Alaska and go to the South Sea Islands — some place like Tahiti, only that place has become like this state: the tourists. The worst thing is the bums who've come up here to loaf and collect welfare, and the crooks, from the Mafia, who are making millions of dollars from the oil companies. Everyone working on the pipeline has to pay some money to the union; and the union is controlled by the Mafia — it's the teamster's union. I hear Daddy tell Mom that he feels like taking all his money out of the bank and getting a compass and spinning it, and wherever it ends up pointing to, we would go there. But if it pointed straight north, we couldn't go live near the North Pole.

"I don't think Daddy really means everything he says. He just sold a lot of land, and he put the money away in a trust fund he's set up; but not all the money, I just remembered, because he went and bought some more land. And he's building a movie house, and he's building a shopping center, so he hasn't given up on Alaska. My mother says he never will — he just gets annoyed, because it used to be one kind of life up here, and now there are so many more people, and Daddy doesn't like a lot of them. I think I'll stay here, too. It used to be that I dreamed of living in California, where my favorite dress was made. I had books about California and a map of the state. I knew a teacher who came from Los Angeles, and she told me to go live there. I knew a friend of my mother's who once lived near San Francisco, and she told me to go live there. But they both are living in Anchorage! I asked them why, and they told me. They just live here! I do too! I guess I always will. I'll travel, I hope, but I'll come back in the end. Mary and her daughter — they don't even think of leaving Alaska. They probably don't know any other place to live. But I don't think the maid and her daughter are unhappy about much. The maid says she'd like to be at home more, but she could be there all the time if she wanted.

"She doesn't like to leave us, she says — even for a day or two. She worries about how the house will look when she comes back. She always tells us, when she returns, how nice it is to be back working for us. I think she's got used to our house. Her own house isn't as nice and she likes her room in our house. Daddy says her husband drinks a lot. Mum says a lot of the Eskimos drink but they don't know how to drink, that's the trouble. It's too bad. They can't stop. Our maid told me once that when she looked at my parents drinking, she could hardly believe it — they take a glass of beer or wine, and then they eat. Even when they drink whiskey, they stop after one or two glasses, and eat. Her husband empties one bottle then another, until he falls on his face. Maybe that is why she

doesn't want to live at home. She says her old mother is the
only one who is not afraid of the man. I'm sure all our maid's
children have learned to stay away from him. Daddy says
Eskimos aren't smart enough to handle their liquor. They're
nice people, but they don't know how to build cities and airplanes and pipelines and steamship boats and bridges and
automobiles and shopping centers. We should have left them
alone. They don't know how to live in the white man's world.
They have no ambition; I think that's the problem. But they
are good people. I remember the vacation I had in the Eskimo
village. Everyone was very good to me. Everyone smiled and
tried to be nice to me. It's too bad about the Eskimos. They
may just disappear."

At twelve Pam herself occasionally talked of disappearing.
Hawaii became attractive to her. She argued constantly with
her mother and father. They did not like her "sloppy" appearance. They also did not like her friends — "a fast crowd," in
her mother's words. It was not only the onset of adolescence
that bothered her parents — the girl's increasing independence, her interest in rock music and in older boys who were
fast motorcycle drivers. Pam's "ideas" began to change, and
even upon occasion became defiant. She kept asking her parents why the Eskimos and the Athabaskan Indians are so poor.
She accused the white man of treating the state's native people meanly, even brutally. She praised the natives at every
opportunity, much to the consternation and increasing annoyance of her parents, who regarded the Eskimos as foils of their
daughter's — a means by which she could, by indirection, ac-
cuse her mother and father and others like them of wrong-
doing.

For the girl, increasingly a young lady, it was a quite different story: "I can't talk to my parents very much these days.
They want me to behave like a little child. I'm growing up. I

can talk with Mary. She understands how I feel. Now *I* know how *she* feels. My parents treat *her* like a child. They order her around and she is always trying to please them. She's as old as my mother, but I was brought up to think of her as my age. It's all wrong, the way the white people treat the Eskimos. I'm not trying to blame the whole world's problems on my parents. They say I am, but I'm not. I just feel sorry for our maid and for the other Eskimos I see here in Anchorage — or in Fairbanks. I've gone up there with my father, and you see them coming out of bars, and standing in the street, and they look so sad. They weren't meant to look sad! They're a happy people. I know; I've stayed in an Eskimo village, and I thought they were happier than all the rich white people like us here in Anchorage. But even in the villages the Eskimos are changing. They're becoming more like us whites, I'm afraid."

Pam began to be afraid of the tension that was developing between her and her parents. They threatened to send her away to school. They weren't sure where, actually, to enroll her. They only knew that their daughter was far too angry, and that even Mary was getting worried about the girl. It was the maid who somehow brought Pam and her parents together. Mary was the one Pam never stopped trusting. The maid could get Pam to dress as the parents wished, to go to church with them, to eat properly. Eventually the mother and father talked with the maid about their daughter, and soon thereafter Pam and Mary once again went to the latter's village home for a week's vacation. Upon their return Pam was quieter, less combative. Her parents were stunned: a miracle. What magic had the maid summoned? But Mary, when questioned, was perplexed. All she had done was enjoy Pam's company. They had had no soul-searching talks. Yes, a remark or two; Pam had turned on Anchorage's white people, and the maid had said that there are good and bad people everywhere.

But mostly Pam had enjoyed an early spring out on the tundra — the delicious and surprising warmth, the sudden burst of flowers and insect life.

Pam's version of the visit was similar. They had a "relaxed" few days, she kept on saying, whereupon the parents would suggest more visits. But Pam never wanted to return to the maid's village. She had in fact felt great pity for the people there, and a melancholy kind of resignation — a sense of the doom facing a people. But Mary had told her not to blame others, not to turn on the white people as the devils: "She told me that it's up to her people. Either they stand up and figure out how to live in Alaska, now that it's changing, or they don't. I began to see that you can't just call one person bad and another good. Anyway, I felt uncomfortable up there with the Eskimos. They're different from white people. I decided when I came home that I should stop giving my parents such a hard time. They're good to me. I'd rather be their daughter than our maid's, even though I love Mary a lot. Up in that Eskimo village I realized how lucky I am, living here in Anchorage in a home like mine. I guess I'm just a spoiled kid! I think our maid has known that for a long time! She told me once, a few years ago, that she often wished her kids could live the way I do. And I've been ungrateful; I've turned on my own parents. They have their faults, but so do all people. The Eskimos want to live like we do. Maybe we should help them to improve themselves. My father says that's the answer."

At the age of thirteen Pam prevailed upon her father to give the maid's village a gift of $100,000, so that a better sewage disposal system could be constructed. He pressured the state government to add much more for the same purpose. And he set up a scholarship fund for the village: five Eskimo children can, one day — if they finish high school — attend any college in the United States. His daughter fervently hopes one of them

will be Mary's daughter. Pam even hopes that one day she and
the maid's daughter will meet in a college, will become good
friends. Unfortunately, the maid keeps reporting bad news:
her daughter doesn't like school; her daughter gets sick every
day she goes to school; her daughter (at twelve) only enjoys fast
snowmobile rides, beer, and music so loud and unnerving that
the younger children start crying when it is played. It is only
a "stage," the thirteen-year-old Pam constantly told Mary in
reassurance. She would then add: "Look at me, how I've already outgrown that stage." She had indeed; she was becoming quieter, more sedate, more fashion-conscious *(Vogue, Mademoiselle)*, more ambitious academically and socially. But
Mary was not convinced, and the months, the years, have
proven her to be right in her skepticism.

PART FIVE

IN, NEAR, AND OUTSIDE THE CITIES OF THE NORTH

I

YOUNG PATRIOT

HOUSEKEEPERS, a parade of them, have taken care of the boy; and he, in return, has been grateful. When he was seven he asked his mother what she would do if there were no more successors to be found for the housekeeper about to leave. When a successor was indeed found, but only stayed eight months, the boy wondered whether finally his mother would throw her hands in the air, as she said she would, and take care herself of the boy and his sister. But no; within a week there was a new "lady." The children, a year apart in age, refused to call her by her name, or by any name, for three months. Finally, she asked the boy Richard (he was never called Dick at home) to use her name, Charlotte — *please.* He said yes, he would try to oblige; but he did not say yes, Charlotte, when he assented. Two months later Charlotte was gone. Richard told his sister, Sally, that he was just about ready to use Charlotte's name — but he was glad that a certain skeptical side of him had held off. But when Charlotte left he drew a picture of her — on a broom. He was being mischievous, and a touch insolent — so his mother said.

The broom took up most of the page, a long black stick, with black bristles at the end. Charlotte was perched on its upper region, a bit awkwardly and ponderously, as if she knew quite well she would not stay there for long. She was given no pointed hat, no cape. She was not explicitly called a witch. She was allowed no features save small eyes. Her blond hair was made longer and fuller — the wind, no doubt. Her feet dangled noticeably. Her hands held on tight. She flew over no land, under no sky, with no sun to warm her. She was just there, suspended, on that rather large piece of paper. Nor would her portraitist say much about her, save to identify her all too pointedly by name: Charlotte, he printed under the picture. (Figure 34.) Shown the picture by the boy, the mother became stern, reprimanding. Then she asked why Charlotte's name had finally surfaced. The boy had no immediate answer, but five or so minutes after the conversation had turned elsewhere, he told his mother that he ought to have drawn pictures of all the housekeepers, and identified them, so that he would have a record of the various people who had taken care of him and his sister. His mother, hurt and troubled, asked once again why he had put "a nice woman" on a broomstick. The boy had no reason; he "just did it." The matter was thereupon dropped.

Richard at eight was pronounced "very bright." He was ahead of his class in reading, but he was especially precocious in arithmetic and in "analytic ability." The parents were called in to the small private school the boy attended and told that he could easily be moved into the fourth grade. They decided against doing so. They wanted their son, a little small for his age, to keep his friends and not be overwhelmed by classmates much bigger, much more adept socially. Not that Richard was a shy or difficult child. He had begun to ski rather well by the time he was eight. He could skate rather well, too. He knew how to play soccer. He rode his bike fast and adroitly. He could ride his pony — trotting, cantering, with great enjoyment and competence. He could swim, and was moving nicely along from category to category in the Red Cross swimmers' course. He had even on his own initiative swung a tennis racket now and then, not with any great success, but as a sign of a future willingness to take the sport seriously. And he had friends; they came over to build with Lego, to construct model airplanes or boats, to play with soldiers, to play *as* soldiers, to run and shout and pretend and watch television. The boy worried about losing those friends, going into a higher grade where he would know no one and as a result feel rather peculiar. His father had observed that new friends would be made soon enough. But his mother had her doubts, and she had the final say.

They live in a town "well outside" and to the west of Boston. It is a town where corporation lawyers, doctors, businessmen live; where the stockbrokers tend to be middle-aged and older, the advertising men senior members in a firm. The town is thinly populated, the homes surrounded by considerable acreage. Many of the business and professional people have what the town's store clerks often refer to as "inherited money." One day Richard heard a clerk in a drugstore use that expression in connection with his parents and asked them later if indeed it was an accurate assertion. The father said he was surprised that anyone would "gossip" that way; the mother said perhaps the boy had misunderstood what was being said. Neither said a word more on the subject. The boy held his ground, insisted that he was not in the slightest mistaken about what he heard, nor had he really felt in the presence of a gossip — rather, a "nice lady" who admired his family because of its money.

Richard has in fact learned to value the meaning of money. He gets twenty cents a week allowance; it is always two dimes — never, for lack of change, a quarter. His father gives him the money and, with it, often a lecture: "Daddy wants me to know how to manage money. That's what he does all day. He's a vice-president of a bank, a big one, in Boston. He knows how to make a trust for people, so they can save money for their kids. He's set up one for me and one for Sally. We don't get the money until we're twenty-five. Even then we only get half! Daddy says it takes a long time to know how to spend money right. I like to spend money; that's the trouble. Our mother will buy us things and charge them; then Daddy has to pay the bills. He gets upset. I've heard him say we're all spendthrifts, including Mother. She taught Sally and me what the word means. I told one of my friends that I'm a spendthrift, and he told me that's what his father says about *his* mother and him! His father is rich, really rich. He owns half the city of Boston, my father says; only he's kidding. My friend's father owns a company that makes electronic stuff, and he also has a lot of property that was left him by his father. I think they've had a lot of money for a long time."

Richard had a savings account opened in his name at the age of seven — "the age of reason," his father told him. By the time the boy was eight he had the sum of eighty-four dollars to his name — small gifts given him at Christmas, Easter, on his birthday. He was anxious at that age to boost the amount to an even hundred. Then he would be "in the three-figure range," his father had told him. Richard kept telling people that when he got in that range, he'd look forward to reaching "the four-figure range." But he knew the climb would be steep and hard, a far slower ascent than the one he'd nearly made at eight. Sometimes, when asked about his extraordinary mathematical skills, he would attribute them to his father's interest in figures, in sums of money. But his father did not like that explanation, nor did his mother. The boy found out from them exactly why: "My parents say it's in the blood — that I was 'born with a good head,' that's what they tell me. Maybe

I'll be a scientist. Next year I'll be nine, and I'll know even more about numbers, and about science. We have a good teacher, who shows us the different kinds of trees and leaves. We've learned how to tap a maple tree and make syrup. I've been reading a lot about ants, the colonies they live in. I told my father I wouldn't mind studying science, and being a teacher of science, like the man who teaches us. My father said he's a good man, but you make very little money teaching in a school, even ours — and it's private, and it has a lot of money in the bank, I think. My uncle — my father's younger brother — teaches astronomy in a college, and my father says it's a good thing my grandfather left each of his children a trust fund. (It's in the six figures, my mother told us.) I told Daddy I don't want to live like a rich man. If I wanted to study the stars, and teach, I'd go ahead and become a professor, like my uncle. Daddy says it would be okay; but he said my uncle needs his trust fund, because you don't make too much money if you're a college teacher. Daddy has warned Sally and me that the money will run out one of these days, so we've got to make some for ourselves."

As the boy has read about ants, or about various mammals or birds, he has wondered out loud whether man needs money. Don't birds know how to care for their young, get food, find respite, move from place to place, without money? Don't ants build "cities," labor hard on behalf of a particular community, without money? Is it not true that families of lions and tigers get on amicably without money? Such questions, addressed to his father mainly — occasionally to his mother — elicit what the boy has come to call "lectures." The parents, without hesitation or embarrassment, use the same word to describe their attempts to teach the boy or his sister "the hard facts of life." Money is what human beings have used for centuries, Richard has been told — and there is no point in comparing the way animals live and the way human beings live, or in trying to judge man invidiously through descriptions of the natural world. In case the boy has any doubts about the importance of money, his parents oblige with aphorisms. He has heard that "without money people go hungry," and that "without money people can't do much in the world," and that "without money people can't buy anything."

The boy finds such a (penniless) life unimaginable. How do the poor live, he wonders; and has wondered out loud. His father has told him; has recited grim stories of bellies that hurt, because they are empty, of homes that go unheated in the middle of the winter, of children without toys or games, without books, without even the barest minimum of clothes. The boy has wondered what such people *do*. Surely they don't just sit and suffer. That is the point, the father replies; a lot of them do just that — experience hardship and more hardship. Why? The boy uses the word often: why, why, why? His parents earnestly try to provide answers, but sometimes their patience wears thin or they feel troubled, even enraged, by the new questions that the answers seem to prompt. Richard remembered, at the age of nine, one rather tense and eventually frightening conversation with his parents and his sister: "They kept telling Sally and me how lucky we are to live where we do. I asked whether there might be some kids who wouldn't want to live here. My father said no, any kid in the world would 'thank his lucky stars' to be here. I said that even if the parents of a kid lived in a bad place, and they didn't have any money, the kid would still rather stay with his parents than come out here and live with us. Daddy said sure, but it's no kind of life, living in a slum. He said some parents who are very poor give their children up, because there's no food for them. I asked him why we don't get some of those kids and have them come here and live with Sally and me. He said there isn't

the room, and he and our mother have enough to do bringing
up Sally and me.

"That's when I got them mad, I think. I said we had all these
extra guest rooms, and they had beds in them, and there are
two bathrooms we don't use. Why couldn't some kids stay
here? We could feed them, and give them clothes. Mother
throws away a lot of our clothes. She sends a lot of our clothes
to the church, and they send them to the poor people. We
could give the clothes directly to the poor people. Dad told me
to stop talking like a fool. Sally said I wasn't talking like a fool.
I said it wasn't fair for us to have so much and a lot of people
to have nothing. That's when Mother told both Sally and me
to leave the table to go up to our rooms. Sally started to cry.
I didn't know what to do; but seeing her cry got me upset, and
I just forgot myself, and I raised my voice at Mother and said
she was just saying she agreed with Dad, but she really didn't.
Daddy told me to shut up. I began crying."

Later there was a "family conference," and apologies given
all around. Richard was especially repentent. He had been
rude, even insolent. He had been ungrateful; his parents have
given him a lot, and he wanted to turn their home into a
boardinghouse or an asylum. Two years later, at the age of
eleven, he still remembered that incident; it was one of the
crucial ones in his childhood. As time separated him from the
actual experience he became harsher on himself, even contemptuous of the very arguments he had set forth so pointedly
and unnervingly. His parents had told him the next day that
they admired his "generosity" and were sorry they had become so angry at him, when he was only trying to "be nice."
But the more they saw his behavior that way, the more he
turned on himself with an increasingly fierce critical eye. Casual remarks his mother and father had made about the poor
— their lack of initiative or self-regard and, often, their "lazi-

ness" — became for him guideposts in the beginning of an
ideological journey. He became a young, vocal conservative,
quick in elementary school to express opinions on the nation's
fiscal crisis, its dangerous leftward drift, its awful struggle with
the "welfare mess."

At ten, in the fifth grade, Richard wrote a paper on George
Washington and his achievements as our first President. The
military victories were enumerated all right, but the paper's
hidden agenda turned out to be different: "It seems to me that
we have lost George Washington's beliefs. He didn't offer
bribes to the people, if only they would join his army and fight.
He had no money to pay them. They fought under him for
nothing. They fought because they believed in their cause. In
the old days people were willing to sacrifice. Now everyone
wants all he can get from the government, and he doesn't care
if he works or not. A lot of people don't even want to work.
All they want is someone else's money. I think that if George
Washington was alive today, he'd be surprised, and he'd be
very disappointed in this country."

He received an A for the paper, with a comment of strong
approval from his teacher, who told the boy several times
during the year that he did not "always agree" with him, but
he admired his forthrightness, his willingness (and ability) to
state "a strong viewpoint." Later in the year Richard wrote a
paper on aircraft carriers — their history and the way they
have been used in specific battles. His father has read widely
in military history and his books were of enormous help (and
fascination) to the boy. The boy had too much to say; he felt
paralyzed, could not begin the composition. Finally his father
told him to forget about all he'd learned, and begin with an
idea — or with a personal statement. The boy did so: "A lot of
people in this country don't want us to build aircraft carriers.
Without them we'd be very weak."

Richard got an A on that paper, too. He brought to school the three aircraft carriers he had built; he was fast and competent with models, had made dozens of them. When asked in class by a student who our enemies were — whom the aircraft carriers might one day fire upon — the boy was by no means at a loss for words: "I answered, the Russians; and maybe the Chinese, and the Cubans, too; they're the communists, and they're jealous of us. They want to beat us. Then they'd be first in the world, and they'd have all our money. We have to be strong, or else we'll end up being beaten in a war." No one pursued the argument. At home his father did: "My Dad said we might be able to sit down and do business with the Russians. They are afraid of us, so they want to talk. That's why the President is talking with them. But you never can tell; the Russians might be up to some trick. Why should we trust them? If they've been bad for a long time, why would they suddenly turn good? They could be laughing at us, and thinking we're real suckers. The President should tell them we're not afraid of them, and we're ready to fight, if they want trouble. The trouble would come if we let down on our spending for guns and boats and planes; then we'd be in no position to argue with them, because they'd just laugh at us and tell us we're silly fools, and we've let ourselves get weak, and we're a pushover, so we can't bargain, we just have to surrender. That would be the end of America. It's scary to think what might happen."

At eleven Richard was precocious enough in math to be given the most advanced of high school algebra and geometry. He had learned how to use a computer. He was doing quite well in English and history. He was seemingly headed for Harvard, where his father and grandfather and great-grandfather had gone. He had enrolled in a "public speaking" course, and was doing quite well in it. He still remembered the incident years ago when he and his parents had a brief but painful philosophical as well as psychological confrontation. As a matter of fact, he was presumptuous enough to believe that the confrontation was not an unusual one — reason enough for him and others who shared his beliefs to feel "scary" about "what might happen." Richard viewed his passing concern for and infatuation with the poor as a representative experience; millions felt and continue to feel the same way. He had soon come to his senses, unlike many others. The country will go broke, in time, unless it begins to understand that (as he put it when he was nearly twelve) "you can't just print money and hand it out to everyone on the street, and tell them to go home and spend it, and forget about working."

He tried to practice in his twelfth year — and others that followed — what he preached. He had become a frugal person, an active, energetic youth. He studied hard and never allowed himself what he called "shortcuts." He was not satisfied with doing minimum assignments; he often consulted books at home, wrote longer papers than required, delved into matters of history, mathematics, or language on his own, and upon occasion at great length. He was good at sports. He would eventually become captain of the school's soccer team. And not least, he had a strong interest in being of service to his community. He helped clean up litter in a conservation area used by the public. He accompanied his father in the door-to-door solicitations for the Community Fund. He and his sister assisted his mother in the Red Cross blood drive.

Most of all, though, Richard was an enthusiastic and successful Cub Scout, then Boy Scout. He won badge after badge, did well in contests, was an obvious leader. He loved to wear the Scout uniform, and for a while talked about going to West Point. When he was twelve it was no mere fantasy, or so he insisted: "I'd like to go to West Point. I want to go in the army.

My father was in the navy, but I like the army. I could become a general someday, if I worked hard. When you get out you're a second lieutenant; then you keep getting promoted, if you do your job well: first lieutenant, captain, major, lieutenant colonel, full colonel, and then general. There's brigadier general, major general, lieutenant general, and full general. There's also General of the Army, but only a few generals have been that: MacArthur, Eisenhower, and Bradley, I believe. Maybe there were one or two others. President Eisenhower wasn't only in charge of American troops; he was the Supreme Commander during the Second World War. If you go to West Point you learn how to be a leader. You study the battles other leaders fought, all through history. It used to be that everyone wanted to go to West Point. Now some people are against it; they want to cut down our army and navy and air force. Then we'll be a fifth-rate power. But I don't think they'll win. This country won't just collapse like that. I told my father yesterday that I'm *definitely* going to West Point. He said okay, but he said I should wait and see how I feel a few years from now: I might change my mind. I told him no, I wouldn't.

"I could do a lot in the army. They need people who are good at math and in science. If you're really loyal to the country and you want a good career, the army has a lot of good jobs. I went with our Scout pack to an army base, and they showed us a film about the army. An officer spoke to us; he was a captain. He said there wasn't a better life anywhere than the army life. You get to travel all over the world, and you learn a lot of things you'd never learn in any other profession. Every once in a while I think I might like the air force. I love to fly; we go on vacations, and the best time is on the plane. But I'm too interested in battles, and in the air force, you're either a pilot or it's no fun, and there aren't the battles you have in the army, only dropping bombs, or sometimes a fighter plane fights with the enemy's fighter planes. But the great thing is to be in charge of a lot of soldiers. You've got to be able to outmaneuver the enemy. It's your brains against the enemy's. And you've got all your men to think about. If you don't do your job well, they'll be in trouble and a lot of them will die, and you'll lose. But if you're smart, and you study your maps, and figure out what the enemy is likely to do, and beat him to the punch, then you'll win, and you're protecting your country that way."

He has never quite forgotten the poor, however; and so when he talks about the advantages and occasionally the outright glories of army life, he thinks of the millions of poor in America whom he hears his father call "a drain on the economy." Why, he wonders, aren't such people — many of them, at least — drafted into the army? Then they would be fed and clothed and sheltered. Then they would no longer be poor; they would be paid a salary. *And* they would at last be doing something constructive for their nation, rather than depleting its resources. He was not just engaging in idle speculation. The Congress would have to pass a law, he knew; and that would not be easily done, because "the liberals" control both houses. But if there were "a good President," maybe he could keep going on television; each time he would show the people how sensible the idea was, how much money the country would save — "no more welfare" — and how much stronger we'd be, militarily, in the bargain.

Eventually, he hoped, voters by the millions would be won over, and for the first time in a long time the country would be "on the right path." He uses that expression with no intent to describe a conservative direction. He is a twelve-year-old boy who is brimming with intense idealism; who worries about a nation he deeply loves — a nation to which he wants to give his working life — and who is very much afraid that "the good side" in America is in danger of losing to "the bad side." The path he referred to, the "right" one, stands in contrast, as he views it, to the "wrong, wrong one." The repetition of the adjective is quickly followed by a brief and dire analysis: "The country is in a lot of trouble, and the people in the army are worried sick. The captain told us that if we don't watch out, we'll be in a war we can't possibly win, because we're ruining our army by cutting back on the money it needs to buy the best possible weapons. That would mean the end of the United States. We wouldn't be the country we are anymore. There'd be a communist dictatorship, that's what we'd have. It's only the army and the air force and the navy that stand between us and communism. But a lot of people don't want to sit down and face the facts. That's how the captain ended his talk to us."

At thirteen Richard was not so sure about West Point. He had talked with his paternal grandfather about a military life, and had been discouraged by the old man, who had been a colonel in the Second World War. The army is important, the boy heard, but so is a profession like law, and so is banking. The grandfather is a retired banker. His father was also a banker. Richard would be the fourth in a direct family line to be a banker, were he to choose that career. The grandfather had often suggested to him a joint career in law and business: international banking, perhaps. The boy had been going into his father's office for several years during school vacations. He knew how to read the financial pages of the newspapers at the age of nine. He knew a lot at about the same age — which stocks are "strong" and which are "risky." He was no stranger to the Dow Jones average when he was eleven; he wrote a short composition about how that average is calculated. His stunning mathematical competence made his father and grandfather all the more anxious to have him join their profession. The boy was often called "a natural" for investment banking.

He had also, at eleven, drawn a picture of his father's place of work (Figure 35) described by the artist as "one of the best banks in America." There was no point drawing the inside, the boy pointed out; but the exterior was handsome and deserved recognition. He worked hard on the columns in front, tried to evoke a building's massive eminence. The name was carefully done, the windows also drawn with care. The sidewalk presented a bit of an obstacle; Richard felt that he had made it too narrow, and so doubled its size. He then decided to put some people in his drawing. They were given little attention, however. They came out as huddled figures, featureless, all in black, utterly insignificant in front of the building. A large American flag hung over them; it was as overstated as they were stunted or dwarfish. But there was one human being who was acknowledged quite lavishly — a policeman. He was in front of the building, tall and well armed and with large eyes, hefty arms, good-sized hands, long legs. He has one hand on a pistol, another hand on a club. He is poised for action, and necessarily so: "Without the police, the banks would have to hire their own guards. Even with the police, Daddy's bank has men who watch the bank, especially when they bring in money or take it away in the armored trucks. I rode in one of them. It's fun. There were guns all over. One of the drivers had been in the Korean War, and he'd got a medal for bravery. He told me about charging up a hill, and the machine guns were blasting away, and the Chinese outnumbered us ten to one. But he got to the top; we had our planes to bomb them out of their bunkers, and the tanks, too. He was wounded, and that was the end of his fighting. They brought him home, and he was in the hospital for a whole year, but he got better. Then he had trouble finding a job. But he got one, finally.

"I think there was an article about him in the newspaper — how he'd fought for the country, and almost got killed, and got the Purple Heart, but he wasn't able to find a job. I think it was then that Daddy's bank wanted to hire him. My grandfather says he remembers the story, but he wasn't in charge of employment. But he said the bank hired a lot of disabled veterans after each war we've been in. It's been a strict policy. My father says some veterans today aren't reliable — the ones from the war in Vietnam. The ones from the other wars are the best workers. There's a guard in the bank who fought in the Second World War, and he was decorated by General Eisenhower. And when General Eisenhower was elected President, the guard wrote to him and congratulated him and reminded him of the decoration; and President Eisenhower wrote the man a personal letter, on White House stationery. The man had it framed, and he says he could sell it for maybe five hundred dollars, but he never will. His wife had a bad disease, and she went into the hospital, and she was there for a long time, and she almost died. The man lost all his money, trying to pay the doctors and the hospital.

"Today the bank has a good insurance program, but I guess they didn't then. The guard told someone in the bank he was going to sell his letter from the President of the United States. My grandfather heard about it, and he paid the guard's bills from his own pocket. The newspapers wrote it all up; I've seen the story. My grandfather didn't want anyone to know, but a reporter found out. Guess what happened! Poor Granddaddy was flooded with letters from people all over the place who wanted him to pay for their medical bills, too. A lot of them were veterans, and they told him about all they'd gone through in the war, and now they had a sick wife or a sick kid. My grandfather thinks people these days are always looking for someone to bail them out of trouble. If they see that someone has had good luck, they want to cash in, and get the same favor done for themselves. It's not fair. The guard still apologizes to my grandfather and my father, because he says he's a proud man and he never has accepted any charity in his entire life, except for that one time. But my father has convinced him that it wasn't charity; it was the bank's duty to a man who was willing to give his life fighting for the country."

As for the picture he had drawn of the bank, Richard declared it to be "not good." It is hard, he insisted, for anyone, no matter how artistic, to draw a bank. The heart of a bank, after all, is the vault, where the money is. Perhaps he ought to have drawn that, rather than the exterior of the building. And there wasn't enough paper either. He had simply suggested what the front side of the bank looked like. There was a wing in the back that he could not show. Perhaps he ought to draw the armored truck; that would be fun. He starts doing so, and is quite happy with the project. (Figure 36.) He makes the wheels rather large — too large, he realizes — and works hard on the main body. Soon most of the paper is full. He decides to decorate the truck with an American flag, even though there isn't one to be seen in real life, and he jokingly adds to the sign "Brink's" a message: "Don't Try to Rob Me!" He has heard often about the Brink's robbery, which took place in Boston before he was born. His father claims there will never be another one, but his grandfather believes that "as long as there is money, there will be thieves who want to steal it, rather than work for it."

When the truck is done Richard decides to put it on the road, literally; he sketches a stretch of asphalt, then makes a sidewalk. He forsakes a sky, as he did with the picture of the bank. He contemplates putting up some buildings, but decides no; he will let the truck be alone, on a part of its travels where buildings are not to be seen. Perhaps he was mistaken, he muses, in putting up a sidewalk. Perhaps the truck is on a highway, outside the city. Perhaps it has even been headed toward *his* house! Why not! He has, in fact, asked his father quite often *why not*. Doesn't he own the bank? Well, if not own, then surely "just about own"? And if things are so dangerous in downtown Boston, if the crime rate is so high, and if the father is quite pleased indeed to be out of the city by four o'clock, before dark, then why not have an armored car, with an experienced guard or two at his disposal? Is he not important enough to warrant that kind of protection?

The father laughs, but not without an edge of apprehension. "The day may well come," he has told his son. "At the rate things are going," he has told his son, never actually finishing the train of thought. Richard has had to prompt him, get him to speak about his fears. Even their home is not safe, the boy knows. He is an authority, it so happens, on "alarm systems." As a banker's son, he is proud about all he has learned — the forms of protection the depositors get without knowing either the cost or the many details. He knows, too, about the dangers that people like his parents face, "out in the country." When he was thirteen he wrote a composition about his hometown and later talked about the composition, the teacher's attitude toward the composition, and, not least, his own attitude toward the teacher, as well as a number of other people: "I wanted to be nice to our town; but I had to face the facts, like my Daddy says you have to. This is a good town; the people here are good people. We're too easy, though, on the outsiders who come in here. Some of them work for us and take our money, then they go home and tell friends of theirs how rich we are, and we're easy targets for a robbery. That's what has been happening. They say in the paper that some of the vandalism is due to our own people, the teenagers. But the worst kind of robberies are different; a truck comes and the house is stripped of everything when the people are away. It's an inside job, my father says. Someone tips off the crooks.

"It's hard to trust the help these days. My mother asks for

three references; she used to ask for only one. She's really afraid when she has a big party and the caterers come and bring their own people to serve. She once joked with my father; she said she wanted some of his guards from the bank to come and help out, to keep an eye on the serving people. But my father said we might need someone to keep an eye on the guards. The younger guards aren't like the older ones! That's why we keep a lot of things locked up in our safe, down in the cellar. Not only the silver, but some gold watches my father has, and some rare dishes, and my mother's jewelry. And we put in the best alarm system there is. Let them try to rob us!

"In my paper I wrote about how the town was settled by people who liked living away from the city, and how the town slowly grew, and then we decided to stop it from growing, or else we'd have a big city out here, with ranch houses almost touching each other. My father is the chairman of the town's conservation board. He's made sure that we're all protected. But he doesn't like what's happening. Besides the robberies, there's a lot of drugs being used, and he thinks a lot of kids won't be the equals of their parents. He says he's lucky, because Sally and I are younger, and he hopes that by the time we're old enough to get into trouble, we'll be away in school. But we won't get in trouble. Dad says at times he thinks of moving away. He doesn't know where. He might decide for us to live all year around in our summer home on Nantucket, but mother says no, it's too far away. Dad says we could have an apartment in the city, too. If you have to worry about crime and drugs way out there, then you might as well live right in the middle of the city and watch every step you take, and at least you're near some good restaurants and the clubs, and you can walk to the symphony. My mother goes to the symphony on Friday afternoons, but she leaves early. She doesn't like to walk even a block in the city when it gets dark, but she thinks she could get used to doing it.

"The teacher didn't like my composition very much. She said I was too gloomy, and I was exaggerating the crime we have out here. She didn't write anything on my paper. She called me in for a conference. She said I was entitled to my opinion, and she thought I did a very good job of organizing my thoughts and saying what I believed. But she wanted me to know that there was another 'point of view.' She kept on repeating that there was my 'point of view' and hers, and I guess she was sure I was wrong. I didn't argue with her. I know what she thinks. She's a liberal. Dad says you can spot them a mile off; they're always worried about someone a thousand miles away. If their next-door neighbor's house is broken into, even if the robber kills someone, the liberal is worried about how good the prison is where the robber will be sent. I don't think some of our teachers really like this town; they try to preach to us about how we did a lot of harm to the Indians and to the black people. My father says it'll always be like that; there are people who are prejudiced against anyone who has tried to work hard and make some money, and prejudiced in favor of the people who don't care if they work or not, so long as they collect welfare."

He distinguishes himself from such people. He sounds smug and self-serving at times when he does so; but at other times he is more earnest and anxious than assured. Often he worries that he is going to become like "them," like the people his mother and father (especially the latter) so often criticize — the poor and their various apologists. He will be sitting in his room, tinkering with his shortwave radio or wondering whether he'll get the phonograph he requested for his fourteenth birthday, three months off, when suddenly he brings himself up short, starts charging himself with "laziness" or with "expecting too much for nothing." Those are the most severe reprimands he has heard his parents make, and though they have rarely, if ever, used the words against him, he has worried over the years about the possibility that one day it would come to such a pass. As a result, he makes sure that he keeps busy, and is applauded for doing so by his family.

His mother at times wishes he would be "a little more relaxed," but she also believes very strongly that "idle hands make for trouble." The boy helps clear the table, even though there is a live-in housekeeper to do the job. The boy rakes leaves, even though a "handyman" comes to the house every week. The boy sells Christmas candy, even though his parents give him an adequate allowance. The boy is very handy with tools, tries to fix things around the house. He also, at eleven, had learned how to put on and remove storm windows, clean gutters, and clip rose bushes. He has always loved riding his bike, and is anxious to go on errands. The housekeeper feels no hesitation asking him to go fetch bread or milk; he will likely as not ask her if she might possibly (he hopes) have a "bike errand" for him to do. And at thirteen the young man was determined to find a job when school was out; not for the whole summer (because the family goes away to Nantucket for a month, apart from weekends) but for "a few weeks, at least."

The modifier is not simply a casual or offhand phrase. There is a plaintive tone in the youth's voice as he speaks. He feels that he must indeed work — *at least* for a while. If he did not, he would be showing himself to be unworthy of the ideals his parents uphold: "My Dad tells me that if ever I decided to become a banker, he hopes I'll have held a lot of other jobs first. He says the worst thing that can happen to you is to be given a lot of money and be allowed to go spend it the way you want. That's what's wrong with the country; that's the whole problem of what's happening to America — that people don't know the value of money. Everyone wants to get money and spend it, but no one wants to work hard and really feel good about the money he's made, and save it and see it grow bigger each year. Then you hear a lot of complaints from people about how they haven't got any savings, in case of an emergency. Well, the reason is they haven't saved a cent, and then they complain that they've got nothing, and they want the government to step in and give them a lot of handouts — money they haven't earned. The country will go bankrupt if it pays out money that no one has earned."

He sounds arrogant at times, but he worries about himself. Is he yet another "spendthrift"? Ought he to stop asking his parents for several gifts on his birthday or Christmas, and instead settle for only one present at a time? Doesn't he, at times, spend his money too readily? And how many times has he gone to a ski camp or on a trip, or permitted his parents to buy him something he very much wanted, without giving a moment's thought to the amount of money involved?

At fourteen he was taken to meet the trust officer who was to manage his "six-figure" account. Richard's father had managed it for a long time, but decided to turn such a private and personal concern over to someone more detached. Richard wanted to meet the man, and so the lunch was arranged. They went to a private club, the same one Richard visited with his father for lunch. The boy said afterward that he had been enormously impressed with the trust officer and only hoped that he, young though he was, had at least managed to prove himself "serious." He had worried in recent months that he was not as "serious" as his father, or for that matter, the others who kept his father's bank "solvent." The boy had heard his father talk about the "struggles" bankers have, and had wondered whether he, Richard, would one day in the future be equal to those struggles.

Richard's father himself became increasingly concerned about the boy's self-critical side. As a result Richard was criticized for being too self-critical! He was told that he was actually quite conscientious and need not include himself in the company of those who are financially irresponsible. But his father's exoneration did not help much. The boy complained of headaches. The mother took him to the pediatrician, to an ophthalmologist. He was declared not only "healthy," but an "attractive" youth, who showed a great degree of interest in each doctor's speciality. The mother was a little concerned when she gathered from the pediatrician that Richard had told him he might himself want to be a pediatrician, and from the ophthalmologist that Richard could easily imagine becoming an "eye doctor" one day. But she reassured herself; she remembered that Richard had always been "enthusiastic," had always been "extremely eager" to be liked, to impress people.

When the headaches persisted, and the reassurance of the doctors was no longer of comfort, the mother went to her minister. She is a devout Episcopalian, and trusts her minister "more than anyone," except her husband, of course. The minister is middle-aged, and fortunately "a man of good judgment." He never allowed himself "to get caught up in all those crazy causes, in the 1960s." Now he is known, "even by the town's minority of liberals," as a wise person, chary of fads, and quite "introspective" in an old-fashioned way. He spent two hours with Richard's mother, and decided that he would like to talk with the young man — but not in such a way that "the treatment would be as bad as the illness." That is to say, he worried that he too would be seen by Richard as yet another exemplary person, not unlike his father, whose questions might well be taken all too personally. The meeting, accordingly, was arranged with great care. Richard was one of sev-

eral young people in the church whom the minister wanted
to talk with. Perhaps a young people's center might be set up,
for certain weekend hours, in the basement of the rectory.
When the meeting was over Richard was chosen to head a
committee that would pursue the subject further, and so there
were good reasons for the minister and him to talk at further
length.

After several "good talks," as the minister described them,
the mother was told that there was nothing to worry about,
that Richard was "just growing up very fast," that he had "a
strong conscience," and that sometimes those so "endowed"
are likely to be susceptible to headaches at "various points in
their lives." The mother was satisfied with the explanation; her
mind was "made easier." The boy was also quite pleased; he
developed yet another "interest." He was, by his own account,
"growing up"; and at fourteen it was proper for him to get to
know the minister. The church has meant a lot to his parents,
and will mean a lot to him, he hopes: "I like the minister, and
he has been very good to me. He's worried, just like my Dad
is, about the town. He thinks people don't believe in anything
— just in buying new cars and new houses and new boats. I
told him what my father said about money — how it's spent
before it's earned. The minister said he knows what my father
means — it's all due to 'materialism.' I didn't know what 'materialism' is, but he explained it to me. He said that it's the
worship of things instead of God; and people are 'materialistic'
when they worry too much about their clothes or their television sets. The minister said he tries to teach people to be
different in his sermons, but a lot of people don't listen the way
they should. There's a lot of competition between people, too.
When people compete too much, they grow to be enemies of
each other. That's how a lot of trouble begins.

"I told the minister that he was right. Even in my class at

school a lot of kids cheat, or they won't help anyone, because everyone wants to be on top. The teachers say we should 'cooperate,' but it's hard because everyone finds out the other person's grades, and you want to be first if it's possible. I try hard, and I'm in the highest third of the class, the teacher told my parents. The minister says we shouldn't even know our grades. I told him I'd still worry what my grades *are,* and he said yes, he could see what I mean. He's nice. I look up to him. I told him I wouldn't mind being a minister myself when I'm grown up, and he said he thought I'd make a good one, but he was sure I'd make a good banker, like my father, or a lawyer, like my uncle. He just makes you feel good, talking to him. It's not only what he says; it's the fact that he's a good person, and he smiles at you when he talks. My father says he's lucky, that minister; he has the time to talk with someone for a long time and he enjoys his work."

Richard's headaches went away within a few months. His mother was convinced that the minister was the one responsible, but the boy's father was not so sure. The boy was growing up, and his headaches were going away, and that was that — a matter of good luck. In the father's eyes the minister, for all his "moderate" social views and political principles, is somewhat suspect. He talks too much about hungry people in Africa, victimized people in South America, or, nearer home, the impoverished of Appalachia. At least he doesn't get himself involved directly in "controversial affairs," which for Richard's father have ranged from the civil rights struggle, the anti–Vietnam War protest, to the matter of fluoridation. On that last score Richard was quite well versed, even when he was nine years old. He had heard his parents talk about fluoridation, had been told what it was all about and why his parents opposed its implementation in their town. He had also been told that his dentist was in favor of the measure — another reason to fear and dislike the man. And he had been told that fluoridation was but a "part of a large puzzle," as his mother sometimes put it.

The boy had grasped by then what the nature of that puzzle was: "If you're free, that means you decide if you want your water pure or if you want the fluoridation. We have our own well. They can't put anything in our water. We don't have town water. My father says that's one of the best things about our house, that we don't have to draw on the town for water. He's been fighting against fluoridation because he doesn't think it's right. Why must anyone have something put in their water if they don't want it there? I'd be upset if all of a sudden I found out I wasn't drinking the same water I used to drink. Daddy says it's an invasion, only you can't call out the police or the army. We could always buy bottled water, that's what my mother keeps telling Daddy. As long as you have the money, you can get around the government. But Daddy says it's not fair, because there might be someone who doesn't have the money to go buy bottled water, but he'd still be against drinking the water that's gone through fluoridation. Dad says he wants to fight for other people, so that they can have the choice. Otherwise they're not free."

The word "free" has come over the years to mean a lot to Richard. He gave a talk on "freedom" to his fellow Boy Scouts, warning them that "almost anytime" they could lose their freedom. He was fourteen. He wrote a composition on "freedom," arguing that we don't "have" freedom, we "fight for it"; and it is a fight that has to be waged continuously. He was thirteen. The year before, he had written a brief but pointed letter to his congressman, complaining that "it's not fair when people don't try to take care of themselves, and they want to take away money from the rest of the people, who do try to stay free and take care of themselves." At twelve he was quite upset by what he'd heard his father say about "welfare" and what it was doing to the United States. He disagreed with a friend, who felt that there ought to be some black people in their town. Richard said no one has a right to be in the town; the only people who *should* live in the town, according to him, are the people who have freely chosen to live there — who have come and bought houses and pay taxes. He was eleven. He got into repeated mock wars with his friends, shooting at them wildly with cap guns or water pistols, calling them communists, saying they *are* dead, or should be dead, or will be, soon enough, given a few more bangs or squirts — from him, a free American. He was ten, or nine, or eight, or seven, or six, or five, or four.

A longtime, fighting anticommunist, he has also been quite knowing about why he fought mock battles as a younger child and what was at stake in those battles. When thirteen, and a bit removed from the kind of open, lawn warfare he had previously waged with friends, he was able to summon some perspective on his past efforts: "They'll be our enemies all my life, I know they will be: the communists. They own Russia and China and Cuba, and they own other countries. My father says when he was a boy they still played cowboys and Indians; but it's stupid to play that kind of game when the Indians and the cowboys aren't fighting now. We're in a war all the time against the Russians; even when there's no fighting, both sides have to be ready. If we begin to trust them, they'll invade us. It would be a bad war, and a lot of people would die.

"The communists have friends right here in Massachusetts. My father says a lot of the college teachers are procommunist. They aren't traitors, but they're not friends of his bank, and of the people who run our businesses. It's jealousy. People don't like others getting ahead. If the communists took over, we'd have a different country than the one we have. We wouldn't be free any more. They tell you what to think. They order you around. They close down the newspapers, and they have only the paper that the government runs. The government is everyone's boss. Whatever the government decides, you have to go along with. My mother knows a woman whose husband wrote a book about the communists; I think he is a professor in a college. He says that the communists want this country to get into real, bad trouble. They want the black people to fight against the white people, and the Indians to fight against the white people; and they want the army to be weak, and the air force not to have the planes it needs, and then when the country seems to be really falling apart, they'll invade us. That's why the communists took over Cuba; it's less than a hundred miles away from our land, and today a hundred miles is *nothing* — not with airplanes around, and missiles, and real fast ships.

"Sometimes I think I'm being selfish by not planning to go to West Point. There's nothing more important than defending the country. But Dad says not to worry; we'll win and you can't think only of a war. My mother says the next war may be the end of all of us; everyone could get killed. But that's probably not what will happen. The communists are cowards. They won't start a fight if they think we'll win. They only fight when they think *they'll* win. I try to win when I fight with my friends. I never take the communist side in a game. Some kids do. My father won't believe it when I tell him that a few of my friends don't care if I call them communists, and declare war on them, and fight them. They even tell their parents that they fought on the communist side and I was on the American side. Their parents don't mind! My father would never let me do that. I told him that someone has to take the communist side when we fight, but he said: 'Not you.' He said he never played an Indian, always the cowboy."

The boy has, in fact, despite his disavowal of the game, played a version of cowboys and Indians. When he went horseback riding, at eleven or twelve, he would imagine himself a cowboy, and peer into the nearby woods: any Indians hiding there? He would even take along a toy rifle and push it partially under his saddle. Every once in a while he would take the rifle out and make some noises that indicated he had seen a few Indians and killed them. When he came home, he would upon occasion be wistful: if only the communists were as easy to spot and shoot as the Indians must have been to our cowboys! The trouble with communists, he had come to learn, is their deviousness. They pretend to be interested in the plight of the black man, in the poor and the jobless, in the old and the vulnerable, even in such causes as fluoridation. Their real purpose is quite something else: the overthrow of our government. But how to spot them, arrest them? More generally, how to be a patriot, how to defend America against its internal enemies? Communists can't be shot, the way Indians once were. Communists are too "smart" for that, he has heard his father say many times. In fact, they are dangerously "smart" — and dangerously influential among those who are "smart": college professors and very bright college students and those who write books or work on television or on newspapers. Even a West Point graduate is helpless when the enemy doesn't use guns, but propaganda. That is why Richard would remind himself, as he grew older, that there are many ways to fight this latest enemy of America's, and his way — mastering the art of debate, speaking out at school, Scouts, church, and among friends — is as important as the soldier's way.

II

A BOY'S JOURNEY FROM LIBERALISM TO SOCIAL DARWINISM

I N THE same town, scarcely two miles from Richard's home, lives another boy of his age and first name. This Richard is the son of a specialist in internal medicine, a man with a professorial appointment at Harvard Medical School, a small but quite well-to-do private practice, and an abiding interest in cardiac research. The two Richards go to the same school and have come to know each other. They have debated. They have argued. They have fought during recesses. They are not "enemies," though — as both hasten to assure their parents. One Richard calls the other "Richard the red," but claims he is only "half serious"; the other Richard refers to his "dinosaur friend Richard" but insists that he is rather fond of the boy, and has to admire his outspoken honesty, and yes, his patriotism. They both belong to the same school band. The more liberal Richard has noticed the emotion his conservative classmate displays when a Sousa march is struck up, or when "America" or the national anthem gets played. It is strange for this Richard, called Dickey since he was a baby, to witness such emotion. The flag, the pledge of allegiance to it, or a patriotic song means very little to him.

He is an American, of course. He has known that fact since

he was four or so, and not in any way been ashamed of it. But he has learned to regard himself as more worldly in the literal sense. His mother has been a great believer in the United Nations. She has bought and sold cards for UNICEF, has joined groups anxious to promote its importance. His father has traveled widely, maintains an active correspondence with friends on several continents, and has visited both the Soviet Union and China, in order to exchange medical information with the leading physicians of those countries. And his father is what the other Richard's father calls a "far-out liberal," a man who is in favor, for instance, of a national health insurance program, as well as various efforts to provide jobs for the unemployed, food for the hungry, and protection for consumers, whom he believes to be the unwitting victims of various large corporations.

For the man's son, Dickey, such concerns have become a part of what life is all about. His compositions, like those of his namesake, have reflected ideas consistently advocated at home. And those ideas have very much determined friendships too. Richard and Dickey have known each other for years but have never become friends. Friendly antagonists, yes; they have argued with one another, and written or spoken from opposite points of view, and especially did so when a voluntary suburban busing program got under way. (The intention was to introduce a small number of black children from a Boston ghetto to good suburban schools.) Neither child was personally involved; their private school would not receive black students from Boston. But their parents were taxpayers, and much involved in the town's affairs. Before the busing (only twenty students were involved) could get under way, the town's residents had to meet and register their approval. They did meet, and eventually they did register their (guarded, hesitant, fearful, not enthusiastic or overwhelming) approval. Dickey was ten at the time; he remembered what he heard at home before and after the town meeting, and what he heard for a week or so at school in the form of casual comments from Richard and others who agreed with him: "I wouldn't want to be a black kid and be within hearing distance of Richard when he talks about black people. He doesn't like them. He even says so! He says they're different, and if a lot of them come out here to school, they'll bring crime with them. They could steal while they're here. I overheard him saying that. I asked him if he really believed what he'd said. He asked me where I got the idea that he'd ever talked like that. I said I just heard him! He said I was hearing things!

"I told my father and mother what happened. They said a lot of people like them — Richard and his parents — won't even admit what they believe to each other, so they certainly won't go and tell me what they think. A few days later I asked Richard what he *did* think about busing; he said he didn't care whether the black kids came out here or not. They aren't coming to our school, he said, and so it's none of his business. And he told me: 'It's none of yours, either.' I told him I wasn't trying to interfere. I just wanted to know what he thought; and I told him I'd be glad to tell him what I thought. But he said he already knew! Then I laughed. He's got a fast mind and he knows how to say something real smart, and you wish you could say something fast, but you can't think of anything to say that's as good as what he's said!"

He was being characteristically modest. Dickey tended to regard himself as no match for a number of other classmates, whom he regarded as more articulate and more sure of themselves. He was in the minority socially and politically, and knew it. The town was a conservative one, but his parents were liberals. And his parents had no real friends among their neighbors in the town. The boy heard his parents talk rather critically of the town, even of the school he attended. When he was nine, and the matter of busing was being argued out all over the town, he drew a picture of his school, showing it to be the pleasant place it was, a country day school with buildings arranged around a quadrangle. Dickey especially liked one "hall," where his homeroom was. The architect's use of glass, of sharp angles, entranced the boy; and he strived to duplicate in his drawing what he approved of. He also worked hard to convey the beauty of the surrounding land. The school was on a gentle, thickly wooded knoll. A long driveway led up from the town's road. Dickey could see the road from his classroom window, and sometimes he would stare out a little longer than necessary, while sharpening his pencil. Once the teacher even noticed and said, "That's enough." In fact, the boy had broken the newly made point because he had turned the sharpener too often. He retired to his seat holding the pencil so that no one would see what had happened. He thought of that occasion as he drew; he decided to put himself at the window. On the road he put a yellow school bus. No one in his school rode on one. They did so "in the public school," a phrase he sometimes heard used by boys and girls in his class with varying degrees of condescension or disapproval.

When he had finished with the crayons (Figure 37), he began to comment on what he had done and what he had in mind: "I wish I could draw better. The school is a very unusual place, especially when you're in a car driving by, and you see that slanted roof of the main building up the hill. My parents had a long debate about the school; they weren't sure I should go. My mother wanted me to go to the public school. She's against private schools. She says they take good people away from the public schools, and that's not good. She says that in a town like ours, where the public schools are good, there's no need for private schools. My Dad says she's right, but if there's one school that's better than the other, then I should go to the better one, even if it's private. I guess it's better at the private school. I've never been to the public one, so I don't know. If I went there I'd be new, like those black kids. They don't have a lot of friends, my mother's heard.

"They wouldn't, in this town. There aren't too many people here who would want black people moving in. There isn't a single black family here. My mother tried to get people together who would change that. She was trying to see if they could build some homes for people who don't have a lot of money, and then some black families could move in. But no one wanted to do much, I think, except my mother and one other lady, and she told my mother it was 'hopeless.' The town didn't want the black kids being bused in here. First they voted no. Then the Boston newspapers criticized the town, and a lot of people felt ashamed of themselves. So, they took another vote, and a lot of people switched, but not enough. Then there was more arguing, and they took another vote, and that time it was very close, but they did agree to let a few, only a few black kids be bused. My Dad says they ought to get a helicopter to take the black kids here and bring them home, because it's nearly an hour, the bus drive, each way.

"When I broke the pencil that day, after turning the sharpener too many times, I guess it was because I was thinking of the black kids. They'd just started coming out here, and I was wondering how they were doing. I was wishing that I was in the public school; then I could say hello to them and try to be friendly. When the black kids started going to school in this town, my mother was all set to take me right out of school and put me in the public school, but my Dad said absolutely no, and he's the boss of the house. He told me, when I asked him why I should stay in a private school, that school was where you go to get an education, and I'm getting a good one where

I am. My mother says no, I'm not; she says I'm not learning how to get along with anyone but kids like that Richard."

That Richard — Dickey occasionally referred to him that
way, and by the age of ten saw him as an antagonist; not a
personal one, but a symbol of all that is wrong about the school
and town. Dickey did not do as well as Richard in mathematics
and science, but he wrote more imaginative if less logical
compositions. He never even thought of trying to debate; and
he was only fair in athletics, though quite conscientious. The
two boys became increasingly explicit political opponents.
When the superintendent of the town's schools proposed to
double the number of bused students from twenty to forty the
town again was in an uproar — only a year, it turned out, after
the whole matter had been discussed for weeks in public and
private. Several parents, including Dickey's, suggested that
the town's private elementary school also receive (on scholarship, of course) some bused children. The handful of parents
who favored the idea were voted down.

But they were joined, for a brief period, by some teachers,
one of whom had both Richard and Dickey in her sixth-grade
English class. She asked all her children to write an impromptu composition one day on what they thought of the
proposal that four or five blacks be bused daily to their school.
Dickey had this to say: "I think it would be a very good idea
if we had some *color* around here. As I look around, it is all
white, and very sad. Why are we afraid of other people? Just
because they have dark skin doesn't mean they are any different from us. I am sure they are different, though. The reason
is, they are poor and they don't live like we do. They can't. If
they could, they would, I am sure of that. I am afraid that if
the black kids came out here, they would not want to stay here
for very long. They would not make too many friends. Maybe

they would make no friends. They would decide that we are not very nice people out here."

Meanwhile, his classmate Richard had been quite blunt in his remarks: "This is a private school. Everyone pays to come here. Why should we let some people come here free, just because they are black? Why not let some white people come here, who don't have the money, but live near the town? Some people are in favor of the black people, without knowing them. That's prejudice, too. If a black family has the money and wants to move in this town, I would be for them. If they sent their kids here to our school, and paid the way we all do, I would be for the kids. That's the right way."

The teacher posted all the compositions, and Dickey read Richard's with special care. Later Dickey went to his art class. He loved to draw and paint. Richard did not take art, preferring skilled carpentry work, for which he won several prizes. That day Dickey painted what he called a scene: the sky is cloudy, with the sun hidden from view; the trees are tall, stately, and it is spring, because they are just breaking out with leaves; the grass is also a mixture of brown, the winter's residue, and green, new life; to the side are the school's buildings — especially, in the foreground, the low athletic building; standing on the playing field are several youths, ready to play, evidently, soccer, hence the round black and white ball; and off to the side of the field, near the woods, stands one youth, small and dark-skinned. One of the black student's feet is on the grass, the other well into the woods. When Dickey was through with his painting (Figure 38) he set it aside, and later brought it home. He put it upon his bulletin board. He also wrote a few lines which were meant to go with the painting, and which also were put up on the bulletin board: "Don't come here. If you do, you'll have a lot of trouble on your hands. Should you ride on the bus for an hour, just to get into trouble out here? I think you shouldn't. Richard is wrong, but he is right when he says what will happen if you decide to come out here."

Dickey's worries were needless; the school's board of trustees said no, firmly and unanimously. One trustee wavered, Dickey's mother heard, but not for long. Then Dickey's parents went through a spell of intense self-scrutiny. Once again, though with the question of racial isolation as a focus, they asked themselves — out loud, and within hearing distance of their son — why Dickey was at the private school and not the public school. This time the boy spoke up, asked to transfer — but also acknowledged that he was hesitant to do so. His schoolwork was good; he knew "the place," as he called it, and it would be especially hard to leave in the middle of the academic year. Still, the mother argued, maybe some sacrifice was in order; maybe a gesture of protest would have some effect on the private school's trustees. The boy eventually said yes, he would oblige. But his father became outraged. Why should Dickey leave? Who would really pay attention to such an act? And as a result, how many black children would benefit? Anyway, were blacks up to the rigorous intellectual demands of the school? Ought they to be bused all the way out to their town, only to go through the agony of academic trial and defeat?

The boy agreed with his father when he spoke, agreed with his mother when she spoke. Her line of reasoning was, by her own acknowledgment, "emotional" and prompted to a large extent by anger. Dickey saw clearly what she felt, and shared her resentment, though with qualifications: "The school isn't bad. You learn a lot. There are some nice teachers. I agree with my father, that there's not much to complain about, as far as the work goes. I'm doing pretty good, I think. My adviser says so. But we're all pretty lucky kids, I guess. My mother says we're in trouble, because we don't have any black kids, and no poor kids, and so it's unreal, she says. My father disagrees. He says there will be plenty of time later on for me to find out what the world is like. He got angry the other day. He told my mother that there are no black people in his laboratory either. What should he do? Should he go and get a black man and call him a doctor, and tell him to do some research? My mother started crying. She said he wasn't fair, the way he was talking. She said we're living in a ghetto here in this town, and she's fed up. She wants us to move into the city, and I could go to a private school there, but it would be integrated. When a school is integrated, that means you have white kids and black kids, and they're in the same class, and there aren't any bad fights, though they may not like each other at first, but after a while they begin to be okay together.

"I'm not going to leave my school this year. My mother decided Daddy is right; and he agreed that we should talk again in the spring. But we're going to do something good this summer; Mom has signed up to have one of the black kids coming to the town on the bus stay with us for two weeks. It's a plan some families thought up, and we've joined them. We'll take him down to the Cape. We have a house on the ocean, and he can swim. I'll teach him how to dive, if he doesn't know. My father said not to be so sure he'll even know how to swim. If he doesn't, I can teach him. I remember how I learned. If we stay here for part of the time, we can use our pool. It's easier to learn in a pool than in the ocean."

That summer Dickey turned eleven, and he was indeed a host to a black boy named Kenny. Dickey was becoming tall, and was quite thin. He had curly light brown hair and blue eyes. He was moderately athletic, preferring activities he could enjoy by himself — skiing and swimming — rather than "group sports." He was a fine artist, a rather talented saxophone player, and a self-styled shortwave radio "fanatic." He had a powerful set that picked up broadcasts from all over the world, and listened to them endlessly. He owned, further, a number of walkie-talkie sets; no fewer than four sets, he was embarrassed to admit, each slightly different in appearance. He had been to England, France, the Caribbean, California, Hawaii, Canada, and Mexico and had in his room pictures of himself standing before various well-known buildings or monuments. He had a large number of metal and plastic cars and soldiers; and there was a large, handsome desk. And there was a fishing rod and paraphernalia. And there was a clock-radio. And there was a large map of the world, on which the boy had put variously colored pins to mark his travels. And there was a small library of books, fitted into a substantial and spacious bookcase. And he had in the room an enormous window that afforded a view of woods, a trail, a pond, and, beyond it, a hill.

If he had a "fault," in his parents' word, it was daydreaming; he loved to stare out the window for seconds that became a minute or two, a long time for a boy of eleven. Once his mother noticed him doing so (she was outside the house) and timed him: four and a half minutes. What *was* he thinking about? He did indeed remember. The snow had gone, and he was wondering whether various animals would soon be coming out of hibernation. Were *they* wondering the same thing? Or were they still asleep? Do animals think? Do they talk to each other, through the noises they make, as we do with words? Might he someday become a biologist, and learn the secrets of animal psychology? Those were the kinds of thought that crossed his mind as he looked out at the late winter, early spring country landscape. What was wrong with "staring" anyway? Nothing, his mother insisted — hurt that she had been put in the role of a critic. But Dickey knew that he himself sometimes became impatient with his own habits, among them the "staring" he did. He would think of classmates of his, like Richard, who were so energetic, so constantly on the move. A few times he had been gazing intently out the window at school and had not heard the teacher give instructions. The teacher had not reprimanded him, had not even appeared to take notice of the direction of his head and eyes. When the boy went up and asked to hear the directions repeated, he met with success — and no lecture on "paying attention." But he gave himself one — then and on other occasions. He would never be a good biologist, or a surgeon, or an electronics engineer — his three choices for a future profession — if he "daydreamed." His father had impressed him with the need for punctuality, attentiveness, and a scrupulous regard for detail on the part of scientists. If Dickey were to be a writer, an artist, his father pointed out, then he could gaze to good effect. But Dickey had always told his father, when he made that last observation, how irrelevant it was. The boy was not grown up, but he knew "for sure" that he would "go into science," some form of it.

He also had some convictions about the future of black children — what they should do with themselves when they grow up. Some should be fellow scientists of his; but he believed that black people badly need writers, men and women who would be able to reach, touch, persuade people like those who lived near him or went to school with him. A casual remark made by his fourth-grade teacher had stayed with him for two years and promised to stay much longer, he was sure: "I remember the teacher reading to us from a writer whose name I forget, but he was a black man. He wrote about how he felt being black. He didn't feel too good, being black. But it was strange; when you thought about it afterwards, you wondered if you would ever be able to speak like that. I mean, he really got to you. He made you admire him. He must have been a very brave man. I don't believe I could be as successful as he was, if I was born so poor, and if my father was shot dead by some white people, and my mother was very sick, and died. His grandmother took care of him, and he had seven sisters and a brother, and five of them died before reaching the age of ten, and the brother got killed by white people, just like the father. I guess they were troublemakers. That's what the teacher told us: in the South, if you were black, you had to keep your mouth shut.

"The man went north, and he decided that he would let everyone know the truth. So he learned how to write, and he got a job in a newspaper, I believe, and then he wrote some books. Even Richard was impressed — and some of the others in my school who don't like black people. There are a lot who don't like black people in this town! Richard told the teacher that he was in favor of anyone who worked hard, and the one who wrote books must have worked hard to get them done, so at least he wasn't sitting around waiting for a welfare check. The teacher said that not everyone can write books; and he told us that we should try to think of what it would be like for us if we didn't live out here, and we had no money, and we had black skin instead of white skin. But it's hard to imagine yourself being someone else. I've tried. I've stood there in my room, and I've looked at myself in the mirror, and I've tried to picture myself looking like a black kid. Then I've closed my eyes, and I've thought of what I'd be like, and what I'd think, and how I'd be living, if I was black. I even painted a picture of a black kid — I made up his looks in my mind; and I said to myself: now he's you, and try to do like the teacher says — imagine what he's like, and where he lives, and what he thinks about life. A lot of the time, I just drew a blank, I have to confess."

He was not always stymied, however. His drawing of the

black boy (Figure 39) was itself an imaginative statement, especially when placed beside one he did of his classmate Richard. The black boy is fragile of body, with large, intent eyes and equally conspicuous ears. He seems to be at a loss to know what to do with himself; his arms stretch out, but his hands are small, his fingers short and narrow, and one begins to think that the figure is impaled or is in flight. The legs are also thin, slightly bent, and inadequate, it seems, for the elongated torso. The clothes are dark, nondescript. The artist wants to indicate an urban setting, so he places the boy in front of an enormous black building, with many windows, irregularly arranged, and four rather thick chimneys, each belching black smoke into a cloudy sky. The building is meant to be a factory, and it has no limits; rather, it ends with the margins of the paper. There is no door. The boy is alone, superimposed on the factory. We learn this about him: "He lives in a ghetto. He has to get a job, so he goes to a factory and applies. He's left school. He's lucky; he gets the job. My father says it's the only hope for the black people, that they'll get more jobs, if only the big companies move into the ghetto. I've never been to a ghetto, so I don't know what it looks like. My mother and father haven't been there, either; but they've seen pictures. It must be bad."

As for Richard, he is depicted as the tall, sturdy boy that he is, and the budding tennis player. The artist wants to make sure that his personal prejudices don't get in the way of a faithful and respectful portrait. It is, as well, a country landscape — trees, shrubbery, and some tulip plants. Richard's mother is known for her tulips, and the boy is placed near them. He has his racket high in the air — a rehearsal stroke, perhaps, for a game soon to be played. He is much bigger and more solid than the nameless black boy; and, unlike the latter, is favored by a cloudless, sunny day and a wide expanse of green lawn, which stretches out before him (and the viewer) invitingly. (Figure 40.) We are told what Richard is up to, at that moment and beyond it: "He's thinking about what he wants to do. He may go play tennis; he'll probably win. He may ride on that racing bike of his. He's fast. He's smart. He'll be a success. I talk about him with my parents, because he's always saying things I don't like to hear. My mother was going to see the headmaster and ask him to put me in another class, but it's no use; there's only one "fast" section, and we're both in it because we both do good schoolwork. I even thought of not doing so well; then, they'd transfer me. But that's no way to get rid of Richard! He's not the only one, anyway. My mother says I'd better get used to him. She says the world is full of people like him. I hate to think that's what I'll find when I'm a grown-up — Richard and a hundred of his friends standing in front of my house and telling me I'm a communist!

"Richard hates communists, but he admitted to me that he's never seen one. He asked me last week if *I* was one! I said yes, absolutely! He laughed and said I was a joker. He's a joker himself! He has all kinds of magician's tricks he's learned. When he grows up he'll become a bank president, like his father, and he'll own a big house, and have plenty of land. My Dad says Richard won't be living in this town then, because two or three black families might move in ten or twenty years from now, and right away Richard's family will move. Richard said his uncle owns an island off the coast of Maine. Maybe that's where he'll live when he's grown up. My father says no, because you can't live on an island off the coast of Maine all year round. Maybe you can, though. If you've got a lot of money, you can do anything. Dad has always said that. But I don't think Richard would want to admit that he's afraid to live anywhere except on an island. I heard him tell a friend that he wished his parents would move into the city, right in

Boston near the water, where a cousin of his lives. Then if a thief came to rob, Richard would fight back. He's been learning how to shoot a rifle. I don't think it's legal for him to have a gun until he's older, but his father is a big hunter, and Richard goes along on hunting trips. Kids say he's a good shot. My father says they ought to outlaw guns, so only the police have them."

Dickey used to want desperately to play with guns — toy pistols and rifles denied him by his parents, who felt he ought not to be exposed to "violence" on television or to "weapons," however harmless. He and a close friend, nevertheless, played cops and robbers, using branches from trees as rifles, and making a lot of noise to indicate bullets going to and fro. They would also play cowboys and Indians; in so doing they were permitted to use bows and arrows. They have had acres and acres of quite lovely woods to use — riding paths, several small ponds, a large one, some swampy land attractive to migrating geese, and right in the middle of it a stunning meadow with tall grass, wild flowers, a gentle slope, rabbits that dart about when approached, hawks that hover overhead warily. The two friends sometimes have invited others, formed shifting alliances, waged "war," united to explore, divided again into opposing "expeditions," each intent on reaching an agreed upon destination through different routes.

At other times the two boys have been content to collect leaves or watch birds — Dickey's father is an inveterate bird-watcher — or keep an eye out for woodchucks or raccoons or snakes or, very rarely, a red fox. Sometimes Dickey will come home and think of the woods, which abut his parent's seven-acre property. What would it be like to live in such a place the way his ancestors once did? (They were early New England settlers.) Could he survive such an ordeal? He doubts so. He is too "soft," too dependent on what his mother often calls, both with admiration yet a touch of disparagement (he thinks), "creature comforts." He has, of course, been a Scout; and he has gone on overnight camping trips organized by the Audubon Society or by his friend's father. He knows how to cook, how to get by on precious little. But he wonders whether there isn't something contrived or false about the outdoors life he has lived — all too cleverly "natural" and "educational," but not what he calls "real." It was "real," he suggests, when the Pilgrims faced the obstacles of New England life, but it is scarcely "real" when he and his friends go into woods not intrinsicially different from the ones the Pilgrims encountered, but a brief safe alternative to Dickey's comfortable life.

The boy at twelve was quite interested in the "real" as against the "fake." He had listened for years to his mother rail against some of their neighbors — the lavish parties they give, the various homes they own (ski lodges, "places" by the sea, even additional "places" by seas far to the south), and the possessions they seem to keep seeking, keep buying, keep needing. Dickey began to turn against one or two families, then a particular neighborhood within the town, then just about everyone within miles of his home. If only the town weren't so wealthy and important, or self-important! If only he and a few of his friends could go back to some earlier, simpler way of life! He expressed his strong criticisms at the dinner table, or while walking with his parents — when they seemed ripe for their more serious conversation. The boy bluntly asked his parents (a week after he turned twelve) why they still lived where they did, and when (if ever) they would move away. They tried to explain their reasons for staying put; and they told him frankly that they saw no reason to leave, not for years to come, maybe never. Certainly they would not consider picking themselves up and departing when he was still at home and going nearby to school. It was the least pleasing

FIGURE 1.

FIGURE 2.

FIGURE 3.

FIGURE 4.

FIGURE 5.

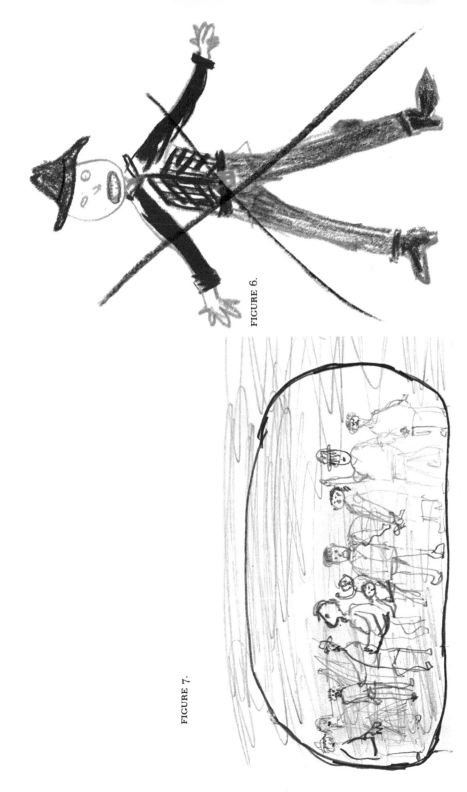

FIGURE 6.

FIGURE 7.

FIGURE 8.

FIGURE 9.

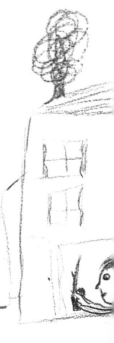

FIGURE 10.

FIGURE 11.

FIGURE 12.

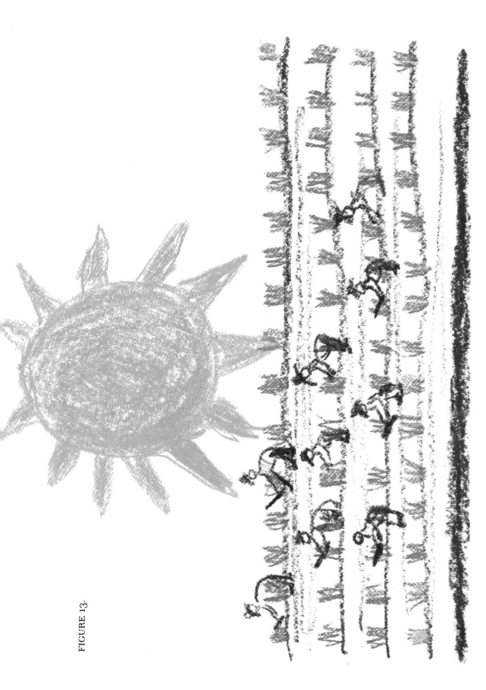

FIGURE 13.

FIGURE 14.

FIGURE 15.

FIGURE 16.

FIGURE 17.

FIGURE 18.

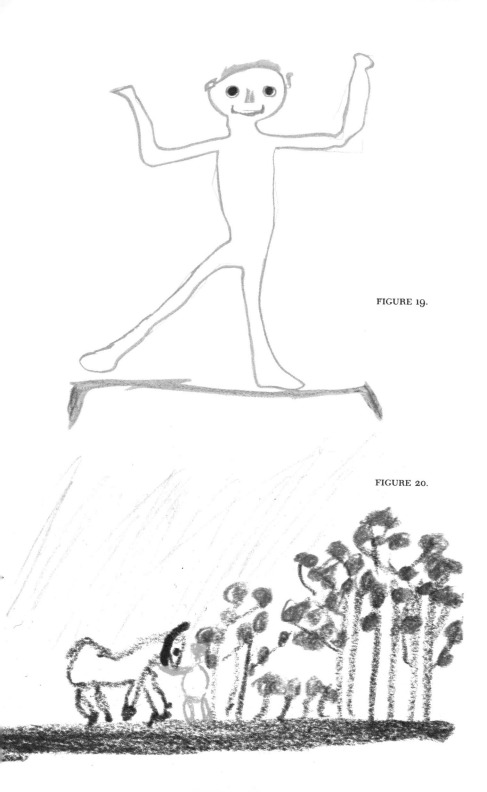

FIGURE 19.

FIGURE 20.

FIGURE 21.

FIGURE 22.

FIGURE 23.

FIGURE 24.

*Taos
Dixon

*Santa Fe

alb u qu erq u e

FIGURE 25.

FIGURE 26.

FIGURE 27.

FIGURE 28.

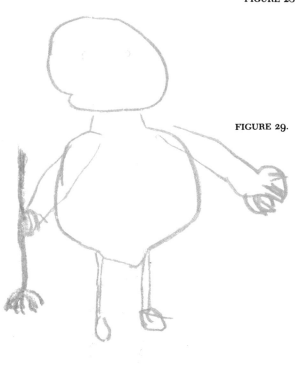

FIGURE 29.

FIGURE 30.

FIGURE 31.

FIGURE 32.

FIGURE 33.

FIGURE 34.

CHARLOTTE

FIGURE 35.

FIGURE 36.

FIGURE 37.

FIGURE 38.

FIGURE 39.

FIGURE 40.

FIGURE 41.

FIGURE 42.

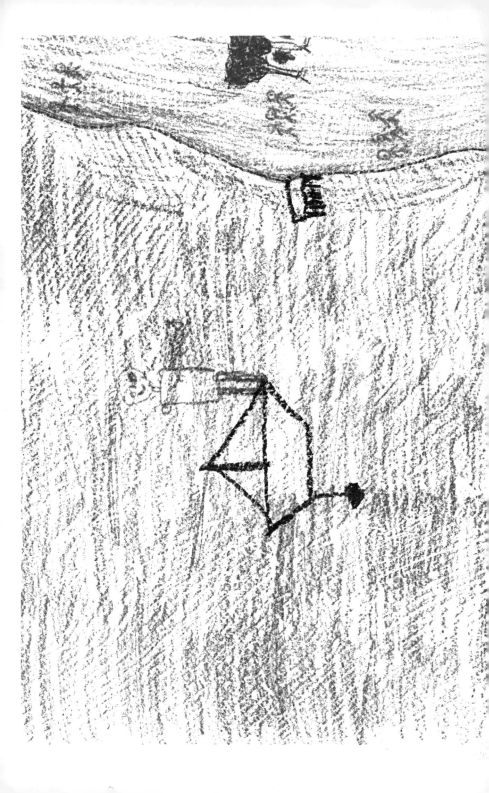

FIGURE 44.

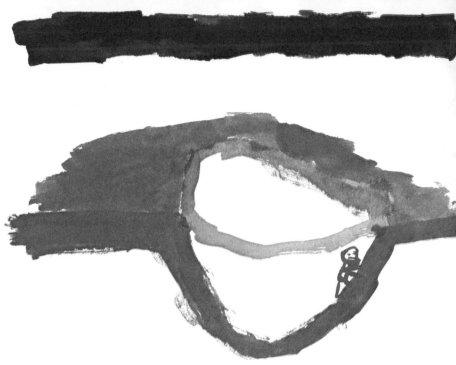

FIGURE 45.

FIGURE 46.

FIGURE 47.

FIGURE 48.

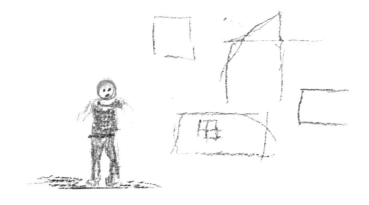

FIGURE 49.

series of observations or explanations he had ever heard from them, and he managed to tell them so. He resented being considered a "reason," and he wished, as a matter of fact, that for his sake, if no one else's, the family would move — and quickly.

But move where? And what did he hope to do — exchange one set of disadvantages for another? He was not surprised to hear those questions; he rather anticipated them. But he had some answers of his own — ones he had put in a lot of time thinking about: "I just tried to be honest. My mother and father have told me all my life that I should be honest and not be afraid to say what I think. When I was in the second grade I didn't do well in one test, and then another. I was afraid to bring the papers home. Finally my parents found out. I guess my mother went to see the teacher. She was surprised to hear that I was having trouble with my arithmetic. The teacher told her she'd sent home the papers. But my mother hadn't seen them. Well, I had to have a long talk with my mother and my Dad. They said they must have done something wrong, because I'd failed to tell them the truth, and the reason was that I was scared, and they were sure they had made me scared. I told them no, I wasn't scared; I just knew they'd be sad, and I didn't want them to be sad. It was bad enough that *I* was sad! But from then on I knew that you'd better tell the truth, because sooner or later the truth comes out. Look at what happened to our President. If he couldn't hide what he'd done, I guess I can't hide what I've done. I broke a window the other day, and our maid said she'd take the blame, and I wanted to say okay, but I was afraid that we'd both get caught. I don't know how. But it would happen. So I told my parents the truth; and they weren't upset. They said accidents happen.

"That's why I wasn't afraid to tell my parents what to do when they asked me last week. I said we should move as soon as possible. I said we should move because if we didn't, I'd turn into someone like Richard, my 'friendly enemy.' That's what we call Richard when we talk about him; but I don't want to fight him, and a lot of the time lately I end up agreeing with what I hear him tell his friends. I don't like to be the one who always argues with everyone. I don't like to be outnumbered ten to one. It's no good. Some of the kids tease me. They say I should ask my parents to give all their money away to the poor people, since they're so worried about the poor people and since I'm so worried too. Up until then I hadn't told my parents what the kids were saying about giving our money away. My father laughed; he said he'd give everything, every single penny we own, if Richard's father gave just ten percent of what he owns.

"I got upset. I said that wasn't fair. My father told me not to worry; he knew Richard's father, and he wouldn't give one dollar to anyone poor, unless the person worked for him. My mother was more upset. She said I should ask the kids at school why their fathers don't give any money to poor people. I told her I'd be laughed out of the building, because the kids think anyone who worries about 'welfare chiselers' and people like them is considered a real idiot. That's when my mother asked me what we *should* do — I mean, where I thought I should go to school. When I had to come up with an answer, I wasn't sure. I said maybe we should move to some other part of the country, where there's no trouble like the kind we have here: the black people and the white people fighting in Boston, and now the trouble here over 'voluntary busing.' Maybe we should live up in Vermont all year round, not just go there in the winter when we want to ski."

He had no further suggestions. He began after that to turn away from discussions of busing or about black people. He told his mother one morning that he was not interested in politics, and didn't really care whether President Nixon stayed in office or not. He went on to insist that it really made no difference who is President: "They are all crooks." When his mother argued with him on that score, he backed down a bit, acknowledged that there have been differences among the Presidents, and affirmed his loyalties to his parents' social and racial views. But he gently reminded his mother that he had to survive in a school where those views are not so popular. And she replied that he was "right" to avoid arguments and try to "get by" in school without "friction." And that is what the boy began to do — with a vengeance, almost. He shunned all controversial subjects. In his compositions he wrote at great length about his camping adventures. In social studies he always chose topics that had to do with the past rather than the present. Asked to research any presidency he wished, he chose Thomas Jefferson's. Dickey had been to Monticello, had saved a number of postcards of the buildings, and did an excellent job of summarizing our third President's many achievements. The boy was relieved that he hadn't chosen one of the recent Presidents, because there had been arguments about their relative merits among his classmates afterward. Everyone agreed Jefferson was "important"; and that consensus of his classmates meant a lot to Dickey.

He was beginning to be known as a future scientist. He knew a lot about chemistry. He was an amateur astronomer. He was especially interested in biology. He was allowed increasingly to take special science electives and to give talks to younger children about their science reading and experiments. At thirteen he was even made an assistant to the school's science teacher; instead of study periods, Dickey helped teach. He also went into Boston's Science Museum rather regularly on weekends, took part in numerous activities there, entered various competitions, and won several. Back at school he became rather immune to criticism; he took no part in the rough-and-tumble of recesses and study periods, and he never had anything to say about politics, social problems, contemporary events. Nor would he have dreamed of leaving his school when he was thirteen or older. It was a "good" school. It was a school that let him show what he knew and learn what he very much wanted to know. He had to take the usual "other subjects," as he came to call everything else besides science that he took. But he didn't mind doing so. Nor did he mind athletics. Nor did he mind any of his classmates anymore.

Just before his fourteenth birthday he came home and told his mother that Richard had asked him to his birthday party and that he was looking forward to going. Any disagreements they had once had were no longer present. Dickey was willing to say that he had done more than try to forget certain sensitive topics of conversation. He had quietly but definitely changed his mind: "I used to think we should try to change a lot of things right away. But you shouldn't be too quick; you should stop and think, and wait for a good long while. Black people are different from white people. That's what black people say, so why is it wrong if white people say the same thing? If you know what Darwin said, you'll be in favor of very gradual change. You can't speed up nature, and you shouldn't even try to do it. It takes a long time for something to change in nature, and the same should go for man; we shouldn't try to rush into something too fast."

His parents now began to hear him present a case for Darwinian gradualism as a philosophical guide to social and political analysis. They tried to ignore the implications of his point of view. They listened in silence most of the time or questioned him in hopes of showing how sad, or even absurd, it could be, in their opinion, to apply Darwin's theory to the racial problem of contemporary American society. But the boy would only repeat his assertions or ask his parents why they were so stubborn or blind or both. It was an impasse that became more and more severe, and has showed no signs of abating. Dickey considers his mother and father "liberals," who may mean well, but "don't understand that nature resists change, and only gradually lets it happen." Dickey's parents hope that someday he will abandon the theory they see wielding its ideological hold on him — and worry that long ago they didn't move away, so that their son would not have found in Charles Darwin's ideas the means of a reconciliation with Richard, not to mention others in the town who think like Richard.

III

YOUNG OBSERVERS

CHILDREN like Helen play right in the heart of Boston and talk about their houses, their yards, even their streets. The houses are town houses, the yards are small, though sometimes quite lovely, with potted plants everywhere, or a small patch of land quite nicely used to support flowers. There are slate terraces, lights that can banish the dark completely, and outdoor furniture that is as handsome as it is practical. The streets sometimes are really small alleys; or a group of houses may make up a "square" or a "court," or something called a "landing." That is to say, there is privacy amid the urban press of traffic and crowds.

Not that Helen is a stranger to the country; her parents own what they call a "country house," as a matter of fact. It is a "farm" on Martha's Vineyard and is near the ocean. But the child doesn't want to leave the city when her parents do, on weekends. Often her parents have asked her to draw a picture of their country home, but Helen has been reluctant. When she obliged, at the age of nine, her parents were dismayed. How could an artist able to evoke city life so carefully and sympathetically fail to be similarly responsive to a familiar and pleasant rural setting? Helen was at the time able to answer that question: "I don't want to go away from home. This is my home. There's only one reason I like to go to our country house — because Daddy is there. All week we don't see much of him. Sometimes I'm lucky if I see him for five minutes in the morning, before I go to school. There are days when he's away. There are other days when he's been at a meeting the night before, and he just can't get up to say hello. Then when I come home, he's at work. And a lot of times he doesn't get home before we go to bed. I miss him. So does my brother, Geoff. He says he wishes Daddy would lose his job, then we'd have him here at home. Geoff says he even *prays* that Daddy will lose his job. Geoff is only seven, and he doesn't realize that if Daddy loses his job, we might be in trouble, because we wouldn't have all the money we do now. Then we might have to sell that country house — but Daddy would at least be home more. Maybe he could get a new job right away, and it would be a better one.

"I once had a bad dream in the middle of the night. I think I was talking in my sleep, and Mommy overheard me. She was still awake. When I woke up, she was standing beside the bed, and she wanted to know if I was okay. I said yes. She asked me what I'd been dreaming about. I remembered; I told her it was about Daddy, and he was in the house we have in the country, and he had to get out, to go back to Boston, but the door wouldn't open. So he climbed out through a window, and then he got in the car, and he drove off; but he left us behind, and we didn't know how to get back to Boston, and we all started crying, even Mommy. She told me I was being silly to have a dream like that; and then I went back to sleep. The trouble with our country home is that you're away from everyone. We've gone there on some weekends when Daddy is in Texas, on some business trip, and then we have the worst time ever, because Mommy is unhappy when Daddy is away. Geoff starts crying and says that he's afraid Daddy may never get back, and then we couldn't get away from here, because he's the one who knows how to close up the house before we leave. But I tell Geoff not to worry, because Mommy knows how to close up the house, too."

Her father is an important young executive in a real estate firm that develops land sites for commercial buyers and also arranges for the construction of all sorts of buildings as well as the rental of space in them once they are completed. He went to Grinnell College, in Iowa, came East to the Harvard Business School, and, as Helen puts it, "fell in love with Boston." He has been on the rise ever since he graduated from the business school. He worked for three other companies before he got a chance to return to Boston: first Procter & Gamble in Cincinnati, then a real estate company in Houston, and finally a textile company in North Carolina. He grabbed the opportunity to return to "real estate development," and swore to his wife that they would not move again, having done so four times in six years of marriage. He has poured his heart and soul into his work since then, and will undoubtedly be able to keep his promise. He has become one of the firm's most successful executives — a planner, a salesman, a coordinator of projects, a shrewd observer of the entire nation's business climate, and a man very much liked by the firm's president.

When he does have time to be with his children, they are grateful and happy — though they ask him, right off, how long it will be until he leaves. They also ask him when they will *next* see him. His wife often tries to prevent those questions, but unsuccessfully. She has known her husband since they were both in the same classroom in high school and has built her life around him and his work as well as her two children. Her older child was able, at nine, to indicate how the family's life works: "My mother keeps Daddy steady. He says so. She became a nurse before they got married, and he says it's a good thing she did. He'll come home late, and he has a headache or a stom-achache, and she knows what medicine to give him. If they go out together, she'll go up to him and pinch him on the arm, and that means he's been drinking too much, and he should stop, unless he wants to get sick. Then he usually stops; but sometimes he doesn't, and there's trouble the next morning. Daddy will be sick. He has to watch out, or he'll drink more and more, and then he'll be in bad trouble.

"He's the one who decides whether we'll go to the country or whether we'll stay home because he and Mommy have to go to a party. Sometimes he tells her he's sick in his stomach and he has a bad headache. But when she tells him she'll call up and explain to the people, he says no, it's important to go out. I wish some weekend we could just stay here and they wouldn't go out, and we could visit the Aquarium. I've never been there with my parents. I came home from school one afternoon and asked Mommy if we could go there with her and Daddy, and she said yes, but it depends on what Daddy has to do. We haven't gone yet. When Daddy comes home, we have to keep quiet. Mommy makes sure of that. She tells us that if we don't help out, Daddy will be upset, and he works very hard. She says that later, when we're older, Daddy will be with us a lot, and we can look forward to the day. But by that time Geoff and I may be all grown up!"

If she had a wish, with respect to her future, what would it be? What about her present life — how pleased is she with it, and what about it would she want different? She is a talkative and speculative child, at times annoyingly so. Her father does not like her questions, or her social and political observations. Her mother may enjoy them, but she also has been embar-rassed by what she has heard. She has been described by her husband as "the source" of Helen's inspiration. But Helen is quite capable of developing her own ideas, sharing them with her brother Geoff, and surprising both parents by the vivid originality (and emotional power) of her mind. Her teachers, too, consider Helen quite bright and perceptive. At the age of ten she wrote a composition which her teacher found almost unbearably personal, and so did not post on the bulletin board, though she ordinarily did display especially worthwhile writing. The title was "My Parents." It went as follows: "My Daddy is going to be president of his company one of these days. I heard him tell my mother that. He said he had to work day and night, but in the end it would be worth it. My mother is not so sure. My brother Geoff and I are not so sure, either. My brother and I wish our father could be home with us, and not at the office or traveling all day and half the night. My mother wants him to keep his job, but she is afraid he could get sick. My grandfather has a farm, and many are the days when Geoff and I say that it's too bad that Daddy doesn't own a farm, and then we'd see him a lot more than we do. But we love our house here in Boston, and it is because Daddy has such a good job that we can have all the toys and live where we do. You can't have everything. Our mother tells us that. I know what she means."

Helen has some ideas about her future. She wants to marry a man who already has a lot of money. Such a person, she is sure, will not have to work as hard as her father does. Such a person, she believes, would be able to spend long hours at home. Perhaps he would work in the Aquarium or the Science Museum in Boston; or in its Museum of Fine Arts. She goes to those places often with friends, and notices not only fish, or wonderfully intricate machinery, or paintings, but grown-up men who work. She is not sure about the kind of work her future husband might do in one of those places; perhaps be the director — "the one who makes the decisions." She has heard her father talk about "decisions," about how hard they sometimes are to make. She hopes her husband will have an easier job of making decisions; but she is not about to consign him to the gendarmes, the sanitation department, or the ranks of salespeople. Her brother has suggested that standing guard in a museum, or selling things in a museum store, or operating one of the rather elaborate and inviting floor waxing and polishing machines would be acceptable jobs for himself in the future. Why not for his sister's husband, too?

Helen refuses to go along with those recommendations. She keeps reminding her brother that they are "fairly rich," and that it would be "very bad" to live a relatively "poor" life. What is that kind of life like? She has a few ideas on the subject: "We wouldn't be able to go to our school. We'd be in a public school. The black kids and the white kids would fight. And we wouldn't have very good teachers. And we wouldn't live on this nice street. And we wouldn't have our friends. And we wouldn't be able to take trips. It wouldn't be a very fun life. Daddy may be away a lot, but he's given us a fun life. Our mother keeps telling Geoff and me that we have to be grateful for the success Daddy has become."

Helen is grateful. She is also compassionate toward others whose parents have been less successful. She has helped her mother wrap presents to be sent to churches in the city's ghetto. She has received Girl Scouts at her home, and gone to their homes — in the ghetto. Each time — a matter of a few hours — she has been eager and outgoing, quite anxious to get along with the black girl. She has told her parents often that she likes black children, that she cannot understand why others of her age who are white don't feel the same way. At ten she drew a picture of her "favorite black girl," who was almost exactly, to the day, Helen's age. The black girl is shown sitting on the steps of the six-family wooden house where she lives. The house is located on a street that once was fairly pleasant

but now has deteriorated considerably. The particular building Helen drew was in fact grayish green, but Helen made it
brown. The front stairs were dangerous to use, and appear so
in the picture. The girl sits on them, small in size, her head
tilted forward. Her arms are short, her feet thin. She is not
given a dress. The windows are not drawn as they appear in
life, but are given an irregular, haphazard arrangement. To
the side of the building we see some nondescript bodies of
youths (not identified by name) who are huddled together.
(Figure 41.) They are using drugs, the artist says.

Helen has seen such young people several times "passing a
cigarette around," and been told by her host Girl Scout what
was happening. When she told her parents, on return home,
what she had witnessed, they were surprised and dismayed.
They were also worried. Her father has several city planners
for friends, has been enthusiastically in favor of various urban
renewal projects, and has told his children that he wished that
"a few blacks" lived in their neighborhood. But stories of drug
use made the father change his mind: "One day Daddy will
like the black people, and he'll tell us how he'd like to help
them, and sometimes he does. But another day will come
when he's changed his mind. Then he's all against them. He
says it'll soon be so bad in the city, because of the black people,
that we'll have to go live in our country home, or in one of the
tall apartment houses that Daddy's company owns; they have
police guarding them all the time, and they have to, because
if they didn't, everyone would be robbed. We have an alarm
system, and if someone tries to break in, the police will come
right away. I think they hear the alarm, or a detective does.
I don't know where he is. He might be sitting in an office
someplace. There are a lot of black kids around who steal.
They use drugs, and they need money to buy the drugs. One
girl I know, she's black, and she came here for an afternoon.

She told me all about the bad people she knew. She says Geoff and I are lucky. She told us why. Geoff said he felt real sorry for her. I felt sorry for her, too. But she's pretty tough. She says she can take care of herself. She says she wouldn't want to be anyone else but who she is. That's what she told me when we were playing with my dolls. She said she didn't like my dolls. She said my room had too much stuff in it, and if she had all that stuff, she'd want to throw it out.

"I didn't like her too much. She may be poor, but she's not so nice. The minister tells us that poor people are very good, and we should be nice to them; and they told us that at the Scout meetings. But Daddy says it's the poor who make a lot of trouble in the city, and that girl might turn out to be a robber one day. She kept on picking up things in my room, and putting them down again. I thought to myself that she should stop that, but I didn't dare say anything to her.

"She said she was tough, and I believed her. She *was* tough! Maybe she stole some of my things. I have a lot of dolls, and things for my dollhouses, and she could have taken something and I might not even miss it. A black boy came here, to visit my brother, and he took three of Geoff's Corgi cars, we're pretty sure, but we can't prove it, and we don't want to cause any trouble for the kid. He's the only black boy in Geoff's class. He's poor, but the school gave him a scholarship. We've got five or six black kids in our school. Our parents say it's important to have some blacks going to school with you, but they should do good work. If they don't, then the teacher has to take a lot of time to help them, and she can't teach the other kids, and it's not fair."

She began to worry a lot, at the age of eleven, about what was fair and what wasn't at all fair. She thought that her brother Geoff was being pushed too much — and at a distance or remove, no less — by her father. Geoff was expected to be at the top of his class and a successful athlete and popular. He was none of those three; he was, at nine, nearly ten, an average student, average at sports, neither a leader nor a popular companion. He was, in fact, a rather shy boy, interested in guinea pigs (of which he had four) and highways — he had many road maps — and airplanes, models of which he constructed endlessly then stored in a large walk-in closet. The boy also tended to pay attention to "current events," about which he felt inclined to talk during his social studies course. He knew a lot about Presidents, senators, governors. He liked geography, and could point out nations others of his age didn't know existed. His sister was also a companion; *they* had guinea pigs, looked at AAA maps, talked about various kinds of jet plane, watched the evening news, or looked at an enormous wall map of the world, located in Helen's room.

A month after her eleventh birthday Helen stared at that map and wondered out loud about others her age, in America and abroad: "They tell us in school that we should give our pennies to UNICEF, and then a lot of kids won't go hungry. The next thing you know we're eating lunch, and there's so much food, and we all go get seconds, and sometimes we even go get thirds, and there are a lot of kids who say they're not going to tell their parents how much they ate, because they're getting fat and they're not supposed to eat so much. I told the teacher we should skip lunch, and the food should go to Africa, where millions of people are starving to death. My mother is trying to lose weight. My father is always trying, but he doesn't have the willpower, he says. They both tell Geoff and me that they wish they could eat as much as we do! I told my mother the other day, and so did Geoff, that it's not right for us to buy so much food and then throw a lot away. She said I was worrying too much about everyone in the world, and you can't do that. Geoff spoke up for me! He said: 'Why not?' Daddy told

him not to talk like that to our mother. Then I said it —
the same thing: 'Why not?' He told us both to go to our rooms
for five minutes.

"When we came back the maid brought us our suppers
again, but I didn't want to eat anything. They made me finish
some of the food on the plate. When the dessert came, I said
I didn't want any. Then Mother said I had to eat it, because
the maid would be offended; she made it. I said no, I wasn't
hungry. Geoff said he wasn't hungry, either. Daddy lost his
temper. He said we're spoiled brats. He said we talk back to
him and Mommy, and we act as if we're a prince and princess,
and entitled to get our way all the time. He said we'd better
'cut it out.' When he says those words, he's angry. He gave us
a long lecture on how hard he worked, and it's all for us, but
we don't say thank you, we just 'pick and choose.'

"He said that he never could eat the kind of supper we had
that night when he was a boy. He remembers saving up pennies to go buy an Oh Henry bar, or an ice cream cone. Once
he dropped the candy bar while unwrapping it, and he picked
it up and was going to eat it, anyway, but it was dirty, and his
father took it away and threw it down a sewer, and told Daddy
he'd learn to be more careful after that. Daddy said Geoff and
I need some discipline, and if we don't watch out, we'll get so
soft we'll never amount to anything. Then he decided to stop
talking. Geoff and I ate the dessert, and when the maid came
and cleared the table, and asked us how we liked what she'd
made, we told her we liked it a lot. Then Geoff and I asked to
be excused. When we went upstairs we looked at a *National Geographic* magazine, and there were some kids from
India shown, and it said they didn't eat very much, and a
lot of the kids there would die. I told Geoff I had a stomachache; and he said he had one, too. But we got better, and
we went to bed, and the next day we went to our country

house, and Daddy came with us, and we all had a good time."

When Helen was twelve she had slimmed down, was preoccupied with the French language, which she had begun to study in earnest, and with France as a nation. She read books about its history, geography, culture. She had on the walls of her rooms pictures of Paris and of the rural landscape to the south. She listened a lot to records of spoken French and to French music. And she dreamed of going to France. She would do so upon turning thirteen — six weeks there with her mother and brother. They were joined by her father in Paris for the last week. That trip did it — the conversion of an interest into a love affair. Upon her return to America Helen became known to the French consulate in Boston, and she loved going to a patisserie not far from her home. She excelled in French, was the best at speaking as well as reading and writing the language. And, after reading an article or two in the newspapers about contemporary problems in the formerly French-dominated parts of Africa, she began to understand the nostalgia of the colonialists: "The French are so smart, and they must have helped the native people in Africa. When the French left, I read, there was trouble, and now there's starvation. If the French had only stayed, then the people there would be better off. I joked with my French teacher; I said I wouldn't mind if the United States became part of the French empire! I like our flag, but I like the tricolor better; and I like 'La Marseillaise' better than our 'Star-Spangled Banner.' In Africa the French tried to bring the tribes together, but then when the countries became independent there, the tribes started fighting with each other, and there's been trouble ever since. It's too bad."

She was no longer worried about the "trouble" hundreds of thousands of utterly impoverished men, women, and children face daily; her worry was directed at the notion of "progress."

When is it genuine, when a prelude to disaster? The result was lively talk at the table, especially at suppertime. Those talks encouraged Helen's parents, who saw her as a girl who was fast growing up and becoming responsible and thoughtful. Helen also spoke highly of her parents: "I used to think my father didn't care enough about us at home, but now I realize how hard he works, and it's all for us. He helps a lot of other people, too. Geoff says that when he grows up he doesn't want to work as hard as Daddy, but I hope Geoff will change his mind later on. That's what happened in the French empire. It wasn't 'progress' when the French left Africa. It was the beginning of a lot of trouble. My mother says I'm not being fair to the natives, because they don't have the education that the French have. But that's why the French should have stayed there, so they could keep educating the natives.

"If France still had its empire, I would try to go to Africa and teach the natives. Maybe I could still go; but it wouldn't be as interesting now. According to our teacher, a lot of the African countries have very poor governments. And if you're white, you can get into a lot of trouble. My mother says there's a real problem they have, the natives: they'd like our help, but they don't always like us! That's not fair; a lot of white people just want to be generous, and they don't want to take anything away from the natives. Geoff and I argue a lot; he says that if he lived in Africa and was a native, he'd want to be the boss and not have to salute my French flag! I told him it didn't make any difference which flag the natives salute. Geoff says he wishes he could have been in the French Foreign Legion, and so do I, but there weren't any women allowed."

She wrote a story for her English class — responded eagerly to her teacher's request that the imagination be used to the fullest. She told her readers about the French Foreign Legion, then had a woman cooking meals for Legionnaires, and finally, becoming their leader — after saving them all from ambush at the hands of some natives, whom she had spotted. Only in France, or among Frenchmen, was such an outcome possible, she insisted, at the end of her composition; after all, France is the nation of Jeanne d'Arc. The teacher was pleased, praised the author highly — but with one reservation. The description of the natives was called "not quite fair, even for a story." The author was asked to discuss the matter further with the teacher, and did.

Helen remembered vividly, even months later, what went on: "We had an argument. I told her the natives were always stealing, and the French had to watch them, and that was the job of the Legionnaires. She said I was being too critical of the natives. That's when I told her that I thought the French are smarter than the natives, and there's been a lot of trouble since the empire ended. She asked where I got my facts. I said from reading magazines and the newspaper. Then I told her to look at our school, and how the black kids aren't doing very well. There are three in our class, and they're all getting special help, and they get bad marks. (We see their papers; they even show their papers to us.) I guess I shouldn't have brought up the subject of our black kids, because the teacher got upset and told me she had another appointment.

"I left the room, and one of the black kids and her mother came in. When I got home and told my mother, she said I should be careful about what I say outside the house. Mom told me a lot of people in the school are beginning to worry about the scholarship students. I said the scholarship students are all black. Mom said it's best to call them the scholarship students, and not the black students. I asked why there aren't any *white* scholarship students, and she said because we don't need any — since everyone is already white in our school. That's when I said maybe there shouldn't be *any* scholarship students anymore, if they're all having trouble in our school. And my mother said, yes, she was beginning to agree with me, though she told me we'd both better wait and see what happens, and not 'go advertising' what we think. Daddy has told us, a lot of times, not to 'go advertising' what we think; he says you should let the other person tell you what is on his mind first."

By the age of thirteen and a half her mind was taken up with schools: would she go away to X or Y boarding school? France remained a preoccupation, if not an obsession — the latter a word her father used, half jokingly, to describe the continuing concern of both his children, actually, with "les affaires françaises." He was not by inclination or habit one to use a psychologically pejorative word, like "obsession," but he had begun to get annoyed with what he regarded as the excessive Gallic pride of his daughter. She had responded with a gradual diminution of interest in "that foreign nation." She would never see eye to eye with him. But she did find it hard to disagree with him outright. And besides, they really did agree "on most important things," as she came to realize quite clearly when they had their first long personal talk, a couple of months short of her fourteenth birthday. He asked her what she anticipated doing with her life. She told him that she no longer thought she would live in Paris and become an actress or live someplace in the French Alps, where she would try to be a "champion skier." Nor was she anymore taken up with dreams of geographic expeditions to central Africa. She wanted to stay in New England and nourish a rapidly developing hobby of hers — one she envisioned turning into a career: photography.

She had received a Polaroid camera when eleven and had largely ignored it for over a year. At twelve she took many pictures, asked for a conventional camera, began to use that, too. At thirteen she felt increasingly competent with the two cameras, and began to learn how to develop her own pictures.

She was taught how to do so at school and by a neighbor who was a rather experienced amateur photographer. Helen was becoming known as such herself by her classmates, and her photographs of Boston, of the rural landscape near her parents' country home, were displayed in the school's library. She was in the eighth grade at the time, and it was then that she announced, in another one of her compositions, her intention to become a fashion photographer. She had for a year or so been taking notice of *Vogue* and *Mademoiselle,* both regularly present in her mother's sitting room. Maybe someday she might be a fashion photographer, and roam the world — combining thereby a life of travel and photography. And maybe she would, in the course of such a life, meet a Frenchman she liked, or maybe an Englishman; eventually she would marry, she speculated, a European.

However, when her brother said that he too might want to go to Europe, and maybe live there, she expressed disapproval. She would in time decide to come back to this country. Europe was fine, but America is best, she told Geoff. He did, as he got older, take up the camera with an enthusiasm to match hers, but he was interested in less romantic pictures. In the country he photographed (at twelve and thirteen) the men who worked on the road, or the local policeman at work. In the city, Geoff walked away from the well-to-do enclave he considered home; he reached other streets, far less attractive, took pictures of stores and storekeepers and ordinary working people. His finest work was done with the firemen who were assigned to a location a few blocks away from his home. He asked the men if he could photograph the engines, then asked them if they minded standing near those engines. He built up a portfolio of photographs that the school judged worthy of highest honors in its annual hobby show.

Geoff was rather more critical of himself than others were

of him. His sister was quite upset with him, as a matter of fact, when she heard what he had to say about the fire station series of pictures: "He told me he was worried, because there's a kid in his room who is black, and he told Geoff that his father can't find a job, and he keeps trying, and he applied for a job as a policeman and a fireman, but he still hasn't heard anything. I told Geoff not to worry; it was silly to worry. If the father wanted a job bad enough, according to our Daddy, then there are plenty of jobs to be found. Daddy showed us once how many pages there are in the newspaper full of advertisements for people to come and apply for a job. Geoff isn't old enough to understand a lot of things. He feels sorry for everyone! I used to be like him. But when you get older you know that people have to help themselves. It's not fair, though, about the black people. They've had a bad time. But they're having a better time."

She thought she might try to follow her brother's lead, do some documentary photographs. Why not go to a black neighborhood and take pictures there? If Geoff could win a prize for his pictures of firemen and their engines, she could win the same prize a year later with the project she had in mind. Her mother offered to drive her to a black neighborhood and stay with her while she used her camera. Her father said no, they might both get in trouble. Helen decided to go see — to drive with her mother down a street where one black classmate lives and see what was there waiting for the camera to catch hold of. But just as they were ready to go, she told her mother that she had reconsidered, had no further interest in the idea, and wanted instead to take some pictures of the houses and people in her own neighborhood. She liked cats, had an idea about what she would do: photographic portraits of cats sitting on the steps of town houses.

IV

WITHDRAWAL

HIGH UP in an office building the boy stands with his father and listens to a political analysis of a city's turmoil. Black and white children are being bused, black and white parents are up in arms, violence has repeatedly taken place, and the boy's father has been dismayed, saddened. The boy has wondered why. The father has tried to explain. Then they enjoy the view. It is part of a ritual they have — looking out the window, picking one part of the view for discussion (a building, a neighborhood, the river, one of several parks, a particular street) and then, when the conversation is over, just staring for a moment. The boy is proud of the view, proud of his father, proud of what he has learned from his father. The boy wishes his father were mayor of the city, governor of the state. Then, there might be less trouble. But his father is no politician, the boy knows. And that is the trouble with the United States of America: the power wielded by politicians — as opposed to men like his father or, for that matter, women like his mother.

A day or so later, the newspapers carried a letter the boy's father had written, urging "reason" and compliance with the federal judge's school desegregation order. The boy had asked for an extra newspaper; he, too, wanted a copy of the letter to

keep. The next day, in school, he wrote his own brief statement as an impromptu composition: "If white people and
black people were friends, we would have a better country. I
think that there's nothing bad about going to school in a bus.
It's good that we have black kids in our school."

He was then nine. His is "a liberal, progressive school," the
boy's mother says. His name is Gordon. He has always been a
bright, committed, forthcoming student. He has rarely de-
scended to B work, yet is not especially bookish. He laughs
easily, is good at sports, is called "a natural leader" by his
teachers. He likes to give oral compositions, has been speaking
up in class rather vigorously since the first grade. The school
he attends is a private urban school just outside Boston. Children of doctors, lawyers, businessmen, and professors go
there; but so do poor children, a substantial number from the
ghetto. Gordon has made a point of befriending those children, has long been encouraged to do so by his parents. When
busing got under way in Boston Gordon not only joined his
father in supporting the idea but offered to be bused himself.
His parents said no. His father, a scientist and college professor, emphasized the importance of staying in a good school
— one which was, besides, integrated. His mother, of a quite
wealthy family, insisted that he owed it to the black students
in the school he was attending to stay and speak or write on
their behalf. The boy agreed to remain, but was not able to still
the voice of his conscience. He wrote a brief comment for his
school's student newspaper: "I believe it is not fair that if you
have money, you can go to a private school, and not be bused.
Only the white kids who are poor and don't like blacks go on
the bus. No wonder there is a lot of trouble in Boston's schools.
We should try to help, but I don't know how. Any suggestions?"

He received none. He went about his business, tried to push

Boston's torment out of his mind, but could not: "If I was eleven or twelve, I'd just tell my mother and father that I was quitting the school I'm going to, and taking a bus over to any school in Boston I got sent to. They might not like what I'd want to do, but they would let me go ahead. My sister is thirteen, and she tells my parents what she's going to do, and they disagree with her, but they don't stop her. She told me yesterday that if I got really upset, and stood my ground, they'd give in. I asked her how she gets upset! She said it's easy — just get upset! So, I tried. I told Dad at supper that I wasn't happy at school and I wanted to leave. He asked me what I meant. I told him I just wasn't happy there. He asked why. I said for a lot of reasons. He said to name one. I didn't. I said I just wanted to leave and go to a public school in Boston. Then he guessed my reason. He said I wanted to be of help.

"But he wouldn't let me leave. He said no, definitely no. My mother said that if I could persuade them, then I could do what I want, but I had to be a good lawyer! I tried. I told them what I'd written for the school newsletter. I told them why I thought I should be bused to a black school. I told them what a black kid told me in school; he said that he felt like a traitor, because he was going to a fancy private school, while other kids on his street were going on the bus into Hyde Park and South Boston and places like that. He said I should be bused and so should he, because we both live in Boston. Then my mother interrupted and wanted to know what difference it would make if two extra children got bused. I said I didn't know. My father said I'm going to a good school and I have black friends there, and he wouldn't take me out, even if I did the best job of arguing in the world! That's when he and Mom had an argument. She said that if I really wanted to leave school and go to a public school, they should at least discuss it, and leave the door open. My Dad said I wasn't old enough to

decide where I was going to school. He said later, *later* I could.
My mother said he was *dictating* to me. He said he was just
being my *father*. That's when my mother turned to me and
asked me what *I* thought. I didn't know what to say! My sister
said I should speak up, but I couldn't find any words. I kept
quiet. My father said: 'That settles it.' If I knew how to persuade them, I think they would have let me switch schools."

Gordon was enough like his sister to stay concerned with the
problem of busing for a long time. He continued to alert his
fellow students and his teachers to the vexing moral question,
as he saw it, of who was being bused and who was not. At the
age of ten he drew a picture of a bus, filled with black children,
approaching a school, in front of which stood some white children. (Figure 42.) The whites seem large, strong, unfriendly.
One has a club in hand. The blacks are mere faces, peering out
of windows. The boy has left half the windows empty. He had
a reason for doing so: "I should be on the bus. Other white kids
should be there, too. It's not fair that the blacks are being
bused and the whites mostly aren't. I'd like to be bused, but
I won't be. It's no fun going in a car pool — the same old
people! I told my mother that yesterday, and she laughed. She
said she could understand why I feel like I do, but I have to
remember that someone else's problems are not always mine;
there's a limit to how many fights we can get into. I said that
I agreed, but this was *my* fight. She smiled and said she was
glad. She told me to tell Dad that I was still in the ring fighting!
I did — at suppertime. He said he was proud of me!

"Dad believes Boston is full of racists, and it's getting worse
rather than better, and the whole country is laughing at the
city. Even at our school there are kids who say that the blacks
aren't as smart as the whites, and they need special help, and
it's all right to have them in our school, but they're not the
same as we are. I got into a fight with a kid who said that last

week. He thinks he's so nice and tolerant, but he doesn't really like black kids. When I told my father, he said that was a good reason for me to be right where I am — so I could argue with the kids who are going to be racists later on, if they're not told to stop talking like they do."

He more than fulfilled his father's expectations. At eleven Gordon was a forceful, incisive spokesman for integration, if necessary through busing. He was also worried about other problems; he wrote a composition denouncing our high military budget, our willingness to support certain dictators, our failure to align ourselves more dramatically and enthusiastically with the world's poorer (mostly African and Asian) nations. The essay was given first prize for the best seventh-grade written exercise. Gordon had supporters among his classmates, but there were those who found him rather more sure of himself than they liked. Gordon was not inhibited by disapproval. He actually enjoyed it. He enjoyed being regarded as a person of strong, uncompromising opinion, as a well-informed boy who didn't hesitate to speak out, even to the point of criticizing his own situation. Who else in the school had called himself "wrong" for not being on a school bus every morning, on his way to a public school in a black section of Boston? Who else had acknowledged that his parents, as quite well-to-do people, had "good reasons" to want to keep the status quo, or modify it only so much? Who else brought in suggested reading about Cuba and China — books and articles that Gordon's older sister had found interesting and valuable and which she recommended to him?

At the age of twelve Gordon even mentioned a desire to go to both Cuba and China. Why? Because he felt those nations to be "the wave of the future." He wanted to see countries where "poverty has been wiped out." He wanted to meet Castro and Mao, because he believed both of them to be "great men." He thought that each was like our Abraham Lincoln, the one president he really liked a lot. His father would ask Gordon what he thought Castro ought to do, or this country ought to do with respect to Cuba. The boy would take a position and argue it out over supper. The father would press hard, take issue with the son, point out one or another issue the boy had overlooked. The mother would eventually ask both of them to stop, to get on with the meal, or turn to lighter, less abrasive conversation. When Gordon indicated that he really did want to go to Cuba, rather than a summer camp he'd been attending since the age of eight, his father expressed approval. Why not? The boy would learn a lot, and begin to see how other people live, other governments operate. The mother became nervous: wasn't the boy too young? But she, too, assented; and both parents tried hard to learn if there was some way for their son's wish to come true. There wasn't. Instead he went to the Southwest, stayed with a Navaho family on an exchange program, toured Arizona and New Mexico, came back full of affection for another region of America and full of concern for the Indians he had stayed with and come to know somewhat.

At school he wrote one composition after another about the poverty he saw, the consequent demoralization of a once-proud people. His teachers were quite pleased with him — both for going to the Southwest and for coming back even more troubled than before about others, less fortunate. At the end of a composition the author was told that if only there were more people like him, this would be a better country. But Gordon was not so willing to be thus complimented. He wondered out loud at supper what difference his teacher's attitude toward him made to the Navaho Indians. Ought he not, in a few years, go out West, live there all the time, work hard on behalf of the Indians? Ought he not to ask his father to send money, a lot of it, the Indians? Why should he, one twelve-year-old boy, have "almost a hundred thousand dollars, maybe more," put away in his name for his future use, while thousands of Indian children of his age are penniless and always will be, things being as they are?

His father supplied answers to those questions, and Gordon listened carefully but not always in agreement: "My father says we've done a lot of harm to the Indians, and he agrees with me, it's been bad that we haven't tried to make up for our mistakes. But it's got to be the government that will change everything. Even if my family gave all its money to the Indians, they wouldn't be much better off than they are now. I think that if everyone who worries about the Indians really started trying to help them, it would make a difference. It's not right that I become a good guy in school, just because I say the right words about 'the poor Indians.' That's what our social studies teacher keeps on telling us — that we've got to realize how bad everything is for 'the poor Indians.' I agree, it *is* bad for them; but we're not helping them by saying so all the time!

"When I asked my mother if she'd mind if I went out West next summer again, she said I was getting 'overinvolved' with the Indians. Her friend — her roommate at college — used to be a psychiatric social worker before she got married, and she was the one who put it in my mother's head that I was 'overinvolved.' My mother told me what she thought, and I got very angry. Then she told me, the next day — after she'd called up her friend, I'm sure — that I *was* overinvolved, and the proof was that I'd become so angry! Isn't that wild! I told my Dad, and he agreed with me; he said that Mom is really upset because I'm only twelve (I'm almost thirteen!) and she is worried that I'm talking like some college student who wants to be a revolutionary. I told Dad that isn't true. I don't want to get into any trouble. But if a lot of people don't try to help out the Indians, and the black people too, then it won't do any good for just me to go and sacrifice. I laughed at her, I guess, when she kept on telling me I was 'overinvolved.' She just walked out of the room; and later she told Dad that she was upset with me. I guess that's why he spoke to me. Maybe next summer I'll go back to my old camp as a junior counselor. I think the director told my Dad I could be a junior counselor if I wanted."

Gordon did become a junior counselor. He turned thirteen that summer, and he began to hear his voice crack and deepen and see new hair appear on his body. He had always loved swimming, loved playing in the sand, loved the sight and sound of the ocean as well as swimming in it. He began to lose some of the intensity of commitment he had felt a year earlier to the Indians. He decided that he really wouldn't be happy living in the Southwest; the ocean is too far away. A lake or two would not suffice. Might he go away to some school located at the edge of the Maine shore? Might he become a sailor one day? How about marine biology for a career? He had an uncle who worked as a marine biologist at Woods Hole, Massachusetts, and perhaps that was the best possible occupation for a boy of thirteen whose parents got obviously nervous when future enlistment in the navy or merchant marine was mentioned.

When he was through with his eight weeks of working in a summer camp, Gordon went to Woods Hole, became familiar with the various ways his uncle pursued his work. He went out on a boat, from which he went underwater in a special cage. He examined specimens from the sea that were under study. He talked with his uncle about the future: what to study, where, and with how much hope or certainty of becoming a first-rate scientist? In the autumn Gordon stopped writing about politics for a while, devoted himself almost exclusively to essays on the ocean. He did not, however, lose a strong social conscience. He announced to his teachers (in one essay) and to his parents many times over the dining table that he was going to try to help the Indians and other impoverished people "in a real serious way" one day; he was going to learn how to take organic matter from the sea and make cheap food for the world's hungry masses.

Let others indulge in empty talk; Gordon was going to be the best kind of idealist and activist — a practical, competent, knowing man who could come up with something of obvious worth: "I'd like to be helpful to others. My mother and father tell me that if you have a lot, then you have to give back to others who don't have anything. That's why I study hard, I guess — so that I'll be able to become a scientist maybe, and then I can really be of help. I might end up being a doctor. I have an uncle who's a surgeon; he does research. I have another uncle who is a doctor; he delivers babies and he does research too. He's my mother's twin. He always tells me that a lot of children never should be born, because they're going to live a bad life. It would be nice if they could all be born, and then have plenty of food. If only we could discover some cheap food that everyone could eat; then no one would starve to death. I wouldn't want to be born poor."

In school, when Gordon was twelve, he had written the following composition: "We are the privileged ones; we have been born lucky, and we'll probably die old and still pretty lucky. We have parents who have plenty of money. They love us, and when we want something they say yes, and they go and get us what we want. That's being lucky. I wish that others were as privileged as we are. I wish everyone in the world had enough food and a good home. My father says that when you're poor, you feel like two cents. There are many people in this world who feel that way, even in our country. If I thought I could help a lot of those people out, then I'd feel a lot better. Then I'd really be lucky. Then I'd really be privileged. Right now, the trouble with a lot of my friends, and with me, is that we are so lucky, we don't even know how lucky we are. I asked my parents if there wasn't a plan we could discover that would help all the kids all over the world who don't have the good luck we do. My parents said they wished we could, but they couldn't think of any plan like that. I can't think of one, either. I hope one day there will be a plan."

He did, of course, think of such a plan — the application of marine biology to problems of nutrition. But when Gordon was almost fourteen, he became disillusioned with that idea and inclined to return to his parents' faith — that political and economic changes might ultimately affect the lives of the poor. He took a new interest in history and in civics, and he asked his mother and father more and more questions about "the government" and how it works. He went with them to the state capital and to Washington, D.C. They visited his congressman and both his senators. He watched the Supreme Court, the Senate, got to see a room in the White House. When he came back he was full of information, but also inclined to wonder even more about his country and how it is run and for whom.

Gordon wrote another composition for his English teacher, and in it he repeated old preoccupations but imbued them with new doubts: "I went to Washington, D.C. I saw a lot of places. I realized that our government has many parts to it. You can't help thinking how beautiful the buildings are there, but you worry about all the American people who never get to Washington, and don't care, because all they do care about is getting enough food to eat. My father said that the government supposedly belongs to everyone in the country, but when you come right down to it, a lot of people don't know how the government works. All over Washington there are lobbyists, and *they* are the ones who know how the government works.

"I asked our congressman if he thought Thomas Jefferson and James Madison ever dreamed there would be so many lobbyists in Washington, and I didn't get a good answer. The congressman said: 'There weren't any lobbyists then.' But my father said there probably were, only they didn't get called by that name. The congressman wasn't happy to hear my father say that! He said that any citizen has the right to come to the Capital and *petition* — that's what a democracy is. We didn't answer him back, but later my Dad and I laughed: a lot of people don't have the fare to get to Washington, and no one would pay any attention to them if they did. But if you've got influence and money, everyone listens to you. That's one lesson I learned in Washington — that there are a lot of interesting places to see, and a lot of lobbyists, too."

Gordon added other comments later on, when talking to his friends. He emphasized the physical beauty of the city, the pleasure he had in riding the Senate railway, and the awesome majesty of the Supreme Court in session. But he kept referring to lobbyists as well. And he wondered what he himself might do, when older, to influence the government. His parents suggested that he could best be of service to his country by choosing an honorable profession and becoming a kind and generous husband, father, neighbor. The boy was not so sure. He talked of writing a letter a day to his congressman and of persuading friends to do likewise. When he read of the Children's Crusade in a history book he asked his eighth-grade teacher whether she thought such a crusade (on behalf of America's poor) would work in this country in this century. The answer was no. His parents also said no. By the end of his eighth-grade year the boy had also decided no. He was "into" marine biology again, but keeping an eye on the front page of the newspaper. When he read in a social studies class about the civil rights movement of the 1960s, he remarked in class that it would be "nice" if one day his generation could become involved in such an effort. His teacher agreed; later, his parents did. But none of them, including the boy, could imagine what such a future effort might be like.

A week before he turned fourteen Gordon suddenly became cynical in a school report he had written on Woodrow Wilson's presidency: "It does not pay to become idealistic. You try hard, but you get misunderstood and destroyed. That is the lesson of Woodrow Wilson's life." His teacher thought Gordon "too pessimistic"; his parents told him he would "change his mind" and realize one day "how many chances there always are" for people to express their idealism forcefully and to great effect: "They tell me to cheer up, and they say that I'm *only* thirteen, or I'm *only* fourteen, and in a few years I'll see what they mean. But I hear my parents talk about things, and I know what they believe in their hearts. They say things to me they only half believe! I say things to my friends I only half believe! The teachers say things to us they only half believe! We say things to the teachers we only half believe! My mother used to tell me that you can't say a lot of things out loud. Now I know what she meant: you don't even admit to yourself a lot of things. My father says you've got to compromise in this world. I used to think he was wrong. I hate to believe it's true, and I wish it wasn't true. I wish everyone was more honest, but you can't be.

"I'm a teenager, my parents keep telling me. I'm supposed to be 'idealistic' because I'm a teenager! Then I'll grow up, and that'll be the end of my idealism! Then I'll become 'practical!' "

After he spoke that last sentence he looked at an old drawing of his, which he had kept on a bulletin board. (Figure 43.) He drew the picture when he was twelve and first developing a strong interest in the sea, in the life within it. A boat is anchored in the ocean. Divers have gone under water. Some machinery will soon follow them. The sea stretches indefinitely in one direction; in the other is the mainland: people, trees, a wharf, a building or two. A person stands on the ship; he is made big, out of proportion even to the size of the ship, let alone the people on the land, who are huddled together in discrete bunches. The artist knew what he intended — a portrait of the artist as sailor, scientist, explorer, and, not least, man removed from others, privileged to have his own activity, while they cling to each other and do nothing, get nowhere. When he had finished the picture the boy had tersely expressed his sadness: if only others had his opportunities, but they haven't and won't.

Two years later Gordon repeats himself, decides he doesn't want the picture near him anymore. After all, he observes with a smile, the boat must have long since pulled up its anchor and gone someplace else. Nor is there any point in drawing such pictures. He has tired of autobiographical writing. He has come to respect more and more those scientists who withdraw from the world's distractions, carve out an exceedingly circumscribed domain for themselves and work it to the fullest. He knows one such biologist who claims never to read the paper, never even to watch the news on television. Why should anyone become acquainted with, agitated by, events over which he or she has utterly no control? It is a question the boy, the youth, asks himself more and more often.

V

PROBLEM CHILD

MAIDS brought up the girl from the beginning. Her mother was a mere drinker when pregnant, but a few months after her daughter was born her husband began to use the phrase "heavy drinker" about his wife. The girl's father is himself rather knowing about alcohol. He has slowly worked his way up in corporate management. He started with a Cincinnati department store, moved to a Chicago insurance company, then to Cincinnati again, with Procter & Gamble, then to an Illinois steel company, then out to California, then back East to Virginia, and finally to a New England electronics firm. He is one of a number of vice-presidents — a man who knows how to manage employees, arrange for advertising, keep an eye on all sorts of budgets, conclude arrangements, deal with various contractors, and, not least, get along with other executives like himself. During twelve years of marriage he and his wife have lived in seven cities — the Midwest, the far West, the upper South, and finally, New England. All the while his alcoholic intake has steadily increased. All the while his wife pretended to be abstemious; at times she claimed to be a teetotaler. She never drank in front of him. When she became dizzy, unstable, slurred of speech, he was likely to be away from home. If he was at home, she took to her bed, worried out loud that she had "a strange neurological disease." He said she ought to go see a doctor. But for periods of a week, even a month, she became suddenly better. Then she urged *him* to see a doctor; he drank too much. Yes, he agreed; but he was getting more and more influential, and so had to face constant pressure. One day, he might well get to be president of a company; then he would have to take no one's orders, and would be quite at ease with himself — and so, uninterested in whiskey, gin, beer, wine, brandy. Meanwhile, he drank them all.

His wife drank only vodka, had been doing so most of their marriage — heavily, and most often alone. No one had ever found one of her empty bottles. She prided herself on her control, her guile, her circumspection, her resourcefulness. She was so smart that she even fooled herself; she would drink a lot, complain of severe headaches and unsteadiness, wonder out loud whether she ought call a doctor, suggest to the maid or her husband that she be taken to a hospital for "tests," then mysteriously lose all her symptoms. The pattern, the cycle, the addiction and apparent remission from addiction lasted for years. Meanwhile there were two children who needed a mother and a father — the older child a boy, the younger a girl. The latter was born when the mother's secret drinking was accelerating; was born in the midst of yet another family move; was born on the way to a strange hospital.

When the girl was eight she was able to describe the experience as if she were a grown-up witness to it, rather than an extremely young participant: "We have moved a lot. We have never lived in the same place more than two years. Daddy is going to be the boss in a business one day, but it takes time. He has to go where there's a good job. Each time we move, he gets a better job. I remember the friends I had in California. I don't remember being born, but my mother has told me how it happened. And our maid has heard the story, and if I forget something, she reminds me. Daddy got a better job, so we had to move to Chicago. I wasn't supposed to be born when they were moving. I came early. My mother and father and brother were driving to Chicago. They said good-bye to our house. Halfway to Chicago my mother began to have pain. My father kept telling her she needed to eat, and that was why she had the pain. She doesn't eat very much. The maid will cook us supper, and Mommy says she's not hungry. Then she tells us to eat. A lot of the time I don't feel like eating, either. The doctor gave me pills to take, so I'll grow. He says I may not be getting all the vitamins I need.

"When my mother kept saying she hurt in the tummy, my father stopped at a Howard Johnson's. He told my mother she had to eat. My mother ordered fried clams, but she didn't touch them. Then she went to the bathroom. When she came out, she told my father she was in real trouble. He went to find out where the nearest hospital was. She was in pain, and she ordered a drink. Daddy says it was one of the few times he's seen Mommy drink out in the open. They took her to the hospital, and that's when I was born, on the way. That's why I have to say I was born in Indiana, even though my parents never lived there. My mother had to stay in the hospital with me; my father left her and drove to Chicago with my brother. He was only two then; my grandmother came to take care of him, but she was sick, and she had to go into a hospital in Chicago a few days after she got there. Daddy hired a maid. He's the one who usually hires the new maid, if we lose our old one. Mommy says she doesn't want any maid around. But we need one. Without a maid, there would be trouble."

The girl is called Susie by her mother, but insists on being addressed as Susan by the maid. When she was seven the maid's name was also Susan; they agreed that young Susan would call the maid Sue. That particular maid was "the best one," according to the girl. On her bureau she has kept a picture of the two of them, taken by the child's father. The maid stayed with the family for a year and a half, and was sorely missed by the girl. When she was nine she remembered that maid fondly: "I liked her the best. She's the only one I liked. We used to take walks. I liked living in that house. I wish we were still there. But we rented it; Daddy doesn't want to buy a house until he knows he'll be staying with the same company for a long time. My mother was sick when Sue was with us, but we didn't know what the illness was. The doctors aren't sure now, either. But they are giving her tests. My brother says it's a mysterious disease. We've heard Mommy and Daddy fight; Daddy blames Mommy for being sick. He says it's her fault. Mommy says that if she is sick, she shouldn't be blamed.

"I feel sick a lot. My old maid, Sue, used to hold me on her lap, and she'd make an ice cream soda, and when I had it I'd feel better. My favorite was strawberry. I wish she was back with us. She was going to move with us, but my mother didn't want her to come, because then she'd be part of the family. It's too bad she didn't. The new maid has a whole suite for her own. She has a bedroom, a sitting room, a little kitchen and a bathroom, and a hall. She has her own steps going upstairs. This is the biggest house we've ever lived in. We own it. We have sixteen rooms, I think. We have nine acres of land. A lot of it is just trees; but Daddy wants to cut some of them down and build a tennis court and a swimming pool. If Sue was with us, she could go swimming next summer. That's when we're going to build our pool, just before it gets hot, so we can swim all during July and August. Sue would have liked our house."

The girl worried her parents when she was four and five; she spent hours with her dolls and their dollhouse, and had scant interest in other children. Her nursery school teachers observed that she had no interest at all in the dolls or dollhouses at school. When the family moved yet again — she was six — Susie abandoned her dolls completely. She went through what her mother described as "a change of personality." The girl, who had been shy, withdrawn, seemingly uninterested in others, became a willful person who was especially interested in outdoor activities. She loved to swing, to run about, and, at seven, to ice-skate. She announced to her mother that she would, one day, become a well-known skater — would make money doing exhibition skating. She had seen a documentary on ice-skating, had dedicated herself to becoming as proficient as possible. She drew a picture, when eight, of herself skating. She was tall, upright, nicely balanced. Her arms were outstretched. She wore a red jacket, a blue hat. Though she usually skated on a pond near her house, or an indoor rink of a private school, she showed herself skating on what looked like a river or highway of ice, lined by fir trees, all under a blazing sun hanging low in a clear, deep blue sky. (Figure 44.)

She was indulging in a bit of fantasy, as she made clear: "I told my mother this morning that I'd like to skate so fast that people would think I have a motor in each skate, and I'm being pushed by the two engines. I woke up and I was a little scared during the night. I must have been crying, I guess, because my mother came to my room and she asked me what was the matter. I'd had this dream. In the dream I was skating so fast I passed all the automobiles. It was real weird. I was on a road, I think. Maybe it was the Charles River. (My mother said it must have been!) But I was passing all these cars, so I think it could have been a road, and it was icy, and that's how I was able to skate on the road. I remember seeing a church, and some stores, and then all of a sudden I saw our old house, the one we lived in before we moved here, and I think that was when I woke up, and I remember being scared, because just when I saw our old house, the ice melted, I think, and I was afraid I was going to fall in the water and drown. I'm glad I woke up. Dreams can be real funny."

She was an exceptionally active dreamer when seven, eight, nine — to the point that her parents were often unnerved by her accounts of what she had seen and heard and said to herself or others while asleep. They consulted a pediatrician: ought the child be dreaming so much, and be so willing to talk about her dreams, and if not, what was to be done? The doctor reassured them: some children do indeed have frequent, vivid dreams, and are not shy about remembering them out loud. When Susan was nine she woke up screaming one night. Her father was away on business. Her mother was in a stuporous sleep, and did not hear the child. The maid came, and tried to comfort the sobbing, frightened girl. In the morning the maid told the mother what had happened, but the mother could not, for a long while, convince her daughter to talk about the nightmare. Finally, the mother did learn what had been dreamed, and so did the maid and the father and even some of the dreamer's friends. In a picture done with paints the girl tried to show what she had seen that night. With brown paint she constructed a rather deep hole; then she built a fence around part of the hole; then she placed herself near the fence. (Figure 45.) That was all there was to the dream — a child climbing up a hole, trying to get out, but not able to do so because a fence blocked her way.

With no one's help the girl had figured out what had happened, and why she had been terrified: "I knew that a tornado had just taken place. Once when we were moving, we almost got killed by a tornado. We could see it coming, and my Daddy stopped the car, and we got out and went into a ditch and just lay there and prayed. My father asked God to spare us. My mother said she'd be a better mother if only we'd be spared. My father said he wouldn't make us move ever again. And we were saved! The tornado hopped, skipped, and jumped all over, but it didn't touch us. Then we got in the car and we kept going. My father said we sure were lucky. We passed a lot of houses that had been picked up — just picked up! — by the tornado and dumped someplace else. You could see the cellars of the houses. I think that's what I was remembering in my nightmare. I was in a ditch or something, maybe the cellar of our house, and trying to get out, but there was this big fence, and I couldn't find a way to get through it. And I could hear my mother and father; they were someplace, but I didn't know where, and I couldn't see them. I think my mother was in the ditch too, and she was telling me that it's best to 'stay put' — those are the words she uses a lot, when she wants me to stop being 'antsy.' And my father was someplace else, on the other side of the fence, and he was telling me to hurry up (like he always says) and get out, and climb the fence and come with him. It was confusing. And I was scared, I guess. Then I woke up, and our maid was asking me if I wanted some warm milk, and I said no."

In her painting she had neglected to show any of the debris scattered by the tornado, but she had made the sky black, and for years she described that sky to friends. When the family moved one more time (she was ten) her first question was about tornadoes: would there be any "there"? Her next question was about skating rinks: were any nearby? In her fanciful moments she wondered whether she might win prizes as a skater, or get caught, fatefully, on a frozen pond when a tornado struck. Would she be able to skate faster than the tornado? She had been told that tornadoes don't come in the middle of the winter or, for that matter, don't come at all where she now lived. Still, she could not forget them, even as she placed great and continuing store in her ability to skate "as fast as lightning." And when her father boasted of her achievements he too emphasized speed as well as canniness: "Daddy says I should learn to skate so fast that people will say I'm gone before I start! He says you've got to stay ahead of all the other people, or you'll be in trouble. There's always someone who wants to win the race! Daddy gets up early and he goes to bed late. He says if he doesn't stay ahead, he'll fall way behind, and then we'll all be in trouble. If you keep your eyes open and watch what everyone else is going to do, then you can get yourself all set, and try as hard as you can, and whiz ahead and stay ahead. Daddy says that if you keep yourself ahead, you win."

She was extremely competitive in school. She would cry, in the second and third grades, when she learned that she had made a mistake or two on a paper, whereas classmates she knew had not. In the fourth grade she stated how assertive she felt obliged to be: "My hope is to have a good Christmas. I would like to win the ice-skating contest at the rink. My mother would like me to win, and my father would. He is almost a president of a company. We will not move, if Daddy becomes president. I would like to be a president of a company later, when I'm big. Daddy says I will, if I keep my eye on the ball."

That expression has always been a favorite of her father's and has become one of hers. In the fifth grade — she was ten — Susan tried to explain to a teacher what she meant when she talked about keeping her eyes on the ball; she meant "knowing what's important." She meant "trying not to lose, never forgetting that if you lose, you'll have no friends, but if you win, everyone will want to be nice to you." At about that time she became aware that her mother was "sick" and that her father was not sorry for his wife or compassionate, but rather, quite angry and self-pitying. She began to tell her friends that her mother would stumble, would speak incoherently, would cry inexplicably, would have wild suspicions or come forth with sordid accusations. She began to tell her friends that her father was thinking of sending her mother away to a hospital — though all his wife had to do was "behave herself," the girl pointed out.

When the girl's teachers heard about her "family problems," they decided to intervene, tactfully. One teacher called Susan aside, asked her what was wrong. She said nothing, but immediately contradicted herself, told everything she knew — a tale of a well-to-do family's "troubles." Susan used that word. A week after her eleventh birthday she drew a picture of a house she wanted — for herself and her cat, Lilly, and her books and her beloved skates, and her clock-radio, which she declared her single most important possession. The house was small, rather quaint; it had plants and flowers on a front lawn and on the window sills; it had a thick brown roof, with hay on top — a thatched roof; it had warmth — smoke curling out of the chimney; a storybook house. Nearby was a pond — frozen over, for skating. The sun was large, kindly in its smiling nearness to the land. The trees bent gently toward the house, protectingly. (Figure 46.) The artist made no effort later to deny the debt she owed to picture books she used to read: "I remember seeing little cottages that belonged to farmers. I think my mother once gave me a book called *The Farm Girl*, and it was the best present I've ever got, because I loved reading about the nice people and their nice little house. For a while I read the book every day! Then my mother wanted to take it away and throw it out, but I wouldn't let her. I hid the book from her! She forgot about it.

"She has a lot of troubles. I don't know what's the matter with her. I wish I did. Daddy won't tell me what her troubles are. He says he would like to go away for a week and just be by himself. He's always going on trips, but that's business, and he has to go to a lot of meetings. If I had a place like this house I've just drawn, I'd go there on weekends, after school is over, on Friday. One of our teachers goes away every weekend to a home she has in New Hampshire. I wish I had a home I could go to — besides the one we have here. Daddy says that even if we didn't have to move anymore, he still wouldn't want to stay in this house for the rest of his life. We have the maid, and we have a woman who comes and helps the maid, because the maid can't do everything by herself, and my mother is in bed a lot, or she goes to the doctor, or she has to have a 'rest.' She goes to a 'rest place,' and then she comes back and she promises us that everything will be different, and we're starting a new slate. But then she gets sick again.

"If I had a little house like this one in the picture, I would watch my favorite programs and make myself sandwiches, and then I'd go skating, and I'd ride my bike. Maybe I'd make friends; maybe there would be a girl not too far away, and I could skate with her, or ride on my bike with her. But if there wasn't anyone, I wouldn't mind. A lot of days, I leave the house and go on a hike, all by myself. The maid jokes with me; she says that I spend too much time with myself, and I should give other people a chance to be my friends. I have some friends, but we get into fights a lot. One of my friends says she wishes she could skate the way I do. Another friend is good in school, but I got better grades than she did last time. She beat me the time before. We went to camp together last summer. I hated the place. I won't go there again. Daddy said I had to go, because he was going to be away a lot, and my mother has all her troubles. I said I'd go if I could be with my brother, but Daddy said no, we had to be in different camps. So, we went to different camps, and we both had a rotten time.

"I cried a lot. When I didn't stop crying, after a week, I guess it was, they called up home. Daddy was away and my mother was in the hospital. I *had* to stay, they told me at camp. I couldn't go home to an empty house. But the maid was there! They let *me* call her up. She said it was all right with her if I came home. But they wouldn't let me, even so. I got up one morning, and I hated everyone in my cabin, and those stupid counselors, and the idiot who ran the camp. That's why I ran away. I decided to leave. The breakfast was awful — more Rice Krispies and hard toast! I just walked to the town, and then I put out my thumb, and a truck driver picked me up. He wanted to know where I was going. I said back toward Boston. He took me as far as Plymouth and let me off. Then I started hitching again; but the state police spotted me, and I was in trouble. They wanted to know where I lived. I told them. They called up, and the maid wasn't home. They took me to a jail. They didn't put me in, though! Finally the maid got home, and they spoke with her, and I guess she told them I was supposed to be in camp. They took me back. I never spoke to that maid again. I finally convinced my mother, after I got home from camp, to fire her."

That summer was a turning point for Susan. When she came home she was fidgety; she ate less and complained of headaches. She turned twelve in the autumn, and talked openly of running away from home — perhaps to an aunt in Jacksonville, Florida. The girl had always liked her, and had learned to imitate her Southern accent rather well. But Susan did not run away to Florida; she ran into the woods near her parents' home, and camped out there for a day, a night, another day. Her mother and father called the police, of course. Everyone looked everywhere — except in the woods in back of the house. At the beginning of the second night she decided to return home, and did — for an hour or so. She almost went unobserved. The maid saw her as she was leaving for the woods again with a supply of provisions. The girl's parents were, of course, glad to see her; but in no time their thankfulness turned to bitterness and anger. Why had she gone? What is the matter with children like her, who have been given "everything" and who still are not "happy," and who keep acting "as if they are kings and queens"?

Susan had no answers. Her grim and persistent silence only prompted more questions from her mother, her father, and eventually the family doctor, who suggested (when he too was met with unrelenting silence) that a child psychiatrist be consulted. The parents were as alarmed and angered by that suggestion as they were by their daughter's behavior and her subsequent moody withdrawal. They did, however, ask the girl whether she would consent to go "talk with someone." The girl asked who. The parents replied directly and briefly: a doctor. The girl asked (right to the point) what kind of a doctor. The mother had no answer. The father began to describe the doctor as "someone who understands children." The girl made his circumlocutions utterly unnecessary: "You mean a psychiatrist." The parents pulled back, asked their daughter if she wouldn't promise to "behave," in which case they would certainly not urge any visits with a psychiatrist. But Susan, in fact, wanted to go talk with a doctor — about her parents. And did. She approached her seventh-grade teacher and asked if she might speak to the school psychologist. She poured out her story to him, pleaded with him not to tell her parents that she had gone to see him. But he did tell them; so did the school's principal. When the girl learned that her parents had been told, she again ran away, this time on her bike.

She filled her knapsack with nuts, fruit, chewing gum, and some Life Savers. She tied her skates on the bike's handlebars, and pedaled away south, toward Connecticut. She almost got there before she was spotted by the police. She cleverly used local roads rather than highways. She had a map and used it quite intelligently. But she had not reckoned on a flat tire. As she stood by the side of a road, wondering what to do next, a state police car pulled up. The girl protested hard, screamed, cried, begged to be let go. But of course she was taken home. Shortly afterward she and her parents jointly took themselves to a child psychiatrist for a "consultation," and shortly after that the girl began seeing the doctor, and her parents began seeing, together, another psychiatrist.

After six months of "talks" with "a nice woman," Susan spoke quite gratefully and reflectively: "I thought at first that I must be nuts. I knew I wanted to go see someone, but I didn't know what I'd say, once I got there. I was sure I was the only one I knew twelve years old who was seeing a psychiatrist. But I've found out that there are a lot of kids who go. The lady, the doctor, told me that she sees kids *all day* — and some of them are a lot younger than me. I asked her how old the youngest is, and she said he's a boy, and he's only four years old. And she said she once treated a kid who was younger than that. I can't figure out what we do in her office, except talk. And I don't know why I feel better after I've left the office, but I do. I guess it's because with the doctor I try to say what's on my mind. With my mother, I can't; she's got her troubles. With my father, I can't; he's always working. With my brother, I can't; he's too young, and he gets scared when I ask him questions about what he thinks of our parents. Like the doctor says, he doesn't want to tell me what's on his mind. I don't blame him, either.

"I don't want to tell a lot that's on my mind to anyone. The doctor said I'm lonely, and I told her I don't mind being lonely! But now that I've met some kids who go to psychiatrists, I don't feel peculiar any more. I met one of the kids from school coming out of the building where the doctor's office is; and we said hello. The next day she came up to me during a recess, and she asked me who I was seeing. I was surprised. I didn't know what to say. She said they're all psychiatrists in that building, so she knew I'd been to see one, but not to worry, because she sees one, and so do a lot of kids. Then she started pointing out some of the kids, right then and there. I was upset. I thought it wasn't fair. But later I realized that the kids didn't mind; it was *me* who minded. I found that out when I met another kid from my school coming out of the doctor's office, a couple of weeks later, and she was like the first girl — she came right up to me and said I could join the 'club.' Well, there really isn't a club; but in a way, I guess, there is one.

"After you've talked with a psychiatrist for a while you begin to realize that it's like talking to someone older, who's nice and is trying to help you. My mother started crying the other day, after I'd come out of the doctor's office and while we were driving home. She said that if she'd been a better mother and if my father had been a better father, then I wouldn't be going to a doctor to talk. But I told her not to worry, and not to feel bad, because I don't mind going to a doctor. She's a nice doctor, anyway. She reminds me of the nice maid Sue we once had. My mother said my father had told her that there are times when he wonders if it's all worth it — the struggle he's had to get on top. Now they are on top, but he feels as if he's wading his way through a big, squishy swamp, and any minute he'll fall, or he'll step into some quicksand, and he'll sink. He asked my mother if she'd be willing to settle for ten thousand a year and him home all the time. She said yes, she would. So would I. But he said it wouldn't be so nice to be poor; and he's probably right. I like my room, and I like my skating lessons, and I like the woods we have, and our swimming pool."

She also liked going to talk with the doctor. But after six months of doing so the news came that her father would at last be the president of a substantial company, at a high salary (well over a hundred thousand dollars a year); but he would have to move yet again, this time to Westport, Connecticut. His wife was upset; she had begun attending Alcoholics Anonymous meetings, a move she made several months after her daughter started seeing a psychiatrist. His son was upset; he had two good friends, and he did not want to lose them. Nor did he want to go to school elsewhere. Nor did he want to give up his room, his wall covered with pictures of animals, hockey players, the Six Million Dollar Man, and Batman. As for Susan, she was quiet, resigned, compliant at first. She pointed out — to herself, to her mother and brother, to her doctor, to her teacher — that there wasn't anything she could do about the projected move, anyway. It was best to go along, try to look at the brighter side, try to emphasize their good prospects — an even larger home, a summer home, perhaps in Massachusetts (Cape Cod), and vacations all over the world. (She had dreamed for years of foreign travel.)

But a week or two before moving time the girl became sad, teary, lethargic, moody, unable to sleep well, and without appetite. The pediatrician pronounced her well physically. The child psychiatrist, saying good-bye, said Susan still had "problems," but was more aware of them than she once had been. The mother rallied around the girl as never before. The mother was determined to be sober, to make amends for her past errors of omission or commission. And the father came into the girl's room one day, sat down, and candidly acknowledged how "rotten" he felt, how much "to blame" he was for the girl's state of mind, and how hard he would work, in Connecticut, to give her everything, *everything* she might want — including an ice rink, if she wanted one, in which she could practice and practice, right at home. After that talk, everyone noted, the girl's spirits seemed to pick up a bit, though no one was exactly sure why, including the girl. She was quite impressed with her father's generosity, even moved by it. But she told him no, she didn't want such a gift. She would be embarrassed by having it. And she wondered out loud whether he was promising her the stars, in order to tide her over a bad period, in the hope that she would forget his offer or shy away from it — as she did.

VI

MONEY AND LUCK

THE BOY Raymond was five when he was told that he was a Negro, and that most people in the United States of America are white. Raymond hadn't seen all that many white people as a baby; just before he was born, in 1958, his parents had built a large brick home on eight acres of land at the edge of a section of Atlanta where the most prosperous of black families live. The boy's father is quite well-to-do. He was the only child of a Pullman porter. He was sent to a school run by a black college for children of upper-middle-class black parents. He went to college. He opened up an insurance agency after he graduated. He married the daughter of a professor. He invested his profits in real estate. He opened up a "finance company." He was the chief backer of a large shopping center, for working-class black families. He opened up a store that featured hi-fi equipment, radios, televisions, records. He expanded, soon owned a chain of such stores throughout black Atlanta — and the black sections of other, smaller Georgia cities. He moved on into Alabama, opened up music stores in Birmingham and Montgomery, bought land near those cities, sold it, bought more land, sold it. He opened up branches of his finance company in various cities of Alabama, and eventually decided to do the same in Mississippi and South Carolina.

No one in his family, however, is allowed to talk about money at the table, just as no one is allowed to call himself or herself "black." When the boy Raymond was three his older brother was about to be one of Atlanta's "pioneers"; leaders of the Negro community had urged that the youth help initiate school desegregation in 1961. But the father, finally, would not allow his son to take part in such an effort. He did not want his son to "suffer." He also did not especially welcome the publicity. He was a private man. But he was willing to spend a lot of money on behalf of other Negro children; he contributed heavily to the NAACP, and to its legal struggles against segregation. And he gave his blessing, as a leader of his people, to those young men and women who did enter Atlanta's all-white high schools in the late summer of 1961. Two years later the city was no longer the same, as the boy Raymond was told when he heard from his father "the facts of life." That was the expression the father had used; and that was the expression the boy remembered a few weeks afterward: "My Daddy told me it was my turn to be told; so we went outside to the pool, and he told me. He said I had to know the facts of life. He told me I was Negro, and I'd never turn out to be white. I guess it was my fault that he had to tell me. I'd seen a television program, and there was a kid on it, and he was nice. So I told my brother I'd like to go play with him. My brother said I couldn't, because it's just a program; and besides, he said, the boy's white, and we're Negroes. I told my brother that maybe we'd turn white, and then there wouldn't be any difference. Then I could play with the boy. It was the next day that Daddy talked with me. He said I shouldn't be expecting to be white, because it won't happen."

When Raymond was seven he was still noticing white children on television and asking his parents why he didn't see them in real life. One day the father took the boy aside and said they were going on a trip together, into parts of Atlanta Raymond had never seen. They left an hour later, and toured the "poor white" section of the city, as the father described the neighborhoods he pointed out to his son. The boy was fascinated: everyone was white, just as everyone was black where he lived. On the way home the father gave his son a "talk," and it was one the boy would never forget. A year later, at eight, he could still vividly remember what the weather outside was like, as his father spoke and he listened without once interrupting: "We kept driving down a road where the white people go to get the bus for work; it was raining, I remember, because Daddy told me some of them don't have cars, and they need a bus to get to work. He told me that a lot of Negro people don't have cars either, but I should never be ashamed of my own people, because the white people, a lot of them, aren't any better than we are. He told me that the most important thing is how you live. If you're poor, it doesn't make any difference whether you're Negro or you're white. If you've got enough money, it doesn't make any difference either — because you've got what you need: money. That's why Daddy works so hard; he told me that. He said that my mother will tell him, a lot of the time, that he should slow down, because he's got all the money he'll ever need. But he answers her right back; he says a Negro without money is in a bad way. My mother doesn't argue with my Daddy; she agrees with him."

At the age of eight he drew a picture of himself. He made his legs quite long, his arms quite short. He gave himself eyes and a mouth, but no nose and no ears — and no hair. He used a brown crayon while drawing his self-portrait. He placed himself on a hill, pleading the desire to see "far off." (His home is located on a hill.) He furnished the hill with a few pine trees, none of which is as tall as he is. There is no sky, no sun. He has a telescope in one hand, but is not using it. No distant (or, for that matter, nearby) view is provided. (Figure 47.) A week later he drew another picture, this one of a white boy, the son of a banker his father knows. Once Raymond had gone with his father to meet the banker at his office, and had met the banker's son. The two boys had talked, but not played. The white boy had actually left rather abruptly, saying he had to shop with his mother. Raymond drew the boy as short, with a small round head, possessed of a mouth, no nose, and eyes located strangely high up on the face — at the roots, virtually, of the boy's yellow hair, which was made rather obvious. The eyes are blue. The boy lacks ears. He also lacks hands. He has short stumps for arms. He is placed on some earth; no grass is visible, no trees are provided. There is, however, a sky above, and a rather fat sun, which also has eyes and a mouth. The boy starts to draw some buildings, but stops and decides that he is done. The result: a bleak landscape of seemingly half built or half destroyed buildings. (Figure 48.)

The boy talked about white people and himself after he finished his drawings: "I wouldn't want to be a redneck. They're the worst people alive. A lot of white people are poor, and they are no good. They live in slums. When they drink beer they call the Negroes bad names. The Negroes have a lot of patience. They're always putting up with the bad manners of the white people. My grandfather worked on the railroads, and he served the white people — the rich ones. Even they didn't have the manners they should have had. He'd have to clean up after them. He used to tell my father: The white man is an animal, and it's best to watch him all the time, and stay clear of him, if you can. My father says once his father came home and said he'd never go back to work, because he'd been waiting on some rich folks from New Orleans, and they kept asking him to do things, and they never said please or thank you, and they were sweet to their friends and real sour to him. But he did go back to work, I know; he died on a train that was going to Washington, I believe, from Atlanta.

"My Daddy was never allowed to go on a train. My grandfather told him he had to be his own boss, and never work for the white man. My Daddy works for himself. He says he'd like to have some white people working for him, but it would only mean a lot of trouble. The police always believe the white man. My Daddy says there are Negro police, but sometimes they will favor the white man too. He's always getting the Negro into a jam, and he's always hurting us, one way or the other. As soon as we try to build ourselves up, he's trying to tear us down. But Daddy says it's getting better and better, and by the time I grow up we'll be living better. Daddy says I was lucky to be born when I was born, and not a long time ago."

Though he has learned to criticize white people and to fear, even loathe, them, he has also learned to keep a sharp eye on them — through television and the movies, through the things said about them by his parents, relatives, friends. A cousin of his, also from a well-off family, attended a private integrated school — integrated in the sense that the boy is one of ten blacks in a school of two hundred white children. Raymond has asked his cousin rather often about "the white kids": What are they like? What do they do in their spare time? Can one make friends with them? Are they loyal friends? Do they all of a sudden turn on you? How do they dress, or talk? What do they read? And are they any good at sports? And do they go to the Cub Scouts, the Boy Scouts?

Raymond received answers; and by the age of nine he had come to the conclusion that there was no point, really, in even asking any more questions. White people are of many kinds, he began to realize; it is risky to generalize. Anyway (so he had also decided) race is important, but class is also important: "I got a railroad set, and Daddy says it cost as much as his Daddy used to get for a salary in a whole year! Well, maybe a half a year! We have a big playroom. It's the best railroad set there is. Daddy has bought stocks in railroad companies. He says he doesn't make much money on the stocks, but he enjoys sitting in his office and getting letters from the president or the treasurer of a railroad company addressed to him, asking for his vote, I guess, or telling him what the company is doing. Daddy wishes his Daddy had lived to be able to see those letters. Daddy says he wishes he could buy a whole railroad company, but he doesn't have the money. He buys a lot of stocks in the airplane companies. We travel first-class on the planes. We get treated like the best. You have these ladies, and they are white, and they wait on you. They keep on offering you something to eat and something to drink. My mother says she has to go on a diet after every plane trip we take. My father tells her not to eat anything, and ask for a diet cola. But she says she gets a big kick out of sitting there and having the white girls come up to her and ask her what she wants and ask if she's happy. We all laugh, but Mom and Daddy get angry at us. They tell us to behave ourselves and act serious, or we'll be in real trouble later, when we get off the plane, and we're away from the white people waiting on us."

When Raymond was nine his father opened up a savings account for him. The boy was taken to the bank, introduced to a bank officer, told about what would happen (in the way of interest accrued) to the fifty dollars his father had deposited and to the future sums that would be added later on. The father was quite solemn with the boy; in fact, gave him a lecture on the importance of money in our society. The boy asked why some people had a lot of money and some people none; he asked why those who have no money don't try to print some up; he asked what happens to those who lack enough money to buy food or pay for clothes; he wondered whether whites have more money than blacks, and if so, why. His father tried to explain the country's economic system; he told the boy about "the free enterprise system," how it permitted "anyone" to work his way up. The boy wondered out loud why so few had actually done so. After all, his father had told him that there are relatively few rich, and many, many poor in the country.

The father explained further: it takes considerable energy, dedication, and intelligence for someone to "rise high" in this country. Those who do so deserve what they get. The boy asked about the Negroes, millions of them, who have given their energy and dedication to the white man — and no small amount of intelligence too. What about his grandfather, who has been described so often as "shrewd" and who gave all he had, for decades, to his job, to the white people? The father was silent for a long time. He acknowledged his own father's many virtues, but insisted that he "might have become a millionaire" if he had been even shrewder, smarter — or luckier. The boy stopped asking questions at that point. He told his father that he was grateful, that he realized how lucky he was, how very lucky. He wished there were more Negro boys and girls of his age who had savings accounts, and lived in houses like the one he had. The father said an amen to the boy's declaration, adding only the conviction that such a life can be anyone's who tries hard enough to obtain it. The boy was in no mood then to disagree.

A month or so later, in an English class of the private Episcopal school he attended, Raymond wrote a composition that surprised and unnerved his teacher. She gave him an A, but worried that he was "too hard" on his family and on his friends and neighbors, not to mention classmates. The composition went like this: "In our country anyone can become rich. All he has to do is be smart and be lucky and be determined. He has to be smart enough to beat the next guy. If he isn't he'll be left behind. He has to be lucky, too. If he has an idea, and it's the right time, he'll hit a home run. If it's not the right time, he'll strike out.

"What about all the people who work all the time, but don't get rich? They may be smart, but they're not very lucky. They're not determined enough. They may be good to have working for you, but they aren't the leaders. It's the leaders who make the money. My mother said that a lot of people who have made a lot of money have cheated, and they've been crooked. But it's not fair to say that everyone who has a lot of money has done wrong. I do know some rich people who have done wrong. I have some friends, and they talk about their fathers. They aren't as honest as the police. But the police aren't so honest either. My father has given them very big Christmas presents. Like he says, he even gives them Christmas presents in July, as well as in December. I don't want to make a lot of money. People might think I wasn't nice to a lot of other people."

The teacher asked the boy to be more "specific." She told him he had indulged in "generalities." She also said he offered a lot of "hearsay evidence," rather than "concrete facts." She told him that he had unquestionably "misinterpreted" what his parents had said, and that it was "too bad" he had done so, because the "subject matter" of his composition was "excellent." She suggested that he go home, show the paper to his parents, discuss its contents with them, come back and discuss them with her; then he would be in a position to write the essay once again. Even so, he received a B−, a good grade from that particular teacher. She waited in vain, however, for the boy to come to her for a discussion of the composition. He did show it to his parents, but they became upset enough to frighten their son. He was told that he had somehow come up with "crazy" ideas, with "communist" thoughts, with "confused" thinking. He was told that he had managed to "discredit" his race — in the eyes of white people, meaning his teacher and the other teachers who (so the parents believed) had read what the boy had written.

The father gave Raymond a long "lecture." He told the boy that he had to be doubly careful; he was black and he was the son of rather well-off parents. For being the former, he was always "on display," so far as white people go; for being the latter, he was likely to be envied and even hated by both whites and blacks who are less prosperous — including schoolteachers. The father and mother also went to Raymond's teacher and talked with her. They wanted to know how their son had managed to get such ideas into his head. They wanted to express their concern, their worry, their disapproval. The teacher was of no help; she sympathized with the boy's parents, told them what she had come to realize, in years of teaching — that children come up with surprising, even shocking lines of reasoning, and that it is not wise to argue strenuously with a boy like Raymond. Best to let him "outgrow" the vexing "ideas" expressed in the composition.

Yet the boy wanted to talk about what he had written. When the father, keeping in mind the teacher's advice, indicated a lack of interest in a "discussion," Raymond sought out his mother, and, in time, his best friend: "I talked to my mother. She said she knew what was bothering me. She told me her Daddy had once swept floors, and she remembers him being glad that he had that job! She said I was right to worry about the poor people. But she said it's not right to denounce people, just because they've made money. It's better to have money than not to have money. I reminded her that she was the one who told me that a lot of rich people are cheaters, and they know how to be crooked and not get caught. She said I was exaggerating what she told me, and that I'd better not go around quoting her, or she'll get in trouble, and then *I'd* be in even worse trouble! My best friend said my mother is right. His father is my father's best friend and he is my best friend. He's ten; my mother says he could almost pass for white, but he can't. If he married a white woman when he grows up, then his children would probably be white. They'd *look* white, at least. He says he doesn't want to look white; he says he's glad he's a Negro. I am, too. I guess I am.

"My Dad always tells us that we should be glad that we can live the way we do — real comfortable. He says a lot of Negro people spend half their lives wishing they were white, or trying to look just a little whiter. They straighten their hair, or they even try to make their skin look lighter. Some dye their hair! According to my father, it's foolish to try to look white if you're Negro. You can't do it. But you *can* make some money, and then you can live as good as the white man — and better than a lot of whites, if you make enough dollars. My friend says he'd like to be a millionaire. I asked my father if he is one. He said it's none of my business. He's set some money aside for me, I know that. He's told me; and I heard him talking to his lawyer. He said that if I ever went to a good college — like Harvard or Yale, someplace like that — then he wanted me to be able to keep up with anyone who goes there. I don't think I get the money until I'm twenty-five, some age like that. I'll be halfway through my life by then!

"They got all upset at school because they thought I was being fresh; they thought I wasn't being fair to all the rich folks! But it was my father who told me not to trust anyone who made a lot of money, because you don't make a lot of money by being honest all day and all night. He joked with me; he said he'd 'turned a few tricks' to get where he was. But he's a real good man. He tells the truth. He doesn't pretend. At the church they gave him a cup, and said he was the best, the most outstanding man in the whole Negro community. We were all there. We were proud of him. They took his picture, and they showed him on television later, accepting the cup. But they didn't show him giving his speech.

"My Daddy got up and said thank you, and then he made everyone nervous, because he said he remembered his own Daddy, and how he'd told him that if he wants people to pay attention to him and recognize him, then the thing to do was make a lot of money. He said that he'd fought his way up, and he wanted to give money to the church, and he hoped the church would give the money to good kids, who are smart and ambitious, and want to work their way up, the way my Daddy did. And he said he hoped those kids didn't make any mistakes, or hurt anyone on the way; but they most likely would, he said, because that's what you have to do to win. He said he was sorry if he'd been bad to anyone; and he hoped God would forgive him, and he asked for everyone to pray for his family and him, and he promised to give more money away. Later he asked me if I'd be worried if he gave *all* his money away. I said he wouldn't give too much of his money away, but even if he did, I wouldn't worry because he'd just go and make some more, because that's how he is!"

About a year after the boy's composition had stirred up confusion and apprehension at school and home, the father agreed with his son's earlier judgment. The boy was twelve, was becoming a young man. His father took him for a walk, talked with him about matters of money, race, class, and sex; told him that he had been right a while back to be suspicious of those with money, but emphasized how vulnerable and sad it was for anyone to be without a substantial amount of money

— "especially Negroes." The boy was touched by his father's candor, by his willingness to subject himself to his own keen, critical eye. It would be no joy being a Negro in America, but with "money and luck," a twosome repeatedly mentioned by his father, it could be "pretty good, most of the time." The boy liked that cautious, guarded, tentative kind of optimism. He made it his own. He kept on telling his close friend that "money and luck" are what matter; that they make all the difference; that a Negro, and especially a poor Negro, needs both badly; that with both one can "forget" a lot of things, and enjoy a lot of other things, and somehow, get the "kick" out of life a Pullman porter once saw white people get, and an Atlanta businessman and his son are sure they are both getting.

VII

RICH IN THE BARRIO

T HE GIRL was named Joan after an Anglo woman who had befriended the baby's mother. At the time Joan was born her parents lived in a barrio of San Antonio. Their house was small, only two bedrooms. Joan was the third child; she has an older brother and an older sister. Their father now owns a store in the barrio. He also owns a number of houses, some vacant land, and a small office building in which a Chicano doctor, two Chicano lawyers, and a Chicano dentist have offices. Joan's mother is the daughter of the dentist; she is a tall, dark, quite composed woman, known to many as "the silent one." She measures her words carefully, speaks slowly and quietly. She prefers to talk in English, though her husband will often not oblige; he is comfortable talking Spanish, and besides, he has to speak it all day with his customers. They are the poor of San Antonio, many of them migrant farm workers who have worked their way to the city from the Rio Grande Valley, in hope of bettering themselves, only to find jobs relatively scarce, and those available menial and poor-paying. To such people Joan's father is an authority, an established figure in the community, a rich and important man, an intermediary with the white world.

When Joan was four her father had a rather large ranch

house built for his family on some vacant land he owned. He spared no expense. A year later, when the last of the decorating was done, the last of the important furniture purchased and moved in, Joan was clearly pleased with the result: "My Daddy told us that he was only going to ask us to move once, and so he made the house very big, and he told Mamma that he would have the best that money can buy, and then we would enjoy our life in the new home. Each of us has a room; our parents have the biggest bedroom. They have a huge color television in it; but we can come and sit on their bed and watch. There is another color television in the living room, but Mamma doesn't want us in there all the time, because the furniture costs a lot of money, and she wants to keep the room looking very nice, for company. My older brother broke a dish in there, and we weren't allowed back for a long time. Now, we can go in the room — if we ask her first. The kids I play with say we have the nicest house in San Antonio. My father says maybe it's the nicest in the barrio; he says the Anglos have bigger homes. They have more money than we do. They are the bosses, my father says. His friend, the priest, came over, and he said the same thing, that the Anglos are the bosses. The only Anglos we see are the people downtown; we go shopping with Mamma, and see them."

A year later Joan was seeing other Anglos — the nuns and lay teachers in a private, parochial school she was sent to. It was about then she began to wish that she could one day become a singer, and appear on television. Joan had a good voice, was taking piano and singing lessons, was described by her father as "ambitious." Even at six and seven she talked about going to Hollywood or New York, carving out a career for herself — so that she might, on a Saturday night, appear on the Lawrence Welk Show. Her brother was bored by that program, and her father agreed. But Joan had her mother's support: Lawrence Welk featured attractive young women, who sang "nice songs" and looked "very pretty" on the television screen. They must live, Joan was sure, quite interesting lives. One of her teachers, as a matter of fact, had left Texas for a stay in New York City, and told the class, from time to time, how "different" it was in the East, and especially in New York City.

Joan listened intently, came home and implored her parents to go to New York City on the next vacation. The parents said yes — someday; but not right away. After all, the girl had not really seen much of San Antonio, let alone other Texas cities, like Houston or Dallas. Her father's younger brother is in Chicago, trying hard to make it on his own, and admittedly not doing too well — but writing proud, stoic letters, full of praise for the city's tall buildings and fast, cosmopolitan life. All right, Joan would settle for Chicago, for a visit to her uncle, who sounds like a real swinger, a happy-go-lucky man who is not afraid of the Anglo world, but rather seeks to be part of it. If she went to Chicago, she was convinced, she would come home different. She would look different. She would be ready, then, for another trip — to New York City. And she would have so much to tell her teachers at school, she kept reminding her parents — as if to make it easier for them to say *yes* (an educational trip, after all!) rather than their predictable *maybe later.*

When she was eight she drew a picture of herself in front of her home. (Figure 49.) She stood rather stiff (she actually had a rather relaxed, casual carriage), her arms straight down and close to her sides, her feet firmly together. She gave herself thin lips, small eyes, a small nose, and very little, black hair — a flat-top of sorts. She wore the black dress required by the nuns. In back of her loomed, it seemed, her home: in her mind, apparently, as enormous and imposing as it was to other

Chicano children of the barrio — "the rich one's house." The roof virtually touched the sky. The sun was nearby, but without a face, only rays. As a background Joan supplied other homes of the barrio — cramped, huddled, nondescript, a blur of poverty. On her comparatively spacious lawn she put her beloved black hound dog. The animal had more freedom to roam than the dozens and dozens of people who live in the houses shown. There is a fence around her home, and it is shown in the picture. No one from the cramped, swollen barrio can use that lawn unless invited.

Joan has known for years that she is granting a privilege when she invites a friend over, as she indicated when she commented on her own picture shortly after drawing it: "I have two girl friends, and they love to come here, because we can run all over the lawn, and we have the swings and the slide and the sandbox and the pool. Daddy says he's going to build a real pool; then we can throw away the plastic one. My friends say they don't care; they like the pool we have. They joke with me; they say I live in a park! When we drive by the old house, where I was born, I can't believe that we once lived there. I don't remember living there. If I had to live there, I guess it was best to spend the first three or four years there, when you're not doing much anyway. I've asked Mamma why we lived there, and she says that I'm talking spoiled, because the old house is a lot nicer than most houses our people have in San Antonio — or in Chicago. I picture my uncle living in a house like the one we have now, but my mother says I'm all wrong there!

"My Daddy says we moved to our new house because he made the money we needed to buy it. He says money is very important. He says I'd better watch out; if I leave here and go to New York City, when I grow up, I might not be able to make the money I'd need, and then there would be real trouble. He

says he'd fly up there and take me home. He thinks my uncle
will soon come back from Chicago. Our people don't like the
cold North, the bad winters. My father says we can have all the
dreams we want about Chicago and New York, but it's not in
our blood to live there and be happy, the way we are in San
Antonio. My mother will agree with him some of the time. She
says that we should look around us, right here in San Antonio,
and see all the poor people here. This city isn't so good to our
people either."

    She stops, she wonders whether there is anymore to say. She
puts the drawing aside. She looks out the window: another hot,
humid day. She is glad that her room is air-conditioned, that
all the bedrooms are. Her father has talked of air-conditioning
the entire house. She remembers those remarks, makes a few
of her own about him and her mother and her brother and her
sister and herself: "We are lucky, I guess. That's what everyone says. I don't like to hear my mother and father keep
reminding me that I am lucky, but they are right, I know. I
wish we lived in New York. I wish I could go see television
programs, and take music lessons from the best people. Maybe
I'll never leave San Antonio. When my mother gets angry with
me for not cleaning up my room, she tells me that she's going
to send me back to the Rio Grande Valley; I have an uncle
there too — well, three uncles, I think. They work on farms.
They pick crops. My mother says if I was down there, I'd be
doing the same thing already.

    "Once she got really mad; my room was a mess, and she told
me to clean it up, and I forgot to. She came into her bedroom,
and I was watching TV, and she started screaming that I belong down in the Valley. My friend was there with me. She
said that when we get older we should both leave our homes
and go there, to the Valley. I don't think we'd like it there. The
nuns try to scare us. They tell us in school that we'll burn in

hell if we don't watch out. That's what my mother says about the Valley — that it's hot, and there's no air conditioning in the houses. Kids go to work at five in the morning to pick the crops, and they come home late, at six or seven at night, and they're all worn out. Maybe my friend and I *will* go there in a year or two. Then we can send postcards home, like my uncle does from Chicago. Who knows — we might end up liking the Valley, and staying there for the rest of our lives!"

It is a passing thought, or speculation: she has no real intention of going down to the Valley nor does her mother plan to send her there, even on a brief, punitive visit. By the time Joan was twelve she had forsaken her New York plans, but very much wanted to go up North, to Chicago. She wanted a career in radio or television. She had been told for years that she had "a good voice"; now she wanted to use it as an announcer or a newscaster, rather than a singer. Joan watched with interest, approval, and a certain envy a woman reporting the news on a local television station. She was Anglo, and Joan had begun to believe that only Anglos could obtain the kind of jobs she had in mind for herself. She had also begun to worry about how she looked. At one point she even talked of becoming a nun — on the theory that nuns don't have to be beautiful, and she saw herself as unattractive, if not ugly.

Soon, however, that ambition faded. The girl became increasingly interested in her father's business. Wasn't there a way she could work for him? She asked him that repeatedly, and he scratched his head, and shook his head, and said no, there was only room for his son and three nephews, and maybe not all of them. Besides, in a few years she would have other ideas in mind — marriage and motherhood. Joan was not so sure; she resented being told exactly how her life ought to unfold. She resented, too, being given one dress after another, along with bracelets, a watch and then another, fancier watch, some necklaces and hair braids and an endless number of shoes. She took to wearing her jeans all the time — or as much of the time as she could. She was now delighted with her school uniform — its somber simplicity pleased her immensely. She felt torn between her desire to dress up (in the future) and talk before the television cameras, and her desire to be utterly casual (right then and there) and lounge around the house, watching television.

She also felt torn between various "lessons" she had heard from her parents: "I can't win. My mother tells me I should study hard. Then I do. Then she says I shouldn't study too hard, because boys do that, and I should try to be 'lighter.' I ask her how, and she says I shouldn't ask her, because I already know the answer, and I'm only being stubborn. My father says I'm not supposed to be interested in his business. Then he catches me sitting in the house watching television, and it's nice outside, and he gets very angry, and asks me why I don't go outside. Then I tell him there is nothing for me to do outside, and he gets very angry. He pulls me! When we get outside he points to the pool, and to my bike, and to the grass. He says I can swim; I can go on a bike ride; I can cut the grass. I said it was for my brother to cut the grass! He exploded. He told me I would get no allowance for a month. I was glad. All I do is put the bills in my wallet, and it gets fatter and fatter! When my father is in a different mood, he won't even let us spend our own allowance. He buys us what we want, and tells us the allowance is for the extras. But a lot of times, I can't think up anything extra that I want, and so I get richer all the time!

"Maybe a few years from now I'll have so much money I can go and invest it somehow and start making a lot of money, like my father did. I could buy some land; he says that land is the best thing to buy, because it always goes up, up. Once he gets

going on the subject of land, and the money you can make
from owning it, he doesn't care what he was telling you before.
He will sit down with us and explain why he bought the land
in this place, and this place, and this place. I wish he owned
the land where the television station is. Then maybe he could
get me a job on one of the television programs, when I'm
bigger. But he says there's a lot of land that only the Anglos
own. They sell it to each other. They wouldn't let a Mexican
own the land, even if he had a lot of money, and was ready to
pay anything they wanted."

She will switch from one ethnic or racial self-description to
another, depending on the subject of discussion. She knew
that Anglos often referred to her people in a derogatory way
as "Mexicans." She herself can unselfconsciously assume Anglo
attitudes and words toward her own kind as if she were one
of "them." She can also be more evenhanded, can talk in a
rather neutral tone about "the Mexican-American streets" in
San Antonio, as contrasted to the Anglo ones. She can also
become fiercely proud of her own ("Chicano") people. At
twelve or thirteen she frightens her parents with her declarations of solidarity — and enmity: "I don't like to hear my father talk about the Anglo bankers. He admires them. He says
he is sure that they like him. Well, why shouldn't they be nice
to him and like him? They make a lot of money off him! First
he makes money; then he borrows more money from the
Anglos; then he makes more money, and so do they! No wonder they smile at him and pat him on the back, when he comes
to them and tells them that he is going to build some stores or
some office buildings or some houses. I wish some of our own
people had as much money as the Anglos do; then we could
go to a Chicano bank and borrow money from Chicanos, and
then Chicanos would be helping each other. The Anglos don't
like us; they do business with my father, but he is just another

'Mexican' to them. He told me that himself a long time ago, and I remember. But when I remind him, he gets angry with me and tells me I should stop talking like a man who is running for mayor of San Antonio!

"I wish I could be mayor! I wish a Chicano got elected mayor; then our people would be better off. The nuns told us that would be good too; and they are Anglos. One nun told us that it's already been too long that the Anglos have run Texas. Once Texas belonged to us, the Chicanos. Now, we are under the Anglos; they are over us. I asked my father the other day, when we were all joking and he was in a very good mood, if he would give me enough money to run for mayor of San Antonio. He laughed. He said he would; yes, he would. He asked me how much money I thought I'd need. I said, maybe five hundred dollars. He said I'd need hundreds and hundreds of *thousands* of dollars! Even he couldn't give me that much! He has a lot of money, but my mother has always told us that when a Mexican-American has a lot of money, it is one thing — you're still in the barrio, even if you're rich. When an Anglo has a lot of money, that's another story. We can lose our money overnight. The Anglos can put the squeeze on us. It's their country."

Toward the end of the eighth grade, when Joan was a few months short of fourteen, she "settled down," as her parents described it. She didn't by any means become, in the mother's words, a "dream girl." She played her hi-fi set louder and louder; her choice of music (acid rock) confused and enraged her parents. Her dress continued to be casual, or provocatively disheveled. She was no better at taking care of her room. She turned sour and petulant inexplicably and remained so for hours, even days. But she indicated to her parents a desire to stay in San Antonio, to go to college, to take there "a business course," and to become, at least for a while, a "business secretary." Her father was delighted. Maybe Joan could, after all, join his business. He had a part-time secretary already; he had for some time felt the need of someone to keep track of his various obligations and commitments, as well as the bills he sent out and received, the payments he had to make and expected to arrive. Why not entrust such important and mostly quite confidential matters to someone in the family?

He and Joan talked about such a prospect with increasing intimacy and relish. The nuns soon heard from her of the plan, and supported it. The father gradually laid bare to his daughter much of his financial situation. On the weekends, especially, he would take her aside for an hour or so, explain what he owned, how he had acquired it, and what he hoped to do in the future with it: hold on, make improvements, sell at the first opportunity, sell eventually. He also showed her how to use an adding machine he kept in his study at home; and he explained to her what he does with the profits he makes — stock investments, insurance, savings accounts. "There is not a *lot* of money," he kept telling her. "The Anglos can wipe me out in a moment," he kept telling her. "The Anglos hold my fate in their hands," he kept telling her — because he believed in "expanding" rather than "standing still," and so he would rather (and constantly did) borrow money to enlarge one or another part of his business.

Every once in a while the girl would suggest to her father that he stop in his tracks, even change direction: give some of his money away to the poor, to the Church, to an orphanage next door to some property he owns. He was not resentful. He even promised at times to remember them when making his will, or rather, revising it. But he did warn his daughter that later on, when she was "all grown up," and so "no longer a trusting child," she would have "different ideas" about what he ought do with his money — while alive or in anticipation of death. If he were "really rich," he told the girl, he would indeed leave large sums to charity. For that matter, if he knew that she would, years in the future, marry a Mexican-American man who himself was quite well-off, then he would perhaps contemplate giving her share, at the very least, of his estate to charity. But he rather believed she would not want him to do that. And when he asked her what she thought, she said yes, he was right, she would "probably" want to receive and hold on to her inheritance. She did hope to have children someday, and her father had quite successfully convinced her that a lot of money is required if they are to live well.

PART SIX

ENTITLEMENT

T HE POOR both are and are not all alike. On the one hand they struggle against the same odds — hunger and malnutrition in the worst instances, or a marginal life that poses constant threats. Yet Eskimos do not regard their poverty in the same way that Appalachian yeomen do, or Chicanos in Texas or southern California. In the four volumes that have preceded this one I have tried to show how the common social and economic vulnerability of the poor does not make for a uniform pattern of child rearing. Historical precedents, cultural experiences, religious convictions exert their influence on parents and children, make boys and girls differ in all sorts of respects, depending on where they live and who their parents are. The same holds for the well-to-do or the rich. It won't do to talk of *the* affluent ones in America (never mind the world!). It won't do to say that in our upper-middle-class suburbs, or among our wealthy, one observes clear-cut, consistent psychological or cultural characteristics. Even in relatively homogeneous suburbs, there are substantial differences in home life, in values taught, hobbies encouraged, beliefs advocated or virtually instilled.

But there are indeed distinct groups among the well-off — equivalent in their way to the various kinds of poor people.

It is the obligation of someone who wants to know how children make sense of their lives — agricultural migrancy, Indian reservation life in the Southwest, the upper-income life of large homes amid ample acreage in rich towns or in wealthy urban enclaves — to document as faithfully as possible the way the common heritage of money and power affects the assumptions of individual boys and girls. Each child, however, is also influenced by certain social, racial, cultural, or religious traditions, or thoroughly idiosyncratic ones — a given *family's* tastes, sentiments, ideals, say. The issue is "class"; but the issue is not only "class."

Many of the influences, even some of the more idiosyncratic ones, that distinguish some children from others are themselves subject to side influences — a "rebound effect," one rather prosperous Illinois Mormon called it. He was anxious for me to know (just as he could not forget) that there was only so much his faith could resist. He took pains, constantly, to tell his children that he was not like his father; that he was not like his brother either, who lives in Salt Lake City and works for a bank. To live near Chicago and be a doctor, to be a Mormon living in a highly secular upper-middle-class world, was to be an exile. He felt stronger in his faith, but also weaker; he felt like his neighbors in many ways, but unlike them in critically important preferences and articles of faith.

What binds together a Mormon banker in Utah with his brother, or other coreligionists in Illinois or Massachusetts? What distinguishes such people, one from the other? Old New Orleans upper-class families are not in certain respects like families who live in, say, Wellesley Hills, Massachusetts, or Haverford, Pennsylvania, or up the hills outside San Antonio. There *are* resemblances, based on class, occupation, religion, common experiences, expectations, ideas conveyed to children. And yet, again, there are distinctions, shades of feeling and thinking, emphases of one sort or another — even within those families and well-to-do neighborhoods.

I use the word "entitlement" to describe what, perhaps, all quite well-off American families transmit to their children — an important psychological common denominator, I believe: an emotional expression, really, of those familiar, class-bound prerogatives, money and power. The word was given to me, amid much soul-searching, by the rather rich parents of a child I began to talk with almost two decades ago, in 1959. I have watched those parents become grandparents, seen what they described as "the responsibilities of entitlement" get handed down to a new generation. When the father, a lawyer and stockbroker from a prominent and quietly influential family, referred to the "entitlement" his children were growing up with, he had in mind a social rather than a psychological phenomenon: the various juries or committees that select the Mardi Gras participants in New Orleans' annual parade and celebration. He knew that his daughter was "entitled" to be invited here, to attend a dance there, to feel part of a carefully limited and sometimes self-important social scene.

He wanted, however, to go beyond that social fact; he wanted his children to feel obligated by how fortunate they were, and would no doubt always be, all things being equal — or unequal! He talked about what he had received from his parents and what he would give to his children, "automatically, without any thought," and what they too would pass on. The father was careful to distinguish between the social entitlement and "something else," a "something else" he couldn't quite define but knew he had to try to evoke if he were to be psychologically candid: "Our children have a good life ahead of them; and I think they know it now. I think they did when they were three or four, too. It's *entitlement*, that's what I call it. My wife didn't know what I was talking about when I first used the word. She thought it had something to do with our ancestry! Maybe it does! I don't mean to be snide. I just think our children grow up taking a lot for granted, and it can be good that they do, and it can be bad. It's like anything else; it all depends. I mean, you can have spoiled brats for children, or you can have kids who want to share what they have. I don't mean give away all their money! I mean be responsible, and try to live up to their ideals, and not just sit around wondering which island in the Caribbean to visit this year, and where to go next summer to get away from the heat and humidity here in New Orleans."

At the time he said no more. It was 1960, and I was interested mainly in what his son and his daughter thought about black children — and about the violence then being inflicted on a few black children brave enough and stubborn enough to walk past mobs into two elementary schools. But as months became years, I came back to that word "entitlement," especially because it was one I had heard years earlier, in Boston, when I was receiving my training in child psychiatry. "Narcissistic entitlement" was the phrase I had been taught to be familiar with, to use occasionally when speaking of a particular kind of "disturbed" child. The term could be used in place of more conventional, blunter ones that everyone else uses from time to time: a smug, self-satisfied child; or a child who thinks he (or she) owns the world, or will one day; or a self-centered child who expects a lot from just about everyone.

I recall a boy of eight I was treating in Boston, before I went South; my supervisor, a child psychoanalyst who had worked with a similar child for three years, and anticipated, alas, another year or two, at least, of thrice weekly office visits, told me that I was being naïvely hopeful, and a touch simpleminded, when I remarked upon the curiosity of the boy, his evident willingness to ask me questions about all sorts of persons, places, things — and so his capacity for engagement with the world around him. Yes, she pointed out, there was indeed a measure of that, but it was best that *we* ask questions about the nature of *his* questions. As we did, they all came back to him — to quite specific experiences he had gone through and wanted to talk about. And he had told me that, actually; he never asked a question out of intellectual interest — rather, in his words, "because I like to know what might happen next to me."

It is hard to describe the special fearfulness and sadness such a child struggles with. He was not the "ordinary" child; he was quite troubled. And I suppose the parents of such children (even if those mothers and fathers have other, relatively solid children, psychologically speaking) must be disqualified as "normal" or "average." They may be like anyone else on the street; may be rather knowing, psychiatrically — able to sense something "wrong" with a child's "behavior" and go do something about it by seeking out a doctor. But the analyst-supervisor I was myself "seeing" once a week was convinced that there was a "special narcissism," she called it, that a certain kind of parent offers a child: "Narcissism is something we all struggle with; but some people have more of it than others, and some children come from homes that have so much that all the money and possessions, all the rugs and furniture and toys and vacations and savings accounts and insurance policies come crashing on the child's head. There is a shift from narcissism to narcissistic entitlement."

I wasn't sure exactly what she meant, or how the "shift" she had mentioned did indeed take place. I know, because she is someone I still discuss psychoanalytic theory with, that she was not sure herself what the exact dimensions were of that childhood journey. But she knew even then, before there were "fields" like "social psychiatry" or "community psychiatry," that at some point a family's psychology and psychopathology engage with its social and economic life; and that when a migrant child or a ghetto child has to contend with narcissism, it will take on a certain flavor (narcissistic despair, for instance); whereas for a child who lives in a big house and whose parents have a lot and want to give a lot to their offspring, "narcissistic entitlement" may well be a possibility. The child withdraws not only into himself or herself but, by extension, into a certain world of objects, habits, and rituals — the comfortable world of a room, a home, a way of life. The child has much, but wants and expects more — only to feel no great gratitude, but a desire for yet more: an inheritance the world is expected to provide. One's parents will oblige, as intermediaries. And if underneath there lie apprehension and gloom and, not least, a strain of gnawing worthlessness, that is of no matter to many children whose "narcissistic entitlement" becomes what psychoanalytic theorists refer to as a "character trait," rather than a "symptom" that prompts a visit to a doctor. That is, the child is regarded by everyone, psychiatrists included, as "normal," as "all right," or different, but not all *that* different. One doesn't send every cocksure, greedy, self-centered child to a child psychiatrist.

In many other well-to-do homes I've visited, parents have known in their bones what child psychiatrists think and wonder as they talk with their children. Will a certain child get too much — so much that he or she runs the danger of turning away from life, forsaking people for a life of passionate involvement with objects? Less ominously, might a mild tendency in that direction become especially evident when things get tough, psychologically, for one reason or another? Will the child be willing to reach for people, and get along with them, but always with certain limits on the involvement?

Often when children are four, five, and six, parents who have felt able to offer them virtually anything begin to pull back, in concern if not outright horror. A son not only has become increasingly demanding or petulant; even when he is quiet he seems to be sitting on a throne of sorts — expecting things to happen, wondering with annoyance why they don't, reassuring himself that they will, or, if they haven't, shrugging his shoulders and waiting for the next event.

It was just such an impasse — not dramatic, but quite definite and worrisome — that prompted that New Orleans father to use the word "entitlement." He had himself been born to wealth, as will future generations of his family be, unless the American economic system changes drastically. But he was worried about what a lot of money can do to a person's "personality"; he uses that word as a layman, but he knows exactly what he has in mind. It isn't so much a matter of spoiling or indulging children; he is willing to let that happen, "within limits." But he knew precisely what those limits were: when the child begins to let his or her situation, the life that he or she lives, "go to the head." It is then that children begin "to act as if they have royal blood in them." And conservative though he is, for him each generation has to prove itself — not necessarily by finding new worlds to conquer or by becoming extraordinarily successful. He has wanted his children to show an interest in the world, to reach out and touch others, to develop their own initiatives, however circumscribed, undramatic, and conventional. It is those kinds of initiative he naturally finds appealing. He is rather satisfied with the life he was born to. He finds each day to be pleasant, interesting, and by his lights, quite useful. He has, however, worried at times that his children were taking *too* much for granted. When his young daughter, during a Mardi Gras season, kept *assuming* she would one day receive this honor and that honor — indeed, become a Mardi Gras queen — he realized that his notion of "entitlement" was not quite hers. *Noblesse oblige* requires a gesture toward others. Had a parent sensed the danger of what my supervisor referred to as a "shift" from "entitlement" to "narcissistic entitlement"?

He would not be the only parent to express such a concern to me in the course of my work. In homes where mothers and fathers profess no explicit reformist persuasions (to say the least!) they nevertheless worry about what happens to children who grow up surrounded by just about everything they want, virtually, on demand. And if much of the apprehension is conventional — that the child will become "spoiled" — there is an element of uneasiness that runs deeper. The parents may begin to regard spoiled behavior as but a symptom: "I don't mind if my children become a little spoiled. That's bound to happen. I worry that they will think that everything is coming to them; that they will grow up with the idea that if they're frustrated, or if they want something, then all they have to do is say a few words, and they'll have what they asked for. When they're like that, they've gone from spoiled to spoiled rotten — and beyond, to some state I don't even know how to describe."

When children are two and three they become increasingly conscious of what belongs to whom. They also become, usually, more and more willing and able to leave themselves behind, so to speak — reach out for objects as well as individuals. They develop their first friends, their first interests or regular and cherished activities. They learn too, most of them, a variety of restraints and frustrations. They must gain control of their bodies, manage without diapers, remember to empty their bladders before going to bed, and get up at night and do likewise in the bathroom rather than on the sheet and mattress. They must learn not to touch hot stoves; not to leave refrigerator doors open; not to spill things, break things, step on things; not to intrude on what belongs to others; not to confuse their prerogatives or possessions with the rights and property of parents, brothers and sisters, friends. At three and four, children from homes like those in New Orleans' Garden District have often started nursery school, have also started making visits to other homes or receiving visitors at their own homes. There are toys to share, games to play, a sandbox or a lawn or indeed a swimming pool or a paddock with its animals. All children have to struggle with themselves for the strength to offer as well as take, or to yield with tact and even a touch of gratitude what has been loaned rather than made an outright gift.

But for some children, a relative handful of the world's, such obligations and struggles are muted. Obviously it is possible for parents to have a lot of money yet avoid bringing up their children in such a way that they feel like members of a royal family. Yet even parents determined not to spoil their children often recognize what might be called the existential (as opposed to strictly psychological) aspects of their situation, and that of their children. A father may begin rather early on lecturing his children about the meaning of money; a mother may do her share by saying no, even when yes is so easy to say — but the child may well sense eventually what the parents know quite well: the difference between a voluntary posture and an utterly necessary one.

Such a child, by the age of five or six, has very definite notions of what is possible, even if not always permitted; possible because there is plenty of money that can be spent. That child, in conversation and without embarrassment or the kind of reticence and secretiveness that comes later, may reveal a substantial knowledge of economic affairs. A six-year-old girl in New Orleans knew that she would at twenty-one inherit a half a million dollars. She also knew that her father "only" gave her twenty-five cents a week — whereas some friends of hers received as much as a dollar. She was vexed; she asked her parents why they were so "strict." One friend had even used the word "stingy" for the parents. The father, in a matter-of-fact way, pointed out to the daughter that she did, after all, get "anything she really wants." Why, then, the need for an extravagent allowance? The girl was won over, told her friends thereafter that it was no matter to her whether she even received an allowance; the important point was the future and what it had to offer. The friends then checked back with their parents, who were rather alarmed — that such young children were talking so freely and openly about family financial matters.

As a result the girl learned from her friends that she had disclosed what ought to be kept firmly under wraps. She decided on the basis of such declarations that her friends may well be "comfortable," but they are not as rich as her parents are or as she will one day be. They in turn explained to her that she had gone beyond the bounds of available evidence. The friends may simply have been told to keep quiet about their family's monetary status — a good idea, the girl was reminded by her parents. The girl agreed, but was not really prepared at the time to follow such advice. She had heard her parents talk with *their* parents about money matters and had been told that it is best that she, too, gradually understand what her financial situation is and will be. That being the case, she wondered out loud why it wasn't appropriate for her to share what she had learned about her future prospects with those she considered good friends. Her parents could only repeat their conviction that certain matters are quite definitely and properly kept within the confines of the family.

Such conversations between young children and their parents help consolidate in boys and girls a conviction of present and future affluence. It obviously never occurs to these children that they won't have food at some point in the near or distant future. Nor do they ever really lack for anything. There are differences in amount, and lectures and sermons may accompany parental acts of generosity. But admonitions don't modify the quite shrewd appraisal children make of what they are heir to, and don't at all diminish the sense of entitlement.

In an Appalachian mine-owner's home, for instance, a boy of seven made the following comment in 1963, after his father's mine had suffered an explosion, killing two men and injuring seriously nine others: "I heard my mother saying she felt sorry for the families of the miners. I feel sorry for them, too. I hope the men who got hurt get better. I'm sure they will. My father has called in doctors from Lexington. He wants the best doctors in all Kentucky for those miners. Daddy says it was the miners' fault; they get careless, and the next thing you know, there's an explosion. It's too bad. I guess there are a lot of kids who are praying hard for their fathers. I wish God was nice to everyone. He's been very good to us. My Daddy says it's been hard work, running the mine and another one he has. It's just as hard to run a mine as it is to go down and dig the coal! I'm glad my father is the owner, though. I wouldn't want him to get killed or hurt bad down there, way underground. Daddy has given us a good life. We have a lot of fun coming up, he says, in the next few years. We're going on some trips. Daddy deserves his vacations. He says he's happy because he can keep us happy, and he does. If we want something real bad, we go tell him or Mum, and they oblige us almost all the time. That's what Daddy always says — that he's glad to oblige my sister and me!"

The father is not *always* "glad to oblige"; he can be quite stern at times, but the children have learned that his lectures have only a limited applicability to their life. Yes, there are restraints; not every request for money or a present is granted forthwith. On the other hand, their life is sufficiently comfortable to belie the parents' insistence on caution, lest there be nothing left. In fact, the lectures only seem to reinforce in the children a certain materialistic preoccupation. Having been told to make do with what they already have in such abundance, the boy and girl (and their counterparts in the homes I have visited in other parts of the United States) retreat to their respective rooms, get out their possessions, and begin to use them as well as simply gaze at them. The boy can be quite pointed and expressive about what he has — and is doing with what he has — at such moments: "I have my soldiers, and my trucks, and the tanks and the helicopters. I get them lined up. I build a fort. I have the blocks and the logs, and I make the fort strong. I have my helicopter pad. I make sure the pad is protected by tanks and some men with machine guns. Some terrorists might come and try to attack, and destroy the pad and the helicopter. It's best to keep a few planes in the air, to scout. You have to keep your eyes open, or there will be a surprise attack. I surround the fort with men, and I have these bushes and trees, and I put men behind them. And I have some men on horses."

He stops and looks at what he has done. He is rather proud of himself. He has thought at times of working toward a military career, but he knows that he "most likely" will follow in his father's footsteps. There is a profitable coal company to run and his father has told him that, in the boy's words, "coal has a big future now because there's an energy problem." That observation prompts him to worry about his fort. Does *it* have enough energy or might there one day be a shortage? No, he is sure that his fort will be able to manage successfully. There is a large stack of wood set aside in the stockade. As for the tanks, helicopters, airplanes, they will not lack fuel; there is an oil well nearby. And in the event that should give out, the boy is certain that oil can be flown in or, if necessary, a "secret pipeline" could be built, just in case some disaster should come upon the airfield–landing pad.

His sister has on some occasions become provocative, even truculent. She has asked him, after watching him "declare war" on an unseen enemy, why he always wins. He has replied that the answer is quite simple; he has the best army. She will occasionally express her misgivings: there might be, just *might* be, an army that could overcome his army, with its nineteenth-century fort and twentieth-century military hardware. The boy replies with scorn that his sister is being far too literal-minded. Anyway, America has never lost a war, he knows for sure, and he is an American and does not intend to lose one either. Nor has his father, when brought into the argument later, been anything but encouraging. True, Vietnam was "a mess"; but the country was never "really determined" to win — and maybe never should have involved itself in such a struggle, waged in "distant jungles." The sister has by then lost all interest in her younger (by one year) brother's "game."

The boy is not obsessed with the war game, either. He has many other opportunities to play — other games or, more personally, friends to have over, to go visit. When he plays the war game with them, however, there is invariably a battle of wits, a stalemate. The boy and his friends are tireless in the resourcefulness they summon to their encounters. If necessary, they find themselves in possession of atomic bombs, supersonic planes, surprise tunnels, magical weapons of all kinds, secret supply bases, hidden contingents of men. Eventually, they each declare the other "a winner." The boy realizes: "I know there has to be a losing side. My sister is right. You can't win all the time. But she doesn't like to lose, either. She's always saying her guinea pig is the prettiest, and she says she can ride her bike faster than anyone. I hope I'll get a five-speed bike soon; as soon as I'm a little taller, I'll get one. Then you can really go zoom, zoom down the roads. They say that when I'm grown up, we'll be landing on the moon all the time and we'll be landing on the planets — Mars, for sure. This country will do it! Maybe I could be an astronaut for a while, and then come back and help Daddy in his business. He says he may buy a couple more mines, and by the time I'm out of college, there will be a lot to do. He says I should plan to be a lawyer, because it really helps you, if you have a business, to know how to go to court and protect yourself. The unions want to interfere a lot, and Daddy has to fight them. He has to give some ground, but he's the boss, and they can't push too hard or he'll close up his mines. Then they'd all be out of work! And Daddy could hire some other miners. There are a lot of people who would be glad to get a job!"

So it goes: an abundance of energy for his fort and air force base and an abundance of workers for his father's mines. Abundance is his destiny, he has every reason to believe. He may even land on the stars. Certainly he has traveled widely in this country. He associates the seasons with travel, among other events. In winter, for instance, there is a trip South, to one or another Caribbean island. Winters can be long and hard in Appalachia, and a respite is invigorating — and "healthy." The boy watches his father exercise, hears his mother talk about certain foods, and remarks upon something else that has to do with his future: he may well live to be over a century old. Why not?

His parents are not health faddists, or unusually self-preoccupied: given exercise, a careful diet, and medical progress, one will do (in the father's words) "right well." As an additional boost to the family's collective health, a sauna has been installed, and the children are entranced with it. They also are preoccupied with their two dogs, and their other animals — the guinea pigs, hamsters, rabbits, chickens. There is always someone in the house, a maid, a handyman. Still, it is sad to say good-bye. Now, if the family owned a plane, the animals could come along on those trips!

The boy doesn't really believe that his father ever will own a Lear jet; yet, at moments he can imagine himself wrong. And he can construct a fantasy: suddenly an announcement, most likely at breakfast, of a "surprise." It is a familiar sequence. The boy has come to associate breakfast with good news. What is ahead for the day? When does a certain vacation start? During one breakfast the father announced that he had a surprise. The children were all ears. So was their mother; she knew of no forthcoming surprise. The father paused, waited for a bit of suspense to build up, then made his announcement: a new car — a red MG, a fast car that takes curves well and seats only two, in which he would take his wife and children for rides, one at a time.

Yet the boy had apparently been hoping for another kind of surprise: "I woke up and it was very funny, I remembered that I'd just had this dream. In it I was walking through the woods with Daddy, and all of a sudden there was an open field, and I looked, and I saw a hawk, and it was circling and circling. I like going hunting with Daddy, and I thought we were hunting. But when I looked at him, he didn't have his gun. Then he pointed at the hawk, and it was coming down. It landed ahead of us, and it was real strange — because the hawk turned into an airplane! I couldn't believe it. We went toward the plane, and Daddy said we could get a ride any time we wanted, because it was ours; he'd just bought it. That's when I woke up, I think. I even forgot about the dream until I looked at my fort and the airplanes, and then I remembered the dream, and once I remembered it, I didn't forget it again."

Dreams evoke a social as well as psychological reality. Dreams show what a child can hope for, unashamedly expect. It so happens that among rich children one day's apparently fatuous, excessive fantasy or dream can turn into the next day's actuality. Four years after that boy had dreamed that his father owned a plane, the father got one. The boom of the 1970s in the coal fields made his father even richer. The boy was of course eager to go on flying trips; eager also to learn to fly. The family owned a horse farm by then, near Lexington, Kentucky, and when the boy and girl were not flying, they were riding. The girl learned to jump well, the boy to ride quite fast. At thirteen he dreamed (by day) of becoming an astronaut or of becoming the manager of his father's horse farm or of going to the Air Force Academy and afterward becoming a "supersonic pilot."

He would never become a commercial pilot, however; and his reasons were interesting: "I've gone on a lot of commercial flights, and there are a lot of people on board, and the pilot has to be nice to everyone, and he makes all these announcements about the seat belts, and stuff like that. My dad's pilot was in the air force, and then he flew commercial. He was glad to get out, though. He says you have to be like a waiter; you have to answer complaints from the customers and apologize to them, just because the ride gets bumpy. It's best to work for yourself, or work for another person, if you trust him and like him. If you go commercial, like our pilot says, you're a servant. You can't really speak your mind. I'd like to fly, but I'm worried about going into the air force. Our pilot says it can be fun, or it can be murder, depending on your superior officer. If I got a bad one, I guess I'd just quit. They can't keep you in forever against your will."

He has only confidence about the future, no real sense of

danger. At times he talks (at thirteen) as if he could simultaneously hold down several jobs. He would run the family horse farm. He would take part in any number of races and hunts. He would also fly his own plane. He would learn how to parachute; he might even become a professional parachutist. He met one at a fair, and found the man not only brave, but "real nice to talk to." In more restrained (realistic?) moments, he forgets the horse farm, forgets airplanes or just plain air; he talks about law school — the place his father would like him to race to, land upon. When only an eighth-grade student he imagined himself, one day, owning an airplane, flying it back and forth from law school (at the University of Kentucky) to his father's horse farm, some fifty miles away.

He has never had any patience for lines, for traffic jams, for crowded stores. Many of the children I have worked with are similarly disposed; they do not like large groups of people in public places — in fact, have been taught the distinct value not only of privacy but the quiet that goes with being relatively alone. Some of the children are afraid of those crowds, can't imagine how it would be possible to survive them. Of course, what is strange, unknown, or portrayed as unattractive, uncomfortable, or just to be avoided as a nuisance can for a given child become a source of curiosity, even an event to be experienced at all costs. An eight-year-old girl who lived well outside Boston, even beyond its suburbs, on a farm, wanted desperately to go to the city and see Santa Claus — not because she believed in him, but because she wanted to see "those crowds" she had in fact seen on television. She got her wish, was excited at first, then quite disappointed, and ultimately made rather uncomfortable. She didn't like being jostled, shoved, pushed, and ignored when she protested. She was only too glad when her mother suggested that they had gone through quite enough. Yes, they had, the daughter agreed. Soon they were in a cab, then on a commuter train. The latter was going to be the limit for the girl thereafter; if she would venture into the world, the train would be its microcosm. She would travel by train to Boston, then turn right around and travel back — unless, of course, she were going to a restaurant or an art gallery or to her parents' club. In those places one is not overcome by people who shout, and step on the feet of others, and ignore any protests made.

A week after the girl had gone through her Boston "adventure" (as she had called the trip *before* she embarked upon it), each student in her third-grade class was asked to draw a picture in some way connected to the Christmas season, and the girl obliged eagerly. She drew Santa Claus standing beside a pile of packages, presents for the many children who stood near him. They blended into one another — a mob scene. Watching them but removed from them was one child, bigger and on a higher level — suspended in space, it seemed, and partially surrounded by a thin but visible line. The girl wrote on the bottom of the drawing "I saw Santa Claus." She made it quite clear what she had intended to portray: "He was standing there, handing out these gifts. They were all the same, I think, and they were plastic squirt guns for the boys and little dolls for the girls. I felt sorry for the kids. I asked my mother why kids wanted to push each other, just to get that junk. My mother said a lot of people just don't know any better. I was going to force my way up to that Santa Claus and tell him to stop being so dumb! My mother said he was probably a drunk, trying to make a few dollars, so he could spend it in a bar nearby that evening! I don't want to be in a store like that again. We went up to a balcony and watched, and then we got out of the place and came home. I told my mother that I didn't care if I ever went to Boston again. I have two friends, and they've never been in Boston, and they don't want to go there, except to ride through on the way to the airport."

She sounds at that moment more aloof, condescending, and downright snobbish than she ordinarily is. She spends some of her time with two or three girls who live on nearby "estates." Those girls don't see each other regularly, and each of them is quite able to be alone — in fact, rather as anxious to be by themselves, do things by themselves, as to be with one another and find things to work on together. Sometimes a day or two goes by with no formal arrangement to play. They meet in school, and that seems to be enough. Each girl has obligations — a horse to groom, a stall to work on. They are quite "self-sufficient," a word they have heard used repeatedly by their parents. Even within one's own social circle there is no point in surrendering to excessive gregariousness!

The girls meet by accident (or unacknowledged design) on various riding trails. On such daily expeditions one learns to be very much alone with one's thoughts. In the beginning they have to do with riding; but eventually they embrace the weather, the landscape, and, almost always, the child's body: "I think of my leg muscles, my hold on the horse. It's funny how you can forget a lot of your muscles until you mount that horse. Once up there you notice your feet and your knees and your hips, and you watch your arms and hands, and you think of your head and back — how straight are you sitting. It's your whole body that's on your mind, like the teacher says. It's a little like that with skiing, and a lot like that with ballet lessons; but for me, riding is when I'm most in touch with my body! And I'm also in touch with the horse's body. We're sort of one!"

Once up on the horse, riding, she is (by her own description) in her "own world." She has heard her mother use that expression. The mother is not boasting, or dismissing others who live in other worlds. The mother is describing, as does the child, a state of progressive withdrawal from people and, selectively, the familiar routines or objects of the environment, in favor of a mixture of reverie and disciplined activity. And when the girl, for one reason or another, is unable to ride, she misses not only the sport, but the state of mind that goes with riding.

Her mother is more explicit about what happens; she tells her daughter, at times, that she wants to "leave everything" and go riding. She tells her daughter that when she is on the horse, cantering across the field or trotting down a trail, she has a "feeling" that is "better than being on a plane." She finds that she can put everyone and everything into "perspective." Nothing seems impossible, burdensome, difficult. There are no distractions, nuisances, petty or boring details to attend to. One is not only away from it all, but above it all. And one is closer to one's "self." The mother talks about the "self" and the child does too. "It is strange," the girl comments, "because you forget yourself riding or skiing, but you also remember yourself the way you don't when you're just sitting around watching television or reading or playing in your room."

With none of the other American children I have worked with have I heard such a continuous and strong emphasis put on the "self." In fact, other children rarely if ever think about themselves in the way children of well-to-do and rich parents do — with insistence, regularity, and, not least, out of a learned sense of obligation. These privileged ones are children who live in homes with many mirrors. They have mirrors in their rooms, large mirrors in adjoining bathrooms. When they were three or four they were taught to use them; taught to wash their faces, brush their teeth, comb their hair. Personal appearance matters and becomes a central objective for such children. A boy of eight expresses his rebelliousness by clinging to sloppy clothes, but leaves the house every day for school in a neat and well-fitted uniform. A good number of these children wear them — shirts or sweaters with a school's name and/or insignia on them. Even when the child relaxes, comes home, and changes into "old" clothes, there is an air of decisiveness about the act — and certainly, the issue is one of choice: to wear *this*, or *that;* to look a particular way, in keeping with a particular mood, time of day, event.

The issue also is that of the "self" — its display, its possibilities, its cultivation and development, even the repeated use of the word. A ten-year-old boy who lives in the outermost part of Westchester County made this very clear. I had originally met him because his parents, both lawyers, were active in the civil rights movement. His father, a patrician Yankee, very much endorsed the students who went South in the early 1960s and, nearer to home, worked on behalf of integrated schools up North. His own children, however, attended private schools — a source of anguish to both the father and the son, who do not lend themselves easily to a description that only emphasizes the hypocritical element in their lives.

The boy knew that he also *would* be (as opposed to wanted to be!) a lawyer. He was quick to perceive and acknowledge his situation, and as he did so he brought himself (his "self") right into the discussion: "I don't want to tell other kids what to do. I told my father I should be going to the public schools myself. Then I could say anything. Then I could ask why we don't have black kids with us in school. But you have to try to do what's best for your *own* life, even if you can't speak up for the black people. When I'm grown up, I'll be like my father; I'll help the black people all I can. It's this way: first you build *yourself* up. You learn all you can. Later, you can *give of yourself.* That's what Dad says: you can't help others until you've learned to help *yourself.* It's not that you're being selfish. People say you're selfish, if you're going to a private school and your parents have a lot of money. We had a maid here, and she wasn't right in the head. She lost her temper and told Daddy that he's a phony, and he's out for *himself* and no one else, and the same goes for my sister and me. Then she quit. Daddy tried to get her to talk with us, but she wouldn't. She said that's all we ever do — talk, talk. I told Daddy she was contradicting herself; because she told me a few weeks ago that I'm always doing something, and I should sit down and talk with her. But I didn't know what to say to her! I think she got angry with me because I was putting on my skis for cross-country skiing, and she said I had too much, that was my problem. I asked her where the regular skis were, and she said she wouldn't tell me, even if she knew! It's too bad, what happened to her.

"I feel sorry for her, though. Like my sister said, it's no fun to be a maid! The poor woman doesn't look very good. She weighs too much. She's only forty, my mother thinks, but she looks as if she's sixty, and is sick. She should take better care of herself. She said my sister and I make big messes in the bathroom. But that's because we *use* the bathroom! And her breath — God, it's terrible. She isn't as clean as she should be. My mother wanted to get her some deodorant, but we were afraid she'd just blow up at us. But she did anyway. So it didn't make any difference! Like my Dad said, it's too bad about her; she didn't know how to take care of herself and now she's thrown away this job, and she told my mother last year that it was the best one she'd ever had, so she's her own worst enemy. I wonder what she'll think when she looks at herself in the mirror and tries to figure out what to do next."

He was no budding egotist. If anything, he was less self-centered, at ten, than many other children of his community or others like it. He was willing to think about, at least, others less fortunate than himself — the maid, and black people in general. True, he would often repeat uncritically his father's words, or a version of them. But he was trying to respond to his father's wishes and beliefs as well as his words. It was impossible for him, no matter how compassionate his nature, to conceive of life as other's live it — the maid, and yes, millions of children his age, who don't look in the mirror very often and may not even own one; who don't worry about what is worn, and how one looks, and what is said and how one sounds, and what is done (in the bathroom) and how one smells.

Sometimes minor details of a life tell more than larger attitudes spoken and duly recorded by outside observers. A boy's fingernails, for instance; or his sister's skin — in each instance, a reflection of much more. Here is the boy from Westchester County, at eleven, talking about the new pair of scissors he has received from his father: "I like them. I didn't want my mother to clip my fingernails any longer. I'd rather take care of myself! I'll be shaving soon. I look forward to that! I've watched my father a lot. He showed me how to use the scissors and end up with nails that aren't too short and aren't too long. There's a kid in my class, he lets his nails get longer and longer and there's a lot of dirt under them, and you wonder how long they'll get, and then all of a sudden, one day, you notice that they've been cut off. His parents have got a divorce, and they have a maid taking care of him and his kid brother, and she runs the house and there's no one supervising her. You have to tell the help what to do, because if you don't, they forget and they don't live up to your standards, and they're acting as if they were back in their own homes."

So it happens — a boy's developing sense of himself as against a collective, amorphous "them." It is a "sense" that has both sociological and psychological dimensions to it. The former are perhaps more painful to spell out but also more readily apparent. The boy has learned that in the ghetto people live who don't use his parents' kind of judgment, and don't, either, have the same personal habits or concerns. The boy's sister has a similar kind of knowledge. At twelve she could be quite pointed: "We've had a couple of maids, and they don't know why I use my mother's Vaseline lotion on my arms and hands — and in winter on my face, too. They say I've got a wonderful complexion; but I don't think they know how to look real carefully at my skin — or their own either. Maybe they don't have the time. But I see them taking a 'break,' and what do they do? They go put on a prize show in the morning or a 'story' in the afternoon. I don't know how they can stand looking at that stuff! I've got a lot of chores. We're not spoiled here! I have to clean out the stalls and brush the horses carefully before we go riding. I have to pick up my room. My mother told me when I was real little, before I was even old enough to go to school, that she wasn't going to have me sitting and looking at television while the maid was straightening out my room. The same goes for outside the house; we have a gardener, but he's not allowed to come into the barn and help us with the animals.

"We had one maid, and she said we spent more time with the animals than she does with her children. I felt sad when she told me that. She has no understanding of what an animal needs. She was the one who was always telling me I was beautiful, and so I didn't need any lotion on my skin. I wanted to give her the lotion. She needs it. Her skin is in terrible shape. It's so dried and cracked. My mother says you can be poor and still know how to take care of yourself. It's not the money; it's the attitude you have toward yourself. If our maid stopped buying a lot of candy and potato chips, she could afford to get herself some skin lotion. And she wouldn't be so fat!"

A child has learned to distinguish between her own inclinations or preferences and those of another person — a whole category of people. This girl was, at the time, not quite an adolescent; for years, however, she had been prepared for that time, for adulthood as well — prepared by parents who not only wanted her to know how to use skin lotions, or choose "tasteful" lipstick, or shun anything but "natural" fingernail polish, or learn how to care for her hair and wash it, and pay attention to the scalp as well. Those parents wanted her to give an enormous amount of attention to *herself* — to her thoughts, which she has been taught are worthy of being spoken, and to her body, which is going to be, one day, "attractive." So she has been told by several maids — far too emphatically to suit the taste of her parents. They prefer a more understated, indirect approach. They remind the girl that she looks like her grandmother ("a handsome lady") or her aunt ("who was quite beautiful"). They let her know how graceful she is as a young dancing student, how agile and accomplished a rider she has become, how fast and accurate a game of tennis she has developed, even at her age. They smile at pictures of her smiling, applaud her once again when watching home movies. Her picture is on the mantle over the living room fireplace, on her father's desk, on her mother's desk, and is on her own desk, for that matter.

When she was six and seven she asked a lot of questions about herself. They were answered patiently, thoughtfully, and often with enthusiastic pride — a contrast indeed with many poor children, whose parents are tired, embittered, sad, or all too resigned to their fate, and hardly able to boast about the circumstances of life. The girl's questions occur to all children, rich or poor — are the banal inquiries we never quite stop asking ourselves: who am I, why am I here, whence do I come, and where am I going — the continuing preoccupations of philosophers, novelists, and painters. Children prefer the painter's approach. They sometimes don't pay much attention to the answers to their questions. After all too verbal family meals they retire to a desk or table, draw pictures meant to suggest what life is and will be about. When the girl mentioned above wonders who she is or has questions about her future, she picks up crayons and draws herself with care and affection — on a horse, in a garden, high up in a tower, surveying the countryside.

In doing so she draws upon her concrete, day-to-day experiences. She also uses those experiences in order to suggest something larger about her particular life. Especially noteworthy is the care she and others like her take with themselves as they draw. So often poor children treat themselves cursorily; they quickly sketch a rather unflattering self-portrait. Sometimes they are unwilling to complete what they have begun — as if they are unsure of life itself. A migrant child once told me in a matter-of-fact way that he had no expectation of living beyond twenty. He was simply a child who knew the score. The children of doctors and lawyers and business executives have learned the score too. The girl mentioned above spends a half hour drawing herself, moves her eyes toward a mirror every once in a while to check on how she actually does look, and is eventually quite proud of what she has drawn. She also spends long periods of time looking at old photographs — of herself, her parents, her grandparents. Such observations and bits of anecdotal family history have become consolidated in the girl's mind. She regards herself — though she has learned to be affectingly modest — as a rather attractive person. No wonder she once posed herself, in a picture, beside a giant sunflower. She was in no way overshadowed by the flower; if anything, it adorned her own luminous presence.

When that girl became ill with chicken pox the anguish of her mental state was noticeable and instructive. She wanted to scratch the many lesions on her face and arms but was told, of course, by her parents that she must not. She heeded their advice. In the beginning she did scratch one pustule midway on her upper right arm. Her mother became quite upset.

Before the mother could say a word, the child spoke up, acknowledged her awareness of the future implications of her deed. She had lost control, and she would suffer. Her description of that talk and of her later, more successful, bout with the disease, has struck me as a classic of sorts: "I don't want to look ugly. If I had scratched my face, like I did my right arm, I'd look a mess for life. I knew that. But I had *such* a bad case! The doctor said it was one of the worst he'd seen in the last few years. He told me he had seen even worse than mine, and I was sort of disappointed. I figured that I'd like to go through the biggest challenge, and come out on top!

"After a day or two, I began to wonder if I'd be able to survive! I got very weepy. I began to wonder whether I'd done anything wrong — to deserve this punishment. I couldn't look myself in the mirror. I didn't want to wash at all. I felt so dirty and horrible looking. I asked my brother and my parents not to look at me! My brother tried to kid me out of my mood. He came in with his Polaroid camera and said he'd take a picture of me, and I could keep it, and when I was over the disease, I could just laugh! Instead I started crying, right in front of him. He apologized.

"The worst part of the chicken pox was the waiting and the trying to keep control. My mother sat with me, and my Dad did too, when he got home. On the worst day, he offered to stay with me and not go to his office. I said no, I'd be all right. But he decided to stay anyway. He just sat there and read to me. We watched some television — the news and a cooking class. We talked a little. Dad kept telling me I was great, and not to worry; he was sure I was going to have a wonderful life, because I've got everything going for me. I told him 'not the chicken pox,' when he said that. But he just laughed and told me that the chicken pox would soon be a bad memory, and I'd forget about it completely in a couple of months. I'm not sure

I ever will, though. I have this scar on my arm, and I'll always have it. My mother says no one will notice; but *I* do! She got angry the other day. She said I was worrying too much. But I've seen her worry a lot too. If a dress doesn't fit her, she sends it right back. She's always either on a diet or coming off one, or getting ready to go on one again. We have scales in every bathroom, and one in her bedroom. I told her I don't need to weigh myself and my brother doesn't; but she wants us to get in the habit, so we'll know later when to start being careful about food. She tells the maid to give us cookies only when she's not around; she doesn't want to be tempted. And her hair — well, that's 'a whole subject,' as my Daddy says. When he was with me that day, I asked him why Mom worries so much about her hair, and dyes it. Who cares if there's some gray in her hair! But Dad said that gray hair for Mom is like the chicken pox for me. I could see what he meant, but it's not exactly the same."

She did not for long insist upon the difference; she went along with her father's comparison. She did so not reluctantly, but with the detachment that goes with complete recovery — a feeling of remove from what was once painful. Her mother has always been regarded as a rather lovely woman; the girl was prepared to emphasize that fact in her mind, and associate her own present and future appearance with her mother's deserved reputation. The girl was also prepared to acknowledge quite candidly what a relatively severe case of a basically benign disease could do to her thoughts about herself: "I began to worry whether I really was as pretty as everyone had been saying. It was a mood; I'm over it now. I do have a few bad memories. Dad says they'll go. I hope so. I look at myself in the mirror and I'll suddenly be afraid that the chicken pox is coming back. I get scared. It's silly. I know I'm never going to get the chicken pox again!

"I wish I hadn't scratched that one place. It's such a small scar. But it gives me nightmares! I woke up the other night and my parents were in my room. I guess I'd been crying or shouting. In the morning my mother said I'd half-awakened, and I'd told them that a cat had been chasing me, and scratched me, and I was afraid there'd be a scar. I wonder a lot about the man I'll marry. Will he have brown hair or blond hair or black hair? My mother asked me if it makes any difference; I told her I like brown hair and green eyes, and I hope he'll be tall and thin. I wouldn't even want to go out once with a man who was overweight!"

This is no petty, superficial, half-witted, or empty-headed girl. She has gone to very good private schools — each of which has high academic standards and expectations. She can be serious, thoughtful, and idealistic — that is, worried about others less fortunate and hopeful that they somehow get to live better lives. As a child she can hardly be expected to come up with solutions for the world's various problems, but some of those problems do at times weigh upon her. Yet she can, all of a sudden, move from writing a composition about "world hunger" to discussing with her mother the virtues of various cosmetics or the appropriateness of certain dresses for one or another social occasion. She can also, rather disarmingly, stop thinking about "the troubles in America" her teacher has asked the class to write about, because her parakeet needs food or water, her two gerbils require new bedding, her alarm clock has to be set, her desk is cluttered and ought be straightened out, or her phone has rung. She has a room with its own demands and requirements, with a bureau mirror and one on the back of the door, a full-length mirror. Sometimes she gets tired of thinking of arithmetic problems and social problems, and spelling problems, of coming up with ideas meant to straighten out society.

The last word, incidentally, has two meanings for her. She started, at ten, dancing lessons. She was aware then that later on she would be going to parties, would become a debutante. Her mother plays down that word, debutante. Her mother is a New Englander who doesn't like "fuss," abhors elaborate, pretentious parties, the stuff of social climbing; but she also has a keen eye for who is acceptable to whom in her social circle, what name elicits deference, and whose "situation" is what mixture of "position" and "real wealth."

Those words are used discreetly, but they do not go unnoticed by a ten- or eleven-year-old child. The girl asks questions about her family, its origins and "place" in the social and economic system. "Our minister tells us to think of others, but it's hard, because I've never seen the poor. I gave half of some money I saved for Christmas to the starving people of Africa. Daddy said he was real proud of me. He gave me the money I'd contributed. He says that when I grow up I should marry a man who is kind and worries about other people, not just himself; that's the type of man who makes a good husband. I agree. It's best to marry someone who's pretty much like yourself, though. Otherwise you might run into trouble. He'll think one way, and you'll think another. There are a lot of divorces that take place. My parents have a lot of friends whose marriages aren't good. If you marry a person who thinks like you, and he has the same beliefs, then you have a better chance of staying married.

"When I leave this room and stay at a friend's, or when we go up skiing or down to our summer house, I get a funny feeling. I really miss my dolls and my bureau — the shells and dishes my parents have brought me when they have come back from trips. I have all kinds of shells, from all the Caribbean beaches. I have dishes and ashtrays from a lot of countries. I have posters; I love French posters. I hope I learn to speak French fluently. It's a beautiful language. It's strange, leaving your room and sleeping in a place that hasn't got much of anything that belongs to you, that's yours, that's *you*."

That last progression deserves respectful attention as a rather forceful, intelligent, and exact analysis of the complicated psychology of class-connected "narcissistic entitlement." She and others like her grow up surrounded by possessions, animate as well as inanimate. They have learned to live with them, to look after them, and to depend upon them for support. They have also learned to give of themselves to those "objects." When they leave for a winter or summer vacation they try to take some of their most treasured belongings with them, but often still experience a sense of emptiness or a feeling of being alone, isolated, bereft. Child psychiatrists use the expression "transitional object" to refer to a child's blanket or teddy bear or doll — taken to bed, carried around, held tight at the age of four, five, six.

Few children are unable to find those "transitional objects." I have seen the poorest of American children, living the most uprooted of lives, cling to a dirty old rag, a stick, a rock, the cheapest of plastic toys, often obtained secondhand, maybe from someone's trash barrel. Children of working-class parents or of so-called "middle-income" families seldom experience such sad desperation. On the other hand, many of those children share rooms with brothers and sisters and by no means assume that they are to be recipients of an apparently endless succession of gifts, vacations, pleasant surprises. In the homes of the rich, in contrast, the children almost invariably have their own rooms, and the quantitative difference in their material acquisitions prompts a qualitative psychological difference: an enhanced expectation of what life has to offer, and with that, a strong inclination to build a sanctuary out of one's room and one's property. The girl is subtle but sharp and exact when she distinguishes between what belongs to her (a piece of property) and what has become hers — an existential psychological transformation. The next step is of course an ironic act of personal surrender: the object and the person merge somewhat — from "that's yours" to "that's *you*."

All children struggle when very young — starting at a little under a year, in fact — to distinguish between themselves and their parents. They begin to realize, at two and three, that it is *they* who exist — individuals who crawl and walk and make noises and talk. As they separate, to a degree, from their mothers, especially then, at two or three, they first know loneliness. Certainly, thereafter, for most children, there are reattachments to the mother, new attachments to other persons — and to things. But the child turns inward too upon occasion, makes an effort to find comfort and even pleasure in a newfound solitariness. Freud, at one point, referred to "the purified pleasure ego" — by which he meant a child's delight in the various excitements or satisfactions he or she can manage to find. I recall a four-year-old boy in one home I visited, not far from that of the girl quoted just above, who slid up and down a wonderfully solid, circular staircase, shouting me, me, me; he was in love with the dizzying speed, with the feeling of control and power he had — with himself.

Later on, at five and six, such a child becomes quite conscious of rights and wrongs, of what ought to be done to please parents and teachers, not to mention one's own developing conscience. Psychoanalysts describe the "idealized parent image" — the part of a child's mind that holds up examples, insists upon directions. The child absorbs from significant persons his or her notions of what matters and how he or she should in general be trying to live — and tries to go along. The "you" that the girl mentioned above at age ten — a summary, almost, of which belongings had become part of her "self"

— was preceded by the earlier "you" comprehended at the age of six: "I'd like to do good in school, and learn to ski, and ride my bike fast, and get to make real tasty cookies with the maid, and then I'll be good, and people will say, she's doing everything she should be doing, and I'll say that to myself. When I'm finished brushing my teeth, they'll be clean, and my mother will soon be upstairs and check me out, and I'll say to myself: you're doing okay. And a few minutes later my mother says the same thing: 'You're doing okay!' "

That child has had ample opportunities — beyond using a toothbrush well — to prove herself, as well as find pleasure in competence. She has been taught tennis and swimming by coaches, cooking by a maid, riding by her mother. The girl has also learned how to draw and paint, play the piano, "do" ballet. She has gone abroad often, has mastered words, used her own passport. She has become acquainted with forms of etiquette, with new protocols. She knows when to defer, when to speak up. She knows how to recognize various songs, symphonies, operatic pieces. She knows how to walk the corridors of museums, recognize the work of certain artists. And too, she has acquired some of the psychological judgment good hostesses have: who is like whom, who belongs near whom at the table, who will be a "disaster" with whom. She used that word sometimes, when eleven and twelve, and in so doing revealed more than a "prepubescent" affinity for a way of talking, or a superficial cleverness about people. In fact, she was indicating something significant about her sense of *herself.*

One such "disaster" was her mother's much younger cousin, and the girl knew why: "She's sloppy. She's always been sloppy. She speaks sloppy. She had a harelip, and that was what ruined her. The parents didn't take her to the right doctor, and the girl became shy, and she didn't want to talk to anyone, and when she was a teenager she became even worse. She just stayed in her room a lot. Then she got religious, in a weird way. She was always praying. My mother says they should have sent her to a doctor. She decided to become a nun, I think. She wanted to convert and be a Catholic, and then be a nun. They talked her out of that. She came to life a little. She began to go out and meet people. Then she met this guy, and he was a music teacher, and he was poor, and they fell in love, and they wanted to get married. He was a disaster, my mother says. He could barely open his mouth, and he didn't know which fork to use, and he wore real funny clothes, and he had a bad complexion, and the worst case of dandruff my mother has ever seen. He just sat there, and it didn't even seem to bother him that he didn't talk. But my mother's cousin was a disaster, too. She was just an oddball, that's what. They got married, and my mother says they've been good for each other.

"They would be poor now, if it wasn't that my mother's aunt left them some money. I think they have enough to get by. We see them sometimes; they come to visit my grandmother. We have to keep a straight face. We can't laugh. That would be bad. You should feel sorry for people who aren't as fortunate as you are. If you don't, then you are rude and you don't have charity. If you're not nice to someone, you've lost. You sink down to the other person's level. That's what Daddy tells us, and he gets angry if we don't pay attention. He says we've got a responsibility to show good manners at all times. I'd never call someone a 'disaster' in front of him; at least while we're having supper. Sometimes he'll be having a drink, and then even he will call someone a fool or *no good;* that's *his* way of calling someone he knows and doesn't like a 'disaster.' "

In "Forms and Transformations of Narcissism" (*Journal of the American Psychoanalytic Association,* April, 1966), Heinz Kohut observes that the "form and content of the psychic representation of the idealized parent thus vary with the maturational stage of the child's cognitive apparatus." Then he adds, significantly, that the form and content "are also influenced by environmental factors that affect the choice of internalizations and their intensity." There may seem, at first glance, a considerable distance in substance if not tone between a child's reflections on her second cousin and a psychoanalyst's theoretical observations, addressed to his scholarly colleagues. But the psychiatrist is trying to formulate what the child is living through and occasionally able to comment upon. Even as a migrant child or ghetto child learns to feel weak and vulnerable, a child of well-off parents learns to feel, in many respects, confident. There are idiosyncratic variations, of course. One can be rich and psychotic, for instance, and instill fear, apprehension, and a sense of worthlessness in one's children. Yet even among the disturbed young children of well-to-do parents there are concerns and expectations that contrast profoundly with the notions other children, from other backgrounds, possess about themselves. At a certain point in every child's life, as Dr. Kohut suggests, and as Freud repeatedly pointed out, culture and class become matters of a child's fantasy life and affect the tone of his or her self regard. The girl who wants to look a certain way, speak a certain way, who anticipates a certain way of life, and who derives personal strength and competence from the sense of herself she has learned to have, is a person whose "narcissism," whose "idealized parent image," has drawn upon many daily conversations and experiences, rewards and lessons.

At another point in his paper Dr. Kohut points out that our "ambitions and ideals" don't just appear out of nowhere. They have a psychological history, not to mention a social and economic background. He refers to their "preconscious correlates" and locates them (structurally speaking) in the "narcis-

sistic self," whose various "ego ideals" have, of course, been
acquired over countless intimate encounters — the family involvements that set the stage for a child's view of what "life"
is going to be like. Dr. Kohut points out that ambitions do not
always coincide with ideals. A child whose parents are poor or
of working-class background may have heard a mother or
father (or, rather often, a teacher) say that anyone can be
President in this country, or rise to the top of a company, or
become a doctor, a lawyer, a "success" — given "hard work."
But the child has seen and heard much evidence to the contrary. The child has seen his or her parents curbed, scorned,
exhausted, frustrated, embittered. The child has heard that
"life" is no picnic, that wages don't keep up with prices, that
the factory is laying off more and more people, including his
or her father or mother. The child has heard, upon breaking
a dish or a toy, upon failing to follow instructions, or falling
short at school, that soon enough the difficulties and tensions
of grown-up life will fall upon him or her. In contrast, privileged children, far fewer in number, are destined for quite
another fate. In his own manner, Dr. Kohut approaches their
lives; speaking of their "ambitions and ideals," he observes
that "they are at times hard to distinguish, not only because
ambitions are often disguised as ideals but also because there
are indeed lucky moments in our lives, or lucky periods in the
lives of the very fortunate, in which ambitions and ideals coincide."

For those "lucky," a sense of entitlement develops —
the merger of what they have learned would be "ideal" and
what they have actually experienced, into an ongoing attitude
toward the world. Let others feel diminished, impeded, burdened; or let them long for a different kind of life, knowing all
too clearly by the age of six or seven the difference between
a castle in Spain and a ranch house in Levittown, or a ghetto

tenement, or a tenant farmer's shack. For privileged children, there is every reason to feel entitlement. But let us not forget that entitlement is perfectly compatible with doubts, misgivings, despair. A child can feel — being realistic — entitled to a certain kind of life and yet have other reasons to be confused or hurt. Even schizophrenics experience the distinctions that have to do with class and caste, race and place of residence. The girl whose words I called upon above had her own thoughts, one day, about these theoretical issues of mental life — after she had heard, at the age of twelve, that her father was sick and required surgery: "I hope he'll be all right. It's serious, my mother told me. I can tell it is; Daddy hasn't been smiling much. He's been worried. He's been talking a lot about his insurance, and he took my brother and me to the bank, and he told us we'll be going there for the rest of our lives, or calling them up and asking them to send us over some money. He says that if we're careful, our children will have the same amount of money we have. It's best to use the interest and not the capital. The bank knows how to keep your money invested in the best stocks.

"Daddy will be all right. He's strong. He has the best doctor in the country; he's the best surgeon. I met him, and he was very nice. He gave my brother and me a book he'd written, about the seashore and the clams and oysters and lobsters you find in the water and the sand. He owns a lot of land by the ocean, and he's a marine biologist, my father says, besides being a surgeon. And he's an artist, too. I wouldn't mind being a doctor myself, but I don't know if I'd want to operate on anyone. The surgeon offered to show my brother and me how he operates; we could watch him — but not when he works on Daddy. My brother said yes, but I said no. I'd rather not be there, if anything goes wrong; then, when Daddy is being operated on, I'd worry even more.

"We'll be all right. My mother says everything will turn out good. Daddy may not be home for a couple of weeks, but we can go and see him all the time. We can eat with him in his room. It'll be like going out to a restaurant. He'll have television and his own phone. We can talk with him any time we want. He says he'll get a lot of reading done. He'll have a nice view from his room, and he'll get all the rest he'll need. Then, when he gets home, we're going away. Daddy says we'll be in Barbados for two weeks. He's promised to take us out of school. We'll get all our homework, and we won't fall back at all. My mother says it may turn out to be a blessing in disguise that Daddy got sick; he'll get a lot of rest, and he'll be much stronger. I hope so."

She was not about to acknowledge, even to herself, how worried she sensed her mother to be. But she (and her mother) had resources that very much ameliorated an anxious period of waiting. The dreaded outcome of the father's illness, a malignancy, did not materialize. All the money in the world could not have converted cancerous cells into normal ones. But during those days that preceded surgery the girl and her brother felt more hope than dread, and had quite valid sources of support for that hope. And during the father's convalescence, instead of hearing their mother and father lamenting bills, expressing worries about the loss of a job, or complaining about the "conditions" in the hospital, their time of trouble became for everyone concerned an opportunity for pleasure, relaxation, new initiatives and accomplishments. The girl and her brother ended up becoming scuba divers in the warm Caribbean water; went on motorcycle rides such as they had never had before; began to realize more exactly than ever how well-off their parents are and they as children are. "It all came out for the best," the girl said, weeks after her father was pronounced able to return to his work as a business executive.

In a sense the words are a slogan of sorts, constantly kept in mind by her and others: life works out "for the best," mostly — and one has a right to conclude that if one has had ample confirming evidence.

For some of these children, the privileged life presents a danger of what clinicians have referred to as "secondary narcissism" — the "narcissistic entitlement" I mentioned at the beginning of this section. However, on the evidence of the privileged children I have come to know, I would emphasize the possibility that a feeling of "entitlement" may develop in a child without the potentially treacherous development of an excessively narcissistic tone. When a feeling of "entitlement" becomes "narcissistic," it has departed from what James Agee called "human actuality." Suppose the girl whose father had taken ill began, for her own reasons, to imagine that her father's illness would be associated with some extraordinary development: a call to the theater or television as a young actress; a medal of honor awarded by the school she attended; a party given her as an expressin of her popularity. Suppose that girl, alternatively, expected the surgeon to cure her father, no matter *what* was discovered upon operating. Suppose that girl began crying constantly before her father entered the hospital; and did so petulantly, plaintively, as if less interested in her father's troubles than her own. At that point her narcissism would have taken its form from her private experiences, although the same child in other moments might lose her despairing self-centeredness. The point to emphasize is the mind's capacity to appreciate the reality of a certain kind of life. The mind can of course undercut a good thing, make a bad thing even worse, or make the best of it.

It is important that a privileged child's normal sense of "entitlement" be distinguished not only from pathological narcissism, but from the more common phenomenon known as being "spoiled." It is a matter of degree; "spoiled" children are self-centered all right, petulant and demanding — but not saddled with the grandiose illusions (or delusions) clinicians have in mind when using the phrase "narcissistic entitlement." The rich, the "well-to-do" are all too commonly charged with producing spoiled children. Yet one sees spoiled children everywhere, among the very poor as well as the inordinately rich. A child can be spoiled by a mother's attitude. What the child is "given" can be called excessive instinctual leeway or, in everyday words, however politicized in recent years, "permissive indulgence." I remember a migrant mother who knew precisely and uncannily what she was doing "wrong" — knew, indeed, to call it all "wrong." She told me one day that she had given birth to a particular child with more pain than usual and had been in lower spirits than ever before in her life during the first months of that child's life. When the baby began to notice the mother and the world, start crawling and separating himself from her, she felt a fierce desire within herself, expressed with unforgettable intensity, "to let that boy have anything he wants, anything he can lay his hands on." She was careful, for all her lack of education and her troubled spirits, to qualify herself. She moved quickly, immediately, from "anything he wants" to "anything he can lay his hands on." She knew that in the first or second year of life the child would have all he could do to reach and hold on to what he wanted.

But soon enough a child begins to see things that others have; on a rented, only half-working television set the migrant child saw a lot, and looked around the room and realized a lot. His was no blessed life! He continued, however, to want to take what little he could get. And of course children (or adults) can want things that are psychological in lieu of what is "material." They can become demanding, possessive, insistent, if allowed to be. They can compete with others for attention, push hard against others who try to assert themselves. They can make every effort to obtain center stage at all times. The migrant mother developed, deep within her hurt and sad self, a pride about her child and his stubborn, indulged, expropriative, loud-mouthed, and at times impossibly egotistical behavior.

He was the child who would shout and scream and swagger, shake his fists, really, at the wretched world he had been born to. No matter that such behavior, whether allowed or even encouraged, is hardly a guarantee of a future rise to success. On the contrary, a child of migrant parents who acts like that one is headed, quite likely, for future trouble. The mother knew that too. She knew that migrants are virtually peons; that they submit to endless demands and manipulations. Perhaps one of her children would be so "spoiled" that he would be utterly incapable of becoming a migrant or lasting as one for very long. She answered along those lines when her husband asked her why she doesn't spank the "spoiled one" as she does the other children.

He in turn mentioned the grim likelihood that the boy would not indeed last as a migrant. He would instead end up in jail — or soon dead. All right, better a last stand, the mother replied. But she knew that really there was no point to such a hope; it would never even come to that, because the boy would either learn to mind his manners, and submit to the only life he would most likely ever know, or go down not in defiant resistance but through the slow attrition of cheap wine and harmless side-of-the-road braggadoccio — the "maladjusted" migrant who works inefficiently, goes to the bars before and after work, dies in a car accident or drowns drunk in one of the hundreds of irrigation canals that crisscross the agricultural counties of Florida, where this particular family spent its winters.

The parallel with spoiled children of upper-income families

is not so farfetched. In one of the first such families I came to know there was a girl who was described by both parents as "spoiled." At the time, I fear, I was ready to pronounce every child in New Orleans' Garden District spoiled.

Nevertheless, I soon began to realize that it wouldn't do to call one set of children spoiled, by virtue of their social and economic background — as against another set of children who were obviously less privileged. Though one meets among the poor any number of spoiled children, one also meets among the rich restrained, disciplined children; sometimes, even, boys and girls who have learned to be self-critical, even ascetic — anything but "spoiled" in the conventional sense of the word. True, one can find a touch and more of arrogance in those apparently Spartan boys and girls, who seem quite anxious to deny themselves all sorts of apparently accessible privileges. But one also finds in these children a consistent willingness to place serious and not always pleasant burdens on themselves. They often struck me, as I came to their homes fresh from visits with much poorer age-mates, as remarkably *less* spoiled: not so much whining or crying; fewer demands for candy or other sweets; even sometimes a relative indifference to toys, a disregard of television — so often demanded by the children I was seeing across the city, on the other side of the tracks.

Those children from prominent families appeared, even at the age of four or five, to put their energies in the service of "constructive" play or "useful" activities. They had begun to learn at two and three how important it was for them to do "right" as against "wrong"; to build rather than destroy; to concentrate their energies, devote them to particular tasks, which were to be finished rather than started and abandoned. They had, in some instances, even learned to take care of their own rooms — keep them neat, pick up after themselves, be conscious of what belongs where. Maids came to help, or lived with the family, but sometimes a particular boy or girl, as young as five or six, was a taskmaster to the maid rather than, certainly, a helpless or indulged child. And sometimes the maid herself became astonished by the example set by such children — and became their strong admirer.

A New Orleans black woman said to me in 1961: "I don't know how to figure out these rich, white kids. They're something! I used to think, before I took a job with this family, that the only difference between a rich kid and a poor kid is that the rich kid knows he has a lot of money and he grows up and he becomes spoiled rotten. That's what my mother told me; she took care of a white girl, and the girl was an only child, and her father owned a department store in McComb, Mississippi, and that girl thought she was God's special creature. My mother used to come home and tell us about the 'little princess'; but she turned out to be no good. She was so pampered she couldn't do a thing for herself. All she knew how to do was order people around. It's different with these two children here in New Orleans. I've never seen such a boy and such a girl. They think they're the best ones who ever lived — like that girl in McComb — but they don't behave like her. They're never asking me to do much of anything. They even ask if *they* can help *me!* They tell me that they want to know how to do everything. The girl says she wants to learn how to run the washing machine and the dishwasher. She says she wants to learn all my secret recipes. She says she'd like to give the best parties in the Garden District when she grows up, and she'd like to be able to give them without anyone's help. She says I could serve the food, but she would like to make it. The boy says he's going to be a lawyer and a banker, so he wants to know how much everything costs. He doesn't want to waste anything. He'll see me throw something away, and he wants to know why. I wish my own kids were like him!

"I wish my kids weren't so lazy; they don't care what's going on; they just want to play and play, and they waste a lot of food, and they break the toys I get them real fast. I even told my children I wish they could learn from these two children here. But these children here are special, and don't they know it! That's what being rich is: you know you're different from most people. These two kids are even more special, because they act as if they're going to be tops in everything, and they're pleased as can be with themselves, because there is nothing they can't do, and there's nothing they can't get, and there's nothing they can't win, and they're always showing off what they can do, and then before you can tell them how good they are, they're telling the same thing to themselves. It's confusing! They're not spoiled one bit, but oh, they have a high opinion of themselves!

"And I'll have to admit, there are times when I have the same high opinion of them! I'll look at them, and I'll say that they could be dropped on an island in the middle of a big ocean, and they'd know what to do, and if they didn't have anyone around to be pleased with them, they'd be all right because they'd be pleased with themselves! And it wouldn't take them long to know where to go and what to do on that island, because they are just so sure of themselves and so full of themselves that they always have their chins up, and they're happy, and they know where they're going, and they know what's ahead — that everything will come out fine in the end. When you have that kind of spirit in you, then you'll always get out of any jam you're in, and you'll always end up on top, because that's where you started, and that's where you believe you're going to end up, and if it's in your mind that it is like that, and it's *going* to be like that, and if you're willing to work hard, like these kids are, and if you're careful about everything, like they are, then you just *can't* lose, and don't these kids know it, I'll tell you!"

Actually the children she speaks of aren't as confident of themselves as she thinks, though she certainly has accurately conveyed their appearance. The kind of children she knows so well are extraordinarily privileged by virtue of background and money, are also intelligent and of attractive appearance; but those children have demons that occasionally urge them on, and their nature is not always easy to divine. Boys and girls may seem without anxiety or self-doubt at, say, eight or nine. Yet, there are moments of hesitation, if not apprehension. An eleven-year-old boy from a prominent and quite brilliant Massachusetts family (three generations of first-rate lawyers) told his teachers in an autobiographical composition about the vicissitudes of "entitlement": "I don't always do everything right. I'd like to be able to say I don't make any mistakes, but I do, and when I do, I feel bad. My father and mother say that if you train yourself, you can be right *almost* 100% of the time. Even they make mistakes, though. I like to be first in sports. I like to beat my brothers at skiing. But I don't always go down the slopes as fast as I could and I sometimes fall down. Last year I broke my leg. That was the first time I'd ever gone to a hospital and stayed there. It was my mother who reminded me that I'd been in the hospital for a week just after I was born! I'd forgotten! I was saying that I'd *never* been in the hospital overnight, and she corrected me.

"My great-grandfather is eighty-four, and he's in the best of health. It worries me that I have bad sinus trouble a lot of times after I get flu. I'd hate to be sick when I'm older. There's too much to do; if you get sick, you can't do much of anything, except stay home and rest. When I get a bad cold, I feel disappointed in myself. I don't think it's right to be easy on yourself. If you are, then you slip back, and you don't get a lot of the rewards in life. If you really work for the rewards, you'll get them."

His teachers have often given him that kind of platitude. In the fourth grade, for instance, his teacher had written on the blackboard (and kept it there for weeks): "Those who want something badly enough get it, provided they are willing to wait and work." The boy has been brought up to believe that it will be like that for him. He knows that others are not so lucky, but he hasn't really met those "others," and they don't cross his mind. What does occur to him sometimes is the need for constant exertion, lest he fail to "measure up." The expression is a family one, used repeatedly. No matter how difficult a task, no matter how frustrating it is for others, one "measures up" when one does it well. One "measures up" when one tries hard, succeeds. One measures up because one *must.* No allowance is made for any possible lack of ability or endowment. The assumption is that one has been "given a lot" (another family expression) and so a "return" is obligatory if justice is to be done. If one slackens or stumbles, one ought take oneself to task. The emphasis is on a quick and efficient moment of scrutiny followed by "a fast pickup," yet another admonitory injunction handed down.

Such counsel is not as callous or psychologically insensitive as it may sound — or even as it may have been *intended* to sound. The child who hears it gets briefly upset, but "a fast pickup" does indeed take place quite often. Again, it is a matter of feeling "entitled." A child who has been told repeatedly that all he or she needs to do is try hard does not feel inclined to allow himself or herself much skeptical self-examination. The point is to feel *entitled* — then act upon that feeling. The boy whose composition was just quoted from wrote again, apparently about his younger (aged five) brother: "I was watching my brother from my bedroom window. He was climbing up the fence we built for our corral. He got to the top, and then he just stood there and waved and shouted. No one was there. He was talking to himself. He was very happy. Then he would fall. He would be upset for a few seconds, but he would climb right back up again. Then he would be even happier! He was entitled to be happy. It is his fence, and he has learned to climb it, and stay up, and balance himself."

The little brother was indeed happy on top of the fence. He would talk to himself with obvious pleasure — tell nameless, invisible people that they are stupid and inadequate because, unlike him, they are unable to climb the fence and stay there and enjoy themselves. Yes, he was obviously talking to himself. He was also speaking to an earlier version of himself, to the boy of four who had wanted to climb that fence, wanted to get on top, and, just as important, stay there and enjoy the experience. Once he had succeeded, he enjoyed his new-found competence. He would practically never be curbed, humiliated, denied interesting or engaging occasions because of the "reality" of the world around him. Quite the contrary; there would be one inviting adventure after another over the months and years. One day, as a matter of fact, he ran across the field after he had shown himself able to climb a particular fence with ease — in search of a taller, slightly more precarious fence on the other side of the corral. And when that climb was "nothing" and the position of balance a giant bore, he predicted quite casually that he would never see a fence that he couldn't rather quickly master. His father did not want the boy to be completely unrealistic, however. To whistle in the dark, to assume that one can always triumph, is to be vulnerable — the weakness of the overconfident. One ought to have a great deal of drive and ambition, a conviction that the world will eventually be made to oblige — but only after a substantial effort.

It is absurd to say that all children whose parents make a certain amount of money or work at certain occupations, or live in a certain neighborhood, possess an attitude of mind (and an attitude toward the world) that might be sensibly tucked into the generalization referred to here as "entitlement." More than once I have insisted that each individual has his or her unique way of pulling together the various elements of mental life. I have wanted, however, to suggest a common manner of response toward life among children of a certain class and background. I realize that the particular word "entitlement" has complicated psychoanalytic implications or, for some, pejorative social or political implications, or indeed, for others, quite defensible and justifiable implications. For the children I have worked with, however, the word is simply a description of a certain actuality. There are both social and psychological dimensions to that actuality, and deep down these children know them rather well.

I have in mind especially the son of a powerful Florida grower. When the child was five he kept using the words "I'm entitled to." His parents were much annoyed. The father did not want his son using such a peremptory, self-important, demanding expression. He began interrupting the boy, telling him that he was not "entitled" to *anything*, that he must ask for what he wanted, and be grateful when he got it. The boy kept asking why, why. The father kept explaining — a litany of oughts and musts. The boy in turn fell back upon his considerable intelligence and powers of observation. He reminded his father of his own words: "If you earn something, you are entitled to keep it." Had not the boy "earned" the right to make his various requests — by trying to be "good" or "quiet"? Had not the father told him on a number of occasions that he was "coming along nicely," that he was "making his parents proud"?

The boy spoke up for himself in fits and starts, but he got his message across, because his father eventually settled for an

ironic statement: "A boy who stands up for himself like that
boy has — well, he's entitled to say every once in a while, that
he's *entitled* to something!" It must be rather obvious —
it was to the grower, for all his lack of interest in the plight of
the hundreds of improverished migrants who worked his land
so long and hard — that not every father can be grateful for
his son's outspokenness, his young son's assumption that he
was entitled to political freedom, social equality, economic
privilege.

PART SEVEN

THE SCHOOLS

MORE than any other American children, the boys and girls of this book grow up with school on their minds. Almost every American child goes to school and has to begin to come to terms with it, if only negatively or indifferently, just when the child, at five or six, has started gaining some consistent control over his or her body, both at day and night, and a stable awareness of himself or herself as a person who exists quite apart from, if also dependent upon, certain significant individuals. Usually the school years don't end until after childhood itself and a good hunk of adolescence as well. "It goes on and on," one child told me when I asked him how school was coming along. He was then ten, in the first months of the fifth grade of a private school located not far from his parents' home in New Orleans' Garden District. He had no "school phobia," no "learning disability," no "problem with authority." He was in fact a rather capable and eager student, who would do well over the years. He simply had moments, then, of boredom or mild dissatisfaction at school. His father would hold forth occasionally about the virtues of education or, at the very least, a series of degrees. The father would list them: elementary school, higher school, and then, as a matter of course, not only college but some graduate school, preferably law or business. The boy listened attentively; he dared not do otherwise. Anyway, he admired and loved his lawyer father. They had good times together. But the boy did, upon occasion, manage a slightly suppressed groan — and those words: "It goes on and on."

The child who makes such an observation has at least shown evidence of a proper "reality orientation" and has also indicated an "appropriate" sense of time — a capacity to live for more than the moment, despite the pain incurred in so doing. A year or so after the boy remarked upon the seemingly endless expanse of time involved in school attendance he was prepared to qualify his reflection briefly but pointedly: "It seems like it goes on and on, but you have to do good."

What did he mean by "do good"? What did his teachers mean? They were the ones who sent home notes to his parents, remarking upon how "good" the boy was, and how "good" his "attitude" always was. He wasn't the "best" student, but he was "cooperative," and again, a "good influence" in the classroom. He was not, however, a "goody-goody" child. The parent were sure of that. The teachers took pains to make that quite clear. The boy himself could be rather assertive, even pugnacious, especially after being publicly complimented by a teacher for setting a "good example" — as if he, too, wanted to indicate that he was still capable of causing a raised eyebrow. But his moments of playfulness or provocative behavior were just that — passing expressions of annoyance, quickly forgotten by a child. It is not a mere matter of "obedience." The deciding matter is the child's long-range philosophical state of mind — perhaps not a pretentious or overblown description, in view of what the boy himself said once, a week after entering the fifth grade: "School isn't like home. School is where you go to start being serious, and where you begin your grown-up life. You can't have a good time all the time. It's too bad. You've got to mean business. That's what they say, anyway."

A rather meditative if not resigned boy, who had already gained a certain long-range perspective on things. That psychological or philosophical distance is characteristic of many children like him — brought up in homes where they have heard, again and again, how important it is for them not only to do well at school, to behave there and earn, if possible, high grades, but, just as important, comprehend what the stakes are. It is a mixture of personal involvement and unyielding hauteur that teachers notice in some elementary school children from exceedingly well-to-do families. The teachers often come to realize that they themselves are a new kind of person for such children — not a servant, but not really an equal either.

Teachers may be on a relatively lean salary and have no claim to social distinction, but they do have a temporary hold on their pupils, and it is precisely that kind of authority or, more crudely, power that is held in high esteem by many of the parents of privileged children. The boy or girl must learn respect at all costs — even if he or she also learns a secret sense of superiority vis-à-vis the teacher.

The same boy at eleven spoke openly and unselfconsciously about the teachers he had come to know in his short, rather eventful and cosmopolitan life: "My father and mother have told me that I go to this school because there aren't too many kids in each class, and we learn French as well as English, even in the first grade, and we're getting the best teaching there is. I've tried to keep on the good side of every teacher I've had. Some are very nice, besides being good teachers; some aren't so nice. My mother keeps reminding me that you don't have to *like* a teacher; you just *learn* from her! I remember when I was a little boy I asked why we couldn't have my second-grade teacher over to the house for dinner. We have a lot of people for dinner. My mother said a teacher is not someone you have over to dinner; she is someone you see in school, and when you get home, then that's a different life you have. Finally my father stepped in; I remember when he told me he had to explain to me that I wasn't getting it straight about the teacher. He didn't want to say a word against her. He just wanted me to know that if we *did* invite the teacher over to our house, she would be real upset, and she probably would find an excuse not to come. I didn't understand, so he had to explain everything to me, and then I did."

A noticeable and important break in the conversation; the boy genuinely does not seem inclined to put what he wants to say into words. Perhaps he learned from his father the risks of speaking out loud about matters best understood and lived with rather than talked about. He will instead move toward more general issues — the comfortable sanctuary of the abstract: "You can't ask everyone you know to come home. The teachers must be glad to leave school in the afternoon; I'll bet the last thing in the world they would want is someone like me asking them to come on over to his house and have something to eat with his friends who go to the same school. There'd be no rest for the poor teacher — just us kids all day and all night! And the same goes for us: you want to go home and forget all the rules and all the lessons you've had to learn, and just go and play. My mother used to have to force me to change my clothes when I came home. She was right when she said I should picture myself peeling off school when I switch clothes in the afternoon, and I did, and it felt good! The teachers tell us the same thing: go home and forget what you've been doing here, and just have a good time. They do give us a little homework, and there will be more and more as I get older; but at least you can work in your room, and you can take a snack with you, and take a break and watch TV, and you're not afraid the teacher will say that you're not paying attention or not following her instructions. It's best to keep home and school separate. If a teacher invited my parents and me home, we'd say we couldn't come, even if we liked the teacher and thought we'd have a good time over at her house. And besides, the teachers don't live near here, and they would be nervous if we came to see them. They'd worry what we thought of them. Even if we liked them, they'd worry."

Children like him are constantly taking the measure of those different from themselves socially — a town policeman, a grocer, a delivery man, not to mention "the help." But especially teachers; they are in a position of authority and yet are often "from a different background," to quote the New Orleans boy when he was ten. For children of families like his, teachers both provoke and elude class-consciousness. Often they become, unwittingly, object lessons for the boys and girls they teach — a means by which those children obtain further confirmation, at home, of their social class and economic condition.

For millions of children whose parents are poor or are of the so-called working class, a schoolteacher is himself or herself a rather privileged and educated person. For moderately well-off children the teacher is an equal of their parents; maybe not a model one holds up, but certainly an acceptably proper and respectable person, in most cases. Among young children from quite well-off or rich families, however, the teacher can be a source of confusion and embarrassment. How does one view him or her socially? How does one react to his or her commands? In some of the rich families I have visited, even lawyers or doctors have been regarded with a certain tolerant good humor as aides of sorts — not servants, but not by any means one's *equals.*

But the lawyer and doctor come and go, and they have little

sustained contact with the children of the family — certainly not the daily acquaintance, hour after hour, that a child has with an elementary school teacher. It is true, especially in the private schools of the Northeast, that some teachers may come from wealthy families. Yet the child usually knows, because he or she has been told, that the teachers, while very much worth listening to and heeding, are (again) of another "background." Though such awareness does not usually get in the way of the acquisition of knowledge, and indeed is rarely given explicit voice in the classroom, there is indeed an element of class-consciousness at work in the private or public elementary school classrooms attended by the children of quite well-to-do parents — an element of considerable psychological significance.

I had best go back to the beginning. The year was 1960, and mobs roamed the streets of New Orleans. I'd been sent over to the Garden District and to Metairie. The teachers there were especially bitter and more forcefully articulate than anyone else. One of them, no doubt sick and tired of my ignorant, crude, morally smug, and patronizing questions about her "attitudes" and about the "problems" in Louisiana or elsewhere in the South, told me rather bluntly: "You might leave us alone, and go talk with the teachers who have rich kids in their classrooms. Ask those teachers a few questions! Ask those children a few questions! Everyone thinks we're the ones who are responsible for what's happening in New Orleans. That's a joke! We haven't a word of say in what happens to this city. The black children think I'm important; their parents are poor, and so because I'm a *teacher,* and went to *college,* they think I can pick up the phone and get everything wrong made right. One of the little colored girls even said that to me; she said that she was sure the principal and the teachers of this school could end all the trouble, if we went outside and told the people in the mobs to go home — because they'd listen to us. And she was sure everyone else would listen to us, too — the mayor, the police people, the men with the television cameras.

"I told her she was very flattering, but she was wrong. That child has a lot to learn! We're not supposed to teach children the real facts of life — only their 'numbers and letters.' That's too bad. But I guess they find out, one way or the other."

Off I went rather quickly, that particular day, to see an important lawyer in the city, who was doing his best to help settle a serious racial struggle. He was the father of the boy whose words I have quoted. The lawyer was interested enough in the work I was doing to express agreement with the schoolteacher just quoted; he offered to put me in touch with the schoolteachers who had taught or were teaching his children. There were few outbursts of frustration or annoyance from those teachers. They were calm, forthcoming. What did I want to know? I wanted to know what they were telling their privileged pupils about the reasons others more or less of their age were going through daily pain and even terror.

They weren't, by and large, telling those pupils much of anything. They tried to forget the trouble, even though it lasted for months and was reported daily on television and in the newspapers. But as I began to talk with the children who went to those schools, I realized that the children knew perfectly well what was happening and were quite able to talk about what they believed to be the rights and wrongs of the matter. They also had not failed, a number of them, to notice the reluctance of their teachers even to edge near a discussion of the school desegregation crisis — or any other social or political issue. The seven- or eight-year-old boys and girls would ask, quite innocently, whether "any colored" would ever be coming to their school. The older children, of nine, ten, eleven, knew that the answer was no, "the colored" certainly would not be sent to their private school or to their rather elegant public school, located in an all-white suburb. All through the city's crisis, several years in duration, virtually nothing was said by teachers about events the children knew very well were shaping their future lives.

So it has been elsewhere, too: among Appalachian children from wealthy families, interested in the reasons for a mine explosion, a strike; among the children of growers, curious about migrants, hopeful that a teacher will shed light upon their way of life; among the children of well-to-do suburban-ites or urban residents, anxious to know "how the other half lives," what it means to be black, live in a ghetto. When Boston in the 1970s began to experience racial turmoil very much like the kind New Orleans had experienced fifteen years earlier, boys and girls in towns to the west and north of the city had good reason to ask all sorts of questions. But often the teachers felt awkward or embarrassed about dwelling on a subject they knew would only prompt extremely difficult discussions, and maybe emotional responses. Sometimes a teacher's wariness or cautiousness can be an eye-opening occasion for a particular child. It is not a matter of a given political "attitude" on the part of a teacher being "discovered" by a pupil whose parents have quite other, and conflicting, "attitudes." It is rather the moment of fear, hesitation, indifference, or hypocritical in-gratiation that the child notices and finds instructive or dis-maying. Children of eight or ten are trying to find safe avenues of personal expression; they are saddened and frustrated when they see grown-up men and women — members of a chosen profession — acting as if they were themselves uncertain chil-dren. At the same time, the child begins to learn his or her lesson — that the schools have made a judgment about getting involved in controversial issues.

As a consequence of such a chain of events the school has forfeited something important in the eyes of the child — especially a child of wealthy parents — and the child has become, sometimes for the first and last time, a serious social and political critic. An important institution has been found compromised, timid, untrue to its own declared principles. The moral result for most privileged children is not usually that of outrage, but a moment of disappointment followed by a quick willingness to fall in line — and to stop asking embarrassing questions. One can regard what follows, psychologically, either as the beginning of cynicism, of disenchantment, or as a start in the child's developing sense of reality.

Sometimes a dramatic incident tells a particular child (and a doctor talking with the child) volumes' worth of theoretical speculation about the relationship between teachers and the institutions they serve or about the relationship between schools and the society of which they are a part. When the Boston schools were ordered desegregated, through a substantial busing program, a teacher in an urban private secondary school that caters to well-to-do Bostonian children briefly suggested in a social studies class for fifth-grade children that they consider their own views of busing. The children went home, did their thinking, came back, offered their thoughts. They also came back with their parents' thoughts. One ten-year-old girl was bold and sassy enough to offer a doctor her sense of what had taken place at school: "In this school what your mother and father say counts. They pay big tuition bills. If the school didn't have parents who can afford to pay the tuition, the school would have to close. Then the teachers would be out of work; so would the principal, and the nurse, and the gym instructor. When my father is really angry, and he wants someone to change his mind right away, he doesn't *tell* him to change his mind and he doesn't argue with him; he just asks him to *think about it* — whatever they've been discussing. Then my father will wait for a few days, and he'll bring the subject up again. My mother says he's never wrong; he knows people will realize, once they think things over, that he was right. That's what happened here at school. He didn't like the way the schoolteachers were getting us to ask all these questions about school busing. He said they had to stop wasting our time with a lot of news stories."

She had decided to write up his viewpoint for a class composition. But she had second thoughts. In order to be tactful, she would have had to write a composition worthy of a Central Intelligence Agency operative — full of suggestion, innuendo, hints, ailusions, but no straightforward narrative explication. Best to avoid trouble. "If you ask me, teachers are always scared. They worry about getting into trouble with the parents. The teachers are always telling us how lucky we are. One teacher said there wasn't a single scholarship student in our school. When we asked her why, she said she didn't know. No one believed her! She had plenty of ideas on the subject! I don't believe a lot I hear in school. I think parents are more honest with you than teachers are. I don't want to be a schoolteacher, because every time I speak, I'll have to hold my breath and think to myself: Will I get into trouble with someone?

"We wanted to know why there aren't any black kids being bused here. They're bused all over Boston. Why not here? That's all we wanted to know. The teacher told the answer right away — that we're a private school. Someone said, *'So what!'* The teacher didn't say anything for a while. Then she told us that we needed to learn our grammar and our manners. She said that you don't say *'So what!'* It's a bad expression. She said that it shows insolence. I wanted to say it again — *so what!* But I didn't.

"In school you learn when to keep your mouth shut! The teachers know a lot about you. When you get promoted, they must send reports about your family to the next year's teacher. They always know that your father has a big job, and so does everyone else's father, mostly. I guess that's why they don't give scholarships. The people who got them would be poor. It would be no fun being poor in a school like this! If the teacher had just said that! We all know it! You don't learn everything in school! You can figure out some things all by yourself. One teacher told us last year when we asked something about black people that there would be time to learn the answers when we got to college. We wanted to tell her that we already knew the answers; we just wanted to see if *she* knew them — or would tell us what she knew. But she wouldn't be honest with us.

"They don't want any black kids here, because they think there would be trouble. I have a friend whose father is a lawyer, and he's always on the side of the poor; and she says that's the trouble with this school — there's *no* trouble! She even told a teacher that once. The teacher said you're not supposed to go looking for trouble. She said we're lucky we don't have to ride a bus, and go to places where you can get hurt. That's what our teachers always do; they never come out and say something, they just give you big hints. If they stood up and tried to argue with my father and the other fathers, they'd get respect from the parents, and it would be a different school. My father says he doesn't expect any teacher to try to argue him down, but he wishes that one day he would be surprised. He'd shake her hand and tell her she's the best teacher he ever met! When they started the busing in the city, my father said it would be nice if the school started demanding that black kids come to our classes, on scholarships. But the school never brought the subject up. I asked my father why *he* didn't bring the subject up. He said, why should he! He said, why shouldn't the principal and the teachers! He said he'd just wait and see, and that's how he'd find out about the school. I guess he found out! He says it wouldn't be any good at all, bringing in black kids for free, if the teachers didn't really want it to happen, and weren't willing to stand and fight for what they wanted."

It can be very hard for teachers to win the admiration of children like her. She is not one to make heroes out of people she sees and hears. She had a picture of Chris Evert, the tennis player, on the wall for a while, until she met her at a tournament — introduced by a cousin who is a tennis enthusiast. The girl decided she ought not admire "too much" someone she has actually met. Then there was Faye Dunaway, whose performance in *Bonnie and Clyde* enthralled the girl — after her parents had finally allowed her to see the film on television. But an actress was also not to be held up too high in esteem. The people to admire are an aunt, who became a distinguished physician — an anesthesiologist — and another aunt, who went to law school at the age of thirty-five, became an adviser to a number of corporations and, later, a college professor.

As for the suburban public schools in rather wealthy suburbs, the parents of the school children in attendance know how to be forthright, vigorously outspoken, and again, if need be, thoroughly demanding — "in the best interest" of their children, of course. All of which — an accumulation of parental words and deeds — a child absorbs and makes his or her own, and all of which becomes very much part of the educational life of a given school.

In the case of some very rich families, or insistently idiosyncratic upper-middle-class ones, children are tutored at home, or a small group of children are tutored at several homes, or a "school" turns out to be as many teachers as students, working in a building set aside on an estate by parents who want their children, and a few of their children's friends, to have the ultimate in "private" education. But even in the less secluded and unusual private elementary "schools" there is to be found, commonly, a special intimacy between parents and school officials or teachers; an intimacy that works well, in the sense that the individual child is thoroughly known at school, his or her every difficulty or achievement discussed; such an intimacy, however, can produce considerable tension if teachers have one notion of what a certain child requires and parents another.

There are confrontations between teachers and children in all schools. But in schools attended by children of rich and powerful parents, those confrontations can have a quite distinct character. Among the children of the working class the teacher is often a hero or, indeed, a devil. Among the poor, the teacher may be feared and resented — her condescension, her barely concealed scorn, noticed and keenly resented by the child. With children from upper-income families the teacher may be liked or disliked, but not so intensely. Often it is a matter of wry observation and shrewd calculation. The girl quoted above is as willing to analyze the attitudes of her teachers toward her parents as toward black people. She can convey her sense that even as the teachers take cues from the parents, those same parents deliberately provoke fear and bitterness in grown-up men and women teachers. The result is a mixture of agitation, awe, and ingratiation on the part of men and women who have a "profession" but who sometimes strike watchful children as being, in the girl's memorable phrase, "not grown-up like some other grown-ups are."

She was not calling her teachers bad names. She was taking stock of the way social position and brute economic power are perceived and used: "I wish there was a teacher who would be like my father. When he gets an idea in his head, he can't be stopped. In our school, the teachers don't have much to say. They have to talk with each other. They have to talk with the parents, and with the principal, and they even have to talk with us! At home, my parents make up their minds, and then we have to do what they want. In school the teachers are more scared than the kids. If the principal comes into the room, the teacher will get nervous. We don't get nervous! I wouldn't want to be a teacher in a school like this one. Even if the school is good, the teachers play favorites. They are very nice to me, but I think it's because they know my father has a temper. He's on the board of trustees. I wish he wasn't. When my mother and he go to a meeting with our teacher, she's nervous. I can tell. She tries to be nice to me and she tells me I'm doing very good work. Even if it's true, she shouldn't be giving me compliments just because she's scared. My friend heard the teachers talking, and they were saying the same thing as we do — that we're spoiled rich kids! But if you asked them if they said so, they'd deny everything. I wouldn't blame them. If they get the parents angry at them, they'll lose their jobs.

"The principal has to be more careful than anyone else. I hear my father say: 'I'll go talk with the principal.' When Daddy sends checks, he gets nice letters back. He's shown them to me — because in the letters the principal always says nice things about me. I only half believe him! He has to say nice things, when he's getting hundreds of dollars — thousands, I think. I asked Daddy how much he gave, and he said it's none of my business. Then I heard him tell my mother that he might have given too much, because it's only a school and not a big hospital. But she said they have high expenses at our school, because there are only a few of us and a lot of teachers, and there's our gym and our language lab. We're learning how to speak French, and some are learning Spanish; they go to South America a lot with their parents."

The narrator is not unaware of the arrogance and condescension she sees about her, and, alas, permits herself to indulge from time to time. She apologizes for the family wealth.
She does so not because she is talking with someone else (besides her teachers) who isn't part of that wealthy world. She
even once wrote a composition meant for her teacher's heart,
perhaps, as well as her head: "I think that if you are born with
a lot of money, you have a burden. You have to be careful that
you don't make other people afraid. The reason they get afraid
is that you can send checks or you can say you won't; and then
the people who need the money will be glad, or they will be
sad. My mother said that the best school would be the school
where you went there, and no one knew your name, and who
your parents are. But my father said you can't have a school
like that. I wouldn't want to disguise myself. I'd be like a spy.
I just wish the teachers could forget about all of our parents.
Then we'd have a better school."

The teacher had asked for it; she had requested criticism
from her pupils, and they had obliged. But her candid remarks
had upset her teacher. She had asked the child if there was
anything "wrong." The child said no, no. Then the principal
called the child in: what had been happening to prompt in the
girl a desire for such extraordinary self-effacement? Nothing.
The girl did become agitated after her disclaimers seemed
unconvincing. Needless to say, the reaction (or overreaction)
of the teacher and the principal only served to confirm the
child's appraisal of her situation, of the school's predicament.
It wasn't easy for her to believe that she was merely one of a
hundred or so, there "to learn," as the teachers kept insisting;
there to achieve the school's standards of "excellence," a word
constantly mentioned by teachers, who repeatedly described
her as "quite capable," on report cards.

The problem for the girl was that she didn't always feel so

"capable." She wondered whether the descriptions on her report cards were meant to be enlightening for her or meant to satisfy and flatter her parents. She wished more than once that the teacher would show some displeasure or, at the very least, some concern. When she makes mistakes she finds too much consideration and support, not enough tough disapproval. But she is a good student, and her desire for a reprimand or two is not "realistic." Her mother has told her that. The mother believes that the girl has been unfair to the teachers; the mother also has insisted that they have been fair at all times. Why, anyway, should a "capable" student from a "good" family complain because she believes the teachers are "too nice," are "prejudiced" in her favor, and are not to be trusted in their appraisals? Why turn school into such a big deal?

Many of the children mentioned in this book, and their classmates or friends, have gone through similar struggles with themselves, their teachers, their parents. It is as if they never quite believe in *themselves;* they are always contending with their families' wealth, status, connections, always wondering whether they can really trust any compliment or take seriously any criticism at school. A child who worries about lavish, ingratiating praise is not likely to overlook the possibility that an all too respectful teacher is also a potentially angry one. It is ironic that children have become suspicious and frightened in schools dedicated to excellence and in classrooms deliberately kept small and intimate. Those same children wonder what it is like to go to a public school or, if they already go to one, they wonder what it is like going to a different kind of public school — a bigger one, usually, located in a large city, where one is not so much on display. At times they allow their speculations, maybe their desires, to become explicit; they speak to their friends or to their teachers. With their friends it is often a matter of fellow sufferers sharing a common out-look. It is astonishing how self-conscious and class-conscious a small group of elementary school children of well-to-do fami-lies can be when talking about their teachers, when sharing suspicions, when expressing plaintive self-pity or honest ap-prehensions, however irrational the basis for those percep-tions or emotions.

Nor are those children willing, always, to be reassured by their own parents. They suspect that their parents are anxious to deceive themselves. They suspect upon occasion that their parents are, quite simply, not telling the truth — denying the existence of a difficulty they know full well to exist. The same holds with the teachers. Although these elements of confusion and doubt ought not to be overestimated, they are at work in the lives of many children of privilege and in many of their teachers. The outside observer, aware of the overcrowded, understaffed, broken-down, badly equipped schools that ghetto or working-class children have to attend, may be tempted to brush aside such tensions. But for certain boys and girls, and for those who teach them, the "moments" are pain-ful and in fact mount up into long days which cause a child to feel a loss of nerve, or cause a teacher to wonder why he or she is teaching in such a place.

Among children of a rather charming and elegant "country day school" to the west of Boston I heard two boys and three girls, all aged twelve, recall in retrospect how their family background had affected their education. They were prepar-ing to graduate, go on to yet other exclusive and expensive private schools. They were not especially angry or discon-tented, but they had gone through some unpleasant times as well as rather enjoyable and constructive ones, and they were not loath to speak up — especially because one of their num-ber, a girl, was rather articulate, and maybe a touch melodramatic. She had fought with several teachers in the course of her academic career, had been sent to a child psychiatrist, first for "evaluation," later for "treatment." At her age she knew to say that she had *not* been "psychoanalyzed" but had received "psychotherapy." She knew to say also and to predict that she might need "an analysis" later on. The reason: she had "trouble with the teachers."

What kind of trouble? She tended to doubt their word, their declarations of approval and sanction — even though she reacted violently (a temper tantrum, a fast departure from school) when criticized even mildly. But she was not as peculiar as she sometimes thought. She had a knack of saying what others felt, teachers as well as classmates. She exaggerated. She even distorted. She gave expression to emotions kept under wraps by others. She was attractive, energetic, intelligent, as well as outspoken, even slightly notorious. Her father was one of the school's largest benefactors; her paternal grandfather was, too — and a "founding member" of the school's corporation. On her mother's side there was another generous grandfather who was constantly giving money to various educational institutions, including her school. His charitable behavior, she was convinced, affected her career.

"They can't just let you know what they think of you, the teachers and the headmaster, when your father and both your grandfathers are sending those big checks to the office. I started crying once; my father was telling my mother that he was going to double his contribution to the school fund, and I suddenly felt real sorry for myself, and the next thing I knew I was crying, and I didn't know why. I had one teacher, last year, for math who kept telling me I was 'catching on,' I was 'catching on,' but I wasn't, and I knew I wasn't. For a while I was happy when she said that, because it meant I didn't have to sit down with my mother and father and offer them explanations and excuses. But after a while I was falling further and further behind. I didn't want to ask for help; I *hate* math. I guess I just figured that if I could get away with it, I would. But I'll bet there were some others who weren't doing much better than I was, and we were all being told that we were doing 'all right.' After a while you get fed up with the teachers and fed up with yourself. You feel like you're a criminal or something."

She has no wish, suddenly, to go on. She sits back in determined, morose silence. Another student speaks up: yes, that is true, that is what happens. And another — in less enthusiastic agreement, willing to acknowledge "a problem": "You shouldn't go too far; the teachers are good here. They really try to get you prepared for prep school. They are the best in their profession. The trouble is you get to know them too well! If one of us misbehaves, the teacher tries to be understanding. There are some teachers who don't know how to say *no*. Maybe they figure that they'll get into trouble if they get our parents upset. I had trouble with spelling, and I had to be tutored. Even so, my father sent in a lot of money, I know. But Daddy thinks the teachers may be a little mixed up. He says he'll go for a conference, and the teacher is too nervous with him, and tries to be too nice. Not all the teachers are like that, but some of them are.

"One teacher left; she resigned. She said that she wanted to go teach in a ghetto. We thought it was too bad she wouldn't stay, because she was one of the best teachers. The teacher told us she was tired of worrying all the time about hurting someone's feelings. I don't know who she was talking about. She never hurt our feelings — except when she left here."

Not an inaccurate analysis of what happens in a number of schools like his. Some teachers in those schools couldn't care less who any child's parents are; and some parents, whatever their means or "position," put on no airs at all, exert no pressure of any kind, try hard to be as considerate, self-effacing, and humble as possible. Nevertheless, there are other teachers and other parents who do, for one reason or another, get caught in a web of guarded statements, concealed dislike, constant edginess.

In some schools the teachers are sophisticated enough, wary enough, alert enough, to make conscious efforts to talk together about "*the* problem": how proud, well-trained, earnest teachers at times find themselves, trying hard to be "natural" and "open" and "honest" while educating a small but rather "important" group of boys and girls.

That descriptive word "important" was used one afternoon by a ten-year-old boy who was anything but smug or self-important. He was the son of a distinguished biochemist attached to an equally distinguished Ivy League university. His parents had money enough. His schoolmates' fathers were considerably richer than his, but he had not become an envious and scornful outsider. He was both popular and bright, qualities that don't always go together. He had a sense of the school — who went there and why, who taught there and why.

He kept coming back to the word "important." He did not want to boast about his classmates, just describe a situation he understood rather well: "I've heard the teachers talk. They didn't think I was paying attention. There's one who has no money except for her salary, and she's in debt because of an operation she had. She says she could make more in a public school in the city. She says she could teach in a junior college — history or English. She says she's tempted. But she stays here because she likes us. She does! She's a very good teacher. When you're through with a year of her class, you know how to write compositions and reports, and you know how to read a book thoroughly. She told us: she was born poor; her father was a farmer in northern New Hampshire and he didn't have much land, and then he died when she was only ten years old. Her mother became a maid. She helped her mother; they lived in someone's house, and got their food free in exchange for work. I guess the people had some money, because they sent her to college and paid all the bills. She got a job here through them; they know the headmaster. She's been here a long time, and she loves each class she has, and she gets upset when they graduate. My friend saw her crying on the last day of school. In the summer she takes courses at college, and gets ready for her work here in September. My father says she gives her whole life to us kids, and he's right. That's what good teachers are like; they don't teach for the money, but because they love to see kids learn and get better and better at what they're doing.

"I have seen her leaving school, and she looks real tired. She told us she goes home and has three cups of tea, and plays her classical music. She says she'll never be able to like Bruce Springsteen! She says she doesn't like any rock music. She goes to the Boston Symphony on Saturday nights. My parents go on Friday afternoon. My father says there is a difference in the audience; a lot of important people go on Fridays. I guess they don't have bosses telling them what to do! She brings in her favorite records and plays them for us sometimes; it has nothing to do with school, but she wants us to get used to good music. She has her 'teacher's pets,' but she tries to be fair. She'll go to dinner at some kids' houses. I think she likes the people and likes the kids, but she must be nervous when she goes to supper. I've been there — to a few of those big houses — and I get nervous. It's different, sitting in those big dining halls and being served. There's a cook, and the mother rings a bell or she pushes a button under the rug with her foot.

"If you're teaching kids from homes like that, you're teaching the really important people. You may be afraid of how important they are, but if you're a teacher, you're pretty important yourself! You give grades to their kids, and they look up to you. There aren't too many people some of my friends' parents look up to! I guess they look up to my father. But he's a college professor. Some of our teachers become our friends, and they become friends of our parents. My mother said that a teacher who works in our school has the satisfaction of knowing that she's going to influence the whole country. A lot of the graduates of this school have gone to the best prep schools and colleges, and later they've become important people, just like their fathers and grandfathers. If you teach them, you get them to think the way you'd like them to think, and then you can sit back, when you're old, and pick up the paper, and see someone's name, and say to yourself: I taught him!"

Though he had received some help, no doubt, in making those observations, his portrait of a teacher was one prompted, really, by affection, and maybe a touch of envy. She gave him good grades, because he was a bright student; but she did not take to him the way she did to certain others. He was not sure that he would have been able to respond, had she in fact singled him out. It takes two perhaps for a "teacher's pet" to emerge — the teacher's gestures and the student's response. Still, he liked the teacher very much, and actually, was glad that she respected him for the kind of boy he was — more his own person than many others.

His mother, herself a teacher in a ghetto school, helped him to think about such matters. The mother had with a certain wry humor pointed out to the boy once that there were two directions a solidly middle-class teacher could pursue: "up or down," meaning a school like the one the boy attended or a so-called inner city school. The boy had quickly insisted that there was a third possibility — to move in neither direction but, rather, teach one's own kind, socially and economically speaking. The mother had forgotten that possibility, and had not made the connection her son was able to offer: that he had been put in an "up" situation, even as his teacher had put herself in that same situation; that they were both thereby leaving their own "people," it could be said, in order to share for a number of hours each day a world that belonged to other people. His mother had accepted the interpretation but, by the boy's estimate, did not like very much the implications. She kept reminding her son thereafter that "the real reason" he went to the school was the teaching — "the excellent teaching." But why wasn't that teaching available to everyone? the boy wondered. This particular school just happened to be "especially good," and so worth the travel, the high tuition fees, the occasional feeling of being in a foreign land. Yet, he still wondered, however shrewd and knowing his analysis of his teacher, why she didn't finally get tired of making *her* extra effort, if not sacrifices.

Such matters of interest or speculation are not confined to alert, introspective children. The teacher he has watched intently goes through her own moments of reflection. She does indeed wonder why she stays, why she doesn't go work with those who perhaps need her most. At times she is all set to go; she will give notice in the spring, finish up the year, leave for good in June. She has gone so far as to visit other schools, inquire after various positions. A well-educated and skilled teacher (with the additional advantage of various "credits" and certificates), she could get a job "anywhere," she knows. She *will* do so, "one day," she says, even when not especially in a mood to contemplate a departure. Her account of the children she works with, and struggles hard on behalf of, is as psychologically sensitive as that given of her by her student. She knows what he knows; but she chooses to put a different

emphasis on her behavior and motives than his. She has
worked for years with children more or less like him. She can
be as pointed as he can be, as aware of his mixed emotions as
he has come to be of hers. Why doesn't he go to any one of four
or five schools she can easily mention, where he would get a
quite satisfactory education? What *are* his reasons, those of his
parents, for sending him "here"? And what about the children
she teaches — how does one do justice to them as individual
human beings?

She especially asks that last question, in many forms. She is
afraid that others will fail to do so: "I've heard for years that
I teach *rich* kids, that I'm working in a *fancy* school, that this
is an *elitist* place, and on and on — until I could scream. These
children are entitled to be seen as something more than members of a *class*, or an *income bracket*. I'm not here to teach
wealthy kids; I'm here to teach kids I happen to like and enjoy
being with. Does that mean I'm a snob, or a social climber?
I've heard myself called both — in a friendly, joking way, of
course! We want each ghetto child to be *himself* — to be *herself*. But these children are not to be given that benefit!

"They are 'future corporation lawyers and bankers,' I hear.
Well, I've kept up with some of the children I've taught over
the years, and they're not going to be so easy to fit into someone's notion of what they should be, or 'have always been.'
That phrase! I'm sick and tired of it: these children 'have
always been' like this or like that. Everyone else is changing;
the whole country is changing — but not supposedly the people who send their children to this school or schools like this
one! I have to laugh when I think about the children I've
gotten closest to; they are as different as can be. They *won't*
all be corporation lawyers or bank presidents! They will have
money, I know; but children are more than future *heirs*. I
have all kinds of boys and girls here. I have spoiled brats and

wonderfully disciplined and imaginative youngsters. I have children who are wild, and others who would gladly sacrifice their own advantages in order to help others — and do, in class, all the time, by deferring to the needs of those less competent than themselves. I am tired of seeing these children regarded as 'poor little rich kids,' or as snotty, arrogant monsters, or as automatons, wound up by greedy, ambitious parents, determined that their offspring will stay perched on the top."

She pauses. She is tired of explaining herself to her friends — to herself. She has found herself apologizing for so much — for where she works, for her "involvement" in the lives of certain children, for her lack of interest in politics, in the sociological interpretation of literary works, in the psychological analysis of historical events. A friend of hers, in a moment of candor, facilitated by whiskey, called her "old-fashioned" and suggested that she would have really been happy in class-conscious nineteenth-century England. They argued. She was appalled at the naïveté of her friend, how ignorant she was of the school, the children — the people she kept hearing called "the rich": "I don't attack other people. I try to look at the individual, not groups of people. I haven't criticized a few of my students who have gone on to the best of colleges and graduate schools, and then all of a sudden turned on everything in their past, and found jobs in the ghettos as organizers or teachers, and came back here and told me that I'm a 'hypocrite' and a 'stooge of parasites.' Even now, with twelve- or thirteen-year-old children, I can spot a boy or a girl who will, later on, turn against everything. That's not my business. I encourage the children to be critical — maybe not to be politically critical, but to read a novel and a poem with open eyes and with *reservations*. I use that word a lot with the children. I tell them that we have to learn to like something with reservations, that we have to get distance on what we read or what we believe.

"Maybe I should go further; maybe I should start attacking 'the giant corporations.' I received a letter a month ago from one of my old students. He's like a few I have every year — from the academic rather than the financial and social aristocracy! He was always disapproving, deep down, I knew; not of me personally, or his classmates, but of the way things work in this country. His parents are quite liberal — yet they sent him here; I suppose because they wanted him to have 'the best education.' In his letter he accused me of just about everything — seven pages of sarcasm and moral outrage. I wondered why I deserved to be singled out! *He* knew why, of course; because he said I should know better, not being a member of 'the ruling class' myself!

"I don't deny the truth of some of his complaints. I was the one who would read to the class from Sinclair Lewis; he was a satirist of the middle class. Now I have a letter from a former student full of satire toward the upper class. He mentions horse riding and phony women wearing dungarees and being 'casual' and using the word 'natural' — everything should be 'natural' and everyone should act 'natural.' He describes the men as preoccupied with golf, tennis, sailing — 'empty heads,' who, like their wives, have their own ways of being cheap and vulgar, while they look down on others and call *them* cheap and vulgar. Well, he's right. There is plenty to make fun of, or be sickened by — plenty of pretense and self-deception and bombast and all the things he describes.

"He's in college now; I suppose he's read John O'Hara and Cheever and Updike and seen *The New Yorker* cartoons. But he isn't happy with gentle satire, or even angry satire. He wants to rage at the very people he came to know through his years here at school — as if those people who run the Soviet

Union or any other socialist country don't develop their own kind of vanities and conceits and illusions and dishonesties. He holds up Cuba and China to me; it's always easy to romanticize and idolize self-proclaimed ascetics who are far away — so that their excesses, their brutalities and prejudices, are safely out of sight. He says I never taught the class how to read the newspapers 'critically'; well, I read recently a book *favorable,* generally, to Castro, in which the author describes the terror visited on homosexuals and the meanness and arrogance of the bureaucrats in that little island of paradise. As for China, I have read that one clique turns on another, and that a man revered one day gets called awful names the next. How is all that different from some of the cheap and tawdry sides of our 'upper-income life,' as he calls it?

"I am not a political revolutionary. But I am not a brainwashed, frightened 'servant' (he calls me), who is always currying the favor of the wealthy parents of the children I teach. He says he doesn't care about me 'personally,' but that he does want to tear down the rich capitalists, and I am 'dangerous,' because I educate those children, and teach them their 'values,' and so I'm as much responsible for the perpetuation of greed and selfishness as any of the self-centered, insolent, and snotty parents around this town. I don't know what to say. Maybe he's right. I was so enraged by his letter that I began to believe he had a point! But that's no way to think. I'm not going to be intimidated by him — or by all that psychology they've been bringing into the schools. One of the things I like about this school is the skeptical tradition; maybe the school is 'aristocratic' because of that tradition, rather than because of the parents who send their children here! The parents may hold on to money and social position as 'values,' but they have given up almost everything else. They don't go to church the way they used to go — only on social occasions, or Christmas and Easter. They go to see psychiatrists, and they end up thinking like them — everything *interpreted*, everyone so *self-conscious*. They read all those books: how to bring up children, and what to say to them about — well, you name it! They talk about joining 'groups,' or 'liberating' themselves. They are no different from the people 'lower down' in the middle class — just a few more airs!

"I hate the way I'm talking! I hate all these *explanations*. I'm beginning to sound like my former student. I know all kinds of individuals in this town. Yes, I've been to their elegant homes and been impressed. Why should I deny that I love seeing a room with fresh flowers, a table with beautiful plates or silver, a house that has fine antiques all over the place! Why should I deny that the land here is beautiful; the meadows and the woods, the pond, the gardens near a lot of the houses! I'll even admit that I like being waited on! It's pleasant to be able to sit and have someone come over and bring you a drink or some food. It's pleasant to be offered your coat expertly, or have it taken from you with a nice, friendly gesture. I suppose that for liking those experiences I've become 'corrupt.' But when I'm at school teaching, I am thinking of the children before me, each of them different.

"In any teacher's classroom there are magic moments; if not she should stop teaching. During those moments it doesn't make any difference what a child's parent 'does,' or what the child's 'family name' is, or where they live or how they live. But when a child is reading about the Civil War, or reading Dickens or Sinclair Lewis, or reading part of a Shakespeare play with me, we end up leaving this school and going back in time and across oceans. We even discuss 'the class system.' We talk about those who are on top and those who suffer. How else would I read Dickens? I don't turn every class into a seminar on Marxist economics or socialist history — that's true. And I *like* these children, most of them — I have to admit that. I'm not prepared to see them as little monsters, or as brats, or as sad and forlorn and abandoned children, brought up by maids and governesses. That's what my former student says in his letter — that these boys and girls here are *victims;* they are destined to be bloated oppressors and meanwhile, as children, they are learning that 'role,' and from *me!* He says they are self-indulgent, and without purpose, and lonely and all the rest, and he reminds me of some of the broken homes he knew about when a student here, and still can't forget, I guess.

"There is no arguing with a lot of what he says — only with his 'perspective,' I guess I would have to call it, even if I do sound stuffy. In any neighborhood, no matter what the 'class' of people there or their race, you will find both attractive and unattractive people — you will find decent and kind and thoughtful parents and terribly self-centered or cocky or foolish people, who don't really give a damn for their children, except as possessions, or objects to be used or manipulated and put aside when boredom sets in or a new thrill or excitement comes along. Maybe there are a lot of people like that among the rich, or maybe we notice them when they are rich, because the rich are on display more, and we envy them or dislike them and notice their faults. I don't know; the whole subject is too much for me. I'd like to scream at that college student for getting me so upset. A few more letters from him and I'll be the useless, insensitive idiot and corrupt social climber he says I am. I've tried replying to him. I can't. All I can remember is that he was one of the brightest children I've ever taught. I really do think he learned a lot in my classroom."

Her remarks were even more extensive. The letter that prompted them was not, however, as specifically upsetting as one might think. Many of the strongly worded allegations made by the former student had in fact been made by her toward herself — and have been made by other teachers like her toward themselves. The former student actually changed his mind; after a five-year spell his political radicalism went away. The teacher eventually received another letter, this one of apology. But it is not fair to dismiss the contents of that first letter, just because its writer, holding politically radical views in the late 1960s and early 1970s, abandoned those views or modified them considerably. The teacher's logic, gained from everyday experience, told her that generalizations may come easily, sound attractive or convenient, lure spiritually or psychologically hungry readers or listeners, but fail wretchedly to do justice to the varieties of human experience, to the complexities of human life, to the ironies and ambiguities and paradoxes that constantly present themselves to anyone interested in how children grow up and become particular men and women. It was unfair, she believed, for the aroused radical to move from abstract historical or class analysis to a psychological and moral assault on one teacher and all of her students. (Karl Marx certainly knew better than to make that leap, to jump from philosophical and social and economic analysis to *ad hominem* psychological judgment or sociological condemnation.)

It would, however, be equally unfair to dismiss out of hand the serious criticisms of so-called elitist secondary school education made by a former student, because a substantial number of the critics have abandoned their previous political positions in favor of others, or even none at all. She was upset precisely because she herself for years had questioned herself: why teach here? She is more introspective, perhaps, and, despite her disavowals, more socially and politically conscious, than other teachers. She knows how difficult it can be for a professional teacher to resist certain blandishments or to respond to an astonishing variety of condescending gestures. Some of her colleagues, she knows, are themselves from quite well-to-do families; "They work for the fun of it, or because they've been taught that they ought to work; they don't work because they *have* to. My paycheck is cashed in an hour after I get it; some of them leave their paychecks around until they 'remember' to 'do something' with them!"

All of this seemed for a long while to me not so terribly important for someone trying to find out how privileged children manage to construct an early and influential notion of where they are going and why. If the nuances or even harsh lines of class are part of a school, they are, after all, part of American life in its many institutional shapes and forms. These are children quite accustomed to seeing their parents rule, command, even bully others. They know that when their fathers pick up the phone, or write a letter, something happens. They often have sensed too that there is another side to servile flattery or eager attentiveness — the resentment of the one who is exploited, treated casually, taken for granted, denied his or her dignity, and given in exchange some cash and a thin smile. What is the difference between a given child's experience at a store, on the street, in his or her father's place of business, or indeed in the home, and the events that take place in school?

The children know the answer to that question. They remember, many of them, how in elementary school — with teachers like the one just quoted — they first realized that others, important and admired grown-ups, live with different assumptions and expectations. What happens when children of one kind of background spend many hours each day with grown-ups of another kind of background? Affection prompts curiosity; and soon enough there are questions. And there are answers from the teachers, too: a brief observation, a suggestive comment, a lengthy explanation. The bolder and more ingenious teachers even have worked those questions into the "curriculum" — have tried to find not only personal answers but statements of writers, historians, philosophers that help explain the disparities privileged children are beginning to ask about and sometimes question.

A thirteen-year-old boy, ready to graduate from this same country day school, remembered vividly a morning's discussion: "It was the most interesting time I've spent in school. The teacher was explaining to us what the Founding Fathers meant when they wrote 'life, liberty and the pursuit of happiness.' One kid told us how much he liked those words, and how glad he was that he lived in this country, where everyone has those rights. I guess the teacher wasn't feeling too good that morning. She asked the boy where he got the idea that *everybody* has those rights. The boy said from reading the book. The teacher started telling us about her father and her grandfather. I guess her grandfather was very poor, and her father didn't make a lot of money either. After she told us about her family, she seemed sorry she'd done it. She changed from being nice to being strict. She told us she wanted us to write a composition, right away, on any subject we wanted. Then she left the room for a couple of minutes.

"When she came back she was herself again. She apologized to us. She said she had a cold. But a few of us could tell: she'd been upset. That was when I wrote my composition about my father being the head of everything, and how lucky I was. The teacher liked what I wrote. She gave me an A, and she said that I'd done a good job of thinking about my family and myself. My father said he was surprised I'd written like that. He said he didn't think of himself as the head of anything; he just tried to do a good job. But he was glad I got an A! He wants me to get good marks. If you don't, you might become lazy. I have a cousin, and they call him a 'playboy.' I don't think my old teacher would like my cousin. That day, when she told us about her family, she said that they worked very hard; everyone in her family, including the women, worked hard. *She* works very hard, I know. The other teachers say she's the hardest-working teacher in the school. If she met my cousin, I think she'd be polite to him, but she'd ask to be excused from the room."

Here is the composition, written when he was eleven years old: "We will be going to Aspen, Colorado. We all ski. It is better to ski out West. The snow is better. There is less ice. My Dad will come later. He's got a meeting. He's the head of a company. He's the head of a lot of boards, I think. I'm lucky. I used to think he was the head of everything. But he isn't. He's got a lot of people who look up to him. He makes the important decisions. I guess it's true, that most kids don't have fathers like mine. With my friends, it's true that their fathers are the heads of companies, or they're important. But they're not better people, just because their fathers are rich!

"It's like our teacher said, so long as you are honest and do your job and work hard at it, then you are a good person. We should think of other people as well as ourselves. Not everyone is as lucky as we are. But you forget. That's why you go to school. You learn about the world. We studied Venezuela last month. There are more poor there than in our country. We are lucky to be in America. Even if you're poor in America, you can work, and you can get a better job, and you can have hope. The teacher talked about hope, and it's important to be hopeful."

He had listened carefully, caught that teacher's message exactly; and she, overwhelmed a bit by her own "momentary slip" (she called it), could only be grateful and respectful. The boy was a bright and impressionable lad, a combination she had always liked. Not always do children make direct reference to what their teacher has just said, as the boy did. The teacher told him that "it might have been better" had he not quoted her, mentioned that "the teacher" said this, or talked about that. Nevertheless, she was not unmindful of the compliment he was thereby giving her. She was also aware that he had been touched by her statements and didn't quite know what to do about them or the feelings they had generated, except to examine his own life a little more scrupulously.

Though the boy has come in daily contact with maids and governesses, they haven't made such personal statements, haven't held his mind up to certain standards of intellectual perception and analysis as a matter of daily responsibility. And he, hearing her quite acutely, showed himself a little more open to the world's diversity, a little less self-centered and self-preoccupied. He acknowledged the element of fate, of chance, in this life. He did a pertinent, substantial amount of social and economic analysis. He placed his father in relationship to others the father worked with, and thereby himself in relationship to many other children. But he insisted upon going from the meditative and the self-descriptive to the admonitory, the prescriptive. The Puritan self emerges yet again in this last third of the twentieth century. That "self" enabled him to become spiritual kin with his teacher; they can at least think alike, hold common aspirations, and yes, prejudices. They could both be "hopeful," though there is a price: the commitment to work. She was not at school to encourage "playboys." He was not at school to prepare himself for a roustabout's life.

The two of them, in their time together, learned from each other. Each taught the other that money both did and did not make a difference. The teacher delivered her speech, insinuated a certain tough, working-class ideology of make-do into her lessons, signaled her willingness to accommodate her life to the needs of particular children. The boy liked his teacher a lot, found her ideas quite stimulating, and yet knew that his life was always going to have its privileged, extraordinary quality. Maybe he could only learn that from someone like her — an outsider.

The boy reminisced upon his graduation from elementary school (grade seven): "Our maid has a son, and he's a good baseball player. He's at a bad school. They don't learn much. He wants to be on the Red Sox team when he grows up. I hope he succeeds. I don't think he'll make the Red Sox. He probably will stop playing baseball when he gets a little older; that's what his mother says. The teacher asked us last week to write about somebody we liked, but didn't know. I wrote about the maid's son. I've never met him. She's shown him pictures of me. I said he might be a good baseball player one day, and that he hoped to be on the Red Sox team, and I hoped he succeeded, but the odds weren't too high that he would. My father has always said that the maid and her son are living in a dream world when they talk about the Red Sox! The teacher liked the composition, and she called me up and spoke to me. She said that if you look at a lot of successful people in history, you'll find out that when they were kids, they had big dreams, and there were people who thought the dreams would never come true, but every once in a while they do come true. So you can't tell. I hope for the sake of the maid that her son does become a big baseball player. Then he'd make a lot of money, and she could live real well. He'd buy her a lot of clothes, and she could learn how to drive and get a car, and he'd buy a house for her — and then *she* would have a maid!"

At home the boy showed his school paper to his parents. The father liked the boy's realism and skepticism — the candid appraisal of life's obstacles. The son countered this praise with the message from the teacher, now made his own: yes, there probably was only a slim chance that the boy would ever become a first-rate professional baseball player on the Red Sox team — but there probably wasn't a very good chance, at one point in time, that George Washington would lead a successful American revolution, or that a poor lad named Abraham Lincoln would end up as President of the United States, or that Henry Ford, tinkering with machines, would emerge as one of the world's great industrialists.

The father did not especially take to the son's description of what success might mean for the maid and her boy. Why would the maid want to leave her job, just because her son had done well? What would she do with her time, even if she did have a new house of her own? And anyway, what did the teacher say to encourage such a way of thinking? The boy replied to his father's question briefly: "I agreed that she probably wouldn't want to leave her job." In effect, the boy recanted. As for the second question, he was now in the realm of pure speculation, because the maid (they had agreed) would never really want to leave. Hadn't she been with them sixteen years, and announced repeatedly that she would double that figure, God willing? The boy tried hard to accommodate his father's views: "There'd be too much time on her hands. The maid wouldn't have us to look after, and she'd probably watch television all day and get even fatter. She should be on a diet now, and she doesn't eat right. It would get worse if she had a lot of money."

With respect to the third question, the boy remembered later on the awkwardness he felt as he tried to come up with an answer: "I didn't think the teacher did anything wrong. I told my Dad that. He said he was sure I was right. He said he liked the teacher. He said she was one of the best in the school.

He said he didn't mind if any of us learned things at school that didn't agree with what we learned at home — so long as we talk to our parents about what we've been told there by the teachers. I don't think the teachers want to disagree with what our parents say. They just want you to 'learn to think.' That's what they always tell us, that if we don't learn to think for ourselves, then we're slaves. I think the Greek philosophers said something like that. My father agrees with the teachers. He says sometimes a teacher will look at a problem differently. He told me about a teacher he had when he was at St. Paul's, and the teacher thought this country was a colonial power, like England and France. When my father told my grandfather what the teacher had said, my grandfather was going to call up the headmaster and cause a lot of trouble. Daddy thinks his father could have got the teacher fired then, but not now. His father never made the call, though."

Even in elementary school children one finds such potential triangular tensions: the teacher, the parent, the child, each struggling to find or uphold a point of view. Again and again one hears privileged children, even when they are as young as eight or nine, trying to negotiate their way between the strong opinions parents may express and the troubling observations teachers may have made: the child as mediator. Usually disagreements between parents and teachers on the issues are not as dramatic or expressly ideological as they become later, in prep schools or colleges. But a remark or two on the part of a teacher, brought home and uttered by a child, heard by a parent, can be the occasion for additional remarks made by the parent, which are brought back to school and put before the teacher: there, what do you have to say about *that?* Some teachers withdraw immediately from a potential confrontation (as they see it) and say nothing. Silence can be rather instructive in its own right.

The teacher may, on the other hand, be silent only temporarily; in a while he or she replies: bland neutrality, or an insistent reassertion of what was said before, or even a somewhat aroused, pugnacious amplification. The child can choose to listen and let the matter drop by saying nothing to the teacher or, after school, saying nothing to the parent; to listen and talk with the teacher, try to get him or her to qualify a statement, so that it will be more acceptable at home; to take polite issue with the teacher, by quoting a parent repeatedly and emphatically; to be sassy, provocative, and sometimes galling by more or less demanding a retraction from the teacher. Needless to say, at home the child in theory has similar choices with his or her parents. But the theoretically possible alternatives rather evidently yield to the realities of a given classroom and a given family.

Those realities are at once psychological, social, political, and economic, and they are realities which children are inclined to appraise in what some older people might wish to describe as a "holistic" manner. Here again is the youth on the verge of graduating from elementary school: "My friends and I were talking the other day. We decided that if you don't watch out, you can get your teacher into trouble. If the teacher says something, and you tell your parents what she says, and they don't like what she said, then they go to the headmaster and tell him. It happens all the time. Then they have one of their conferences. The teacher tells her side, and the headmaster tells what the parents told him, and then the other teachers say what they think. I know how it works, because one of my friends' mother knows one of the teachers, and she told his mother. I guess there are some parents who never complain, but there are some who always do. My parents are in between. When my father hears me say something he doesn't like, he wants to talk it out with me. He says that's the way you do something if you're civilized. A lot of poor people, they're always fighting; they use knives and guns, or they scream a lot. We saw them arguing on television. They don't know how to reason; that's the problem, my Dad says. It's the same with the unions: they want to fight, and they make threats if they don't get their own way.

"In school the teachers try to be nice to you, and I'm sure they don't want to fight with our parents. I don't blame them! I wouldn't want my father as an enemy! He tells us that he's tough when he sits down with the union people. My father says he will never have a fight with a teacher, even if there's one who wants to fight. He says they're entitled to say what they believe, so long as what they say is connected to school-work. The teachers don't want to cause trouble. They like the school, and they come out here because they like teaching us. One woman drives an hour each way.

"It's the English compositions that have caused some trouble in the school. There are one or two kids whose parents get upset if the teachers don't agree with them. That was in the past, though. I've heard the stories. Now they've got good English teachers, and there's no trouble. The teacher says we should try to be *independent* in our thinking; we shouldn't agree with her just because she says something is right. We should even question our parents, if we're wondering whether something they said might not be right. That's what an education is all about — to have your own ideas. But she admitted that everyone wants to know how the guy in the next seat or across the room thinks, and she said the same goes for her; she thinks of her friends and her family and the other teachers when she decides what she is going to believe in, or who the candidate is she'll vote for. You can't divorce yourself from other people; and if you don't want to be a hermit, you'll have to change some of your ideas some of the time, so that they'll agree with the ideas other people have."

He had not just come up with that resolution. He had long

ago spotted a few inconsistencies he had heard — like "always think for yourself," on the one hand, and on the other, "never hurt or offend others, who may not have the same ideas you have." But children are not by and large (unless they are for various psychological or sociological reasons "exceptional") inclined to challenge the prevailing moral orthodoxies. They are usually interested in going from one minute to the next, rather than taking some "long-range" view, and they are usually anxious to make do with people or situations. And they are quite comfortable with inconsistencies, whether verbal or acted upon. They have for years been told to be vigorous and adventurous, but also careful, if not cautious. A few elect to become all too much the daredevils, and another few emerge as rather too timid or hesitant, even for their fearful parents' taste. Most, however, fall somewhere in between those two extremes — each child with his or her own blend of circumspection and boldness. And so with other emotional "polarities" — including that of loyalty to one's parents, versus the attachment to a certain schoolteacher or to a school and its avowed moral principles.

Since children, like adults, only at times a little more extensively, prefer to hear what it pleases them to hear and pick up especially those implications that serve such a purpose, it is no wonder that the remarks of a given teacher get quite a varied hearing from the listening members of the class: some don't even "get," in any significant way, what was spoken; others listen and nod enthusiastically; still others turn their heads away in worry or incipient disapproval.

Class and culture never impose themselves uniformly on family life. No matter how rich the parents, the children may be working hard, competing fiercely — as if their very future depended on a steady rise to the top, academically or athletically or both. Other children, apparently from the same background, are indifferent to or bored with school; they know rather early in life that so far as they are concerned, school is no necessity and may even be a waste of time, given the possibilities open to them. Still other children struggle with a mixture of those two attitudes. The child has been told to "do well" in school — as a matter of family pride, as a matter of moral obligation. The child may also have been told, or may have realized on his or her own, that there are many inviting ways to spend time; and some of them require precious little educational preparation.

A child may, for instance, not merely be interested in scuba diving as a hobby but may have become by the age of ten or eleven an extraordinarily expert diver — interested in underwater photography and exploration. Those interests often begin at the age of eight or nine and can compete strenuously in the child's mind, in the minds of parents, with the demands of schoolwork. A girl isn't "just" a well-trained equestrienne, she is interested in pursuing a life that is somehow connected to riding: shows, competitions, hunts. She knows fully grown women who are doing precisely what she has in mind — and who left school for long periods in order to cultivate riding skills, enter certain shows, "go on the road" at certain times: from one hunt to another, in the spring. The boy too knows men who have spent their lives being gentlemen-oceanographers or have turned an "interest" in deep sea diving into a controlling passion.

Those privileged children who for one reason or another begin early to develop strong interests that compete more and more with the demands of the schools usually find sanction at home for an emotional and sometimes even physical withdrawal from school. A child not only takes advantage of every vacation; he or she takes days, weeks, even a month or two, off and begins to say that school "doesn't count," or that it is a "waste of time," or that it serves only to distract from what matters so very much.

The teacher I quoted earlier in this chapter remembers several youngsters in recent years who virtually dropped out, for intervals of time, from elementary school and who continued their further education only in fits and starts: "Among these children — they are so rich compared to others — I have to be flexible with my standards. Some of them haven't been brought up to think about the usual requirements of the world — the world outside their own tight world. Their parents make rules for themselves. If they feel a burning desire to stay in the Caribbean, they won't come back at the end of a vacation, even if it's a two-week one. Why should they — just because a kid or two ought be in school? And if that kid is interested in underwater photography, his parents might even let him stay down there a month. If they have a daughter who wants to learn French and be a journalist — one of my students got *that* in her head when she was ten! — they see no point in encouraging her to spend her time learning arithmetic and science and even a lot of American history or English literature. They are willing to hire a tutor or two, or send her to a special school in France, or arrange some living situation for her there. If a child from another family got such ideas in her head, and her parents went along with them, we'd say that the whole family needed to be hospitalized for psychiatric treatment!

"I had one student who is going to be a great tennis player, I guess. Besides, he knows more about fish, the different kinds all over the world, than many college professors of biology know, I'm sure. His parents kept taking the boy out of this school for long stretches. They would get workbooks, find out what we were going to accomplish, hire a tutor, and go to the Caribbean, or out West to southern California, or down to

Florida. They'd come back, and the boy wasn't doing top
work, but he'd kept up with us. Maybe we shouldn't have
promoted him or graduated him. But he *was* learning; he had
a decent elementary school education when he graduated,
and we were right to let him by. I suppose some people would
say it was because his family is rich, and we were allowing
ourselves to be pushed around. But I think some of these
children here *are* 'special children'; they live in a special
world, and a lot of people don't understand that world, and so
don't understand these children — how they grow up. I'll say
this: they grow up differently from most other children. You
have to know that, as a teacher. Maybe that's why their parents or grandparents have set up these country day schools
and private *lycées* and small community schools near their
homes — because they know that it would be hopeless to try
to live their lives and have their kids go to public schools. Or
is it that they want to segregate themselves — to use that word
— from others and keep their children's school lives as 'private' as they try to keep the property they live on?"

The teacher never answers her own questions — only goes
on to ask more of them. She had learned to stop "figuring out,"
as she put it, the children she taught, or their families. She
became plaintive or a touch self-righteous only when she felt
others refused to recognize the "special" nature of the teaching she did. Those peculiarities of habit and desire, of language
and dress, of taste and perception, of fantasy and daily commitment, may or may not deserve the categorization, in sum,
of a "subculture," but they do exert their spell in the classroom
— the place where, more than any other place, boys and girls
like the ones mentioned in this book get to meet children of
their own age.

These are not, after all, children — many of them at least
— who go playing casually or with "supervision" in the streets

or in neighborhood playgrounds. They are children used to a rather private life. They are children whose idiosyncrasies may for the first time have to yield to the requirements of the classroom. Some don't at all like the prospect, the necessity. Others like school so much that they begin to dream of becoming teachers, college professors. A few even ask about going to school in the summer as well: a whole new society beckons a child who may otherwise feel virtually condemned to a select number of people, young or old. These children may have in common membership in a certain social and economic class, but they often enough demonstrate the particularities of their mental lives; and they eventually discover that teachers and classrooms also vary widely. In that respect at least they become the comrades of other children, born to quite different circumstances.

PART EIGHT

ETHICAL STRUGGLES: IDEALISM AND PRAGMATISM

E VEN by the time children go to nursery school, they have
learned a number of dos and don'ts, oughts and ought
nots. Sometimes such knowledge is dearly purchased. Every
child psychiatrist is familiar with the boy or girl who seems
fragile and vulnerable — and has been giving himself or herself the roughest of times by transforming parental injunctions
into stern, unrelenting self-accusation. The continuing hold of
the "superego" over many of us until our last breath needs no
documentation. (I refer to the more irrational and excessively
demanding side of that agency of the psychic apparatus, to use
psychoanalytic terminology.) Freud knew that the melan-
cholia of an adult can be but a continuation of an earlier despair — that of a child who wants to oblige various outside
injunctions that have in the mind become inside voices, possessed of striking power. Thus three- or four-year-old children
get grim and reproachful with themselves — insistent that
they not only do "right," but "pay" for any "wrong" that has
been done. Such moralistic self-punitiveness sometimes
becomes converted, out of a need for some relief, into a smug
self-righteous criticism of others.

Even in nursery schools one hears children denouncing a
particular "them" — an individual or a group who are the

faltering or errant ones. Sometimes apparently random, inexplicable nastiness or wrangling among such young children has as its source a stranger's passing remark or a brief outburst of activity that mobilizes an intense, contagious response. For example, one child doesn't do what he's supposed to do, or says something that is "bad"; other children nearby see and hear what has happened; all of a sudden, a fight breaks out, for no reason anyone can figure out. In fact, one or two children have smiled their approval of the "bad boy" and one or two other children have become quite angered by that boy's behavior. Yet the teacher, conscientious and concerned, can't manage to "get to the bottom" of the trouble. She has heard one child, who endeavored successfully to stay at a remove from the turmoil, observe that "everyone was wrong." The child meant "obsessed with wrong," and said as much too by explaining that not only *was* everyone wrong, but everyone had *called* everyone else wrong, and *that* had been wrong too! So ironies mount among children who at the age of four are not altogether different from some of their parents, who also manage to blame others unfairly, find scapegoats, rush to join moralistic and self-indulgent bandwagons, fight possessively and accusingly over various "truths," and so on.

The exacting if not punitive side of the child's conscience or superego has been emphasized by child psychiatrists, who have observed the ways various children learn to deal with the imperatives handed down by their parents. And as clinicians, child psychiatrists do indeed see the victims. I remember all too well the very first child I ever treated, a boy of six who had been strictly brought up and who had started at five to hurt himself by poking at his arms with a fork or scraping the skin of his legs with a metal toy army tank, which he rode up and down from thigh to ankle with merciless pressure exerted on his own flesh. The parents feared he was "going crazy"; they could make no sense of his behavior, and had tried earnestly and valiantly to persuade him to stop it. The boy, however, made quite a bit of sense of his own behavior. He had been called clumsy and sloppy, and he had decided to condemn himself — as if his parents' judgments were not quite enough.

He had also learned to be quiet and obedient — ready at any time to go along with criticisms directed at him. His parents could not understand how "such a good boy" had suddenly, at five, become "such a problem child." The boy couldn't understand, either. He had been trying harder to pay heed to the warnings, advice, reprimands he received, but with no success. Demons within him, it seemed, took over; he found himself doing injury to his body, then would cry and call himself "bad" for behaving (in his father's word) "crazy" — a vicious cycle, like so much human activity that goes under the name of "neurotic" or "psychopathological." It took several years for the cycle to become obvious not only to the parents but the child, and for the boy to begin to learn how to get along with himself in a different way. And for his doctor to comprehend how stubborn and unyielding a child's conscience can be.

Not all children, of course, suffer the tyranny of disordered and vindictive consciences. The "tone" of a child's conscience is, to a large degree, a function of his or her family's psychological makeup, as well as its social and cultural character — and its relationship to a certain region and to a historical era. As children have grown up in the South in past decades their parents have had to teach them racial dos and don'ts as well as the more private ones that enable a child to get along in a family, a neighborhood playlot, a school. In Appalachia the sons and daughters of mine owners have to be taught about farmers in the hollows, about miners — or those children may begin to ask questions about what is going on below the surface of property owned by their parents. Similarly for Anglo children in the Rio Grande Valley or the children of growers in Florida: how to teach young people an "attitude" toward a whole group of strangers who are obviously near at hand, whose work might well excite the curiosity and interest of a comfortably brought-up child in possession of eyes and ears and a mind that begins to wonder.

Some of our well-to-do suburbs are protected from *all* factories or offices. A corporation lawyer or a surgeon or a business executive does work that is less dramatic and directly connected to a parent's home life than that of a grower, a plantation owner, or a mine owner in eastern Kentucky or in West Virginia. But children of those "distant owners," dominant stockholders who live in Eastern cities, are capable of asking a question or two about what their parents believe, and those children, too, have to be told what is desirable or forbidden with respect to a "social outlook."

In New Orleans during the school desegregation crisis of the late 1950s and early 1960s a prominent lawyer had wondered *why*. Why was it that mobs roamed the streets, that grown-ups heckled small children, that the television screens were full of ominous and violent images, reports, prophesies? The lawyer had decided that his children, boys of ten and seven, had to understand something about what was going on. He announced repeatedly at home that each person has a "social outlook," and that the nature of the "outlook" determines the way he or she regards other people. Then he became specific with his children; he told them about white people and black people — about "them," the poor and working-class people of both races who were in such bitter confrontation.

The children listened, took notice, and began to develop a "social outlook" of their own. They became opposed to violence, and they especially wished that their city would be spared continuing trouble. They started to worry about the individuals caught up in that violence. Shouldn't the black children be kept at home, rather than face such awful and dangerous threats? What kind of parents did those "poor" children have, after all? As for the white members of the mobs, why did they behave in such a crude and nasty way? Shouldn't they stay at home, too — mind their own business, stop trying to cause so much "trouble" in the city? Nor did the children let themselves be idle observers, all too ready to repeat what their parents had said. The oldest boy, in particular, wanted to generalize; and when he did, he by no means confined his remarks to the issue of race, or even social equality. He insisted on talking about himself and what he believed to be important. He preferred to be confused rather than consistent; he had tried for the latter, but had failed.

This failure troubled him considerably: "I wish I knew what to do. If I was mayor I'd be all mixed up. My father keeps telling me that I should try to decide what I believe is right, and then go ahead and say what I believe. But I'm not sure what he believes, because he says he changes his mind a lot, and so do I! When you look at the colored kids on TV, being called all those bad names, you feel sorry for them. When you hear white people talking, you can understand their side. I hope that they settle this; then our city won't be ashamed of itself.

"When you grow up you see that the world has a lot of troubles. If it hadn't been for all the riots we've been having, I wouldn't know about some of the troubles. But now I do. In school the teacher asked us what we thought. My friend said his father was opposed to colored kids going to school with white kids. Then the teacher asked him if *he'd* mind if a few colored kids came to our school. He said he wasn't sure. I raised my hand and said I didn't think any could come, because it's expensive. The teacher said I was right. I've heard my father complain about the bills. He says we're lucky Granddaddy gave us the money before he died. If he was alive, he'd probably be paying the big bills. Before he died he told Daddy that he didn't mind a few nigras going to school with me. Daddy told my mother, and she told me. I told our teacher; I said that if there was someone colored, and his father had the money to pay, then he could come here, and it wouldn't be the end of the world. That's what my father keeps saying — that he can't figure out why those white people are acting as if it's the end of the world, just because a few little colored girls are coming to their school.

"When I grow up I hope we'll be over this trouble, and I hope people won't be saying bad things about the city of New Orleans. I'd like to live here. It's one of the best cities in the country, my parents say; and they've been all over the world. My Daddy says that the city needs leadership. Then it would be an even better city. If you live in New Orleans, you're lucky. I wouldn't want to move away, even if I could get a better job someplace else. We can walk to the levee from our house. We go away in the summer. If the colored had more money, they could live the same way we do. I wish they did have more money. Then they'd be equal. That would be good. Then we wouldn't have the problems we have now in the city. Then the city wouldn't look bad to everyone. Daddy says it hurts the city, the riots and the news stories."

The boy has learned to repeat his father's opinions, sometimes word for word. But upon occasion there are variations. Especially interesting is the sequence at the end of the above quotation. The boy had learned from a "liberal" private schoolteacher (in the early 1960s in Louisiana) that the "colored children" had been treated somewhat unfairly during the previous decades. The teacher had, of course, hedged, qualified — to the point that my description, "somewhat unfairly," is probably, in retrospect, itself somewhat unfair. She simply pointed out that it wasn't "right" for riots to take place, nor was it "right" for whites to forget that "the colored" render a great deal of useful "service" to white people "all the time."

But that was enough to set a few young minds going. The boy heard similar comments from his parents, who would nevertheless have been judged or categorized at the time as "segregationists." It was not hard for him, his parents' social views notwithstanding, to declare himself in favor of "equality," though he was far from unequivocal about such ideals. He was willing to uphold the notion of equality, but his reasons were not exactly the best: if a city one loves, like New Orleans, doesn't correct certain inequalities, trouble will evidently break out, persist, and ultimately hurt more people than "a few colored girls."

It is possible to ask whether any "idealism" was truly at work. The boy does say that it would be "good" if black children lived as he did, had as much money as he expects to have. But how carefully had he thought out the implications? He seems to be saying that New Orleans had better watch out; either it changes the social, racial, and economic status quo, or that status quo gets altered by conflict. And, no doubt about it, the boy has learned from his parents to take New Orleans seriously in a certain way. When New Orleans prospers, his family prospers. When New Orleans is in trouble, his family may not be financially distressed (the whole country would have to collapse for that to be the case) but they are saddened and, very important, embarrassed. It is a loss of pride easily scorned by others — the pride of the rich about a city they regard as their province, if not their backyard. It is a shame that sounds, and often may well be, either homely and aesthetic or, just as often, shrewdly calculating about the loss of dollars that follows social unrest.

No question the boy's "shame" contained those elements.

But the boy was responding to unspoken considerations. Children can indeed be very forthcoming emotionally, but are often disinclined to be so with words or "ideas." Anyway, the boy was not issuing self-important pronouncements. He was trying to make clear his budding convictions, with all their inherent contradictions. Some he took over without hesitation or qualification from his parents: he was not reluctant to use their very phrases. But he was an observer himself; and, since he had no decades of living and learning to defend, he knew that at least some of the protagonists in the current social struggle were children only a few years his junior — were members of his generation rather than that of his parents. He was especially touched and troubled by what he saw on television — the spectacle of a lone girl, in one instance, and three girls in another, being heckled, threatened, made afraid for their lives every single day. Not that his parents also weren't made uncomfortable at first and disgusted later. But again, when they felt too much ashamed at what they knew to be happening in *their* city, they came up with arguments that, by the father's own description, "evened the scale" — the Southerner as a victim of arbitrary federal power.

The boy, however, was only then learning to balance his loyalties. Nor was he prepared, emotionally, by his parents (since they were scarcely prepared themselves) to deal with the sights and sounds that television brought into their homes. The look on one black child's face as she braved the jeering mob especially affected the boy. He asked his parents why — even as they had asked the same of themselves. They eventually came up with answers; though they were never fully satisfied by what they assured themselves had to be true. However strongly they argued for the South's traditions, and against the arrogant and ill-timed "interference" of the North through the federal judiciary, there was still something about the picture of a small girl walking into a school past a large crowd of near-violent grown-ups who mouthed threats and obscenities, that prompted dismay (at the very least) in the boy's parents. The boy noticed their dismay. He spoke openly on behalf of the girl, but also paid attention when his parents not so much defended the mob as explained the reasons for its continuing passion.

The boy had learned that it was "bad" to use foul language, to attack others weaker or more vulnerable than oneself. The boy had learned to be polite and respectful toward the black people who have worked for his parents and grandparents or for the parents of his friends. And, like many Southern children of well-to-do families, the boy had been especially close to a maid who had cared for him since he was born. When he saw those children being heckled on television, he thought of the maid's children, especially her young daughter. And he thought of what he had heard: that the powerful ought not take advantage of their strength; that there are standards of public behavior which both children and men and women ought hold themselves to; and that even someone who is doing wrong (initiating school desegregation!) deserves, at some point in time, forgiveness and a degree of understanding. Why did the mobs show no charity?

The boy's increasing worry about the national reputation of New Orleans was not *only* a response to the commercial anxieties of his parents. Their young son could "read" his parents well, because he was himself going through a similar struggle: "I hear Daddy get angry at the mobs, and I'm glad. Then he gets angry at the NAACP. He says they're always asking for something. Then he says we'll have a lot of trouble here in New Orleans if they don't stop the mobs, because no one will want to come here and visit, and businesses will stay out. I don't blame anyone for wanting to keep away. It's bad when the police can't keep the streets safe. I wouldn't want to go to a city where there are a lot of mobs. The judge is scared for his life. He ordered the integration, and now they're defending his home; the police are there all the time. I went with my friends and saw them. Daddy said it's been the worst possible thing, all this trouble. And he even apologized to our maid. He told her he was really sorry. I was proud of my father. I apologized too. She said she didn't want to hear any apologies from my father and any apologies from me. She said if all the white people of the country behaved like us, then the colored would be much better off than they are. I was glad she said that. I felt better."

The father and the boy were judging their beloved city harshly, but also trying to defend its reputation. Each of them wanted to speak for himself — to set himself off ever so slightly or quite emphatically from "others," be they residents of New Orleans or Yankees. The boy speaks: "I think it's wrong what the mobs are doing; and even if it's wrong the way the government is pushing on us, the more people who don't like the riots, the better it'll be for New Orleans." He has already acquired a set of values; he believes something is "wrong," not only for reasons he has learned from his parents, but those he has learned on his own. *He* has talked with his maid. *He* has heard the teachers speak. *He* has put himself in the shoes of those black children, even if only for a few seconds, while watching them on television.

No doubt we all develop our "defenses," learn to become bored, jaded, indifferent, or numb in the face of such a tide of trouble. But children are not so well protected emotionally; if that is why they are more vulnerable to the vulgarities and indecencies of television, it is also why they are more responsive to some of the moral dilemmas implicit in certain news stories. A child who is upset by a bizarre and violent detective story or a confusing and frightening cartoon, because he or she has not yet learned to be detached enough, is the same child who can watch a social or political crisis unfold on television and become quite swept up by it. The boy in New Orleans was moved enough by what he saw on news programs to ask his parents unsettling — and morally quite pertinent — questions; and he was not easily deterred with a casual reply.

For instance, the boy asked his father, "Why do those people say those words to that little girl?" The father told the child that he didn't know "those people," but he was reasonably certain that "they" were angry and afraid. The boy persisted: "Why are they so angry and afraid?" The father tried to explain that New Orleans had certain customs, so far as the way white people and "colored" people had been getting along, and that now those customs were being directly challenged. The result was alarm and even rage. But the boy was still not satisfied — as children often are not, when they sense in grown-ups moral uncertainty. He wanted to know why his father, as someone prominent, did not step in and do something. Surely he could. Surely his advice would be heard, his words taken seriously. And in the schools the teachers were also asked such questions: couldn't *they* do something to make New Orleans once again a peaceful and law-abiding city? It was not always enough, some teachers knew, as did the parents of the boy being quoted here, to come up with vague pieties in reply. They might serve their purpose one day, but be utterly inadequate the next. The boy who asked his father why he didn't try to stop the riots was the same boy who had heard his father mention, on various occasions, how much he could do with respect to many kinds of troubles. The boy had even heard his father talk with other grown-ups about what ought to be done, what might have to be done, what could be done — given continued street violence. When would that "moment" arrive, the young listener naturally wondered — to himself, and, finally, out loud.

Children who had heard their teachers say that one or another kind of behavior was right or wrong, in life or in the classroom, were quick to ask about a public spectacle. Shouldn't the teachers in those boycotted schools go outside and tell those men and women to leave right away, various children kept wondering out loud. When the teachers in a fine, private school said that it wasn't "easy" for the teachers in the beleaguered, mob-threatened schools, the children were astonishingly fast with suggestions: why didn't all of them, in the private school, children and teachers alike, go help the more unfortunate ones, the harassed "colored" girls, and their teachers? Those same children, of upper-middle-class and quite wealthy parents, had differing opinions too. They would follow a suggestion of assistance with a statement of reprimand: if only the "colored" weren't so "pushy," or kept in their "place," or didn't listen to "a lot of Yankees." And if only those "Yankees," those "outsiders," minded their own business, stayed away. Maybe if the riots had got over quickly or not been covered so constantly on television, the children could have kept themselves removed psychologically from the crisis, and so *only* full of annoyance for "outsiders" or for those in New Orleans who persisted in being social and racial protagonists. But the riots didn't stop for a long time. A social reality develops its own, eventual psychological authority.

In Appalachia, when serious coal mine disasters took place, one could hear the children of corporation lawyers or mine owners get caught up in a similar kind of moral conflict. They sensed the sadness and unease of their parents as they talked about a particular tragedy and also heard their parents, not rarely, attribute the "cause" to the carelessness of miners or to "unavoidable" influences. They would also hear — and hear discussed on television — the tearful allegations and embittered accusations of the wives and children of the dead. And sometimes, in the privacy of a home, a lawyer or business executive would shake his head and acknowledge fault, or come perilously close to doing so. The child would pay heed, would be doubly sad — for a parent, and for the dead parents of other children. Not that the parents of such a child always welcome that kind of broadminded, generous sorrow. A girl of eleven, whose father's Kentucky mines experienced repeated explosions (with deaths the common result) kept telling her father that she was praying for the dead miners at night before going to bed. He let her do just that for days, weeks. He said nothing. But there comes, eventually, one time too many — coinciding, tragically, with one disaster too many. Eight men were killed on a certain Friday afternoon, and on the weekend the girl complained that she "prayed too hard for the men, and so couldn't go to sleep." She was tired and irascible on Saturday and Sunday; but so was her father. He exploded on Sunday evening, when his daughter came down for the third night in a row in her nightgown, sadly announcing how reluctant sleep was in coming to her. He told her to stop her "nonsense," to "cut out that prayer business," to go to sleep, and no more ifs, ands, buts. She burst into tears. He gave her an extended lecture on why she must stop saying the kind of prayer she recently had been offering to God. She said yes, she would comply. Then the father went back on himself, told her that she could pray as she had — within limits.

The limits of evening petition became also the limits of Sunday attention and faith. The Presbyterian minister's prayers on behalf of the dead miners and their families were too impassioned, the girl's father complained. He cut back on his weekly donation, and at home let everyone in his family know that he was mightily displeased. He talked of going elsewhere on Sunday, though he also acknowledged that there was no-where convenient to go — and that "their" church was the "best" one in the county. He took pains to explain once more and at great length to his children why it was foolish to blame God for mine accidents, or pray to Him that they be pre-vented, stop happening. The father scorned those who claim to speak for God, those who try to summon the Bible as a means of indicting and convicting people, or sanctioning the activities of other people. As he talked he discerned the per-plexity of his children. They hadn't realized when they were in church that the minister was "against" their father, and now that they were home they weren't able to understand exactly why he was angry. And when he saw the bewilderment on their faces, he misunderstood it as evidence of sympathy for the miners, hence reason for a new outburst of anger: be-trayed at the hands of one's own (misled) children.

After awhile they came to understand one another. The father was told by the mother that he wasn't being fair to his children; that he was interpreting their ignorance and plain curiosity to be evidence of provocative or accusatory behavior. The children were told by the mother that their father was terribly upset, and they had better try harder than usual to appreciate what was happening to him and, through him, to them. The mother was a messenger and mediator; she saw how upset her husband was. She also saw how troubled her children were, especially her daughter. The girl loved her father very much. The girl was also an attentive student at school and a model one at Sunday School. She had done sev-eral "social studies" projects in which Appalachia's "poverty" had been discussed. She had also heard recited, rather often, Christ's Sermon on the Mount and other teachings of His. She had at the time a desire to be a nurse — perhaps join the Frontier Nursing Service, located in her home state of Kentucky. Thereby she would attend to the poor, help those who lived up hollows, far from the possibility of medical care. Her father had looked benignly on her ambition, until the serious mine explosion. He began to wonder why she was so interested in "the subject of poverty." He began to feel that she had become a victim, almost — taken in by a collection of ministers and teachers who worried about "the poor," but never really faced the "practical" problems of society.

The daughter had no intention of becoming a future rebel, a stern critic of the society her parents were an important part of. She even insisted to her mother that her idealism and compassion for the poor were her father's; that he liked giving money to charity, liked helping those who by virtue of illness or old age or disasters of various kinds can't help themselves. He had shown his daughter the brochures of various charitable organizations, explained to her what they try to do for whom. She had never forgotten the moment, the experience of being a confidante of his; nor had she overlooked his usual largesse on Sundays — ten-dollar bills in the plate, to supplement checks sent through a bank so as to be anonymous. It was that last gesture she found so touching and impressive. Her father, she knew, did not want to be known as a person easily approached for money.

Such a child has struggled hard to do justice to demands upon her conscience — demands, ironically, made by the very person, her father, whose moral behavior, as a mine owner, had prompted a family crisis. It is not quite true, however, that parents like him are inevitably seen as hypocrites by exquisitely honorable and sensitive children. There are some children who do indeed relish exposing the frailties of their parents. But there are also a good number of children who upon discovering those frailties feel not only disappointment but a kind of incredulity, which soon enough generates its own psychological sequence: the boy or girl insists that a family's values or standards of behavior be *selectively* upheld — and justified as the father's or the mother's "real" ideal.

The flaws discovered are not quite forgotten. The child who recalls a certain example knows that he or she had better explain to himself or herself why it has seemed best to be selective. It can take months, years, for those selective appropriations of parental words or deeds to be securely defended in a given child's mind. In fact, it can be argued that a considerable part of the childhood of certain children is spent on just such a psychological effort. At twelve or thirteen, especially, one hears certain boys and girls who live in quite well-off circumstances begin to indicate a sense of success — they have learned how to reconcile apparent contradictions of intention or desire and are relieved as well as pleased at the reconciliation. The alternative, they know, is not a thorough, honest psychological scrutiny, but sadness and anxiety and a nagging sense of personal failure — as if the perceived moral downfall of a parent condemns the child to a fate even worse: actual, "real life" downfall in the future.

Why do children come up with such a grim forecast — rather than take courage from their own quite evident capacity to be shrewdly and correctly observant, to free themselves from earlier, pietistic warnings or commands? During the first decade in the lives of many children from well-to-do families the child is regarded as an important, indeed tell-tale, challenge: an infant with a certain biological endowment is expected to become a reasonably well-behaved, well-"adjusted," well-organized, and competent person — or else the parents will hold themselves responsible. There are regional variations, subtleties of encouragement or disapproval within the upper-class world, depending upon the religious and educational and social and racial background of the parents.

But even though the sociological and ideological variations, within the nation as a whole and a given class too, are numerous, there are certain psychological themes that are relatively constant. Children have to learn how to control themselves, how to get along well enough at home to make regular attendance at school possible. They have to learn how to dress in the way their parents, neighbors, and teachers find acceptable. They have to learn how to talk in a certain way, get along with others in an approved way. They have to learn various styles of initiative and exertion that a particular family and community find desirable. In the earlier sections of this book some of those habits, styles, preferences have come across rather insistently in the children's own accounts of what they do or don't do, and indeed in their drawings — which are, after all, efforts to represent the distinctive psychological reality of a given life. Put differently, a young artist perceives not only the external or "objective" world, which gets drawn, but the inner world as well — with all its rhythms, rituals, and imperatives, as they are being absorbed and given the influence parents deem suitable.

Each of those children is learning the hurdles and virtues of social accommodation, psychological development, and moral compliance — as mediated through parents who live at a given time in a given place and themselves have a given personal history. In his paper on narcissism mentioned above, Heinz Kohut points this out: "If the pressures from the narcissistic self are intense and the ego is unable to control them, the personality will respond with shame to failures of any kind, whether its ambitions concern moral perfection or external success (or, which is frequently the case, alternatingly the one or the other, since the personality possesses neither a firm structure of goals nor of ideals)."

The polarity Dr. Kohut mentions is one especially evident

in the lives of the children of America's wealthier families. For these boys and girls "external success" is no distant apparition, no much-sought-after dream. Their parents offer them every day tangible, here-and-now evidence of that success; it becomes the basis for dozens of psychological as well as social assumptions, the former of which it is this book's task to convey, at least within the limits of one writer's capacity to do so. But children don't learn only to expect a gilded journey and a promised land of milk and honey. They learn that they *must* do many things, and that insofar as they do as they have been told, they are "good." They also learn, especially as they get older (say, at seven and eight), *why* they ought behave in certain ways, uphold certain values. It is not only a question of strict obedience, or of clear rewards, or of a responsiveness to the wishes of others, or of a faith in a code of right and wrong. It is a more complex faith that the child now finds — personal but grounded in a given social and economic reality, and in some religious or ethical system whose tenets are less consistent than either the child or the child's parents may be willing to recognize. It is not always easy to unravel the various threads; they are part of a whole cloth, a blanket the child holds close and very much relies upon.

In a rural town to the north of Boston, where thoroughbred horses and fine, large sailboats are much in evidence — farms near the water — a boy of twelve talks as if he had attended a psychiatric conference and thereafter realized the last-ditch narcissism at stake in the ethical conflicts he was already experiencing: "I'll be going away from home soon. I don't know if it'll be Groton or St. Paul's or Exeter or Andover; probably not the last two, because they are too crowded. I'm not ready for a prep-school Harvard! My father doesn't like the idea of my going to visit a lot of schools. He says that the more I visit the more I'll get confused. My mother says I ought to look around, but she'll go along with him. She usually does go along with him, except when she's got her own thing to fight for. He has to give in, then. They've divided up the world! The trouble is, there are a few times I get caught in the middle! A couple of years ago I wasn't doing so well in school. But they put the heat on me. They hired a tutor, too. It was hard for a couple of months, but I got much better. I'm glad now that my parents really have standards. My father always uses that word; he says that if we don't demand a lot of ourselves, then we'll become fat and stupid — and we'll live off our capital, and we'll amount to nothing, and we'll become rich bums, and our children will become comfortable bums, and our grandchildren will become poor bums 'of good families,' or 'of families that *once* were good'! You don't just walk into a good job and walk into a successful life, Dad says. He can hand us the money; he can tell us how much we'll get when we're twenty-one. But he keeps telling us that he wants to know what we'll be *like* when we're twenty-one!

"I used to think he was just talking. I wasn't sure what he wanted me to *do*, except obey him and try to be good at school and win in the games and be respectful — things like that. But he and I have had some good talks, and I've gone to his law office and seen him with his partners, and I think I know what he's been talking about all these years. Maybe I've always known. He wants me to have *principles;* that's the word he always uses. He says you should know where you'd draw the line, and not budge an inch. If you don't know, you're in real trouble. I think I know; I mean, there are things I won't do, even if other kids do them, and there are things I won't say, no matter how many kids say them. I hate to be in that kind of a bind, though. I hate it when everyone is doing something or saying something, and I don't feel like joining up. I don't want to act like I'm superior, but I know my principles. If you stay away at times like that, the kids might turn on you, and even your best friends won't like what you're doing. I just try to get away. I make up an excuse. I'll tell them I have to go to the bathroom; or I don't feel good. I once said I was afraid I'd throw up! Then I went to the bathroom in the school and stayed there for about ten minutes. I kept looking in the mirror, wondering if I looked sick, so no one would think I was fooling. The reason was they were picking on a kid real bad, and then they started writing all those swear words on the wall, and I didn't want to be with them, but they were my friends, some of them, and I could tell that two of my friends, my two best friends, weren't any happier than I was, but they were going along. I really was sick, I think. That's what I kept telling myself when I stared into the mirror!"

He had experienced the "shame" Dr. Kohut and other psychoanalytic theorists have described: a shame that prompted him to withdraw from a crowd — and face a mirror. He had for years been learning that his own self-regard was very much connected to the "standards" his parents upheld for school. The parents did not want their children to become self-righteous or smug or prissy, however. They often told the boy that it was as important to get along with others as to know where to draw the line of no compromise. He had accordingly become frightened, anxious, impelled to seek isolation at a time when he felt hopelessly in conflict. He wanted to be a member of the gang. He was not sure which was more important — that he hold on to his friends or shun behavior he had been taught was "beneath" him.

That preposition "beneath" was one his parents used rather often. Another word they favored was "high." They had not only "standards," but "high standards." One must be careful, lest one "sink." Where does a child find himself when he "sinks"? He is not sure. His father has talked about "most people" with a certain disdain: they intimidate one another, "sink to the lowest common denominator," exhibit no real independence of thought. That last quality is important, the boy knows. When he was in the school bathroom staring into the mirror, he was assuring himself that he had demonstrated a capacity for "being himself." Nevertheless, he had a "bad dream" that night; he forgot most of it, but remembered one strange vignette: "I was with my friends, and we were playing lacrosse. We were winning. The other side was losing real bad. Then I fell down and cut myself. I thought it was on a sharp rock, but they found pieces of glass in the skin. I don't know whether I got back into the game or not. There was more to the dream, but I've forgotten everything else. Maybe my mother and father were there, watching the game. Or maybe they came and took me to the hospital. I don't know."

What he did know was that he felt scared in the dream, more so than a mere cut justified. He had hurt himself before — playing football and soccer, skiing, falling off a horse. He was not a physical coward. He was tall for his age, had always been so. He knew what it was to look down on people — his own friends or others his age. He knew what it was like, also, for others to look up at him — with considerable respect for his obvious physical prowess. In the dream he had been knocked out of commission in the middle of a game, yet not hurt all that badly. The dream described rather nicely the injury to his sense of himself — a narcissistic injury rather than a serious physical one.

The glass connected a dream's pain to that of a previous day's real pain. The worries for himself (Kohut's "pressures from the narcissistic self") came close to overwhelming him in that school's bathroom mirror. He *was* sick; he didn't tell a lie. He knew so at the time, had told himself as he stared at himself that he was "sick of the school," that he could hardly wait to graduate and go away to boarding school. He would then (so he hoped) be with his friends and away from various class-mates whom he regarded as "jerks" or maybe (though he would never say so directly) "beneath" him. Asked for any common characteristics they had, the boy shook his head, said "None," but went on to mention that "a lot of them are the first ones in their families to be here." How did he know? He wasn't able to give a clear-cut answer. He just knew: "Anyone can tell." Perhaps it was a certain roughneck quality in those boys — though he refused to make a categorical generaliza-tion. He was rather tough himself, he had to admit. But one can on occasion be somewhat vulgar, without going "over-board" — another word he kept using, though he was unable to follow it up with any specifics: "Those guys just went over-board, and I guess I couldn't take it."

He was, weeks later, interested in forgetting the panic he had experienced. It had been "nothing," he maintained — even though he had mentioned the incident to his parents, a relatively unusual step. No doubt the minor difficulty at school had achieved special psychological impact precisely because it signified what might be ahead of the boys — more trying challenges or provocations. Would he always be able successfully to appease the conflicting demands of his conscience, or figure out their relative importance to him? He had managed to get himself out of one, rather minor, moral collision; and later, that night, had dreamed himself injured and a bit surprised and worried about himself. His father had always said that "life" could be "hard" — yes, for people like them, so obviously graced by social and economic privilege. And now he realized that he was nearly a teenager, and soon to be out on his own.

But children grow up with more than worries and appre-hensions that they will do "wrong" and be punished. Even before Freud had written about the superego, he made reference to the "ego-ideal," the child's developing sense of what he would like to be and do, whom he would hope to emulate. Most children live in a degree of fear; they have learned that they can expect explicit punishment, or, more devastating, the withdrawal of their parents' affection and support, if a certain kind of behavior is pursued. They have also learned that they will be given praise, even rewards, if they go along with various rules and codes of conduct; and so they try hard, as they grow older, to do just that. But children of seven or eight, and certainly those of nine or ten, have also started to have definite notions of a future life. Especially is this the case with upper-middle-class children or those whose parents are wealthy. Such boys and girls develop plans for themselves. The psychoanalytic literature contains many discussions of the vicissitudes of the superego — the demands of conscience a child learns painfully and anxiously to heed. Much less space has been given in psychoanalytic journals and books to the "ego-ideal" — the child's growing hope for a certain kind of life. At one point the Boston analyst Helene Deutsch observes that "the group situation seems to be the condition for the functioning of the ego-ideal." She is referring to what she calls a "social ideology," which works its way, she knows, into a child's conscious and unconscious mind. But she gives us no clinical documentation of how such a process works in particular instances; and, alas, others have not rushed to do so either.

Yet nothing more significantly marks children off, one from another, than their developing sense of their destinies. In many children whose parents are well-to-do, there are pictures of successful relatives to look at. There are, too, remarks to be heard and overheard — declarations by parents of what they desire for themselves and their children and pietistic avowals of what, exactly, the "good life" is like. And there are friends who have come to certain conclusions about the future — and how that outcome can be secured. Before a child has become a teenager, years of observations and impressions and experiences have congealed into a distinct "social ideology," which is, as analysts note, deeply fixed in the mind's life.

Over the years I have tried to understand the elements of those ideologies particular children learn. The "social ideology" Dr. Deutsch mentions keeps coming up in the dreams of children, even as those dreams enable expression of the fears, lusts, resentments that exist between parents and a child, or between brothers and sisters. It can be arbitrary, at times, for a child psychiatrist to decide where, in a dream, the so-called private or idiosyncratic ends and the "public" or "social" begins.

When an eleven-year-old boy whose father is the president of a bank has nightmares in which, repeatedly, a large building collapses and everyone inside is badly hurt, including the dreamer, the doctor listening may decide that there isn't much of a "social ideology" at work in that dream — rather, a son's rage at a parent. But what if the boy has a number of things to say about buildings? "The trouble with a lot of places is that anyone can go visit them. My father doesn't like to stay in a lot of hotels, because they are big and crowded. He likes to find a small place, and if it's good, and they only take a few people, that's what he likes. He belongs to clubs. If he goes to New York, he stays in a club. If he goes to Washington, he stays in a club. He doesn't like to go to a city where there's no club. If you go to a big hotel, you can get robbed. There are crooks around. They hold up banks, and they break into your room in a hotel. My father's bank is insured. If anyone held it up, the bank would get the money back. A bank can't go broke. Banks used to go broke, my Dad says, but no more. They have guards in our bank. If someone tried to hold up the teller, he would press his foot on a button, and the police would know something is wrong, but there'd be no alarm going off, because then the crooks might get angry and start shooting. It's a good idea to build a bank so that if some crooks try to hold up the tellers, they can push buttons, and lock the doors, and get the police. I had an idea once: build a trapdoor. No one would know it was there but the tellers. It would be right in front of the tellers, where you stand in line to get your money. If a crook came up to the teller, and asked for money, and pointed a gun, the teller could just press a button, and the trapdoor would open, and the crook would fall down. Then they could call the police, and that would be the end of the crook."

He knows his idea is not especially feasible, but he likes to think of ways to foil greedy crooks. His mind works like an architect's — the design of a building is important to him, and a challenge: how to dream up a bank that would frustrate every robber? But the boy has other dreams and fantasies. He does not always wake up in a cold sweat, because a "downtown building" has blown up, and he in it; nor does he always speculate about cops and robbers, or rather, robbers, and later, cops: "I had a funny dream, but it was nice. I built myself a tree fort. It was a big one. I got some wire, and connected the electricity in our house to my tree fort, so I had a television set in my fort. I had a toaster there, and I could make English muffins. I had a little refrigerator. I could make myself snacks. I had a telephone there, and a walkie-talkie. There were some kids standing near the fort. They wanted to come up. I told them to go build their own tree fort. They said they didn't know how. I told them that no one taught me; I just learned. I taught myself.

"If you build a building, it's yours. No one should try to take something that doesn't belong to him. I'd like to build a house one of these days, when I'm older. I could do a lot of the work myself. I could clear the land. I'd like the house to be way up on a hill; you could see for miles and miles. You could have trails going down the hill. You could go riding, and hunting. You could pick up a lot of stations and voices on your walkie-talkie, because you'd be high up. I'd have my friends over. I'd have a lot of room. I'd have a big kitchen, and we could have plenty of snacks. Maybe there'd be a maid there all the time, to keep everything looking good. We have someone who looks after our summer home all year around, even in the winter. We go to it on Thanksgiving and Christmas, so we don't close the place up. My father helped design the house. He said he hopes I *do* become an architect. He says there are people who want a house that's different from anyone else's, and you have to be a special kind of architect to please them, and I would be that kind of architect."

The dream gave him pleasure; the thoughts he had while talking about the dream also gave him pleasure. If he occasionally woke up terrified by his mind's desire to destroy a building, he also could wake up pleased at the side of his mind that wanted to build. Even at night, when at sleep, he could build. He knew at eleven that he wanted to be an architect. He had loved to build with blocks when younger. He had gone through a succession of tree forts. He had built with sand in the summer, with snow in the winter. He had helped his father plan an addition to the family's summer home. He had watched construction of a new building for the father's bank. He had visited many cities, in America and Europe, taken note of styles of architecture. He liked dramatic, modern buildings — ones with much glass. He especially liked a new skyscraper built in Boston by the John Hancock Insurance Company.

Yet the building was no great success; glass panes fell out. Millions had to be spent in correcting errors of judgment or construction. The boy was not dismayed, however. He knew who was at fault, and he was sure that the problems would be solved: "A lot of people don't do their work the way they should. They want to get paid, but they don't want to do the best possible job. I'd like to get a job on a tractor, or a crane. I'd like to design buildings, but before you do that you should know how to build them. You should start from the bottom and work your way up. My Dad says if you want to get someplace, you should make up your mind, and never be satisfied until you've won. My mother says that she'd be happy, no matter what work I did, so long as I was good at it."

The boy is determined, ambitious, strong-minded. He is willing to work hard, to start out low on the ladder. But he has (and will have) limited patience; eventually he expects to be in charge of things. The "group situation" (in Dr. Deutsch's words) for him will be an architectural firm perhaps; maybe a law firm or a bank or a corporation. He imagines at ten or eleven what he will be doing at twenty or twenty-one, thirty or thirty-one. He knows that his aspirations are reasonable and will one day turn into an actuality. He is not simply driven by guilt or fear, hounded by a potentially lacerating and always peremptory superego; he is already drawn along by strong hopes for himself and convictions about himself. And when he is less hopeful about others, less convinced about the moral character or capacity for work of others — the ordinary workers, for instance, who build skyscrapers like the John Hancock building in Boston — he is not simply projecting his own fears or "negative self-image" on others, but has come to an accurate estimate of what others, less fortunate, often do indeed feel. In his own terse words, spoken just after his twelfth birthday: "A lot of people don't want to do much; all they want is to keep their jobs, so they can get a salary. I want to have fun when I go to the office."

He can become, for a moment, now and then, curious about

working people rather than all too sure about them (and of himself). He can say that he feels sorry for people who don't have the sense of themselves he does — the sense of life as welcoming and affirming: "I'd hate to be poor. That's no good. If you're poor you're in trouble. If you don't have money in the bank, you can be wiped out. Someone gets sick, and you're in big trouble. You can't pay the doctor's bills. My Dad says most people don't have much money in the bank. They put in a hundred dollars, and they take it out. Most of the money in his bank comes from businesses — big companies. He says he'd sell a savings bank if he owned one. He likes commercial banks. He likes to lend money to the companies in downtown Boston. His bank owns a lot of property, and a lot of stocks and bonds, and a lot of stores, I think — and the land that shopping centers are built on. It's too bad everyone can't have a lot of money in the bank. If everyone did, the banks would have more money, and the people who had the money would be happier. It is no fun being without money. One of the people who works in Daddy's bank told me when I was there last year that money isn't everything. But it's a lot! I guess a lot of people think it's everything. That's because they don't have it, but they want it. Our maid said so."

What shrewd, weary cynics some children are, already able to piece together a capitalist philosophy of life out of a maid's comment here, a bank official's comment there, and, not least, the day-to-day observations of parents who not only tell a child what he ought not to do, or must at all costs do, but also give him reasons to feel pleased with himself as he is, or reasons to work so that he will years hence have a good opinion of what he has amounted to. But not only cynics; some children can suddenly move out of the self-congratulatory vein — wonder instead, as this boy did, about those who (he knows) will never have the chances and luck he has.

The same parents, it has to be remembered, who talk tough about "the unions" can be generous to a maid, a "handyman," a person who "helps" with garbage, with the lawn, with maintaining the swimming pool: "If I had a lot of money, I'd give some of it away. I mean a real lot. Daddy says we don't have so much that we can just give when we want to give. He's put his money in trusts, and he can't spend some of it, even if he wanted to. He didn't say no to our maid, though, when her husband got sick and nearly died. My father said it cost him a lot of money, thousands of dollars. He said he didn't like paying the big bills, but he couldn't live with himself if he didn't. There's a man at the bank who pays a lot of the bills; my father signs the checks, and the man keeps our records straight. He was surprised when Daddy said to pay all the hospital bills. Daddy jokes, and says he's a miser — and he doesn't have any money! The maid says Daddy is the kindest man in the world! I guess he is!

"I don't like spending my allowance. I'm not a miser, but I like to save up money, and then buy something I really like, after I've waited for it. It's no fun just wasting your money on one little thing after another, and you have nothing to show for it. If I got twice the allowance I do, I'd put more in the church plate on Sunday. I *think* I would! Maybe I wouldn't, though! You can always find something you've wanted, but you thought you couldn't get the money together to buy it, and then you get extra money, from a stock dividend, and you can buy what you wanted, so you don't put the money in the plate. My grandfather gave me some stocks when I was born, and mother used to cash them and give them to the church when I was a baby, but now she lets me spend the money. She says it's real good practice for me to get the checks and cash them and figure out what to do with the money."

The boy gives a listener ample evidence, over a period of

years, of the "social ideology" that influences his "ego ideal."
The boy's outlook on life, his sense of what matters in this
world, his estimate of his own future, and his self-regard are
all constantly being shaped by a set of secular and religious
pieties, which in turn reflect the ambiguities and inconsistencies of a nation's social and economic system. He likes to be
kind to people. He also has no wish to "be taken for a ride,"
or to be known as "an easy target." He doesn't even want to
get the reputation of an open-hearted person — though,
again, he prides himself on being thoughtful, considerate.

The boy has learned not to talk openly or casually about
money — to be tight-lipped and *apparently* indifferent to the
subject. The boy has also learned to think carefully about his
modest allowance, the dividends he gets, and the money he
someday will get. He is anything but relaxed about his "attitude toward money," a phrase both parents have used in talks
with him. One doesn't just spend money, or rejoice in having
it, or lament not having enough of it. One ought devote a good
deal of time to thinking about what money is and what it will
mean in the course of a life. And it will mean a lot, the boy
knows. He is convinced that an utterly essential, maybe crucial, part of himself is something he describes with the phrase
"banker's son." He is not being matter-of-fact; he is trying to
tell how much of his mental life has become connected to his
father's position.

The constraints the boy has learned with respect to money
are especially significant; they would be mind-boggling for
millions of other children, who would not understand a boy
when he talks of the need for being "careful" with the hundreds of thousands of dollars he will inherit — to the point of
having another person "manage carefully" not only one's investments but (later on) one's day-to-day spending habits.
There is a wariness about the world that informs much of the

boy's perceptions — almost as though one has to be exceptionally on guard, because the entire economic fabric of the society might collapse. Like the poor or the working-class families I have worked with, the well-to-do and the quite rich keep harkening back to the Depression — sometimes more insistently than those far more vulnerable. At times the boy (and he is not alone) talks as if he is, or might well soon be, poor. He also talks as if he will never really be wise enough to know how to work his way through a financial maze: the ups and downs, opportunities and dangers, of the stock market.

A child of twelve may have heard his parents say that they, too, don't know a lot, will never know what they would need to know if they were to be "on their own." But that is the point — and what certain children get to believe: one is not "free" or "independent" (or on one's own) when it comes to money. One has to ask for help, and be prepared to take it. If one doesn't, disaster is a possibility, maybe a likelihood. A child who lives in Westport, Connecticut, and summers in Nantucket and winters on the slopes of the Colorado or Utah Rocky Mountains or else the island of Captiva off the western coast of southern Florida was apprehensive enough at the age of eleven to worry, during a relatively minor setback in her father's economic fortunes (one bad stock market investment), that she would soon be "poor," because her father would be "in trouble," and his trust officer would be giving him rather stern lectures. Such a child learns the limits of her future self-confidence, and the importance of relying upon others for counsel all through one's life. And paradoxically, such a child can grow up feeling not only apprehensive about money, but in constant jeopardy.

No wonder idealistic impulses in such children are more than balanced by various considerations that have to be kept in mind. The girl just mentioned was a thoughtful but self-effacing person who felt frankly puzzled by contradictions of idealism she was shrewd enough to pick up. The more she applied her intelligence to the matter, the more frustrated she described herself as being: "Maybe when I'm sixteen, and old enough to have a big party, and dance half the night with my boyfriend, I'll know what to believe in. Or, maybe when I'm twenty-one and I've graduated from college and I've gone to see the trust officer and he's told me all about the money, and at last it's mine — maybe then. I don't think I'll ever really know what the right way to behave is — not when it comes to our servants, or the charities that come to you and they want a lot, and you can't give them everything, or there will be nothing left for you.

"I asked my mother once why we have all the food in the freezer and in the refrigerator and in the cabinets, and there are those people dying. You see them on television. They are the majority, the man said — most of the people on this planet. He said we throw away more than most people eat every day. That sounded bad. I asked Mother why it's like that. She was mad with our governess, because we weren't supposed to be watching that program or any other program like it. My mother says it's terrible, to sit and watch all that sad news. She says you get 'morbid.' My father says it's always been true, for thousands of years, that there are a lot of poor people, and they don't eat the right kind of food, and they eat a lot of potato chips and drink Cokes all day, and that's no good for you. According to the Bible, the poor will go to Heaven. Daddy says not all the poor will go there; only the *good* poor, just like the good rich. Christ didn't want people to look down on the poor, so he promised them Heaven, but not if they are lazy, or they don't try to take good care of themselves and lift themselves up. Then they are being bad, and they won't go to Heaven. Then they are in trouble.

"My father said he didn't want my sister or my brother or me to look at any more of those news programs; and if the governess lets us, we should tell him, and he'll fire her. I think he warned her, because she has cut down on all television, even the good programs we used to watch all the time. She says it's my parents' orders. On television you see people you don't see in real life. There are a lot of crooks, and the police have dangerous jobs. They talk different on television, and you wonder if there are people who are like the ones you see. My brother wants to be a cop, but he'll give up the idea. It's no fun, chasing crooks all day. This would be a much better country if we didn't have crooks. They shouldn't let a lot of people have guns. There are bad people around, and they hold up people and stores. But Daddy has a rifle, and he uses it when he goes hunting. He says that the robbers would get guns even if there was a law that said they have to get permission, before they bought a gun. That's the trouble: there are the nice people, and all they want to do is go hunting, and have a gun in case a robber comes near the property; and there are the robbers, and they don't pay any attention to anyone, and they ignore all the laws, and it doesn't make any difference what they're *supposed* to do. They do what they feel like doing.

"A lot of people are like that. My mother says that the trouble with this country is that people are becoming soft; they want a lot of things, but they're not going to work as hard as they should to get them. They want jobs. But do they really try hard on the jobs? They want things for nothing. But do they know that you can't get something for nothing? There has to be *someone* who pays for everything. It's getting so that the people who work hardest and make the most money end up paying for everything, and the people who want to loaf all day end up expecting to get anything they want just by snapping their fingers. If it keeps on being like that, you won't see many people with any money left, and then the country will fall apart, because there will be millions and millions of loafers, and the ones who don't loaf won't have any money left, because of taxes."

What she says about millions of others she has heard said about herself too. When she has been lazy or sloppy, left her room disorderly, failed to dress neatly, forgotten to feed her hamsters, neglected her horse's currying, omitted an evening of violin practice, her mother or father has called her to account, cautioned her lest she become a "loafer." And she has also been told that she, too, seems to expect virtually everything as a right, rather than a privilege. It is a distinction many privileged parents constantly make — the difference between, in her father's words, "having something because it is yours, no matter how you behave, and having something because you belong to a good family and are willing to live up to its ideals."

Precisely what are those "ideals"? The girl can recite them as well as — maybe better than — her father. One must be orderly, neat, properly active in sports, and reasonably able in schoolwork. One must look appealing. One must know how to get along with a maid, a gardener, a man who does odd jobs, be polite yet not overly friendly; able and willing to issue instructions without demonstrating a crude and self-defeating kind of authority. One must be cordial but finally aloof — not only with the "help" or the "staff" but also with a lot of other people: storekeepers, town employees, and yes, schoolteachers. The girl remembers that when she was nine she wanted her mother to invite an especially friendly and likable fourth-grade teacher home for supper. No, that would not "work," the mother had to say. The child wanted to hear the reasons. The mother would not elucidate, told the child to shut up and change the subject. The child eventually did, of course

— though not before telling her mother that she was a "snob." The mother wanted an explanation. The child gave one: "I told my mother that if the teacher was rich, we'd have her over."

We came across similar dilemmas in the previous chapter — social class and its bearing on education. Here the point is social class and ethical conflict — as in the familiar reconciliation that girl had with her mother: "You have to think of the other person. It can be hard for people to come to supper, if they don't know most of the people. The teacher would only know me. She would feel she had to come, because she was invited, but she might not really want to come. You can't be selfish. I like the teacher. I'd like to teach one day. My mother does volunteer work at the school and at a hospital. I'd like to be helpful to others, when I'm grown up. My mother says a good volunteer program can make all the difference at a school or a hospital. You can't interfere with the teachers, or with the doctors and nurses. You're there to be of help. But you can't let them push you around, either. They've got to know that you are a *volunteer*.

When she talks about the tact a volunteer needs — really the velvet glove that covers a fist of iron — she reveals how attentively she has watched and listened and absorbed an entire social ethic: *noblesse oblige*. There are variations of that ethic, of course. In that regard, everything is tone. One can brusquely try to help others, and care little for them, only for the experience of looking down upon the helpless or the weak — thereby gaining a sense of personal strength and confirming any number of prejudices about those in need of "help." One can be tender and giving with people; glad to offer a skill, eager to lend an open hand. Those who receive such assistance feel better for it, not used and abused, or the targets of condescension. The girl quoted above has never been *told* all of that;

she has absorbed in her heart an unwritten message, made it part of her "being." That is, her response to the sick she visits upon occasion with her mother — the way she feels toward them and the way she moves toward them when near their hospital beds — indicates a natural, spontaneous spirit of thoughtfulness and compassion.

The girl even thought of being a nurse for a while, but changed her mind. If she did so because she was gently persuaded that someone of her background had "other opportunities," as her mother did indeed put it, there was also an element of genuine self-doubt at work, in turn the consequence of considerable admiration for nurses, who are so crisply efficient, yet warm and supportive. And too, the girl wondered if she would be able to make the kind of commitment a nurse makes.

It is true that some privileged children do end up quarreling dramatically with their own past. It is also true that some young children show early signs of a later political or cultural rebelliousness. Still, it is not easy, and maybe it is impossible, to make any kind of precise or safely predictive connections between an elementary school child's self-assertiveness, say, and an eventual ideological disenchantment or rupture with parental values. Anna Freud has warned repeatedly that clinical observations of children, sustained over many years, prove only how hard it is to prophesy. One child's independence, even pattern of disobedience or outright defiance, sets the stage for a youth's strict conformity; another child's quiet acceptance of most instructions, and apparently happy willingness to go along, no questions asked, with a given kind of life, is but a prelude, it seems, to years of intense, critical questioning and even overt truculence: the radical young man or woman of relatively wealthy background who has turned, not rarely with a vengeance, on everything associated with his or her "class."

In many of the homes I have visited there are precious few mixed feelings about the quite privileged way of life enjoyed — or, at least, mixed feelings that seem of significance to the child. The mixed feelings that this chapter is meant to document, yes; a number of parents let their children know that they should be considerate of others, even rather idealistic — up to a point. One is charitable, but not masochistic. One gives, but keeps a lot too. One worries about others, but also about oneself. One tries to do good works, but there is a life to be lived, a way of life to preserve. One curbs oneself — if for no other reason than to live longer; but there are many pleasures available and they require time, energy, and a spirited justification.

Sometimes that justification stops short of turning into an apologia; becomes instead an effort to weigh the ethical importance of different courses of action. A child whose father owns a mine wonders whether the miners' safety isn't important — just at the moment when his father announces a trip to an especially good ski resort, where the slopes aren't too steep, icy, and dangerous. A child whose father owns a large tract of fruit and vegetable producing land, on which work hundreds of agricultural migrants, wonders whether a balanced diet isn't important for those migrants and their children — just at the time when his mother announces the prospect of an evening out at a swank restaurant with a large menu and a reputation for the best cooking around. A child whose father owns a lot of urban real estate, some of it working-class three-deckers and some of it ghetto blocks, wonders whether her parents ought not keep the thermostat down in their seventeen-room home, including six baths — just as her mother declares how wasteful "a lot of people" are with food, how much heat they require in "a lot of apartment houses." But those children are not likely to submit willingly to no vacations, restricted diets, chilly homes. They may want a lot for others, may even, as in the last instance, be willing to deprive themselves a little, but they know also how to complete a statement that begins with "This is what I like to do," or "This is what I would like to do."

Those particular sentences were given a class of fifth graders in a private school in the most distant suburbs of Boston. The children in the school belong to parents who are called, in newspaper accounts of the town, "high-income" or "upper-income" or "socially prominent," or sometimes, quite simply, "rich." The teacher had been anxious to get the children "going." Whatever they decided to offer as a completion to her inviting sentences was satisfactory to her. But, in fact, she was not unaware that the "answers" were of interest, and revealing. Boys wrote that they liked to ski, hunt, go to the Caribbean or Europe; girls wrote that they too liked skiing, international traveling, and riding rather than hunting. But one child of ten, a girl not really in any observable way different from her classmates, or of a family all that distinguishable from its neighbors, had this to say: "This is what I would like to do: be poor so that I could go to Heaven, but be rich, so that I could live the way I do, and not be poor. No one wants to be poor. If you are poor, you can't help it, I guess. If you are rich, you would mind a lot being poor."

I wanted to hear more from that girl. She made no bones about her preferring to reconcile her various hopes through living a life rather than through introspective analysis. She could tolerate in herself a touch of the latter, but only enough to justify a bike ride, a horse ride, a trip downtown with friends or family for a purchase or two. On her eleventh birthday she commented on what she "likes to do," as her teacher put it: "I'm always riding, and I'm always going on trips. I wish my father didn't like to travel. Then we could stay home during school vacations, and I could look out of the window and watch the pheasants. I like to do that more than anything else in the world.

"I think of the birds around our house a lot when I'm walking the dog, or riding. I don't mind riding alone. I prefer to go out on the trails alone. I like to walk. What I like about the pheasants — well, they are pretty, and they like to move fast, and they like the woods. So do I. I told my mother that I wanted to learn to run, like my older brother does. He's at Yale. He's a fast runner. He's on a team, I think. He goes like lightning. My father jogs, but my brother runs. He says we live too fancy here. He says he's embarrassed to bring people home. He has a roommate from Pennsylvania, and his father is a coal miner down there. My brother heard me talking about my horse and the pheasants, and he got all upset. He asked me to go for a walk, and he said I should stop and realize that there are a lot of people in the world who don't eat as well as the pheasants do, or my horses. I told him I would give my allowance to those people. But where are they? He said I'd have to go a far way to find them! I asked him if he would take me, and he said no. There isn't anything *I* can do to change the world. He said he'd like to change the world, but he didn't know what *he* could do, either. I think he'd like to bring that friend of his, that roommate, home, only he's ashamed. I heard my father say that when *he* was at Yale they didn't mix up all kinds of different kids. I wouldn't mind living with someone poor. I wish I could. My mother and father have told me all my life that I'm lucky, and that if I was born somewhere else, and my parents didn't have any money, then I'd be in trouble. I'm sure my parents are right. But I'd like to have a roommate who's poor, like my brother has. He says his eyes are always being opened; and I'd like to have my eyes opened, too."

Her words on paper inevitably come across as more frivolous, patronizing, and insensitive than they were meant or than they sound. Her brother, ten years older, started Yale as a political conservative, a first-rate soccer player, a future major in economics, with a business career in mind. He never really changed his political ideas or his idea of what he wanted to "do" or "be," but he did become, in his own words, "more aware of what other people are like"; and the sister noticed the change, began to wonder how she might emulate him in that respect. There was no way for her to do so. One morning her country day school received ghetto children — the beginning of a monthly Saturday visit for those children. The girl asked why she and a few of her friends couldn't come over and be hosts and hostesses. She was told that the visits were taking place on a Saturday, when there was "no school" — and besides, it was "hard" for children who are "different" to get on without "careful preparation," and the point was to give the ghetto children "a good time" and not cause them any "pain" or "embarrassment." The girl remembered her brother's remarks — his feeling of "shame" at the prospect of bringing a college roommate home. She told her mother, but the mother pointed out with patience and concern that those ghetto children would feel far more comfortable if left alone.

The girl "understood." She "understands" rather more than her parents and teachers may at times fully realize — and (at the risk of our condescension) a bit more, perhaps, than she herself realizes about the significance and implications of the class structure in America. She has come to sense that the phenomenon of class is real, is important, is influential in its effect upon everyone — but has to be talked about gingerly. She has felt herself almost in the presence of a shadowy figure: the class system and its discontents.

She did say a few things a few weeks after the "Saturday Program for Inner City Children," as it was called, got under way; and her words are very much like those of other children of her background and not all that different from those of her Yale brother: "I guess it wouldn't be good to bring us together with the poor kids on Saturday. My parents are right. If we just showed up, after a while we would start to play. I just know it. It would be awkward if some of us went on Saturday and met the kids from the city, but I'll bet that if we thought in advance about what we'd do, and if we tried to be nice, and came up with some games, and started to play them, and acted friendly — then the city kids would relax and they'd play and it wouldn't be so tense after a while. You have to give kids some credit.

"My brother says that he wonders sometimes why they put him and his roommate together. Even if they do get along together now, they're going to be headed in different directions after they graduate. They don't have any friends in common even now. If we went to our school on Saturdays and played with the city kids, I don't think it would make too much difference to them. I think we'd like it. We'd feel better. But they might feel worse. They might not like us. They might wish they had a lot of the things we have. It's better not to know the people you don't like — or the people who live better than you do. That's how I'd feel if I was poor. We drove by the school last Saturday, and I asked my Dad to stop for a second, so that I could look and see. The city kids were running all over the place. It was like they were in their own neighborhood. The trouble is, I heard, that they broke a lot of equipment, and they ruined the lawn."

A year later, at twelve, she would be less inclined even to try spending a few hours with "them." She was immersed in the quickening momentum of her own life. There is just so much time any of us has, just so many claims for its attention that the mind can honor. In a child like her, the issue may not be callousness, selfishness, or ignorance, but rather an absorption in a succession of days. A social observer with a critical eye can find hypocrisy and greed aplenty, but for the child there is what the girl just quoted referred to, upon becoming thirteen and a bona fide "teenager," as "a lot of fun." She was saying that she had much to do, see, hear, feel, experience, learn, enjoy. She was not quite flooded with "stimuli," but she was, in her mother's apt description, "living a full, full life."

There is just so much room in a child's heart for compassion toward others burdened by problems never actually seen, or heard personally described. When a moment of reflection has come, or when a crisis has prompted uncertainty, sadness, and worry, I have heard these quite fortunate boys and girls remark regretfully upon their own provinciality, their lack of awareness, their all too self-preoccupied days. Not with tears, and not with outrage, and not with shame or guilt, but with regret — perhaps an all too self-assured response — that there is a side of life that ordinarily escapes their notice and confronts them only suddenly, dramatically, often through their parents' anguished or agitated talk.

A child whose father's mine exploded wondered why he had never been told that "such an awful thing can happen." A child whose father's agricultural workers, ten of them, were killed or badly hurt in an awful highway collision — the men herded in a pickup truck like cattle — asked why there wasn't "a car pool" like the one she enjoyed twice a day; and why too she had never even seen those pickup trucks or the migrants who travel in them. A child whose father owned a lot of urban property wondered why so many fires take place in the city, and none, it seems, in her town, and why (after six people, including four children, had died in a city fire) there were "all those bad stories about the owner" in the paper. The owner was a corporation, in which her father was an office holder. The more the girl expressed interest in the matter, the more her father told her to mind her own business. Since she was only ten, she did. The other children just mentioned learned to do likewise, even if less brusquely admonished. Of course, no child ever completely obliges his or her parents. There are dreams, passing thoughts, occasional moments of interest, more active curiosity, even a prying kind of inquiry. But the mine owner's child spoke for many others when she observed that "you're not supposed to get everyone in the family more upset than they already are, and if you do, there will be trouble, and even if you find out what was wrong, there isn't anything you can do."

She has learned to be rather plucky, assertive, and confident about other issues or matters of interest. She has pressed her parents hard with questions about sports (including the nature of and reasons for the Olympics), about clothes, about manners — why is some behavior "good" and other behavior "bad"? — and even about war and peace. She has learned to hold her tongue as well as to use it — exercising, one comes to realize, the principle of enlightened self-interest.

Not all enlightenment is of the explicit, rationally stated, and thoroughly analyzed variety. There are many children, and maybe as many grown-ups, who have come by a rather coherent and sensitive estimate of one of those "social ideologies" Dr. Helene Deutsch mentioned when writing about the "ego ideal." America's "social ideology" was all too briefly described by the girl whose father owned Appalachian mines: "Try to be nice to everyone, but look after yourself, because if you don't, you'll have nothing to look after, and then you'll be in trouble." She knew not only the virtues of caution, but the dangers of loss. She knew exactly how much "idealism" would be sufficient, how much "pragmatism" always had to be kept in mind, kept ready for use. Her parents often called her "sensible," and there is no reason to believe that other parents like them would in any way argue with the judgment.

PART NINE

WHAT PROFIT UNDER THE SUN?

HOW DOES one compare the psychological side of the lives of various children: lives different one from the other by virtue of fate or family circumstance, of wealth or poverty, of race, of residence in a particular region? How does one compare the various "crises" children go through — a boy's struggle with the consequences of poverty or racial prejudice as against a rich boy's struggle with a self-centered, possessive parent who is lavish with gifts but unyielding with demands? How does one compare suffering — a migrant girl's effort, against enormous odds, to find some place, or objects that signify constancy, in contrast with another girl's wish that for at least once her corporation executive father will stay put for more than a year or two, so that she won't be moving, always moving, from suburb to suburb? How does one compare nightmares, those most private moments in a child's mental life: the nightmares of a black child from the Delta of Mississippi, crammed with fear and resentment of the white man, versus the intense fears and resentments and nightmares of a white child from the upper-income countryside well to the west or north of Boston? How can anyone really presume to place side-by-side the nightmares of a sharecropper's child with those of a bank president's — nightmares that anticipate a lifetime of arbitrary exclusion and brutal exploitation versus nightmares that reflect the pressure of a millionaire for his offspring to do well in a country day school? Perhaps it is best to move away from bad dreams and into broad daylight. Surely there is quite a difference between, on the one hand, an Indian girl, sick in body but not being treated, hungry, but with an inadequate diet, sad and forlorn out of the knowledge that her people, and she as one of them, have no prospects at all, and on the other hand, a girl who lives in a wealthy suburb, who is trying very hard to lose weight so that she can be a better rider, a more agile skier, and, not least, a more appealing girl in the eyes of her parents and their friends. But how does one *measure* that difference? Ought we to try to quantify "levels" of anxiety or fear, as expressed in response to Rorschach cards or those that go to make up the Thematic Apperception Test? Might it be useful to examine what I heard called, when I was a resident in child psychiatry, "interview protocols," in the hope that they reveal differential intensities of "affect"?

There are indeed measurable variations in the depth and range of psychological pain that children experience. Certainly clinicians — pediatricians in one way, child psychiatrists in another — know that some children are quite troubled, and say so, whereas other children at least say that they feel just fine. Why, though, use that modifying phrase "at least"? We have learned in this century to have our reservations about the merely apparent, to equate it often with the superficial. Yet if all surfaces are misleading, or at best a reflection of more important psychological truths (namely, what goes on below or deep down, to use the everyday clinical imagery), then all appearances are suspect — whether the expression of contentment or the assertion of a complaint.

Some children, we know, only *seem* to be cheerful and at peace with themselves. Catch them at an unguarded moment,

or again, hear them in their sleep, tossing and turning, shouting and crying in the midst of a bad dream or a nightmare that
makes them sleepwalk or wet the bed or rush to parents in
explicit terror, and the hidden psychological reality of their
lives appears. Other children, paradoxically, have learned to
summon and use adroitly, manipulatively, an array of psychological complaints, even outright clinical symptoms. The leg-
endary child who cries wolf once too often is not only a boy
who says he is hurt because he wants attention, or a girl who
has learned to get out of a chore by complaining of an ache,
but all too often these days a canny young psychologist who
has discovered that at home or at school a display of apprehension, of well-timed tearfulness or fear, will earn wonders of
attention and "understanding" — and maybe a few previously
denied opportunities, previously forbidden gratifications. Of
course, one has to acknowledge that such a child is even more
troubled than he or she knows — else why the pretense, the
contrived call for consideration, if not special regard? Carry
that line of reasoning just a few steps further, however, and a
malingerer, a truant, a delinquent is "sick," and a petulant,
spoiled child, always complaining, and always getting off one
or another hook, is also "sick."

As for the child who smiles a lot, eats and sleeps well, keeps
busy, claims to enjoy hobbies, activities, friends — in sum,
"life" — what may "really" be going on, a doctor might wonder, or a teacher, not to mention a social or educational critic.
Whistling in the dark? Crass insensitivity to the plight of others? Craven smugness? A child's version of "I'm all right,
Jack"? Or a normal, so-called developmental stage of childhood being experienced and observed in full display? And
what about the child who shows compassion for others, a concern for human suffering, a constant worry about the world's
serious problems — what ought we to make of him or her? Are

we in the presence of a neurotic, whose own serious suffering has precociously prompted social awareness? Is the child responding to an especially thoughtful and sensitive home life? Conversely, is the child reacting against a callous and self-serving upbringing — generosity and mercy toward others as a form of rebellion, or as reaction-formations, a means by which rather egotistical children can parade a new psychological makeup, much to the confusion, even the anger, of their parents? As child psychiatrists find out from time to time, even a boy or girl brought up in a home much dominated by liberal or radical politics can become troublesome in his or her inclination toward self-sacrifice on behalf of others. When does seemly kindness or extension of the "self" toward others turn into an "unrealistic" or damaging renunciation of one's own future — or "masochism"?

In the topsy-turvy world of child psychiatry it is hard to come up with consistent or unqualified answers to the foregoing questions — often, embarrassingly enough, asked by children themselves. It is no secret that parents and teachers often shrug their shoulders in response to some pointed inquiry from a particular child, or tell that child that enough is enough. As I look back at my two decades of work with all kinds of American children, I realize that it has been a history, rather too often, of questions asked of me, but not given serious attention (questions I ignored in favor of my own questions, which of course I expected to be promptly answered). A child of migrant farm workers wants to know why there aren't "a lot of grownups" who are willing to fight a grower unto death, and I am ready to take an interest in why the child asks that question, and why the child has one or another view of herself, and what the child sees ahead as a likely future — but I never really address myself to the given question put to me, perhaps because I don't think I have the answer or don't dare answer what I know full well.

If I were to answer the child directly I would still wonder why such-and-such a child, at a certain point in her life, and in the course of an "involvement" with me, should come up with *that* question. Is it a straightforward pursuit of knowledge, or is my presence tempting the child to be difficult, shy, hostile, suspicious, challenging, provocative, and all the other nonclinical words many clinicians use in the service of our psychological appraisals of children? And if such a question from a migrant child may strike even the most experienced of clinicians, after years of contact with "case-material," as a matter of genuine inquiry, quite able to stand on its own merits, rather than to be interpreted psychodynamically, then what does one do with the question of a bank president's child: why don't "a lot of grown-ups" (again!) try to take away from the rich and give the plunder to the poor?

Too much Robin Hood on television — that was my discreet answer when I heard such a question asked years ago. And in fact I had watched that program repeatedly with the child — a good way to spare both of us awkward silences at the start of our stretch of time spent together. I was made much more uncomfortable by the migrant child's question, because I was sure that the child was sick and tired of my efforts to find out how her sad, unruly life was going. The mother had told me that the girl was difficult to control, combative, testy, given to tearful explosions out of the blue, or moods of glowering silence. I wanted to know why. It was easier to search for hidden psychological explanations of "behavior" than answer the quite reasonable question put to me by the child — a question that has psychological merit. Why *do* so many of us stand by and watch others being exploited, hurt badly, made to suffer? As for the bank president's child, I noticed that he wondered about the disparity between the rich and the poor after hearing not only Robin Hood's words on television but also his father's angry outburst in the dining room: a new branch bank would be opened soon, no matter what the trouble with the city's building codes.

The web of psychological determinism touches and to a degree affects or constrains all of us, certainly including the social critic or psychological observer, whether psychoanalyzed or not, whether trained in psychiatry or investigative journalism or responsive to a tradition that would include the work of James Agee and George Orwell. If it is those "unconscious factors" that make an irritable, especially truculent migrant child rail against nameless "grown-ups" for their lack of compassion and political activism; and if it is those same "factors" that prompt a banker's son to speak out — only for a single moment in his life — indirectly but persuasively on behalf of the poor, then what causes a research-minded child psychiatrist to listen to those children in such a way that the "manifest content" (as it is put at clinical conferences) is given less attention than a presumed "underlying symbolic purpose"? One falls back on clinical knowledge, on years of "training," on a personal psychoanalysis and the experiences it generated; one has an intuitive hunch, or a not-to-be-challenged doctor's conviction that when a child says x, there is y in the background, in the foreground, in the psychological "context." The migrant child was angry at her strong-minded mother, but ended up accusing other grown-ups. The banker's son resented his father, but could express that rebellious discontent only through a Robin Hood "fantasy."

Meanwhile, a given child has no intention of being so sure of himself or herself, or so quick to figure out what is happening within another's head. Or else the child is indeed anxious to employ guile, resort to cunning, use indirection. Here is that migrant child talking about a schoolteacher, rather than a child psychiatrist: "If you say anything to him, he is likely to correct your language; he doesn't pay any attention to what you're saying. Sometimes he hears you all right, but he doesn't hear what you want to say. He hears what he's afraid the principal will hear. He hears the principal, more than you — he hears the principal getting ready to say: 'You're fired.'" Not bad for a twelve-year-old "child"; but then, she had been mostly working in the fields since she was six, a full half of her life, with school an occasional and quite unsettling, insulting, humiliating, disruptive experience — a month now, a few weeks then. She had learned the score, though her score on one aptitude test after another was consistently low.

As for the banker's child, he was indeed, for a while, all taken up with Robin Hood "fantasies." He drew numerous pictures of Little John, of Robin, of "companions," as the book called them, who assisted in a task the boy was quite willing to cast in a certain "relevance" to our own, American situation, much to the chagrin of the teacher for whom the following composition was written: "When I am twice as old as I am now, I'll be twenty-four. I might try being like Robin Hood, but I don't think I could win, like he did. I'd be arrested. It's good to help the poor, but the rich don't want to lose their money. They have it, and it's theirs. A lot of rich people are selfish, really selfish. My sister says I won't give her my allowance money, so I'm not really like Robin Hood, and I'm selfish. But she's not poor! If Robin Hood came to our town, I'd offer to join his side. It's not fair that a few have millions of dollars, and most people don't have much of anything. My father says I'll change my mind later. He says he wouldn't let me take the side of a man who thought he was above the law. My father studied law, before he joined the bank. He's the head of the United Fund this year. My mother said he's being like Robin Hood. He's getting people to give money to the people who don't have it. I gave a dollar of my allowance money to the United Fund. My father said even my sister and I should give a little. It's good to give."

So it goes — back and forth from a radical activist creed to the self-congratulatory pieties of the wealthier suburban life. The teacher gave the boy an A, told him that she agreed "it's good for each of us to do what we can for others." As for Robin Hood and his merry peasant-socialist men, they may for a time provoke difficult moments, embarrassing questions or remarks, but even an exceptionally idealistic child is likely to "outgrow" the political and economic message of Sherwood Forest. If there is to be a redistribution of wealth, let the haves choose when, where, how much, and to whom. Anyone who has other ideas had best watch out. But watch out for what? This particular child for a month or two almost learned the answer. His parents began asking themselves, and eventually their pediatrician, questions of their own. Why was the child taking Robin Hood so seriously? Ought they to stop him from viewing the program? If so, what should they give as a reason? Do other children go through such a "stage"? Was there something "wrong" with him, with them as parents? Had they, in other words, made some ill-advised comment that set in motion a wave (at least they felt it was such) of rather critical and "inappropriate" social and economic observations — surely not "typical" of what boys of eleven or twelve "ordinarily" come up with? And finally, was there something that could be done — someone who would be able to "help"? The boy's teacher recommended waiting. She was not unaware of the "problem." She had read and commented on his various compositions. She had heard him talk during recesses. But she knew — so did the doctor — that children "outgrow" a number of preoccupations that develop, out of nowhere, it seems, and then disappear somewhere for good. If such an outcome did not take place in a year or so, there would be plenty of time to worry.

Eventually the boy abandoned his interest in Robin Hood, even as the migrant girl stopped even questioning the status quo, never mind thinking up ways it might be altered to the point of paying migrant workers a half-decent wage. I will never know how effectively she removed from her consciousness a revolutionary thought or two. When I knew her best, talked with her most (1963–1965) I didn't think to ask her questions that might have given me a clue about the ways she and other children deal with any number of economic or political ideas. Would the girl or the boy really "outgrow" their respective moments of social protest, or "repress" them, or simply learn or choose to keep some thoughts quiet? Was there no point trying to discuss issues that had ceased to interest those children? Or was the "problem" more mine than theirs? That is, was *I* the one who wanted to ignore or forget about certain subjects, if not "repress" them?

A great deal is made of the patient's "transference-neurosis," and yes, the "countertransference" that even the most knowing and well-analyzed of psychiatrists develops. In the case of work with children, those responses are sometimes quite vivid and explicit. A child may not even need an "interpretation" or "clarification," may realize full well, early on, that the doctor is getting the kind of attention one or both parents usually receive. As for the child psychiatrist, he has spent years preparing for such developments — lest a child's affections or animosities be taken all too personally, in which case "therapy" becomes, alas, a game of blindman's buff. But unfortunately, those words "transference" and "countertransference" have not been given quite their due. What is happening to a migrant farm worker's daughter when she looks askance at teachers or a doctor well stocked with toys, crayons, paper — or at a grower and his foreman? Is she afraid for rational reasons, of which she is consciously aware? Is she hearing and responding to opinions supplied by her father — who in drunken fits of despair regularly curses the entire white, middle-class world? Or have those grown-ups become feared and resented not because of what they have actually done to that girl, but because they have come to be associated in her mind with the bitter and sometimes dangerous outbursts of her father? His alcoholic tirades have frightened all the children, have sometimes been violent in nature. He is regarded as a volatile, unpredictable person by his daughter; and it is surely no great psychological jump from him to those he denounces but characterizes as dangerous, wily, and threatening.

As a doctor tries to understand a child's mind, surely there are just as many questions for him to ask. If the girl has good reason to fear her father, and if the girl's mother is melancholy, aloof, the victim of extreme suspicions that even descend upon her children (they are set to destroy her, she has believed for a spell or two), then it is near madness in a family that deserves all possible scrutiny. But madness caused by what? An impoverished black migrant family is under the most serious of social and economic strains. Each grown-up, each child carries an awful psychological burden, the dimensions and subtleties of which require close and careful documentation. It turned out in fact that the girl had other reasons to feel as she did about growers, about our economic system, besides those prompted by her father's drunken tirades. She may have hated him, linked him in her mind to the growers. But she also knew what the concrete behavior of those growers meant, so far as her life was concerned. In fact, she died when only twelve of untreated pneumonia. I was up North at the time; she was on her way South, after the long annual northerly trek.

I will never be able to find out what went through her mind afterward. But I did come to know her sister, younger by a year. One day in 1973, when she was seventeen and herself a migrant farm worker and two times a mother, she told me this: "I know how I used to feel when I was younger. I hated the growers. I hated them with all my heart. I hated the teachers and the foremen and the police and the gas station people; I hated everyone white, and I hated the crew leaders, our own black bossmen. My father didn't hate them *enough.* I hated him for getting drunk and *telling* us he hated them, instead of staying sober and trying to kill them. That's what my sister and I used to ask each other when we were kids: why doesn't Daddy go and get a gun and shoot them? Why don't all of us go and take away the money from all of them? There are more of us than there are them. There are way, way more poor people in the world than there are rich. There always have been more poor people, and there always will be; that's what the priest says, and he's right.

"A lot of the time I used to hate him, too. He'd come and smile at us; and we'd see him going to the growers, and they'd give him a hundred dollars, and he'd bow before them and kiss their feet. I wonder what Jesus Christ thinks of all this! If He came here, I'll bet He'd tell the rich off. He might take the land away from the growers and let us try to make a living on it. But I can't talk like that in front of my kids. They can't hear you saying those things. When Daddy got drunk and upset, he'd scare my sister and me. We knew he was right. We got angry with him for talking cheap but doing nothing. My mother used to say his talk was as cheap as the wine he drank. I remember my sister saying the same thing. Now they're both dead, and Daddy, too. I don't want my kids to think I'm a coward. There's not very much we can do here; the growers and the sheriffs, they're always together, and they have the guns. You have to teach your kids to know that. They'll end up in jail or dead if you don't. The sheriff, he'll just push you in the irrigation ditch and pull you out an hour later and say you were drunk and fell in. That's what happens to troublemakers around here who try to stand up for the poor man."

It did not take me a decade to learn that migrants are the most vulnerable, endangered, and impoverished of this nation's people. But it did take that long, and longer, for me even to begin appreciating the blunter emotions felt by migrant children, never mind the nuances of their psychological life. And it took me longer to acknowledge the dignity of that psychological life — the considerable social awareness, the political savvy, the powers of economic analysis demonstrated by these "culturally deprived" or "disadvantaged" children, from homes full of tension and turmoil. Yes, their tension and that turmoil require documentation. But so do their lucidity and penetrating acuity of vision.

More recently, in connection with the work done in well-to-do suburbs, the same kind of difficulty has come up, only too gradually appreciated by me. The boy who carried on a love affair with Robin Hood had a better fate than the migrant girl or her sister: he survived, prospered, became in time a Yale student interested in maritime law. I assumed for years that Robin Hood was but one of many passing fancies that he had at a certain moment in his life. Exactly why did the banker's son put to rest his interest in Robin Hood? Did he even, as a matter of fact, do so?

Yes and no; he certainly stopped watching the television program after some eight months. His parents never told him outright to do so, but they did begin to suggest that there were "better things" to see: "Nova," for instance, with its fine expositions of scientific issues. Why dwell interminably on a story meant to amuse "young children" when there is something aimed at "older children"? The boy responded, of course. He was a sturdy, athletic youth, as anxious as anyone to "grow up." It's time to "pay more attention to what the world is really like." That last statement was made by the boy's father in connection with Robin Hood, and was quite enough, it turned out, to assist in the "psychological maturation" of yet another American child.

Soon thereafter, the boy was wondering whether, in fact, there ever had been someone named Robin Hood, or whether he was a legend, pure and simple. He wondered whether there was a small core, at the most, of actuality enclosed in a persisting myth. And finally, he began to think his former hero a bit self-serving and dramatic — out to take care of himself as well as the needy. That way of seeing Robin Hood did not come to the boy spontaneously. One of his teachers gently but pointedly made a suggestion, in response to a composition — one ought "think a little" about Robin Hood's dramatic, adventuresome side. Did he "use" people in order to show off? Was he "really" interested in changing the world around him?

The boy threw in the towel rather quickly. So did some of his friends. He did his best to forget the Sherwood Forest struggles, became immersed instead in "Gilligan's Island." No one objected to that switch of interest. His father even joined him on some evenings. The program was funny. Life is too serious these days. So many people have forgotten how to sit back and laugh. Of course, Gilligan was a protester in a way; he was trying to get people to stop being so harsh and grim, to start smiling, relaxing, forgetting about "a whole mess of troubles no one can do anything about, anyway."

Next came a thought or two of the mother's, expressed in her own kind of personal questions: "I don't know what to say to my children about the world. They ask me why there are poor people, or why black people aren't liked by white people, and I draw a blank. I ask them questions back, I guess. I ask them whether they think anyone will ever be *all* nice. The children shake their heads. They know the answer is no. I ask them if they'd rather be in the best country in the world, even if it's not perfect, or in some other country where most people are much worse off than even our poor people here. The children hear me! I want my kids to feel sorry for others who are unlucky, or poor, or have black skin. But I don't want them thinking they have a lot of *answers*. There have been too many answers in my lifetime. We've oversold the government. We don't even know the right questions. I keep telling my children that they have to learn what to ask. That's why I thought we handled the whole Robin Hood business wrong. My husband didn't like the way the kids kept saying that they were going to 'be' Robin Hood! Robin Hood! And they said they would 'fight for the poor,' and 'take away from the rich.' He finally let the kids know that there are 'better' television programs. I would have said nothing. Children come up with a lot of things and forget them the next day. I just want my children to grow up so that they're open-minded; and they know how *complicated* everything is. Then they'll learn how to think carefully, and not go rushing toward some *answer*. Ask the right questions — that's what I keep telling them. I wish that Robin Hood had done more *thinking*. He was too infatuated with himself. I believe my son came to realize that!"

He did. A year later, two years later. He had become by then a promising student in the seventh grade who, in his teacher's words, "knows how to ask just the right question at the right moment." Still, some of the questions centered on the story of Robin Hood. Even when the boy was fourteen he wondered what would happen if someone like Robin Hood appeared on the American scene, and tried hard to change the United

States decisively — apply military action to the realm of politics. But he wondered about many other possibilities, too. He was constantly wondering, inquiring. He suggested alternatives rather than solutions. He acknowledged doubt. He proclaimed continuing confusion or, at best, uncertainty. He had achieved the tone, the spirit, his mother wanted.

He could still make his father nervous; he could still surprise his teachers. They would have preferred an end not only to mention of Robin Hood, but all the associated "involvements" — the poor, the black, the matter of "world hunger" — which for months caught the youth's attention. It was not until he was a junior at an old, respected New England college preparatory school that the boy signaled himself "safe" — by developing a consuming and, it has turned out, lasting interest in oceanography. He would later combine a career and a passionate hobby: maritime law. His parents were pleased. Had Robin Hood tried harder to figure out what his England was going through, his "adventures" might have been less personal, less quixotic, more significant. "True change" has to do with finding a way to make the country "richer," meaning more productive, hence with more to be spread around. So the young man would believe through school, through college and law school — until, at least, these words were being written and, one suspects, well beyond that time.

Nor would the migrant girl — the sister of the one who died young — turn into a fiery labor organizer or political activist. As indicated, the drift of her life was toward work and motherhood. Later, she would have to bear the anguish of a bad marriage. She grew to hate her husband. He was as drunken as her father. They worked together in the fields, sometimes had gigantic brawls over the pittance he got at the end of each day for the crops he picked — money he wanted to spend on rotgut wine. When she was as old as the rich boy was upon graduation from secondary school, she had two children. She looked ten, maybe fifteen, years his senior. Her hands, had a photographer like Dorothea Lange chosen to picture them, might have impressed the future Yale undergraduate as those of an elderly woman, maybe someone in her sixties. Like him, she came to terms with "life" and its terrible injustices. She learned to accept what she once said "had to be" — her life. She learned to teach her children that kind of acceptance.

When her children began to bother her with those disarming, simpleminded inquiries that require hours of anguished explication, she responded with a firm dismissal: some other time, when you are older. Once she asked her husband for advice. He called her a fool for asking. He might have been a grower, or a foreman, or a sheriff, she thought at first, when she heard his answer: there is no point in even asking such a question. He would not let the matter drop, however. He called her all sorts of names for being "stupid," for asking "stupid questions." He wanted to make her realize how impossibly hopeless their situation was, would always be. It was bad enough walking through the muck, kneeling all day in the muck, living in the muck — the shacks they lived in had no sanitation, no pavements; but to rub things in, to "throw muck" at her with his words, his half-drunken but shrewd and sad and enraging analytic comments, was more than she could take. She picked up his bottle of wine and smashed it — whereupon he went after her with a jagged piece of glass, stopped only inches short of her neck.

She would eventually call him "right": "I blame myself for not being as smart as my husband. He is a no-good drunk, but he is smarter than I will ever be. He sees things out of the corner of his eyes. He lies there on the floor and he thinks. I wish he would talk to me when he's thinking. Then I would know what to think myself! The only time I have for thinking is about four in the morning. That's when I get up. The sun is getting up, too. We have to be in the fields about five-thirty. I wonder what it would be like to be someone else. Why are we born to be ourselves, and not other people? My kids ask me questions like that. I remember having questions like that on my mind when I was a kid. Once I asked my mother whether I could turn white and become rich — if I agreed to die very young. I think I'd heard a fairy story, and in it the girl was told she could be anybody or get anything she wanted, so long as she agreed to die when she was very young.

"I can read my kids' minds. They don't even have to talk to me. I can tell when they're about ready to start crying and tell me that they're tired, and they don't have much hope left in them. I can tell when they wish they could have that lady Barbara Walters for a mother. They figure that she'd be able to give them everything, and I can give them nothing. They're right! That's what my husband told me. don't try to convince them that everything is going to be good later on. Don't tell them lies. Don't tell them we're going to change the world, and they're going to have a new life. Let the priest talk about 'a new life'; we're not going to have any life but this one, and that goes for our kids and their kids — not while we're here on this earth. That's what my kids have to know, and that's what I tell them.

"If they want to die, they can. I've told them that! Let me tell you, I have! I say to them: you can die if you want — anytime you get tired of this life, and you're all upset, and you realize you're never going to get the treats and favors and breaks you've been dreaming of and asking me about — anytime you want to end your life and go and check it out, Heaven, and see if it's there, and if the priest is right in what he says, *anytime,* you can die. I never can go on. I start to cry.

I hate those questions. I'd rather have my husband's fist in my face — even a piece of glass in my eye — than those questions from my children. It's the biggest relief of my life that they've stopped asking me what they did, before they were born, to be born to me! I felt like killing them and then myself when I heard them ask me *that* one for the first time! My husband said he could understand why they asked a question like that. He said he thinks up questions like that all the time when he's drinking his wine. I would drown myself in the irrigation ditch if that's what my mind did to me!"

An especially dramatic and, some doctors would insist, a somewhat hysterical woman, dangerously close to severe depression. Yet she struggles hard to make do, to bring up her children, even as the banker does. Both parents, assisted by their spouses, have earned a measure of "relief," as the migrant mother put it; have obtained from their children a reliable kind of compliance. The children in question came to that state of "understanding" without everyday prodding or formal, explicit instructions to do so. Even the desperate migrant mother found it easier to suggest suicide or threaten murder rather than sit down and talk in detail about the workings of a particular social and economic system — whose structure, whose limits and requirements she knew as well as any economist, political scientist, or sociologist. And maybe, too, she knew a lot about the psychology of child development; she had a parent's sense of pacing, timing — an awareness that a child can absorb the most awful realities and make them lifelong assumptions, if only the parent is willing and able to make it clear that there are indeed answers to the questions their children ask, answers that are sometimes best provided gradually, cautiously, implicitly — but if necessary, with overwhelming bluntness.

The migrant mother knew how to draw the line, end all doubts, portray a stark reality; the banker had his own way of making it clear that "The Adventures of Robin Hood" is a piece of fiction, and would have to remain just that — no inspiration for contemporary, heroic behavior. There was a critical moment in the boy's life when he asked what would happen if the Robin Hood on television started addressing himself to the condition of today's humble people. The father told him, abruptly, that the program would go off the air; then corrected himself: no such program would ever be shown in the 1 -st place. The boy objected; surely it was within the realm of possibility that a television producer would want to let American boys and girls know that Robin Hood's struggle is not unconnected to twentieth-century problems. The father got that message, saw it for a warning as well as a request for information, spoke out loud and clear, and a year afterward remembered what had taken place with a measure of "relief" akin to the migrant mother's, when she was able to take it for granted that her children were thoroughly resigned to being themselves, and no one else, for the duration of their earthly stay.

Both the banker and the migrant mother had come to terms with "life," with their ideological as well as practical responsibilities as parents. And in fact each had directed a child toward the utterly concrete "things of this world." A migrant child often has to start picking crops, alongside his or her parents, when six or seven. A banker's son has a lot of occasions to meet, opportunities to take advantage of, obligations to fulfill. I have tried to indicate some of the central elements in the daily lives of migrant children in the second volume of this series; I had best try to do likewise for the privileged children I have been presenting in these pages, and up to now have been trying to fathom psychologically, educationally, and ethically.

Best to start with just the point made by the banker — that his son had a lot to do. One sees the *busy* nature of the

lives such privileged children live. One sees it on the calendars
of their parents and, in many instances, by the age of eleven
or twelve on the calendars of the children themselves: ap-
pointments, times set aside, whole days bracketed or crossed
out, memoranda set down, reminders scribbled. I used to wonder how young migrant children could possibly learn to be so
efficient, so well organized out in those fields — so damnably
intent, hardworking, careful. The awful press of injustice upon
a child's all too "adaptive" mind, one decides with a certain
resignation of one's own. But the boys and girls whose words
appear in this book are no less agile, dedicated, industrious,
and conscientious. These are children who often are on the go
all day and into the evening — not like migrant children,
working the crops, but working hard at meeting expectations
of their own, or expectations inspired by their parents. They
are children who possess an almost uncanny mixture of matu-
rity and sophistication at, say, ten, along with the childishness
an upper-middle-class culture allows, even encourages. One
minute a girl is talking as if she were a tourist guide to London
or Paris; the next minute she is surrounding herself with old
dolls and stuffed animals, watching television in her room, and
refusing the offer of something to drink or eat made by a maid.

Privileged children clearly possess numerous options —
escapes, alternative plans, layers and layers of preferences.
Privileged children can be conventional in some respects, but
also quite unconventional. They may feel powerless in the face
of demands made by strong-minded (and, occasionally, nar-
row-minded) parents, but they also may feel quite sure of
themselves. They may also feel quite above or at a remove
from so-called middle-class morality or customs. Is not their
life different from start to finish from that of more ordinary
people? Some children have explicitly learned to ask and answer such questions affirmatively. Others have assumed the

gist of the message without feeling the need to put it into words — perhaps the ultimate in a casual sense of one's own importance.

Still other privileged children have learned that they belong to rich, important families, all right — but ones in peril also. Their parents feel themselves holding on to what they have against high odds — the grasping, demanding, meddling fingers of the federal bureaucracy, the liberal ideologues. Who is to measure fear — a migrant child's sense that he can be arrested at a sheriff's arbitrary will, harassed unremittingly at the behest of a grower by his foreman, as against the conviction a banker's son learns that planners, officials, and activists are out to undercut the authority of his parents, take away their money, render them weak and powerless? Many migrant parents say with no prodding and with no sense of self-accusation that they and their children alike have become prey to various demons, slipped into excessive anxiety, doubt, and worry, because of the life they lead. Some privileged parents worry loud and clear that they are being "hounded" by bureaucrats, that their children are paying a toll — a family's consequent fearfulness or agitation.

No matter what their parents' attitude toward their own money, these are children privileged to have a quite distinct and extraordinary sense of space and time. Many of the children of working-class background I have worked with have never left home at all, or have gone only on brief car or bus trips — to a nearby beach resort or to visit a relative in a city not all that far away. Migrant children do a lot of moving about, of course, but hardly the kind that involves first-class air travel, and the rest. A boy or girl who has, at ten or twelve, seen the Atlantic and Pacific oceans, the Caribbean, maybe; who has heard French, German, and Spanish spoken; and who has become familiar with distant places, customs, habits, is likely not only to be rather hopeful about the prospect of future trips but sophisticated about the world's problems and shrewd or imaginative about what might be done by an American who wants to work or study abroad. Countries whose very names mean little or nothing to many, if not the majority, of American children become objects of anticipation to certain privileged children — who have every expectation that this year or next year or two years hence will see them here or there.

That notion of "next year" is somewhat unusual for other elementary school children, who tend to live in the present and consider the next *day* quite enough time ahead. For a lucky few, however, there is an apparently limitless supply of places to visit, each of which has to be matched up with a spell of time — and done so, mentally, well in advance. In fact, for a number of these privileged children time is just that — a benefactor, a source of wonder, amusement, excitement, and mysteries that soon become casually amassed memories.

For a migrant child sunup is the beginning of a working day whose hours stretch almost indefinitely. "I don't know when this day will end," one hears from such a child, who is being not only plaintive or sad but quite sincerely informative about what time means for her — a demanding, insistent, tireless taskmaster whose power is never to be questioned. Sundown is an interlude, but one doesn't anticipate it too strongly. There are some migrant children who, at seven or eight, wonder whether even that respite, even the night itself, can be presumed a certainty, an inevitability. Might it not one day happen that the sun will say: enough! Then there will be endless days, endless work — "no time but sun-time," as one migrant child put it.

Richard Halliburton's idiosyncratic, even eccentric, adventures of the 1930s have become for the children of the well-to-do the assumed, the required. A girl of nine with cerebral palsy, substantially retarded, is moved on to planes, helped from hotel to hotel, gets to know when and how to show or use her passport, fusses over the picture of herself used in it. Her sister, two years older — they are daughters of a New England insurance executive and stockbroker — observes, out of earnest consideration and affection, that "it would be terrible if she couldn't travel with us." Why? Very simple: "If you don't see the world, you won't really know much. You'll be missing a lot, and you won't have any idea of what's happening. It's like staying a baby, instead of becoming a grown-up. You just *have* to travel, even if it's hard." So much for one view of a certain "variable" in "child development" and psychological "maturation."

Such a privileged child is likely to be removed, however, from the very world she also is getting to be so familiar with. Built into the childhood of these boys and girls is isolation — the distance that land provides, the distance that hills or islands provide, the distance that a "private way" in a city provides, or an elevator that rises, rises to the very top of a building. The summer home; the winter ski lodge; the hotel; a seat on an airplane that is big, comfortable, and, not rarely, next to an empty group of seats; a large and well-appointed suite in "the quiet part of the building," meaning that one's eyes don't get distracted by ugly sights, sore spots, but have unlimited access to the broadest, least cluttered view. How restricted is the life of people who have the fewest restrictions on them, how secluded the life of people who range farther and wider than any of their countrymen.

The children of such men and women get to feel at a remove in some psychological or spiritual way. At times a particular boy or girl talks like a black or a migrant or an Indian — as if seclusion has prompted some pervasive and unregenerate notion of *difference*. "I am not like a lot of kids; I know it," one child announced, and went on to say why plainly and wryly: "We live away from other people, and we don't see too many people. My parents like their privacy. My father hates to answer the phone. He says he'd rather answer a letter. He just talks into a machine, and his secretary types a reply. He says you should be polite, but not get friendly with those who aren't your own kind of people."

She is not yet old enough, at eight, to be self-consciously snobbish or even, really, aloof when she makes such remarks. She is being candid, matter of fact. She is neither bragging nor complaining. Some children do either or both as a consequence of their relative isolation. They find it difficult to break themselves of long-standing habits — an introspection that derives from aloneness or solitude rather than a strong need to avoid people or an active fear of them. They find themselves resenting such a psychological fate — especially as they become adolescents — and trying hard to become more open and responsive to people, more in touch with those they do meet.

"I'd like to talk with a lot of different types of people," a fourteen-year-old boy who lives on a ten-acre estate thirty miles north of Boston comments. He has had his fill of Europe, Latin America, even Asia. He has been all over America. But he has no real confidence in his ability to get on with people. He has gone, so far, to an exceptionally small, cozy school run at great expense for a small number of children, each like himself in family background. Yet, in that school, the social and economic problems of other children, including those who belong to migrant farm families, have been studied from time to time, at the instigation of one teacher who has, with some success, reminded her students of how "far away" her students are from millions of others. Each year, the teacher knows, a few take her "almost too seriously." She tells what happens: "They wake up to find themselves living on an island — almost. They start wondering how to go ashore. It is sad in a way, but inspiring — because they really do try to break out of a certain mold, and that's hard for any child to do. Some fail; some succeed. It is fascinating to watch — and sometimes I've thought to myself: these are 'culturally deprived' children too, and maybe they are psychologically stunted in a way."

She retracts the last part of that comment; it is, perhaps, "too strong." She will settle for the word the children themselves use most often, in those moments of self-recognition she has encouraged in them: again, "different." And they certainly are that, with respect to "most others," a phrase they also learn to use when talking about themselves. They are, as indicated, rather intensely curious, at certain points in their young lives, about how the rest of the world manages to get on. It may well be in many instances that the drive to "break out" is really a drive to learn about areas of experience hitherto excluded, for all a given child's worldliness and sophistication. These children are brought up not only to "have" manners, but to use them as a means of distinguishing themselves in several senses of the word. They must of course measure up to the demands of their family life. High emphasis is put on politeness — as virtually the keystone of one's way of acting in the presence of others, even sometimes one's own kin.

Politeness, however, becomes *politesse* — a code of behavior that excludes as well as includes. It is not "polite" to speak with people one does not "know," one has not formally "met." It is not "polite" to ask questions of so-and-so, or talk with someone else in any but a certain prescribed, almost ritualized, fashion. Even within the home, it is not "polite" to get "too friendly" with a maid or a cook or a gardener or a handyman. One learns to restrain curiosity; one submits to a rather measured and regulated form of human relatedness. When "good manners" are found lacking in others, they become a "them." The child develops a socially connected sense of himself or herself as a person who is aware of and does certain things unfamiliar to others. "Our maid's children don't know about finger bowls," a seven-year-old New Orleans girl says. She also says — the year is 1960 — that "the kids going into those [desegregated] schools don't know about finger bowls, either; and they don't know how to smile and say thank-you to the people in the mobs."

An astonishing remark, that last one; it is hard, within the limits of good manners, to find out what such a comment possibly could mean to a child who was, after all, talking about terribly harassed and threatened (and grievously unprotected) black children, only four of them, every day confronted twice by unruly, abusive mobs of full-grown white men and women. The girl, it turned out, came up with a plan of action to help those four black children, so ignorant about the purpose of a finger bowl. It was an instructive plan, indeed: "If you show people that you know how to behave, then they won't bother you. If you don't show them, you can get into trouble. They will tell you that you're not good, and they can give you a talking-to. Maybe if one of those colored girls showed the people standing in the mob outside the school how nice she is, and how she can be polite, and smile a lot — polite to *everyone* — then, after a while, she wouldn't be in any trouble. If you really learn your manners, then you can be sure of yourself, my mother says; you can go anywhere and you can be with any sort of person, and you know how to behave, and no one can get you all upset, and you won't be standing around or sitting around, not knowing what to say or what to do. That's the worst thing that can happen — you're not sure what will happen, because you're not paying attention to your manners, and so you get upset. My mother says that when you 'mind your manners,' you're in the driver's seat, and no one can scare you off. But if you don't 'mind your manners,' then you can get thrown off any second, because you don't know what you're doing — what you *should* be doing — and so a person can say something, and you can slip up, and the next thing you know you're in trouble."

That particular "moment" in my New Orleans work was especially decisive and clarifying. I began to realize then that a city's social and political crisis can bear down psychologically on more than the all too vulnerable (or hate-obsessed) participants. I also began to see that I had been obtuse and dismissive about a child's interests and preoccupations, when in fact they were a matter of great importance to her. She had been trying to tell me more about herself than I had cared to (been prepared to) comprehend. For months, on and off, that child and several others like her I knew in the Garden District of New Orleans had spoken to me of the meaning of "etiquette," "good manners," "correct behavior." I had listened with, at best, half-interest. I wanted to go well "below" such conventional and essentially hollow and trite conversation (so I was convinced it was). I wanted to know what those privileged boys and girls thought about blacks, about the poor, about themselves as members of a given social and economic class, and so on. Instead I was given brief sermons on the importance of being earnestly gracious, courteous, refined. But a girl who spoke of finger bowls as the one quoted immediately above did has been struggling in a certain way to imagine herself in someone else's situation; has been struggling to figure out what she would do: what resources of mind and spirit would she have? What had she learned to do, when threatened by uncertainty or danger, however slight? What was she afraid might happen to her — the worst fate possible? And was there any avoiding it?

The answer is evident; for all the privileges of her life,

the girl felt her own kind of insecurity, precariousness, jeopardy. She must not ever be at the mercy of others; she must keep herself aloof from them, protected by a veneer of manners, which actually amount to a complicated and tenacious defensive network of words, gestures, rituals. With manners she felt reasonably secure, able to respect herself and come to terms with others. Without them she felt very much exposed to danger. Those without manners, meaning the lower orders of New Orleans, might harm her and her family. Manners for her had become, implicitly, a symbol of class power. If one "has" manners, one has the prerogatives of one's class situation. If she should "forget" her manners, she would fall, find herself part of a nameless, faceless assortment of "others."

In the homes of many young privileged ones, the servants show their own mastery of etiquette, and receive from the child a similar response — increasingly "correct behavior" as the years advance. Those servants also get many other responses from the children they are likely to feed, help dress, wait on, assist, and, not least, teach. The role of maids, governesses, butlers, gardeners, tutors, handymen, cooks in the nurture and education of privileged children is easy to ignore, simplify, or romanticize. These are complicated involvements, and vary enormously. In one home a governess is, for all practical purposes, a child's mother. In another home, a governess tends the child, but under the careful and determined supervision of a mother who has no intention at all of relinquishing her psychological or political authority to anyone else. And there are all sorts of idiosyncratic nuances — a function not only of a particular servant's personality and that of a mother, a father, a child, but of what is happening in the life of a given family. Unquestionably many children work out complicated emotions with these men and women who are both strangers, yet curiously intimate members of a household. A child who sees little of his parents clutches hard at a nanny. A child who gets on wonderfully with his parents gives a nanny hell all the time. A child who fears his father relies heavily on a gardener for friendship. A child who seems to be his father's best friend struts around the house shouting obscenities at a handyman, the husband of a maid, who also catches a rough time from the boy.

Often a child's class-consciousness first awakens in response to a servant. A maid is friendly, a boy or girl grateful and affectionate. Soon things begin to get out of hand. At five or six, say, the child doesn't clearly know the difference between his parents' social and economic position in the world and that of his nanny or the cook, or the foreman who works on "the place." But such a state of affairs must not last indefinitely, parents know. Well before children get to high school or college and take courses in sociology and political science, they get to appreciate who has what power and why in the immediate world of their family's domain.

For certain privileged children it is a servant who unwittingly becomes a teacher, or whose situation in the family becomes instructive. Southern whites for years have remembered how they first began to learn about the meaning of skin color (their own, the black person's) in the home, when a "mammy" told them a few things about the world, or the mammy's child did, or their own parents had to — lest there be what might be euphemistically called a "misunderstanding": a white child of well-off parents not aware of the significance of race, caste, class. The same holds up North; the same holds when a servant or a staff of them are white. As a matter of fact, in some privileged homes the children learn the specifics of race and class more explicitly and pointedly than any other American children do.

The first child of upper-income parents I came to know in the course of my work — in New Orleans, in the late 1950s and early 1960s — could remember at ten what she had discovered at six: "I used to play with the maid's boy, and with the cook's girl; they were always around, being fed out of our refrigerator. They got fatter and fatter. The cook had special food for her girl, because she wouldn't eat what my mother wanted me to eat. I had fresh-squeezed orange juice, and the cook's girl had Kool-Aid or Coke. My mother tried to get the cook to give fresh orange juice to her daughter, but she wouldn't. Anyway, there came a day when my mother took me aside, and she said I had to understand a few things. She told me that I was getting too old to play with the colored kids, and too old to be hanging around the kitchen and wasting my time. I had my lessons and my things to do, and I should tend to them, and I should be more polite with the maid and the cook, and say please — but when I want something, *ask,* and expect to get it! My mother showed me how she does it. I pretended to be the cook, and she talked to me! After a while I guess I learned! It took time, though. I was too young, I think, at first, to know about the colored and the white — that the colored have been working for white people like us for a long time, and they like it, and they are lucky, because they get all the food they want, and Daddy is very generous to them. They get good salaries — and he would do anything for them.

"A nephew of our maid got into trouble with the police. He robbed a store, I think. My Daddy went and talked with the boy and his parents, and he went to the police and he talked with them. He got the kid off. The maid was very happy. She told me that she's the luckiest one in the world, working here for us. But sometimes she'll forget what she said, and she'll complain or she'll drag her feet. My mother has to speak to her. She tells her to do something, *right away.* The maid *does.* I have to be a little firm sometimes myself. That's what my mother has taught me — that you get 'firm' with servants, when you think they're not doing what needs to be done, or they're not as fast as they should be. My friends and I compare notes on our colored help."

All that may well smack of the cruder form of Southern *hauteur* — a child's still unpolished and all too blunt acknowl-edgment of the facts of race and money, vintage 1964 and Louisiana. But in certain upper-middle-class towns of the North, and in the 1970s, and even among families rather "lib-eral" politically, certainly on the "race" issue, one finds chil-dren getting ideas about servants not so different. Over a long enough time, during the course of a conversation that to all intents and purposes has nothing to do with the subject of "class," one hears scattered comments about a "biddie," or "our Irish cook," or "Jim, who does everything around the property." "Jim" ends up being characterized as "an Italian," or as someone who "comes from Canada, and he's French," or, much less commonly than in the South, as "a Negro," or "a black man."

Those men and women may be objects of fascination as well as thinly veiled condescension; they may be individuals whose affection is earnestly sought and gratefully obtained, or men and women watched warily and coldly. Such people may be-come not only familiar to a boy or girl but unwitting symbols in his or her psychological life. A boy feels concerned about or attached to a servant or an employee — or indeed a mine or factory full of workers — because he feels a bit helpless him-self, or manipulated, or not so much consulted and asked as *told:* what to do, when, and for how long. A girl is very posses-sive of her father, and ready to fight on his behalf anyone who seems in the least threatening, even complaining. There are,

in a sense, two families for many of these children: their
"proper" one, and the larger one occasionally called a "staff"
— of varying size, length of tenure, commitment to a given
home or a piece of property. The psychological complexities
are no less remarkable. A particular "servant" may for even
the same child be a rival, a judge, a negotiator (with the parents), an oppressed one, a loved one, a person who *both* re-
conciles tensions in a home and stirs them up, a reminder of
the outside world, a source of confusion, curiosity, puzzle-
ment, embarrassment, shame, guilt, annoyance, fear.

Privileged children are family-conscious. A family's name,
its traditions, its position in the world, may conspire to produce in a child's mind all kinds of sentiments, hopes, worries.
A young person develops a notion of time, for instance, that
is strongly influenced by the stories, if not legends, he has
heard about his or her ancestors. They may have preceded
him or her for a generation or two, a century or two. As the
child contemplates a life ahead, it is one fitted into a larger life,
that of a certain family's. The result is a certain detachment
as well as a persisting and distinct self-consciousness. There is
a mythological element in some family histories that may especially engage the imagination and the emotional life of the
young.

Whether the stories handed down are literal truth, apocry-
phal, merely anecdotal, or grossly exaggerated and distorted,
the child senses the stuff of romance, dramatic struggle, hero-
ism — and proceeds accordingly to spin fantasies that in turn
enable symbolic expression of what is as well as what was.
Even children who come from the poorest of families have
occasional dreams of glory, of being special, of triumph, or of
a bitter but noble defeat in an imaginary struggle. Even children who know that their parents and grandparents were
factory workers or farm hands or coal miners or migratory

laborers experience a spell or two of grandeur in their day-dreams. For children surrounded by luxury and told repeatedly how valuable and remarkable their various relatives were or are, it is an understandable temptation to construct beliefs out of a mixture of the real and the imaginary.

Quite normal troubles, experienced by most children, get worked into the child's sense of family. A boy, nervous or insecure about himself, begins to be afraid that his family will lose its fortune, that his father will be robbed, that a kidnapping will take place, that a servant will betray the father, that something "wrong" will occur in the cook's kitchen just before an important dinner party, that the whole staff will quit, leaving a growing mess inside and outside the house. Usually such intimations, apprehensions, of disaster are reassuringly brief. Sometimes they persist longer — aided, ironically, by what the child has heard from a parent. If the father distrusts his "help," his workers, if the mother is suspicious of her servants, hires and fires them one after the other, talks behind their backs, badmouths them to her family, the child is likely to follow suit — use the fears and resentments and qualms expressed by grown-ups as vehicles for his or her own worries or misgivings. Again, all children have mixed feelings, contend with antagonistic attitudes toward others or, indeed, themselves. For children of privileged background those personal moments of conflict or contrariness take on a special flavor: self-assurance, for example, is turned into an expression of *noblesse oblige* — followed all too quickly by self-doubt and even a touch of panic, which come across in a stated fear of political or social change and consequent familial decline or ruin.

It is astonishing, as a matter of fact, how many boys and girls of upper-middle-class or rather wealthy background begin to experience somewhat apocalyptic ruminations at various intervals in childhood. At the dinner table they may ask what would happen *if* — and what follows may be a talk about the economy, the class system, racial tensions, the danger of a severe drought, a terrible mine disaster, a flood, depending on where the child lives and the nature of his or her father's occupation. Words or expressions or phrases like political consciousness, social consciousness, oedipal desires (and consequent fears), a developing regional sensibility, or racial self-concept suddenly come to life, get free of their abstract existence in order to become active participants, it seems, in a child's searching, quizzical, perhaps alarmed, certainly aroused, mind.

How does a child, furthermore, settle in his or her mind the contradictions between an anti-intellectualism that can become fierce and contemptuous and a parental concern that the house have books, records, pictures, and that children go to the best schools, learn a lot — even if a considerable amount so acquired will be regarded as "a waste of time"? How does one live in one's mind with memories of hard times and terrible struggles, handed down from generation to generation, and, as well, with memories of singular triumphs, achievements, successes — and a present-day reality that confirms them, even if one hears, also in the present, talk of dangers, threats, tragedies, a possible end to a social and economic system? How does one mix in one's mind a sense of being on top, being the envy of others, a knowledge that one has much, and will have more, much more, in the future, with a good deal of conversation about social unrest and economic decline? How does one try to be self-reliant, cautious, and even tight or stingy, so far as money goes, and yet also be grateful for receiving so very much? How does one enjoy gifts showered so willingly, then respond to accusations that include a word like "spoiled"?

That is such a child's task: to assemble a host of pieties,

banalities, inconsistencies, contradictions, ideological frag-
ments, religious or philosophical constructs, sincerely upheld
beliefs, guiding principles both obeyed and ignored, or
defined outright — and do so in such a way that life feels bear-
able, at the very least, and, a lot of the time, rather pleasant.
Over and over again, one hears from these quite privileged
children a version of this: I'm all right, Jack! Over and over,
one learns of lucky chances, wonderful occasions, delightful
moments and longer — the continuing exuberance of a full,
interesting, advantaged life. A girl in a country town well to
the north of Boston admits to "troubles" at home, to unhappi-
ness because her parents "don't agree," her father "drinks too
much," her mother gets "scared" and has to take "a lot of
pills." But "most of the time," the girl estimates repeatedly,
candidly, and I think fairly, she is "too busy" to feel sad, to
have complaints, to call herself upset, to fret. She thinks at ten
(prophetically? wrongly?) that she might at twenty "worry
more." Why? Her parents do, so she no doubt will too. She has
wondered why her parents "worry": "Is it because they have
so much to look after? Is it because Dad is having trouble with
the people at the factory? Is it because Mother and Dad don't
agree on where we should go for a vacation? Is it because the
stock market is way, way down? Is it because our horse died,
and he was very expensive, and we just got him?"

One pulls together questions like those, asked over the
months, the years; asked tersely, then rather quickly abandoned for affirmative statements of one kind or another. This
particular girl is getting on fine. She can tuck away her doubts
and her considerable apprehensions, in the many folds of a
rich, active, interesting life. Others are not so fortunate. They
live in severely troubled homes, and have become themselves
troubled children. They have perhaps been moved about endlessly — upper-class migrants, at the mercy of corporate deci-

sions. They have, maybe, fathers who drink and drink, who are constantly absent from the home, who have no real interest in their children or, for that matter, their wives. They may have mothers who also drink, who feel desperate, useless, lonely, intimidated. Such children may withdraw into their comfortable rooms, indulge themselves with increasingly elaborate and sometimes weird fantasies, become too much obsessed with certain dolls, toys, stuffed animals, games. They are children whose parents for one reason or another and in one way or another have walked away from parenthood, turned their backs on it, made an elaborate pretense of it. They are children who have learned to become withdrawn, isolated, all too self-sufficient. They are children who may appear "happy," "well adjusted," quite industrious and capable, yet who harbor secret resentments, confusions, sadnesses.

Sometimes such children, well before adolescence, break down. They become anxious, frightened, morbid, severely isolated, antagonistic. I started my work with those particular boys and girls — the ones I saw as a child psychiatrist *before* I began my years of "fieldwork" in the South, then Appalachia, then the North, then the West. There are, as mentioned, only a few hundred child psychiatrists in the United States and, rather often, their time is claimed by those who have money. After a while, if one is not careful, the well-off and the rich get seen exclusively through a clinician's eye: homes full of bitterness, deceit, snobbishness, neuroses, psychoses; homes with young children in mental pain, and with older children, adolescents and young adults, who use drugs, drink, run away, rebel constantly and disruptively, become truants, become delinquents, become addicts, become alcoholics, become compulsively promiscuous, go crazy, go wild, go to ruin.

There is obviously another side to the lives of upper-middle-class and wealthy families in the United States. The crazy, the eccentric, the bizarre, the "sick," the aberrant, the uncontrolled are understandably the ones clinicians see. Unfortunately those same hurt and bewildered young people get wide coverage in the press, are talked about at great length when panelists or "experts" appear on television, are written up extensively by those who want to point out "problems" or "trends" and account for their "reasons." Some obviously troubled homes don't produce half-destroyed children. Some apparently troubled children grow out of their difficulties rather surprisingly, conclusively, inexplicably. And then there are the able, intelligent, thoughtful children, graced with not only substantial trust funds and high social position but a psychologically sound family life. They are children envied as well as admired. They are on a lot of people's minds. No doubt there is substantial psychological trauma and moral squalor in many homes of relatively rich people, but emotional traumas, and yes, serious moral flaws are also to be found in working-class homes, or among the poor. We blame the alcoholism, insanity, meanness, cruelty, apathy, drug usage, despondency, and, not least, cruelty to children we see or are told exists in the ghetto or among the rural poor upon various "socioeconomic factors." All of those signs of psychological deterioration can be found among quite privileged families too — and so we remind ourselves perhaps that wealth corrupts.

How in fact ought we to come to terms with the many psychological ironies that keep cropping up at the theoretical intersection of social class and personal or family life? Anyone who has worked in Harlem, or among migrant farm workers in Florida and up the Eastern Seaboard, or on Indian reservations, or up certain hollows of Appalachia, knows how forlorn, cheerless, apprehensive, and embittered even young children can be — victims of hunger, malnutrition, and the meanest of circumstances, which affect the spirits of parents, the way they get along with their children, and, consequently and subsequently, the way those children regard themselves, the world around them, their prospects. But some poor children, especially when young (say, up to eight, nine, ten), are also capable of liveliness, energetic play, humor, intelligent observation — in sum, a strong and continuing effort at affirming themselves, becoming somebody. If there are the broken, deranged poor, or the marginal and harassed, hence nasty and edgy and hateful and spiteful members of the working class, there are also the tough, resilient, proud, and unbowed poor, and the decent, kind, thoughtful, working people of this country.

It is in the nature of babies and elementary school children especially, given the least encouragement, to hold on to hope, to cling tenaciously to the stronger, more confident side of their psychological inheritance. In the first four volumes of *Children of Crisis* and in other efforts *(Still Hungry in America, The Wages of Neglect, The Middle Americans, The Old Ones of New Mexico)*, I have struggled to convey the way various children grow up — responding to particular social, economic, political, regional, historical, racial, ethnic, cultural influences, as they become mediated in the home. I have, again, not shirked giving an account of the serious psychological consequences for children of severe hardship. On the other hand, I have by no means portrayed the interesting and in many respects quite appealing children I have met as a mob of future mental patients.

Nate Shaw knew he was not unique; he was one of "All God's Children." He had his demons, many of them stirred into destructive action by the conditions of life he and other Alabama tenant farmers had to take for granted, or contend with bravely, constantly, and with scant hope, most often, of any success. But he was a man of dignity and compassion, of psychological as well as moral and spiritual integrity. Any account of his life, of the lives of others like him, that turns him into a caricature of himself, a bundle of twisted impulses and distorted thoughts and mad seizures of mind or spirit, would be a grossly unfair rendition of what James Agee kept calling "human actuality."

I have taken up such matters at great length in connection with just about all American children — except those described or discussed here in this book. They come last in this particular series, though God knows they are first in so many respects. I happen to believe, and have made clear my convictions in many places, on numerous occasions, that it is unfair that a few be so very privileged and that the overwhelming majority be either hard pressed or barely able to make do. But I am not about to allow my social, political, and economic views to distort a presentation of the lives of a number of children, as I have come to see and know them over the years. There is plenty of room for error or worse, though — misjudgments of fact, misinterpretations of what has been heard and seen, omissions or distortions of emphasis in what is eventually written up. One has to be especially mindful of one's views, biases, prejudices, and yes, ideological purposes. And, very important, one has to distinguish between social criticism and psychological observation.

It may well be that from a cultural critic's point of view these privileged children are "growing up absurd," are eventually to be engaged in "the pursuit of loneliness," will become members of a "lonely crowd"; it may be too that their "moral development" is restricted, constrained — or, at the very least, limited by various social, cultural, and educational forces. But my purpose in two decades of visits to homes in various parts of the United States has not been to turn particular children into cannon fodder for a particular ideological or psychiatric theory. Younger children not yet teenagers, still growing in leaps and bounds both physically and psychologically, especially elude — maybe later defy — categorization and prophecy. Anna Freud, I noted above, has repeatedly emphasized how dangerous it is to make predictions about children under ten or twelve — whatever their social or racial "background." They don't come out, all too often, the way they seem likely to come out, and they often surprise even the most intent and learned of observers. Best to describe carefully, Miss Freud suggests — and only after sustained, long-term "direct observation." And best to summon theoretical restraint when considering and writing about large numbers of boys and girls who, after all, deserve from clinicians a recognition of life's fatefulness, its chancy and by no means inevitable or predetermined character.

A number of radical critics of American society have commented sternly, harshly, on its well-to-do people — have observed that many of us are curbed, pinched, all too self-important and self-possessed. I would not argue with a good deal of what they say. There is plenty of arrogance, condescension, narrow-mindedness, and worse abroad this land, *as in others*. There are plenty of desolate, terribly fearful — and reactively truculent — men and women living in this country, *as in others*. Perhaps the world's richest and most powerful nation ought be asked to bear special, critical scrutiny. We have so much and therefore might share so much. We can do so much, and therefore might enable others, elsewhere, to do so much. And we have made mistakes that for a nation as wealthy and strong as ours have been especially awful. Nevertheless, to judge this nation without reference to the behavior of other nations, other empires, other "principalities and powers," in existence now or once in existence, is to run the risk of engaging in a reckless moral diatribe.

The same goes for our wealthy families, the socially,

economically, and politically strong, whose children I have tried here to give an account of; they are boys and girls whose lives may turn out to be ethically suspect, psychologically disastrous, socially corrupt, economically privileged to the point of exploitation of others, and culturally barren. But they may also be boys and girls who, at least during childhood, show no such ruinous inclinations — and perhaps show, at least in some instances, quite contrary tendencies. In a number of cases, they may be boys and girls who stand up well, when compared to various "others" of their age, and who come from quite stable, hardworking and ethically concerned families — children who strike even the most persistent and not necessarily uncritical visitor as reasonably lively, competent, kind, thoughtful, imaginative, compassionate, and "happy," whatever that word means.

The longer the time I have spent with these privileged children, the harder it has been to come up with assertive, confident generalizations. I mentioned earlier that Karl Marx, no apologist for capitalism or feudalism, insisted on distinguishing between a given economic and social order and the individuals who happen to live in a particular world at a particular time. He had an exceedingly long view of things, a desire to understand the curious and vexing zigzag of events, as they work themselves out. He saw the world's people, any nation's citizens, as individuals both struggling to make do and find meaning in life, and as inevitably and inextricably caught in the workings of a certain society. The rich as well as the poor, the so-called powerful as well as the obviously weak, were for him part of a vast historical drama — actors whose roles have been determined by forces often only dimly, if at all, comprehended. He abhorred injustice and exploitation, yet viewed those who profit from them as themselves victims — minions, really, of a dialectic that seems to brook no interference.

If such a view is cold, abstract, all too sure of itself, there is implicitly in it a measure of ironic compassion: one sees the lord of the manor and the serf, the capitalist and the factory worker, and yes, the dictator wielding his arbitrary (and cruel) power in the name of the proletariat and the individual proletarian as all slouching toward a Marxist, utopian Jerusalem — that ultimate, elusive, communist nirvana when a massive bureaucracy will "wither away," yielding a kind of localist paradise such as the Bible offers: Eden. Meanwhile, in our time, in history's time, there are the social and economic "systems" Marx with considerable detachment described and analyzed. And there have been, are, will be millions of children who are born and grow up and inevitably and unwittingly (as he saw it) fall into line, take their foredestined places, submit themselves to imperatives they either don't know of, or only faintly sense, or know a lot about, yet cannot at all alter or even tame.

Not that Marx would deny social critics or moralists the right or obligation to criticize what they see before them. His own social criticism and moral judgment were at once devastating, utterly farsighted, and unnervingly impersonal. If anything, he allowed himself compassion of an evenhanded kind; in his scheme of things, the manipulated bourgeois entrepreneur keeps company with the hurt and suffering workingman — the blind leading the blind, as it were. Even the observer or critic of a given social order, he knew, is very much part of what is criticized; is limited with respect to his or her vision, analysis, interpretive outlook, by a given era's "material conditions."

From a quite different, and even antagonistic, perspective Kierkegaard — no friend of anyone's self-appointed dialectic, unless it be God Almighty's unfathomable one — could also be detached about Copenhagen's mid-nineteenth-century *haute bourgeoisie,* whose assumptions he did not at all share but whom he wanted to understand psychologically and not so much condemn as fit into God's mysterious scheme of things. Marx saw each of us a cog in the works of History; Kierkegaard saw each of us as a desperate wanderer — more on the run than we ever really, for any length of time, can bear to realize. Most of the time we are caught in life's humdrum and extortionate grasp: the "everydayness" he keeps mentioning. At a certain point we emerge, as if out of nowhere, from early childhood, a moment or two of which we remember hazily on our later journey. We suddenly are old enough to know that we *are*, that we have a name, a body, a mind, a particular life — one to be lived, most probably, here and not there, now (certainly) and not sometime in the past or future, and under this kind of (social, economic, cultural, political) circumstances rather than another kind. Rather quickly we learn about the tug, the shadow, the vortex of "everydayness." We wake up, our stomach growls, our conscience stirs, we get up, and we are presently lost to ourselves: teeth brushed, face scrubbed, down the stairs to breakfast, then to school or to work or to the next errand, or to a sport, an event; and then, more stomach pangs, and lunch, and so on; soon, all too soon, we are in bed, lost to ourselves in quite another way — though in a dream or two, maybe, we for a few seconds only do manage to get our bearings. And so it goes, day after day — until over us the words are pronounced: "world without end," that final statement of continuity, of mystery, of man's fateful submission to the nature of things.

Meanwhile, one struggles for a moment, now and then, of reason. Kierkegaard might occasionally have acknowledged that his books offered a few of those moments to a few readers, even as he himself must have fought hard, and only with partial success, to transcend not only bourgeois

Copenhagen but his own crafty, ambitious, arrogant, self-serving, analytical, circumscribing mind — surely quite as much tempted by Hegel's dialectic as appalled by it. He turned his back — knowing that he who plays God with ideas has yielded to his own version of a narrowing "every-dayness": the cloistered weaver, spinning out propositions meant to tidy up (in William James's words) life's "bloom-ing, buzzing confusions." As Marx pointed out, feudalism gave way to capitalism — lonely weavers to interdisci-plinary teams of them.

All the children I have been writing about in this book and its predecessors are trying to come to terms with what one child born to great wealth in New Orleans referred to as her "one and only chance," by which she meant nothing less than her life. She will never be a latter-day Marx or Kierkegaard. She is today well on her way to being a member of upper-crust, conservative New Orleans society, a perfect foil for a person like me, I suppose: the preoccupation with dinner par-ties, flowers, dances, and clothes, not to mention a suitable suitor. She has read nothing I have written, as far as I know, since I met her almost two decades ago. She reads very little, actually, except the New Orleans *Times Picayune* and a news weekly or two, which she only "browses through" at that. She has read her share of textbooks in school, but they don't "at-tract" her, she is frank to say. She is, it's not unfair to say, a vain, self-centered, flighty person who cares not a whit for her fellow man or woman, unless they be part of a small circle of relatives, friends, neighbors: her kind.

Yet, when she was eight she had a habit that puzzled, wor-ried her parents, short time that it lasted — a few months in a girl's long years of childhood. She would, as her mother put it, "sit and stare." In fact, the girl liked looking out the window of her parents' Garden District mansion. Across the street was one of those striking (and to visitors, hauntingly unique) New Orleans cemeteries — the graves, the elaborate and various tombs, all above ground. The tombs cast shadows, and in the early evening or morning the girl would notice them. She wondered about who "those people" were, the departed. She wondered what kind of lives they had lived, what they could tell her now about those lives. Maybe what she was making, in retrospect, a feeble and ultimately futile effort to avoid coming to was herself. She was really struggling hard for a few seconds of detachment, perspective, humor about the world she was part of. She would smile when she looked out and caught sight of an especially ornate, imposing, assertive monument of stone. She would, in her own way, meditate about life's meaning.

But, alas, she told her parents what she liked to do in an occasional "off moment." They were hardly reassured. They were quizzical the first time; annoyed the second; admonitory the third; worried the fourth; and ready to consult a doctor the fifth — those "off moments" indeed! They did call a doctor; he urged intelligent restraint, and his advice proved correct. Not that there was actually restraint. The girl was implicitly and sometimes directly told to get on with it — life. She was, her parents decided, "a little too introverted." She had best be made "busy." They knew the enemy — inwardness. They knew the point of life: the headlong rush; the ferris wheel at the age of six, the assembly dance at the age of sixteen; the full calendar; the school choir, everyone beautifully, expensively, similarly dressed; the clock that keeps moving; the dream that is promptly forgotten; the sigh before retiring that registers satisfaction and congratulation — no wasted time. No wasted time. No time heavy on one's hands. No time to spare. No time left. In no time, no time at all — world without end.

The girl felt the push. It took her a little time to stop being part of some bad time her parents were convinced she must be having — else why the "funny time" she was for a while reported having. So the mother put it: "She still has a funny time up in her room, looking at that cemetery. She tells us she talks with the people in the tombs! I was horrified. She smiles. I thought at first she was teasing me. I guess she's all right. She's just growing up. All children do a few crazy things before they get sensible." She was right; just about all children do have their strange, wondrous, luminous, brooding, magical, redemptive moments. The girl described hers in a way Clarence John Laughlin, mystical and messianic photographer of her native city, would likely find helpful to remember as he stalks the light and shadows, the memories and bizarre actualities of a place, a time: "I don't think there's anyone there, across the street, inside the cemetery. I just like to look at the place. I used to walk in there with my grandmother. I was little, and she was still alive. She told me she had lived a nice long life, and she had been happy, and she was ready to leave us, whenever God decided she had been with us long enough. She would be glad to go. One day we found her asleep, and it was late in the morning for her — nine o'clock. She was dead. My mother said there was no need to call the doctor, but we had to. I never saw her. I wanted to go in the room, but they wouldn't let me. I tried to sneak in, but they said no.

"The maid said they should let me in. The maid almost convinced my mother. I heard them arguing. I never heard the maid speak back to my mother like that. But my mother won. The maid came out crying. She wasn't upset because of my grandmother. The tears were for me. The maid wanted me to say good-bye to someone, but I never could. They didn't bury my grandmother in that cemetery across the street. I'd hoped they would. She and I had always been close — 'real tight,' she said. If they had buried her across the street, we'd still be 'real tight.' But there isn't any room left, my mother says. I don't think that's exactly right. The maid says it's exactly wrong! The maid says she's done some listening, and she knows what's true — that my mother didn't want someone in the family buried there so near to us.

"Some of the time, when I look across the street, I might be wishing my grandmother was buried there. A lot of the time I just wonder who someone was — someone who's inside one of the little buildings. And I wonder if a long time from now there will be a girl like me, and she will be sitting, maybe, right in my room, and she will be looking at the cemetery, and I'll be there, and she'll be wondering about me! If I want, I can be buried there. The maid told me so. I guess I have a lot of time to make up my mind! It's funny, looking at a cemetery. It's funny playing there. We play there, some of us. It makes people nervous when we do; but they let us. You wonder if there are ghosts. I know there aren't, but I wonder. You hear a sound, and you think someone might be talking to you. Even with the window closed, and you're inside the house, you'll hear a noise, and you wonder. It'll be the dog, in the next room, shaking himself. But you wonder."

She stopped all that wondering within a few months. She had gone through her worrisome time, had "recovered." So the mother had it: "Thank God, she's better. She's recovered from her interest in cemeteries." An "interest"? Or was it, perhaps, a brief spell of release, of openness, of escape from Kierkegaard's, Walker Percy's "everydayness"? And maybe a dialectal moment or two — such as Thomas de Quincey, with Clarence John Laughlin approving, once described: "When one feels/oneself sleeping alone,/utterly divided from all call/or hearing of friends,/doors open that should be/shut, or unlocked that/should be triply secured,/the very walls gave, barriers/swallowed up by unknown/abysses, nothing around

one/but frail curtains, and/a world of illimitable night,/whis-
perings at a distance,/correspondence going on/between
darkness and darkness,/like one's deep calling to/another, and
the dreamer's/own heart the center from/which the whole
network of this/unimaginable chaos radiates . . ."

As for that child's maid, she was, as the girl's mother often
said, and as the girl would grow up to say herself, "not always
in control, the way she should be." So much for psychiatry, its
normative judgments, and the uses to which they are put.
Nevertheless, the maid surely deserves a little space, if not
equal billing; she deserves to speak on behalf of herself, and
maybe a lot of other maids. This book could, of course, go on
and on; maids could speak about children, and so could cooks,
and grocers, and druggists, and tennis instructors, and hockey
coaches, and camp owners.

But this particular New Orleans maid, let free for a few
lines, will help us as we come toward the end, here — because
she has never lost sight, really, of "the end of things," as she
has repeatedly put it: "I look at these folks, and my heart goes
out to them. They feel sorry for me. I know they do. I hear
them talking. But I feel sorry for *them*. Mind you, I feel sorry
for myself, too. I'm not fooling myself! It's no good being Mr.
Charlie's maid. It's no good working in the white man's
kitchen and cleaning up after him, and getting his few dollars,
his pat on the back — and because of the pat you're supposed
to act like you've seen God's face, at last you have, and He's
smiling down on you. But who is Mr. Charlie? My Momma told
me who he is; he's a sad one, that's who he is. They're all right,
these people here. I've worked for them for fifteen years. I'll
stay with them, most likely, until they carry me out, and that'll
be the end of things. My Momma told me: remember that
you're put here only for a few seconds of God's time, and He's
testing you. He doesn't want answers, though. He wants you

to know how to ask the right questions. If you learn how to do that, then you'll do all right when you meet Him, and He's there looking you over. You have to tell Him that you've learned how to question yourself, and when you show Him what you know, He'll smile on you. God's smile, that's the sunshine. God's worries, that's the night. We have to face the night. We have to face the end of things.

"These people here, they've got all that money, and all .iis big house, and another one out in the country, and still they won't let that little girl just be herself. She's eight or nine, and she's got an independent spirit in her, but they're determined to get rid of it, and they will, let me tell you, and soon. The girl asks me a lot of questions. That's good. She looks out on that cemetery and she starts to wondering about things. That's good. She wonders about life, and what it's about, and what the end of things will be. That's good. But she's stopping now. That's what they want: no looking, no staring, no peeking at life. No questions; they don't want questions. They go to a church a couple of times a year, Christmas and Easter, and no one asks them any questions there. No one asks them questions anyplace they go. The people who are gone, who live across the street there in the cemetery, inside those tombs — they know what's important, they've discovered what's important, they've reached their destination. I'm poor, but at least I know that I should ask myself everyday: where's your destination, and are you going there, or are you getting sidetracked? A lot of days I wish I was them; I wish I was rich like them. Then I ask myself: would you be any different? I don't know the answer. I mean, it's like the minister keeps saying to us in church: 'Who knows whether he's going to be a wise man or a fool?' And then he'll remind us that 'all is vanity.' And he'll remind us that 'there's no profit under the sun.' I wonder if there is any. I wonder a lot if there's any profit under the sun.

I read the Bible and I wonder. I'll ask myself one day, and I'll ask the next day, and I'll just decide not to be too sure; just keep on asking."

Best to let that black woman have the last word. Like that child, the maid meditates, wonders, takes notice, keeps her eyes and ears open, knows to think about "the end of things," and never stops praying. She prays that she be able to keep her mind and heart and soul, as she always says it, "open to God." She wants to know whether she is a wise person or a fool. She wants to know whether she will always be able to believe that "wisdom excels folly," and "light excels darkness." She knows the ambiguities of life — even of words like "light" and "darkness." She can talk of "light folks" and "dark folks." She can talk of the rich who are light — and yet succumb to vanity; and the poor who are dark — and yet *also* succumb to vanity.

I said I would give the black woman the last word, but I had best take a certain "responsibility" upon myself. *The* answer is a prelude to many further questions. I placed it at the end of the first volume of this series — a sentence James Agee wrote as he sweated and struggled for the words of a language. Hope against hope. And despair all the time a threat, a temptation. Those Alabama tenant farmers, amid their wretchedness and worse, gave him, finally, this victory: "All that each person is, and experiences, and shall never experience, in body and mind, all these things are differing expressions of himself and of one root, and are identical: and not one of these things nor one of these persons is ever quite to be duplicated, nor replaced, nor has it ever quite had precedent; but each is a new and incommunicably tender life, wounded in every breath and almost as hardly killed as easily wounded: sustaining, for a while, without defense, the enormous assaults of the universe." To have been presented that statement is to be privileged. We are "privileged ones" by virtue of that possession, allowed us by a certain grace. It is a start — Agee's message, and our struggle to prove him right. The rest is life: particular human beings — and those questions from Ecclesiastes that one American black woman, under the Louisiana sun, the American sun, will not ever, it seems, stop asking.

PART TEN

REFERENCES

REFERENCES

THE WELL-TO-DO and the rich have the means to obtain privacy. Anthropologists have put in a lot of time with Indians or Eskimos but they have not studied upper-middle-class or wealthy American families. Social scientists have set up "projects" to study Appalachian families or black families in the rural South or in northern ghettos — and come up with plenty of conclusions about those men, women, and children. But how many field workers have taken themselves to communities where corporation executives, physicians, and laywers live? Where are the long scholarly bibliographies that tell us about the values and ideals, the customs and habits, the beliefs and practices of the well-off, the quite well-off, the almost-rich, and the rich indeed? There are essays and articles and some very important books, but the contrast in the "literature" devoted to the Indians, say, is striking.

Since it is the well-to-do, by and large, who buy books, and who don't lack an interest in themselves, one wonders why they have been so forsaken by field workers of various kinds. In Goronwy Rees's words, "The condition of the rich, though it inspires the passionate curiosity of men and women, is on the whole a question serious writers and sociologists have chosen to ignore." This, from the author of *The Multimillionaires: Six Studies in Wealth* (Macmillan, 1961). And so with the quite well-off people who may have hundreds of thousands of dollars, rather than millions but, arguably, have even more successfully kept away from the curious, or been denied the kind of inquiry Mr. Rees refers to. Not that the rich — some of them, at least — have lacked for attention, notoriety, and a genre of books. One can be protected from the careful scrutiny of observers, yet be the subject of endless comment written from afar, so to speak — some of it mere gossip, some of it quite intelligent and thoughtful social comment or criticism, but rather little of it based upon what Anna Freud means by "direct observation": a sustained involvement with a person or a family, maintained long enough so that the observer has some basis in experience, in words heard and actions observed, for coming to whatever more general conclusions seem warranted.

As early as 1848 the upper-middle-class and rich families of Boston were the subject of an observer's shrewd comments: *The Aristocracy of Boston*. The author chose to be anonymous. He described his book as "a History of the

560 REFERENCES

Business and Business men of Boston"; his time span was the forty years that preceded the publication of his book. It is a fascinating book, if brief by our standards — published by the author himself. He documents the ways various Boston families have made good and tried to keep their position. He comes up with clever psychological asides: "Under a demure, almost bashful exterior, he possesses great shrewdness and dry humor" is the way one Boston socially prominent physician was described.

Books like Charles Francis Adams's *Autobiography, 1835–1915* (Houghton Mifflin, 1916), or Andrew Carnegie's *Autobiography* (Houghton Mifflin, 1920), provide a glimpse or two of a socially prominent family and a very powerful man's life — from rags to rather a lot of riches. William Alexander Percy's *Lanterns on the Levee* (Knopf, 1941) gives an autobiographical account of one Southern aristocrat's family, values, attitudes; Bliss Perry's *Life and Letters of Henry Lee Higginson* (Atlantic Monthly Press, 1921) offers a similar exposition of a Yankee aristocrat's assumptions and beliefs.

In contrast to the autobiographical, literary, or historical narrative, there is the sociological essay or book on big business, a substantial though relatively impersonal tradition. The relatively well known books of authors like Cleveland Amory or Stephen Birmingham are in a class all themselves, as indeed many of their subjects are, socially and economically. Good examples of the sociological text are *Man in Business*, edited by William Mitler (Harper & Row, 1962), and Mabel Newcomer's *The Big Business Executive* (Columbia University Press, 1955). An interesting article that describes some of the life lived by a significant number of upper-middle-class American families is "Social Mobility and the American Business Elite," by Reinhard Bendix and Frank Howton, in *British Journal of Sociology*, December, 1957. An important article, Gabriel Kolko's "Brahmins and Business, 1870–1914; A Hypothesis on the Social Basis of Success in American History," is to be found in *The Critical Spirit*, edited by Kurt Wolff and Barrington Moore, Jr. (Beacon Press, 1968). The author points out that the link between money and social standing is never really absent, even if particular aristocrats, like Charles Francis Adams, insist upon separating themselves ideologically or spiritually from the crasser rich of the old order, never mind the *arrivistes.*

Less academic portrayals of the rich or the very well-off are, as mentioned, Cleveland Amory's well-known *Proper Bostonians* (Dutton, 1947), which has an excellent bibliography of books, pamphlets, and magazine articles that touch upon Boston society, and his other two books on the same theme (if of geographically broader concern): *The Last Resorts* (Harper, 1952) and *Who Killed Society* (Harper, 1960). Stephen Birmingham has been even more zealous and comprehensive. What Mr. Amory did for the Boston Brahmins, Mr. Birmingham did for upper-class Jews, mostly from New York, in *Our Crowd* (Harper, 1967) and *The Grandees* (Harper, 1971). He also pursued upper-class Americans of various regions and tastes in *The Right People* (Little, Brown, 1968) and *The Right Places* (Little, Brown, 1973).

A more learned study of the Philadelphia segment of our "National Upper

Class," as the author E. Digby Baltzell puts it, can be found in *Philadelphia Gentlemen* (Free Press, 1958). The book provides a first-rate sociological analysis of the structure of upper-class life. Other efforts along the same lines, but more informal, are *The Private World of High Society*, by Lucy Kavaler (McKay, 1960), and *The Upper Crust*, concerned mostly with New York, by Allen Churchill (Prentice-Hall, 1970). The same author's *The Splendor Seekers* is devoted to the very rich all over the nation (Grosset & Dunlap, 1974). Matthew Josephson has concentrated on a segment of time in his *The Money Lords: The Great Finance Capitalists, 1925–1950* (Weybright & Talley, 1972). A book such as his tells a lot about those who work under or on behalf of various "lords" — the stockbrokers, the corporation lawyers, the not so rich but quite comfortable people who take their cues in many respects from the ones at the very top. In his well-known *The Robber Barons* (Harcourt, Brace, 1934) Mr. Josephson goes back in time to the period of 1861–1901 and lets us know what some of those cues were in the nineteenth century — various forms of acquisitiveness without restraint.

Other books ought be mentioned — not so much for what they tell about specific people as for the more general information they provide about the values of the wealthy and those in business or the professions who aren't doing so badly themselves. *The New Millionaires and How They Made Their Fortunes* (Geis, 1961), for instance; it was written by the editors of *The Wall Street Journal* and offers a series of profiles on successful businessmen — and more: portraits of Americans struggling hard not only for more money but, by their own descriptions, for personal affirmation of one kind or another. The various studies I mention in this essay, many of which have their own references and bibliographies, invariably imply more than they state with respect to the children of the well-to-do, but if the reader should pick up some of these books, like the last one mentioned, he or she might find it helpful to keep asking: what kind of parent would this person make, and what kinds of values would he hold up and try to see his children live out?

With that in mind, one mentions *The Inheritors*, by John Tebbel (Putnam's, 1962), which tells what has happened over the generations to certain family fortunes and, by indirection, what the children of the rich have been like as they have grown up. Kenneth Lamott's *The Moneymakers* (Little, Brown, 1969) also is helpful in that direction, because the author has a shrewd psychological eye for what those "moneymakers" do to others around them as they go on their merry way upward. Stephen Hess's *America's Political Dynasties: From Adams to Kennedy* (Doubleday, 1966) is similarly of great interest; in between the lines, and occasionally quite explicitly, the author shows how men of great power have transferred their desires and preferences to their children and grandchildren — to the point that money and political power do indeed generate a dynasty, something that has enormous momentum. Another helpful volume, because it is a little more "psychological" in its approach, though by no means a series of case studies, is George Kirstein's *The Rich: Are They Different?* (Houghton

Mifflin, 1968). His book is not unlike Frederick Lewis Allen's *The Lords of Creation* (Harper, 1955); both authors admire well-to-do and wealthy people, yet are not afraid to criticize them — individually, however, rather than as a group or class.

Neither Kirstein nor Allen is willing to look at the capitalist system critically, systematically. John Kenneth Galbraith does so in *The Affluent Society* (Houghton Mifflin, 1958); C. William Domhoff does so even more in *The Higher Circles: The Governing Class in America* (Random House, 1970) and *Who Rules America* (Prentice-Hall, 1967). Galbraith is, of course, a marvelous social essayist as well as economist; he is especially sensitive to the ways in which an economic system is affected by, as well as affects, the tastes or preferences of the people who live in it. C. Wright Mills was another brilliant essayist; his books are indispensable: *The Power Elite* (Oxford, 1956); *Power, Politics & People,* a collection of essays (Oxford, 1963). Needless to say, *The Theory of the Leisure Class,* by Thorstein Veblen (Modern Library, 1934), is also indispensable. Very important, too, are *Social Mobility in Industrial Society,* by Seymour Martin Lipset and Reinhard Bendix (University of California Press, 1959), and, from quite another viewpoint, Paul M. Sweezy's *The Theory of Capitalist Development* (Oxford, 1942), which contains a carefully constructed survey of who owns and runs this country and other capitalist nations.

In the C. Wright Mills tradition, though more traditionally sociological, is Suzanne Keller's *Beyond the Ruling Class: Strategic Elites in Modern Society* (Random House, 1963). In that same sociological tradition Lipset and Bendix, mentioned above, have gathered together a large number of essays under the title *Class, Status, and Power* (Free Press, 1966); it is helpful for the reader who wants to learn how various theorists have tried to make sense of the different ways people live in a country like ours — and especially the way important or well-off people exert their authority, lay claim to influence, are regarded as successful, influential, *on the top.* Once there, the competition or drive for distinctive self-expression, if not mad self-display, does not quite disappear, as Lanfranco Rasponi shows in his *The International Nomads* (Putnam's, 1966), and as writers like Hoffman Nickerson (*The American Rich,* published in 1930 by Doubleday) and Floyd Hunter (*The Big Rich and the Little Rich,* also published by Doubleday, in 1965) both have indicated at substantial length in their books for the general reader.

It is important that one realize how many Americans are quite well-off, how many are poor or belong to the working class or the largest portion of the so-called middle class — the portion made up of men and women who live reasonably comfortable lives, by the standards of many other countries quite luxurious ones, but who really have virtually no "capital" and are quite sensitive to even minor fluctuations in the economy. Herman Miller's *Rich Man, Poor Man* (Crowell, 1971) tells how many families, for instance, made $50,000 and over in 1968: some 150,000, or .3 percent of all American families. Add to them the 1.2 million who earned between $25,000 and $50,000, and one has 2.3 percent of the families in the United States really comfortable — some, of course, much more than "really comfortable." In

1968 there were 6.1 million families with a yearly income between $15,000 and $25,000. At that time, interestingly enough, the highest fifth of American families, so far as income goes, received 40 percent of the total income that went to all American families. Miller keeps pointing out an important fact — one that readers of this book ought to keep in mind when they wonder how "representative" as Americans the boys and girls in the preceding pages are: "The figures show that until you get to the very top the incomes are not so high." The top 5 percent, he indicates, were families that received incomes, in 1968, of over $23,000, annually. But inflation has in the decade since then eroded the value of those dollars, even as the top 5 percent, obviously, makes more of those dollars annually. The really well-off, let alone the rich, are about 100,000 to 200,000 families — in a nation that (as of 1968) had over 50 million families.

Who are the "wealthy"? At one point Miller defines the wealthy as those "with a net worth of $100,000 or more"; the "very wealthy" are "those with holdings over $500,000." (Again, one constantly has to correct for the effects of a continuing inflation on any set of figures, even those from a book published in this decade of the 1970s.) Miller tells us that the majority of the relatively wealthy or quite well-off people in our country have their own businesses or are salaried executives. Many too are professional men — doctors or lawyers or architects or writers or artists who make more money than others in their own profession, not to mention the overwhelming majority of their fellow citizens. About 10 percent are exceptionally able salesmen or "craftsmen" who have managed to make a good deal more money than most other craftsmen. Only 17 percent are retired. Significantly, about 40 percent of those who are quite well-to-do claim to have become so on their own rather than to be the beneficiaries of inherited money. If one wants to go back in time, Edward Pessen has written a social history of the early nineteenth-century upper class that provides the kind of statistical and analytical information Miller's book offers us with respect to our own wealthy families: *Riches, Class, and Power Before the Civil War* (D.C. Heath, 1973).

The economist Howard Tuckman's book *The Economics of the Rich* (Random House, 1973) gives an account of how capital is accumulated in contemporary America. He writes with a light touch, for all his charts and graphs (as does Herman Miller), and he makes quite clear who our "affluent minority" is and how the people who belong to it got there — and, courtesy of our tax laws as well as their continuing work and ingenuity, manage to stay there. For readers of the first four volumes of *Children of Crisis*, this observation might prove of interest: "Pockets of wealth still exist throughout the United States. Pikeville, Kentucky, is an example. Conventional wisdom holds that everyone in Appalachia qualifies as a prime candidate for the welfare rolls. Nonetheless, the *St. Petersburg Times* reported that Pikeville, a town of 4,700, represents a veritable showcase of wealth! According to local bankers, the area has more than 50 millionaires and claims 25 doctors, 35 lawyers, a Cadillac dealership with a waiting list, and a 7 million dollar hospital under construction."

At the same time, of course, more than half the people of Pike County,

Kentucky, lived in poverty, as defined by the federal government, and many others were barely getting by — certainly not ordering Cadillacs. Meanwhile, the mine owners not only pay wages to their employees but fight the unions for control of the miner's life: the conditions under which he works, the various benefits he gets — all of importance to a mountaineer's family, his sons and daughters. Once more: the way a coal owner's children grow up to think about coal miners will decisively affect another generation. Today's rich children in Pikeville will be tomorrow's coal owners.

If one wants to find out just where America's wealthy people are — that is, where they live and how they manage to keep their position intact and, usually, better than intact — books like Ferdinand Lundberg's *The Rich and the Super Rich* (Bantam, 1968) and Gabriel Kolko's *Wealth and Power in America* (Praeger, 1962) are of help. The authors document the presence not only of the extraordinarily rich, but of thousands of merely affluent but enormously influential families. And as other books do, these two show how all sorts of laws, ordinances, and regulations, not to mention informal arrangements in businesses, even in schools or colleges, conspire to ensure the continuing "power" that Mr. Kolko takes such pains to analyze. Another series of essays on "power," as it is exerted here and abroad, is to be found in *The Rich, the Well Born, and the Powerful,* edited by Frederic Cople Jaher (University of Illinois Press, 1973). The book contains an excellent bibliography. And finally, I would mention two valuable articles: "Nineteenth Century Elites in Boston and New York," *Journal of Social History,* Fall, 1972, by Mr. Jaher; and Edward Pessen's "The Egalitarian Myth and American Social Reality," in *American Historical Review,* No. 76, 1971.

The word "suburbia" has become linked in many of our minds with the well-to-do — those who have escaped the social and racial strife of the city. There are, of course, suburbs and suburbs — even as there are cities and cities. And land once considered "the country," to which well-to-do people took themselves in the summer or on holidays, or where they lived year round, has now become part of a suburban sprawl, or even absorbed into the smaller, somewhat industrialized cities that cluster around many of our larger cities. If working-class families and not a few rather poor families live in suburbs, then is the sociological literature on suburbia — substantial, and in some instances, compelling to read — of any interest to observers of the comfortable upper middle class or the wealthy? Interestingly enough, most of the studies of suburbia do in fact take up for scrutiny "working-class suburbs," or the somewhat better-off suburbs where those who make from about $15,000 to $20,000 a year live — the middle middle class, I guess research papers call them. It is those suburbs I visited in connection with the third volume of *Children of Crisis: The South Goes North,* and *The Middle Americans.*

In all suburbs, it seems, one finds parents and children earnestly looking "upward": how do "they," better off than we, live, and how might "we" do likewise? A working-class parent, for example, in one suburb has an eye on another suburb; and there, a parent has an eye on yet *another* suburb, and so on. Meanwhile a parent "way out" — that is, in the "country" — talks to his children about "moving back," returning to the city, where residence would be taken up not far from, say, a black ghetto, or a working-class white neighborhood "in transition" — meaning that the people there are hoping to "move out," join a suburban community. Such geographical circularity is, of course, only the beginning of a description of what happens — a game of musical chairs played hard and for keeps by people who "mean business" when they choose a place to live.

The best specific study of a well-to-do suburban community is *Crestwood Heights*, by John Seeley, R. Alexander Sim, and E. W. Loosely, with a wonderfully sharp and spirited introduction by David Riesman (University of Toronto Press, 1956). The authors are engaging, psychologically sensitive, eager to walk the tightrope between their own ideological objectives (as political liberals) and the need as observers to be detached, factual. A less fluid and speculative book, and one less preoccupied with matters cultural and philosophical, is *The Affluent Suburb: Princeton*, by George Sternlieb, Robert Burchell, Lynn Sagalyn, and Richard Gordon (Dutton, 1971). The emphasis is on problems of housing — who lives where, in what kind of home, and for what stated and implicit reason. A more political orientation is to be found in Robert C. Wood's *Suburbia: Its People and Their Politics* (Houghton Mifflin, 1959). The author is at times quite critical of the suburban "mentality," seeing in many of our towns and villages a virtual state of siege, taken up by people in flight *from* something, rather than positively in search of a way of life they have thought out for themselves.

William Dobriner's *Class in Suburbia* (Prentice-Hall, 1963) is an important sociological study. He is shrewdly willing to cut below surfaces, show the subtle and, it turns out, not so subtle tensions, rivalries, currents, and countercurrents that characterize communities that seem to be thoroughly conformist and in many respects similar. The same author has gathered together some remarkable essays, to form *The Suburban Community* (Putnam's, 1958). The major problems that face the suburbs — education, housing, conservation and ecology, industrial penetration, and, not least, governance — are taken up; but so are delightful and not so "minor" matters like gardening — as a way people find to amuse, affirm themselves, and come to terms with the judgments they fear others make when "driving by." Even though this book is now two decades old, it deserves attention; there are prophetic moments in it, one knows now by hindsight: the prophesy of eventual dissatisfaction with suburban life; the warning, issued when the country was riding high on its innocence and self-satisfaction, that ugliness in the form of pollutants and contaminants (or indeed, racism and resurgent class tensions) would come to bear upon the utopian dreams, the *lives*, of those who had settled into various suburban communities.

On the other hand, it is possible to be so critical of various American suburbs that they emerge as caricatures of themselves. Scott Donaldson's *The Suburban Myth* (Columbia University Press, 1969) is an effort to redress what the author believes to be a contemporary ideological emphasis on the negative side of suburban life. It is a well-written book and a nicely, judiciously argued one: not an apologia for nervous boosterism or smug indifference, but an argument by a historian who wants us to look hard at the concrete realities of American life, as opposed to the recurrent dream of a return to some mythic past, when there were fewer people, and all of them, supposedly, "individuals." He is especially inclined to argue against William H. Whyte's *The Organization Man* (Simon & Schuster, 1956), a strong and lucid assault on middle-class working and living practices. Another important book meant for the general reader, and a companion to Whyte's in many ways, is A. C. Spectorsky's *The Exurbanites* (Street & Smith, 1955). The author was a vivid and knowing social critic, and put in a lot of time with well-off people in quite elegant communities; he wrote with both affection and sarcastic disapproval. Harlan Paul Douglass, also a sensitive social critic, used the word "suburban" long ago in the title of a book of social comment: *The Suburban Trend* (Century), published in 1925, when the author saw our growing towns at the edge of the cities to be yet another frontier, full of hopes and dreams, only some of which would be realized. In the same tradition — from Douglass to Donaldson — one finds *The Suburban Society* (University of Toronto Press, 1966). The author, S. D. Clark, is well aware of flaws in the "dream" but, like Donaldson, sees no alternative, given the complexity of American social and industrial life and our still-growing population.

Though the work of Herbert J. Gans and Bennett M. Berger has had to do primarily with so-called lower-middle-class suburbs, the men are both intelligent and wide-ranging social observers who have influenced others in their profession and the general public as well. Their analysis of lower- and middle-middle-class suburban life, at once skeptical and appreciative, has implications for the student of the wealthier suburbs. *The Levittowners* was Herbert Gans's finely wrought study of "ways of life and politics" in a (then) new suburban community (Vintage, 1967). Berger's book is *Working Class Suburbs* (University of California Press, 1960). A more strenuously academic approach to a somewhat similar issue — the movement of upwardly mobile blacks and Puerto Ricans into an older suburban community — is *The Zone of Emergence: A Case Study of Plainfield, New Jersey* (Dutton, 1972), by George Sternlieb. Also of interest and in the same genre is *On the City's Rim: Politics and Policy in Suburbia*, by Frederick West, Benjamin Walter, Francine Rabinovitz, and Deborah Hensler (D.C. Heath, 1972). The book offers some valuable survey research data that has a bearing on "the suburban state of mind" — the fears, worries, and desires, say, of suburban voters.

Historically, the story of working-class suburbs has been well told by Sam B. Warner in *Streetcar Suburbs: The Process of Growth in Boston, 1870–1900* (Harvard University Press, 1962). History comes alive in the book. Graham Taylor covered some of the same territory at a closer interval in *Satellite Cities* (Appleton, 1915). A more limited study of suburbia is to be found in *Housing the Poor in Suburbia: Public Policy at the Grass Roots*, by Charles

Haar and Demetrius S. Iatridis (Ballinger, 1974). This is at first glance a technical, scholarly study, full of graphs, tables, and charts — and not especially well written. But it is also full of information about suburban housing problems (and struggles); and through it runs an unrelenting, probing examination of some of the important ethical issues children of well-to-do suburban families hear their parents struggle with: who shall live where — and who should not, under any practical circumstances, come even remotely near. Especially revealing and instructive is a chapter that deals with the turmoil in an upper-middle-class suburb in response to a proposal that would have enabled some relatively less well-off (and some poor) to live there, through subsidized housing. Not that those same upper-middle-class suburbs tend to welcome large numbers of poorer children into their schools. The relationship between education and privilege is complicated but important to consider — as Christopher Jencks makes abundantly clear in *Inequality* (Basic Books, 1972).

In a more personal or psychological vein, Vance Packard for some time kept a sharp journalist's eye on America's business executives and those professional men who have an eager eye out for money and power, status and privilege. His *The Pyramid Climbers* (McGraw-Hill, 1962) is full of wise, candid observations about the active, intelligent, and ambitious men who are working their way upward, ever upward, in the corporate world. (A more scholarly analysis of the same climb is to be found in *Personality and Organization*, by Chris Argyris, published in 1957 by Harper & Row.) There have been two other similarly penetrating studies by Packard: *The Status Seekers* (McKay, 1959), which essentially provides an update of Thorstein Veblen — the various class-connected desires and lusts of the contemporary well-to-do; and more recently, *A Nation of Strangers* (McKay, 1972), which takes up the psychologically important matter of mobility and its effect upon family life among many upper-middle-class families — the constant changes in address prompted by transfers from one plant, one office, one city or state to another. The personal consequences of such upper-class nomadism on the wives of businessmen are mentioned by Packard and are examined in great detail by a thoughtful psychiatrist, Robert Seidenberg, in *Corporate Wives, Corporate Casualties* (Amacom, 1973). Michael Maccoby's *The Gamesman: The New Corporate Leaders* (Simon & Schuster, 1976) also shows, with psychoanalytic penetration, what a certain kind of business ethic can do to family integrity.

Along with anxiety and occasional moments of despair in men and women to all apparent purposes living the best life in the world, materially at least, there are other emotions: among them a strong sense that one ought to obey the laws and strictures of a given society — or else. Nietzsche referred to *ressentiment* — the burgher's insistence that if he is going to conform in dozens of ways, then no one else ought to get away with anything. The Danish sociologist Svend Ronulf has done an important study on this one aspect of the middle-class mind: *Moral Indignation and Middle Class Psychology* (Schocken, 1970). What he describes comes across also in Paul Wilkes's portrait of a middle-class American family: *Trying Out the Dream:*

A Year in the Life of an American Family (Lippincott, 1974). The people Wilkes brings to us are not at the top of Mr. Packard's "pyramid" by any means, but they know how to look nervously, anxiously (and finally, angrily) at others: those envied, those admired, those feared, those (God help them) "below." One wonders in connection with them, in connection with so many people who are described in this country as belonging to the middle class, how their apprehensions differ from those of the poor, or the so-called working class. Obviously there is a blur, an indefiniteness to that expression: the middle class. Maybe it is an illusion, a myth — as in Richard Parker's *The Myth of the Middle Class* (Liveright, 1972), a vigorous social and economic analysis of how vulnerable the majority of Americans are. Maybe membership in the middle class is a state of mind, backed up by, these days, about $14,000 a year, the approximate present (1977) mean income for all families in the United States. But what a Danish sociologist and an American journalist sense in middle-class families is the psychological jeopardy that goes with being in the middle — and the accompanying rage. More money doesn't always solve the problem, either. One can have three, four, five times the mean income and still feel precarious socially, not all that secure financially.

Perhaps the single most important book I can recommend to the reader in connection with this volume (and all the others in the series) is David Riesman's *The Lonely Crowd* (Doubleday, 1953). He captured a mood in that book, evoked a mentality, portrayed lives being lived both usefully and vainly. He is one of the most fertile and vital thinkers the United States has — a constant, attentive observer of his fellow citizens. He has seen and felt, he has *known* (but never said so dogmatically) what has been happening in the comfortable neighborhoods inside or way outside our American cities — and in the minds and hearts of the many-sided men, women, and children who live in those neighborhoods. He has walked a certain middle path — between particularity and abstraction, between social criticism and ethical affirmation. *The Lonely Crowd* has molded the thought of a generation; it is a lasting contribution to social theory — and the best presentation, still, of the social psychology of American well-to-do people. Riesman's *Abundance for What* (Doubleday, 1964) also comes to terms powerfully, in essay after essay, with the contradictions and ambiguities of American life — including its upper-middle-class segment, whose virtues and vices the author both knows well and has an artist's capacity to bring alive vividly, yet with no sacrifice of complexity.

In a sense, almost anything important that has come out of the social sciences in recent decades contributes to an understanding of the lives of the American people who belong to the upper classes; and perhaps the plural form is the most satisfactory, because, as I keep mentioning, it is so hard to do justice to the complexity of our class structure — a complexity David Riesman knows enough never to "resolve" with a formulation or two. Almost the entire literature in my own field, for instance, has come about through work with rather well-off children: Anna Freud's writings, Erik Erikson's, D. W. Winnicott's. Not that they and others (August Aichhorn, for instance)

haven't worked with or observed the poor, the delinquent, the racially ostracized. But it is clearly those from the middle class — the upper middle class and the rich, actually — who have been able to afford prolonged psychiatry and psychoanalysis and have, too, known about the help such disciplines sometimes can offer. Once again, in that regard, as in the other volumes of *Children of Crisis,* I mention *Social Class and Mental Illness,* by August Hollingshead and Frederick Redlich (Wiley, 1958), an important analysis, with respect to the psychologically troubled, of who gets called what and treated by whom (and in what way). A study that specifically directs its concern to the upper-class young is Burton Wixen's *Children of the Rich* (Crown, 1973); a touching series of psychological case-histories is quite clearly presented. And Kenneth Keniston's books and essays on young people, especially *The Uncommitted* (Harcourt, Brace & World, 1965), have similarly made clear that at the top of that "pyramid" are to be found a good deal of fear and trembling — and at times, a fatal loss of nerve.
The growing literature on the family, on the education of children, and more precisely on moral education tells us a lot about well-to-do parents and their children. The work of Philippe Ariès (*Centuries of Childhood,* published in 1962 by Knopf), of Lawrence Cremin ("The Family as Educator: Some Comments on the Recent Historiography," in *Teachers College Record,* December, 1974), of Edward Shorter (*The Making of the Modern Family,* published in 1975 by Basic Books), and not least, of social critics like Paul Goodman, Edgar Z. Friedenberg, and John Holt are all worth mention, as is Lawrence Kohlberg's important research on moral development. (See his "Education for Justice," in *Moral Education,* edited by T. Sizer [Harvard University Press, 1970], and his "Collected Papers on Moral Education," published as a large monograph by the Harvard Graduate School of Education, 1973.)
There is, finally, the genre of literary commentary — the wry and sardonic and telling and apposite observations of comfortable America made by novelists and poets, and yes, artists, because *The New Yorker*'s drawings (Stevenson, Richter, Saxon, for instance) have been on target, week after week, have shown many of us ourselves as precisely as dozens of articles or books could have managed to do. For children, John Ney's stories have been quite directly about the wealthy: *Ox: The Story of a Kid at the Top* (Little, Brown, 1970) and *Ox Goes North: More Trouble for the Kid at the Top* (Harper & Row, 1973). For youths, J. D. Salinger's *The Catcher in the Rye* (Little, Brown, 1951) continues to strike chords, even if Holden Caulfield's "alienation" takes different social forms in the 1970s. Holden was from "a certain background," as it is put, and his confusions, rages, worries are class-connected as well as quite all his own.
It was William Dean Howells, in 1871, who published *Suburban Sketches* (Hurd & Houghton), an autobiographical series of recollections of his life in Boston's "country." It was Henry Adams who contrasted the pleasures of the then suburban, even country, life of Quincy with that of Boston in *The Education of Henry Adams* (Houghton Mifflin, 1907 and 1913). It was John P. Marquand who brought us closer to banks and those who run them

and live off them in *Point of No Return* (Little, Brown, 1949). It was F. Scott Fitzgerald who gave us *The Great Gatsby* (Scribner, 1925); Gatsby's dreams, less eloquently and poignantly worded, perhaps, have been shared by thousands of other bright and promising (and fatally flawed) young Americans. And it has been John O'Hara and John Cheever (with his Wapshot family) and John Updike and Wright Morris and Peter DeVries whose stories and novels and essays have done so much to show America's well-off people themselves: their foibles and obsessions, their quite human inclinations, and, not least, the structure of their lives — where they live, where they work, what (so much!) they can take for granted. And again, *The New Yorker*, week in, week out — an unrelenting, amused, yet serious onlooker. Or a poet like Richard Wilbur, in *Ceremony and Other Poems* (Harcourt, Brace & World, 1950), telling us how callous we have become, how wantonly materialist. And before them Henry James and Edith Wharton, and later, Sinclair Lewis and William Carlos Williams (in his Stecher trilogy) and Sherwood Anderson — all interested in catching hold of the rhythms and pulsations of American middle-class and upper-class life.

Sherwood Anderson's *Poor White*, for instance, is not about material poverty, but about the Industrial Age and what it did to the town of Bidwell, Ohio — a less symbolic and grotesque version of Winesburg, Ohio; did to Bidwell not only destructively (drabness and more drabness) but did psychologically and ideologically to the people of the town, of America. Hugh McVey came out of the unspoiled countryside bent on rising; he was as determined as the immigrant Stecher family in William Carlos Williams's *White Mule*. A visionary but also a calculating and ambitious man, McVey rose, became well-to-do in Bidwell. Yet he saw a new poverty about him, "the white faces of drowned men and children," the death that industrialism, in various ways, can visit upon the people of a nation. He turned from the commercial world, which had rewarded him for his inventiveness, helped him move on up the social and economic ladder. He turned to dreams, to art, to using his hands patiently and in a way that made sense to him, struck him as proper and attractive. *Poor White* is no *Man in the Gray Flannel Suit;* Anderson was not intent on a romanticized portrayal of upper-middle-class urban, suburban, or exurbanite life. He wanted, perhaps, to suggest the considerable psychological price many of us who "do right well," as it is put in the South, have to pay, day in and day out. The perplexed Hugh and his wife, the quite troubled Clara, are not to be regarded as caricatures of the rest of us, as peculiarly craven or misshaped. They feel pain, because they know deep down that things are wrong for others, even if right for them; and that knowledge, fought off but never decisively banished, makes for continuing tension (and drama) in their lives — and maybe in the lives of many privileged Americans.

INDEX